TORONTO'S GIRL PROBLEM:
THE PERILS AND PLEASURES OF THE CITY,
1880–1930

With the turn of the century came increased industrialization and urbanization, and in Toronto one of the most visible results of this modernization was the influx of young, single women to the city. They came seeking work, independence, and excitement, but they were not to realize these goals without struggle.

Carolyn Strange examines the rise of the Toronto 'working girl,' the various agencies that 'discovered' her, the nature of the 'girl problem' from the point of view of moral overseers, the various strategies devised to solve this 'problem,' and the young women's responses to moral regulation. The 'working girl' seemed a problem to reformers, evangelists, social investigators, police, the courts, and journalists – men, mostly, who saw women's debasement as certain and who appointed themselves as protectors of morality. They portrayed single women as victims of potential economic and sexual exploitation and urban immorality. Such characterization drew attention away from the greater problems these women faced: poverty, unemployment, poor housing and nutrition, and low wages.

In the course of her investigation, Strange suggests fresh approaches to working-class and urban history. Her sources include the census, court papers, newspaper accounts, philanthropic society reports, and royal commissions, but Strange also employs less conventional sources, such as photographs and popular songs. She approaches the topic from a feminist viewpoint that is equally sensitive to the class and racial dimensions of the 'girl problem,' and compares her findings with those on the emergence of the contemporary working woman in the United States and Great Britain.

The overriding observation is that Torontonians projected their fears and hopes about urban industrialization onto the figure of the working girl. Young women were regulated in factories and offices, in streetcars and dancehalls, in an effort to control the deleterious effects of industrial capitalism. By the First World War, however, their value as contributors to the expanding economy began to outweigh the fear of their moral endangerment. As Torontonians grew accustomed to life in the industrial metropolis, the 'working girl' came to be seen as a valuable resource.

(Studies in Gender and History)

CAROLYN STRANGE is an assistant professor at the Centre of Criminology, University of Toronto.

STUDIES IN GENDER AND HISTORY

General editors: Franca Iacovetta and Craig Heron

CAROLYN STRANGE

Toronto's Girl Problem: The Perils and Pleasures of the City, 1880–1930

UNIVERSITY OF TORONTO PRESS
Toronto Buffalo London

© University of Toronto Press Incorporated 1995
Toronto Buffalo London
Printed in Canada

ISBN 0-8020-0598-5 (cloth)
ISBN 0-8020-7203-8 (paper)

Printed on acid-free paper

Canadian Cataloguing in Publication Data
Strange, Carolyn, 1959–

Toronto's girl problem : the perils and pleasures
of the city, 1880–1930

(Studies in Gender and History)
Includes bibliographical references and index.
ISBN 0-8020-0598-5 (bound) ISBN 0-8020-7203-8 (pbk.)

1. Single women – Employment – Ontario – Toronto – History.
2. Young women – Employment – Ontario – Toronto – History.
3. Single women – Ontario – Toronto – Economic conditions.
4. Young women – Ontario – Toronto – Economic conditions.
5. Single women – Ontario – Toronto – Social conditions.
6. Young Women – Ontario – Toronto – Social conditions.
I. Title. II. Series.

HD6055.6.C32T67 1995   305.48'90652'09713541
C95-95930501-7

This book has been published with the help of a grant from the Social
Science Federation of Canada, using funds provided by the Social Sciences
and Humanities Research Council of Canada.

University of Toronto Press acknowledges the financial assistance to its
publishing program of the Canada Council and the Ontario Arts Council.

To my parents, Mary and Arthur Strange,
teachers in spirit and fact

Contents

APPENDICES

Acknowledgments

The debt one incurs in writing a first book is particularly daunting. Not only are there academic contributions to recognize, there is also the encouragement of people along the way who make you believe that you are capable of the task. In my case, they were only partly right: I could not have written this without them.

My early mentors include Margaret Gillespie, who taught me that women could be historians (before I ever dreamed of becoming one). Tom Sea tricked me into applying for graduate school by having me take his Reformation history course. My master's supervisor, Susan Mann, set an example as a rigorous historian and smoothed my path with her quiet but solid support. Suzanne Lebsock, who 'coached' me through my doctoral thesis, was not only an excellent teacher but a fine writer who always inspired me to 'hit one out of the park.'

My colleagues have been equally important in helping me turn random thoughts into a book. My fellow 'turkettes' at Rutgers, and Anna Clark in particular, stimulated an intellectual growth spurt and simultaneously assured me that history (and historians) could be fun. In Toronto I was fortunate to be a member of several study groups that sustained and encouraged me while I was working on my thesis. Mary Louise Adams, Deborah Brock, Christina Burr, Karen Dubinsky, Ruth Frager, Julie Guard, Franca Iacovetta, Margaret Little, Lynne Marks, Janice Newton, Becki Ross, Mariana Valverde, and Cynthia Wright all read and commented on various incarnations of this project, and many of them shared their own work with me. Jennifer Stephen was most generous with her research as well.

Some of these women made contributions for which I am especially grateful. Mariana Valverde has been an adviser, an incisive critic, and a generous friend through good times and sad ones. Cynthia Wright introduced me to many of my Toronto associates and has always been ready to listen (and talk) when I needed to work out ideas. I also had the pleasure of working with her at an earlier stage on some of the material that appears here in the sections on businesswomen's leisure. More recently, Franca Iacovetta has been an ardent booster whose enthusiasm for this project is nothing less than infectious. Gail Reekie, whom I met while doing my post-doctoral work in Australia, read the manuscript and encouraged me to write something more than a social history. In a random act of kindness, Lorna Weir read the manuscript and managed to tell me what I was writing about at a point when I was no longer sure.

Other friends and colleagues have assisted in various ways. Jim Phillips cleared up a few legal historical mysteries and, equally important, gave up his cool office and thereby saved me from trying to write in my kitchen during a heat wave. This book might have taken even longer to appear had Roy Schaeffer, then the archivist of the Law Society of Upper Canada, not found ways to keep me employed at work that complemented my interests in criminal justice history. John Beattie, in a typical act of encouragement towards a younger scholar, told me that I should affiliate with the Centre of Criminology at the University of Toronto. I followed his suggestion and, as neither of us would have predicted, have made it my interdisciplinary home.

A small army of archivists and librarians who work at the institutions listed in the bibliography were instrumental in helping me to find the disparate materials that make up the sources in this book. At the Public Archives of Ontario, Richard Ramsay first introduced me to prison records and Catherine Shepard opened my eyes to the complexity and richness of legal historical material. More recently, Jack Choules has alleviated some of the pains of research. My former colleagues at the Law Society, particularly Ann-Marie Langlois, have been as efficient and knowledgeable as they were when we were co-workers.

Gerry Hallowell at the University of Toronto Press solicited the manuscript and helped me to see beyond its limits. In the latter stages of the book's production, Rob Ferguson helped to make it a reality. I am also grateful for the eagle eye of my copy-editor, Kathy Johnson.

Because human beings, not automatons, write books, the emotional support that writers receive is invaluable. Patty Barclay listened to my stories of murder, botched abortions, dancehalls, and brothels with forebearance and, I hope, interest. Julie Stacker has nursed me through writer's block and always, through her unrealistic estimation of my abilities, inspires me to improve. Not only has she buoyed my spirits but she has also shared her skills by tracing references, searching for pictures, and teasing idiosyncrasies out of my writing. It is a debt I look forward to repaying.

TORONTO'S GIRL PROBLEM:
THE PERILS AND PLEASURES OF THE CITY,
1880–1930

1

Introduction

If historians had found the study of single wage-earning women nearly as compelling as turn-of-the-century urbanites did, this book would have joined a chorus of studies on the topic. Instead, it asks questions about working women and cities that most Canadian women's, labour, and urban historians have not pursued, questions about the rise of the single woman as an economic and social actor and the various responses to her entrance on the stage of urban life. Because the 'working girl,' as she came to be known, was not a career woman, was only rarely a unionized worker, and was never involved in the power structures of urban life, she has fallen between the cracks of conventional historical inquiry. Paradoxically, in her own time, the working girl's political and economic marginality in urban life endowed her with enormous cultural relevance, for contemporary observers saw in her struggles the troubling side-effects of industrial capitalism. Her vulnerability to exploitation, her attraction to the material temptations of the city, and her imperilled journey towards marriage were all scrutinized and eventually elevated to the level of public debates. How this closely observed sector of the workforce in one industrializing city – Toronto – came to be understood as a moral problem and an inspiration for the deployment of new regulatory, reformative, managerial, and medical techniques is the subject of this book.[1]

When single women left Ontario farms and small towns in the late nineteenth century for paid work in Toronto, they came in search of wages, not notoriety; yet they attracted it all the same. Young women who sought jobs in artisans' shops and small factories unwittingly placed themselves at the leading edge of economic and social change in Canada. The country's first working girls were its pioneer urbanites in an era when less than one-quarter of Canadians lived in large towns or cities. Montreal was the premier urban centre in the late nineteenth century, but by the 1910s Toronto had largely caught up through the expansion of its secondary and tertiary economic base.[2] Although Canadians cultivated a sense of national pride as conquerors of nature, they could see by the late nineteenth century that urban Canada had become a dynamic source of economic growth. While the harshness of the frontier threatened the physical survival of those who set out to tame it, the city presented a moral threat to urban and rural Canadians alike. Reports of crime, poverty, and immorality in the industrial cities of England and the United States hinted that urbanization and industrialization were likely to be mixed blessings in Canada as well. The congregation of young, single working women in cities was a visible byproduct of economic change and an unsettling harbinger of the future to Canadians who found it difficult to reconcile their vision of the True North with the emergence of industrial cities.[3]

The expansion of Toronto's light industries, such as paper-box making and various forms of garment work, allowed wage-earning women to leave their traditional niche in the urban economy as servants. Although that movement began slowly, it quickly attracted attention. As early as the 1880s, barely more than a decade after the emergence of industries, royal commissioners pondered why women would prefer to work in ill-ventilated, dirty factories around men whose language was even filthier than the shop floors. The answer they offered was that young women apparently desired waged work that did not entail round-the-clock supervision as live-in domestic work did. As the growing service sector drew women into department stores and offices as well as factories, the trickle of women leaving domestic service became an unstoppable torrent. By the early twentieth century it was evident that single women could not be kept on the farm, nor would they be confined to the home.

Throughout the initial phases of industrialization, exploring the appearance of the single wage-earning woman and the moral consequences of her presence in the city preoccupied moral rescuers, journalists, and social surveyors as well as medical and psychiatric experts. Working girls manifestly violated behavioural norms set out for marriageable women, not so much because of the work they performed but because of the social conditions in which they worked. Shop work and factory labour ruptured the connections to women's working pasts in one crucial respect: non-domestic work drew women from the confines of home and family and provided an individual wage. The migration of single women to the city (in significantly greater numbers than young men) for wage labour weakened patriarchal controls over women's leisure time, their earnings, and, it was suspected, their sexuality. Although those constraints persisted for the majority of Toronto's female industrial and sales workers who lived with their family or kin, waged work that did not require young women to live in their workplaces nevertheless disrupted the continuous flow of supervision between families and employers. The abiding complaint about non-domestic labour, from the early years of women's employment in small industries to the 1920s, when women could be found in every sector of Toronto's economy, was that it left young single women free to do as they pleased outside their work hours.

This obsession with working girls' time off, rather than their wages or their time on the job, was inspired primarily by the minority of single women who lived on their own, apart from families. This version of the wage-earning woman, the most compelling illustration of urban industrialization's impact on family cohesion, was nevertheless considered the archetypal working girl. More than any other women workers, from scullery maids to doctors, single women who performed non-domestic waged work and lived independently captured Torontonians' ambivalence about the social and moral consequences of industrialization and urbanization. As an icon of unsettling change, the working girl was a figure freighted with meaning that wage-earning women themselves scarcely imagined until they encountered well-meaning philanthropic ladies, self-important industrial commissioners, Morality Department policemen and earnest settlement-house workers.

The late nineteenth and early twentieth centuries hardly marked the first time that wage-earning women in cities had been viewed with suspicion. As early as the Middle Ages, single working women who toiled in the trades in European cities were considered 'masterless' and hence in need of restraint through the regulatory powers of town councils and guilds.[4] Once industrial capitalism began to draw European women workers into non-domestic wage labour, similar responses – calls for the restriction of women's work and the stricter moral regulation of women workers – were voiced as industrial commissions in France and England evaluated the social costs of women's work. Investigators in both countries agreed that urban industrial work had led single women to abandon the moral standards that supposedly prevailed in small towns and among domestic workers.[5] This same pattern of young women's recruitment into industrial waged labour, its analysis

by expert observers, and its assessment as a moral danger was replicated in Toronto, albeit under conditions unique to the social and cultural peculiarities of the city.

Why all the fuss? From the vantage point of our post-industrial,
mobile society, the notion of young women leaving school and parental
homes for paid labour in cities fails to raise eyebrows. But the perfect
ordinariness of such economic and demographic patterns today should
not dull our appreciation for the extraordinary impact of turn-of-the-
century working girls on cities like Toronto. Through sheer force of
numbers – impossible to ignore when hundreds of young women
poured out of Eaton's department stores or the Crompton Corset factory
at shift changes – they stood out. But filing out of workplaces was not
the only way they made their presence known. Whether flocking to
lakeside amusement resorts or window shopping along Yonge Street,
their unselfconscious public presence was a vivid reminder that they
did not adhere to the traditional norms of restraint imposed upon single
women. Domestic service, long the staple employment of girls and
young women, could no longer be relied on as an anchor for women
adrift in a city that offered working girls so many alternatives.[6] As tens
of thousands of women in Toronto sought out and found alternative
forms of employment, they forced their contemporaries to confront their
deepest fears: the uncharted and turbulent waters of economic and
social change.

Historians have established a variety of approaches to the study of
working women and female singlehood, and this book complements
rather than follows in the traditions of that earlier work. The US and
British literature provides a rich source of information on the material
conditions of women's work in domestic service, factory labour, and
white-collar work. As well, a considerable amount of writing on women
and unions has accumulated over the past two decades. Most of these
histories focus on the workplace and, to a lesser extent, the household
economy and the role of women's work within it, while the history of
unions concentrates on organizational agitation and heroic individuals.
Perhaps the overriding theme that unites these works is the marginality
of women's labour, reified through the restrictions on women's work
and sex-based pay scales and in the consequent economic imperatives
towards marriage and the hoped-for security of a male breadwinner. As
Barbara Taylor stated and as subsequent studies have shown, union
'men were as bad as the masters' in their rejection of women's equality

as workers with a right to a living wage. The ideological patterns of patriarchy, meshed with the economic forces of capitalism, trapped women in low-paying, low-status, insecure jobs that gave them little ground to establish identities as workers and greater cause to seek their futures in family life. In spite of the few women who did organize and strike against working conditions and wages, most faced their hardships as individuals with little power to protest, save to leave.[7]

A great deal of the historiography on women and work actually focuses on single women without making marital status an explicit subject of analysis. Arlette Farge and Christiane Klapisch-Zuber are blunt in their observation of the absence of single women's historiography: 'La femme seule est dans un angle mort de l'histoire,' they complain.[8] This silence is curious, particularly in regard to the history of working women. Until the mid-twentieth century in North America and Britain, the majority of wage-earning women were single and in their teens or twenties, and many occupations were restricted to single women. Most historians who have looked at marital status critically have concentrated instead on married women and working mothers.[9] The exceptions to this pattern have typically been works that examine the role of daughters in the household economy.[10] The importance of young women's contribution, particularly in immigrant and poor families, to the household economy was crucial. Parents as well as siblings kept a close watch on working daughters, ensuring that they did not compromise their virtue or squander their wages on their own desires.[11] Bettina Bradbury's excellent account of working-class families in Montreal indicates that while both boys and girls were expected to contribute to the family economy, women's low wages complemented parental expectations that daughters were more valuable as temporary workers whose primary duty was unpaid domestic labour. Thus, the conditions of women's labour under capitalism coalesced with cultural notions of proper behaviour for marriageable females to circumscribe working girls' independence. The illness or abandonment of the primary breadwinner, the absence of brothers, or extreme poverty frequently drove daughters from home; however, parents generally felt more comfortable, in emotional and material terms, having daughters under their own roof until suitable marriage partners placed them under theirs. However much parents hoped their working daughters would be dutiful, working girls did not behave well all the time, and some never behaved. Furthermore, those who did not live at home when they worked – in some North American cities, as many as one-third of wage-earning women – evaded the vigilant eye of parents, older brothers, and villagers.[12] These young women certainly appeared to be independent actors, untethered by family obligations and left to float adrift in the city. Although most women workers remained integrated into family economies, those very obligations to contribute wages could inspire the rejection of familial responsibilities in favour of the wilful pursuit of independence.

This does not mean that working girls were career women on the march towards self-determination. That avenue was the preserve of single women, whose labour, for the most part, did not make the difference between penury and survival for their families. The stories of those women – daughters of professionals, businessmen, and aristocrats who self-consciously broke down barriers to higher education in pursuit of knowledge and professional status – are better known but atypical of working women.[13] In Canada, like other industrializing nations, it was not 'redundancy' or debilitating boredom that drove the first generations of women to waged labour, but poverty. Working-class families (and the general public) expected the daughters of farmers, labourers, and artisans to work; in contrast, bourgeois families were apt to oppose their daughters' search for paid work, although their resistance softened after the First World War, by which point more 'respectable' occupations in the tertiary sector multiplied opportunities for women with high school and university educations. Church communities, professional organizations, women's colleges, and settlement houses provided independent women with alternatives to family living and dependence on the financial support of parents or wealthy relatives. This cohort of 'New Women' supplied many of the leaders of the first-wave women's movement, particularly in Britain, but they did not number among the chocolate-dippers and cigar-rollers in city factories (except when they worked incognito in order to spy on working girls). As much as they revolted against their political restrictions and economic disadvantages, they enjoyed a vast array of options for self-fulfilment in comparison with their working-girl counterparts. As daughters from middle-class families took up comparatively well-paying jobs in commerce, education, government, and the professions, the gulf between different classes of wage-earning women widened. 'Business women's' crisp white blouses and tailored skirts signalled not only their class position but their adherence to a code of respectability different from that followed by factory girls, whose flashy dress styles made them notorious. In sum, the majority of single wage-earning women did not work out of a mission to establish new opportunities for women or to create alternative communities of independent women: at the turn of the century, most single wage-earning women worked because they had to.[14]

While conservative opponents to women's emancipation were warning New Women that studying Greek or casting votes overtaxed the female reproductive system, middle-class monitors such as the infamous journalist C.S. Clark badgered working girls about their inappropriate pastimes. Important recent additions to the literature on wage-earning women have explored these reactions to shifting patterns of women's use of the city and its pleasurable diversions. In New York, Chicago, and London, moral pronouncements about working girls' leisure were linked to reactionary responses to changes in the nature of city amusements.[15] Urban leisure pursuits, such as promenading on commercial strips or frequenting dance halls, were not merely activities that some working girls enjoyed: they *defined* the women who indulged in them. Thus, 'Bowery gals,' 'charity girls,' and the generic 'good times girls' were labels that identified young single women who unabashedly partook of pleasures unique to the city. To their moral overseers, commercial amusements were snares that threatened to trap reckless young women in vice; to pleasure-seeking working girls, however, commercial amusements were sites of self-expression and escape from the dreariness of standing behind sales counters and sitting in front of sewing machines. Single working women's continued economic oppression and vulnerability to sexual exploitation left them without a solid footing for true autonomy; however, their leisure pursuits did permit them to push 'at the boundaries of constrained lives and shape ... cultural forms for their own purposes.'[16]

Both the New Woman and the working girl conjured up fears of sexual disorder, though these two archetypes of female independence were linked to discrete fields of concern. As Sheila Jeffreys has argued, the 'spinster' made a great many enemies in early twentieth-century Britain by rebuking heterosexual marriage and attacking male sexual licence. Numerous studies have shown how professional women's intense relationships with other women were 'morbidified' in Europe and North America in the 1920s, when an ideal of companionate marriage was promoted by sexologists and psychologists as the only healthy alternative for women.[17] The admonition to marry and bear children was also a necessary antidote to the problem of 'race suicide,' as the declining birth rate among middle-class Anglo-Celtics was named.[18] Working girls, in contrast, represented the flip side of the race-suicide equation. The form of sexual disorder associated with these wage-earning women was exclusively heterosexual in character. Working girls seemed altogether too interested in men, and some eugenicists, such as Toronto's own Drs Helen MacMurchy and C.K. Clark, leaders of the Canadian eugenics movement, claimed that 'subnormal' young women were inordinately fertile. While the independent professional woman's asexuality or suspected lesbianism was a matter of concern, working girls' alleged hyper-heterosexuality drew the attention not only of psychiatrists but of clubwomen, medical experts, the police, and the courts.[19]

In this book I have concentrated on the working girl as problem, while remaining mindful, unlike most of turn-of-the-century Torontonians, of her material problems.[20] I have looked at the construction of a moral discourse that linked women's pleasure to immorality and their independence to danger, and explored how those links were made in a variety of contexts, from white slavery narratives to self-management advice for the white-collar workers who dominated the female workforce after the 1920s. Although working girls were portrayed as indiscriminate consumers of city amusements, their apparent independence from family also sharpened their image as potential victims of moral danger. At the same time, their poverty, a direct result of the systematic undervaluation of women's labour, rendered them a potential source of moral danger. Women were paid so little that doubts about their ability to survive without bartering their sexual services (and thereby jeopardizing their progress from singlehood to marriage and respectability) were well founded. In the economy of the industrializing city, young women's sexuality commanded a higher price than their licit labour. Lurking beneath the surface of every report on women and work was a subtext (or perhaps the metatext) of prostitution. The search for causality in these explorations – were women thrust into commercialized sex through economic privation, or did pleasure-loving, self-indulgent women merely prefer the luxury and idleness of prostitution to the rigours of work? – plumbed the depths of unease about the rise of working girls and the morality of urban life. As Mary Ryan has observed of nineteenth-century US cities, 'the dangerous as well as the endangered urbanite was often portrayed as a woman, who in turn preyed upon both sexes.'[21]

The city, in other words, was a site of dangers as well as delights for city people and for working girls in particular. Judith Walkowitz argues that women in public in the metropolis (and working girls, by virtue of their work and play, were, along with prostitutes, the most public of women) lacked autonomy: they were 'bearers of meaning rather than makers of meaning.' Thus, although they were identified through policing practices as sources of disorderliness and contagion, urbanites could feel pity for 'public women' who stood also for urban anonymity and vulnerability to danger.[22] White slavery narratives captured this more sympathetic side of the working girl's portrayal dramatically, because they spoke to women's and men's fears about the dangers of urban life and the seeming ease with which villainous strangers preyed upon innocents. Agencies that were devoted to the moral wellbeing of working girls and the reform of the city generated these narratives of sexual endangerment, though courtroom dramas and newspaper coverage of trials were also significant sources. Finally, women who confronted dangerous strangers or intimates spun their own tales of their vulnerability and improvised strategies for resistance and survival. Some, like the confessed murderer Clara Ford, tried to manipulate the melodramatic convention of the innocent maiden beset by the rapacious villain to earn her acquittal. We will never know how many working girls encountered sexual danger, particularly when they were attacked by men they knew; however, it is fair to say that few women, like Clara Ford and, in 1915, Carrie Davies, fought their attackers by taking the law into their own hands. The stories of working girls' endangerment that were delivered in courtrooms were filtered through layers of legal proceedings and transformed by lawyers, judges, and juries, who proved stingy when it came to granting working girls the benefit of the doubt. The working girl, as court records confirm, was implicated in a paradoxical understanding of urban danger: she signified the perils of the city, both as its chief victim and as its source.

Toronto's Girl Problem is based on a disparate group of records analysed through a variety of methodological approaches. Very little of the evidence concerning working girls was generated by women workers themselves; yet that limiting factor is turned to advantage. Authoritative texts, such as state investigations and various forms of advice, from 'confessions' of business women to release contracts signed by parolees, do not offer direct access to working girls' experience or subjectivity, nor do they constitute a stable ideology imposed upon them. In this book I explore the social, political, and cultural contexts in which those texts were produced and deployed without, as Bryan Palmer has warned, sacrificing a materialist understanding of the past on the 'altar of an idealized reading of discourse and its influence.'[23] Historians' acrimonious debates about the uses and abuses of poststructuralist theory versus historical materialism seem to have given way to an appreciation of the complementarity of these approaches in the study of language and social practices. To argue that texts operate to organize meaning and social action does not, as the detractors of poststructuralist analysis charge, closes off questions about authorship, authority, context, reception, and resistance. As Judith Walkowitz argues, it is possible to seek out cultural meanings while paying attention to the historian's traditional concerns: 'power, agency and experience.'[24]

The class position of working girls renders the capture of their experience difficult, though not futile. Court documents, for instance, allow one to hear the voices of women, both victims and offenders, that otherwise would have vanished into the vast silence that consumes the history of women and the working class. My attempts to listen to those voices led me to criminal court records (the York County Court of General Sessions, the County Court Judge's Criminal Courts, and the Supreme Court of Ontario) that involved working girls who were either defendants or complainants. As well, I have studied the case files of juvenile and women's reformatories located in Toronto.[25] It would be naïve to assume that mining prison case files and court transcripts would turn up evidence of the 'real' life of working girls; however, we can listen to their stories with an awareness of the mediating factors of legal discourse and courtroom practice. Complainants in rape cases, for instance, often tilted with defence lawyers under cross-examination, struggling to redefine the terms of heterosexual encounters that they claimed had turned into criminal assaults. Many broke down in tears, but some matched lawyers' insinuations about their respectability with acid retorts about their right to seek pleasure without confronting danger. The verdicts in such cases generally, though not invariably, led to acquittals, but the record-keeping practices of the courts and the coverage of trials in newspapers leaves a residue of working girls' version of their perilous encounters. Probing the reasons why some stories were given credence and others were discounted is not so much an idealistic search for 'the truth' as a way of demonstrating the conditions under which authoritative voices gave or denied working girls' experience the stamp of legitimacy.[26]

The pleasures of working girls, unfortunately, are much more illusive than their perils, and *Toronto's Girl Problem* is consequently weighted towards the dangers of city life. Young working women did not, as a rule, sit around contemplating their diversions or recording details of their time off the job for snooping historians. But there are other ways in which we can discover what working girls did for fun. Photographic evidence of groups of young women cavorting in the waves of the Scarboro Beach amusement resort or piling onto sleighs in High Park displays the energy of youth and the occasional cheeky glance at the camera. Advertisements for commercial amusements and the movies seduced an audience of working girls, who readily turned over a precious portion of their wages for a few hours of pleasure. The records of YWCA houses and other subsidized boarding-homes offer sketches of official recreation programs as well as evidence of the unofficial highjinks of the residents. We can also read through, and past, the words of those who took on the task of reforming working girls' taste for amusement into a desire for healthy recreation. Philanthropic ladies, parole officers, and Children's Aid workers reportedly described their failure to teach working girls to appreciate the higher purposes of leisure time; spicier diversions, such as car rides with young men, exerted a stronger pull. Finally, it is possible to discern working girls' pleasures through the unlikely source of criminal records. Abortion, infanticide, and sexual assault trials hint at the possibilities of alternative happy endings to these tragic tales of heterosexual relations. We can only imagine how young women who met men while attending band concerts at Queen's Park or taking in vaudeville shows may have found romantic partners rather than rapists, suitors who later abandoned them, or bumbling boyfriends whose clumsy attempts to induce abortions resulted in death. While it has become a truism that crimes against women, as well those committed by them, largely remain 'secrets,' we should not proceed to the conclusion that every chance encounter with a man at a dancehall or every dish of ice cream shared in a downtown parlour must have been a bargain with disaster, for that line of reasoning reproduces the moral discourse on women's pleasures.[27] Working girls adopted their own strategies to negotiate their paths through the world of city pleasures, and as a result called into question the dire predictions of social purity advocates. Many clearly had fun in the process.

Toronto may seem an unlikely place to study either danger or pleasure, given its historic reputation as 'Toronto the Good.' It is precisely this image, a fiction consciously constructed in the late nineteenth century, that makes it an especially appropriate context for the study of the girl problem. Toronto was far from a dynamic metropolis of the order of New York, London, or Paris: its population barely topped the one-half-million mark as late as the 1920s, and its Anglo-Celtic cultural hegemony and infamous blue laws caused bon vivants such as Ernest Hemingway to flee to Europe for stimulation. It took Morley Callaghan, in *Strange Fugitive* (1928), to reveal that there was more to Toronto than its civic boosters (or its later chroniclers) cared to admit.[28] Callaghan painted an underworld that included crooked bootleggers, silent 'Chinamen' in dingy chop-suey joints, and lusty Italians girls, who for a few drinks might dispense a few favours. This version of Toronto as a heady concoction of dubious pleasures and mysterious 'foreigners' had actually appeared earlier, in YWCA meetings on the girl problem and in white slavery tracts, and was in fact a stock dystopic image in nineteenth-century literature on city life. Literate Torontonians were familiar with the writings of Dickens and Mayhew, writers who inspired nostalgia for a vanishing rural past, an idealized vision of social harmony when women stayed happily at home and families worked together.[29] Pessimistic Torontonians viewed their city in archetypal terms, as a centre of social disorder, 'of oppression, of crime and squalor, of a reduced humanity.' The extraordinary efforts to create Toronto the Good sprang from a concerted civic effort to ward off the evils of urban life.[30]

The historiography of women in Toronto is considerably sketchier than the historical accounts of the city's underbelly. Most histories of the city ignore women altogether, with the exception of prominent organizational women, professional pioneers, and society women. Even histories of working-class Toronto treat women's labour as a sidebar (granting them a handful of pages out of the text, much like earlier investigators of industrialization did), although they do include census material that reveals at least the statistical importance of working girls.[31] Toronto was one of the principal destination points of young English-Canadian women (as well as of recent immigrants from Britain, Italy, and eastern Europe) searching for paid work. Like New York and London, albeit on a smaller scale, Toronto provided a diversified economic base and a wider range of women's employments than cities like Hamilton, where heavy industry dominated.

Toronto hosted more than its share of organizations committed to the moral reformation of the city and to the moral reclamation of the working girl. The city was the national headquarters of the social purity movement, a loose coalition of Protestant activists and educators who set out to '"raise the moral tone" of Canadian society' in the late nineteenth and early twentieth centuries. Leading figures in the movement, such as Rev. John Shearer, the head of the Presbyterian church's moral reform department, were based in Toronto. Social purity leaders did not need census reports to alert them to the migration of working girls to the city: they had only to look out their windows at the streets of Toronto.[32] The city's infamous Morality Department was equally aware of the girl problem as a key factor in the city's vice scene. The most visible targets (thanks in large measure to the complaints of journalists such as C.S. Clark) of police-enforced reform campaigns in Toronto were illicit pleasure spots, such as saloons and brothels, that capitalized on the ready market of customers willing to pay for diversions. In the 1890s the debate over Sunday streetcars in Toronto, for instance, exposed the contentiousness of workers' leisure as a site of struggle and gave truculent defenders of working men's right to pleasure an opportunity to grumble about the oppressiveness of Toronto the Good. What has received less attention, however, is the place of the working girl in those struggles over legitimate amusements. Working girls were in fact rigorously controlled by the civic agencies that monitored city amusements, from amusement parks to dancehalls, where unescorted women (but not men) were vulnerable to arrest on delinquency charges. Efforts to make Toronto 'good' were played out not only through the suppression of men's gambling and drinking but through the regulatory mechanisms imposed on working girls' pastimes. Even the periodic crackdowns on commercialized sex were felt more keenly by the female suppliers than the male consumers of pleasure. New forms of regulation, such as the city's first policewomen, who monitored public amusements, were introduced specifically with the girl problem in mind, and new agencies, such as the Big Sisters, carried informal yet coercive powers over young single women. The more working girls 'pushed at the boundaries' of sexual respectability by participating in commercial amusements, the more they were apt to find their pleasure-seeking redefined as vagrancy, prostitution, delinquency, or even sexual psychopathy.

With the rise of commercial amusements geared towards working-girl customers, then, the wage-earning single woman became less a focus for pity than a target in the campaign to establish moral order in an urban industrial context. Toronto provided a home for the North American urban Progressive movement as well as the English-Canadian Sabbatarian and social purity movements. Although some writers of white slavery tracts perpetuated the image of the innocent country girl in the city, by the turn of the century the working girl's prominence in city life overshadowed the older image of the woman adrift. The growing numbers of women in industry, sales, and, increasingly, office work proclaimed that working girls could be self-confident urbanites, able to avoid the perils of city life through skilful management.

Although civic reformers worked towards a goal of a morally upright city that required strict codes of behaviour for all city dwellers, the discourse of moral regulation that targeted wage-earning single women was part of a greater campaign to purify and regenerate 'the race.' As Mariana Valverde and Angus McLaren have demonstrated, Anglo-Celtic Canadians in the late nineteenth and early twentieth centuries were eager exponents of the Spencerian concept of racial hierarchy and, more important, white hegemony. Canadians contributed to these notions of racial stratification and the ever-present threat of degeneration by formulating the concept of a morally and physically superior Northern race, cultivated through British lineage and nurtured through the adversities of the Canadian climate. Thus, the Canadian 'race' was invented as an amalgam of biological, cultural, and geographical qualities. Eugenicists were the most notorious promoters of the racial purity concept, but the racist belief in the inferiority of 'lesser' races, ethnic groups, and non-Christians pervaded all levels of civil society. Prominent Torontonians, such as the long-reigning police magistrate George Taylor Denison, openly subscribed to a racial schema in which Jews were 'neurotic,' southern Europeans 'hot-blooded,' Chinese 'degenerate,' and native peoples and blacks 'savage' and 'primitive.' In contrast, Protestant Anglo-Celtic Canadians sat at the top of the racial hierarchy, principally through their civilized sexual mores (Catholic French Canadians, with their higher birth rate, were accordingly assigned a lower rank). In the eyes of the Anglo-Celtic élite that dominated Canadian economic and social life, 'foreigners' (non-British persons or those who did not speak English, as opposed to non-Canadians per se) and the working girl threatened to upset the politically reinforced racial hierarchy by 'mongrelizing' the race – working girls through their alleged lapses into prostitution and foreigners by propagating in greater numbers than the sexually circumspect Protestant Canadians. The devastating losses to Canadian manhood in the First World War boosted government and social hygiene lobbyists' worries concerning racial degeneration to unprecedented heights. The working girl's sexual morality, not only the 'occasional prostitute's' but increasingly the non-criminal wage-earning woman's, stood on the front line in the war against national decline.[33]

Toronto's Girl Problem opens with the 'discovery' of the woman adrift and the creation of the image of the helpless and friendless wage-earning woman that would prevail during the early decades of industrialization. Most official investigations of industrial capitalism and its social costs focused on working men, and relegated discussion of women workers to short comments or separate appendices. In these official texts we can trace the connections between language and social context. Just as the working girl was marginalized through the superexploitation of her labour, so she was literally shoved to the margins of industrial reports and shunted into separate moral categories of analysis. When investigations were devoted exclusively to women workers, as was the case with the commission that studied the 1907 strike of Bell telephone operators in Toronto, the moralization of the working girl and her problems was reinforced through the deployment of a medical discourse that framed the management of single women's work and play in terms of the future of 'the race.' In spite of the overwhelming evidence of women's preference for factory, shop, and office work over domestic service, authoritative observers persistently extolled the virtues and benefits of work in service for single women. Census evidence provides stark evidence that working girls disregarded that advice.

From this general map of the girl problem I proceed to chart specific points of concern and controversy over the rise of single women working in the city. Beginning in the 1880s, evangelical reformers established rescue agencies, and the police devised new practices of monitoring urban morality. In that decade the YWCA established itself as the chief overseer of the wage-earning single woman in the city – or what the ladies of the YWCA understood to be 'the Devil's Kingdom.' In the first decades of its work, the YWCA built homes for working girls but made distinctions between respectable women, who struggled to make ends meet, and 'fallen women,' whose only hope for reform lay in piety and the sole form of work deemed appropriate for them: domestic service. The Morality Department of the Toronto police force, an invention of the reform mayor William Howland, had a very different law-and-order agenda, but it too was involved in making distinctions between chaste and unchaste working women. As the annual chief constables' reports repeatedly complained, the growing number of working girls in the city made the identification of prostitutes a tall order: it was no longer clear whether a young woman, living alone and partaking of urban amusements was a prostitute or a wage-earning worker relaxing after a day's legitimate labour. These exercises in moral identification were carried out in courtrooms whenever women appeared as victims or defendants. Court records suggest how criminal trials, no less than moral rescue, police work or newspaper accounts of crime, were discursive contests in which trial participants and the press juggled images of innocent maidens, fallen women, and the perilous city.

The middle chapters of this book focus on the 1890s to the 1910s, the period when North American-style Progressivism inspired an all-out assault on urban immorality. By the turn of the century a proliferation of discourses on the working girl emerged as professional reformers, including doctors and settlement house workers, as well as clubwomen (in the YWCA and the local chapter of the National Council of Women) and social purity advocates, led by Rev. Shearer and Rev. T.A. Moore, set out to impose sexual order on Toronto.[34] Conflicting and complementary solutions, including the police crackdown on the city's red-light districts, the introduction of legislation aimed at ending the white slave trade, and the stricter supervision of commercial amusements, were among the various approaches to the problem of urban vice. Proponents from different reform camps agreed, however, that the wage-earning single woman was a key figure in the city's attempts to turn Toronto into a 'City upon a Hill.' The 1915 commission charged with surveying 'the social evil' in Toronto summed up more than a decade of pronouncements against the unregulated commercial amusement industry and the lackadaisical enforcement of vice laws. Medical members of the commission reported that the inadequate supervision of urban youth had led not only to the growth of prostitution but to its attendant evils: venereal disease and 'feeblemindedness.' Like race, feeblemindedness was a purportedly scientific category that was fused to moral concepts. Both men and women could be feebleminded, according to medical experts, but because the feebleminded female was sexually profligate and extraordinarily fertile, she was nothing less than a social menace.

As Toronto's growing amusement industry pitched its offerings for the vast market of working-girl consumers, the city's social workers, penologists, and clubwomen felt that young single women would inevitably find themselves vulnerable to the lure of pleasures that their wages alone would not buy. Their antidote for the disease of commercialized sex was not higher wages for women but a pleasure discipline intended to cure working girls of their taste for doubtful amusements. The first guinea pigs were young women who ended up in reformatories after being branded 'occasional prostitutes,' 'moral delinquents,' or – an old standby – 'vagrants.' Both convicted morals offenders and young women termed 'pre-delinquents' were drilled on the ethos of proper recreation and work habits. In contrast, the problems that brought them into conflict with authorities, including abusive families and low-paying dead-end jobs, remained matters left up to individuals and abstract market forces. Ironically, the programs first devised for delinquent youth were later replicated in recreational schemes promoted for respectable white-collar workers. By the 1920s the pursuit of the 'right sort' of recreation became a hallmark of good citizenship for single female wage-earners.

In contrast to the pervasive regulation of working girls' pleasures, the policing of sexual danger was spotty and inconsistent with the idealized image of Toronto the Good. Chapter 6 explores this theme by analysing criminal trial records and the arrest tallies of the Toronto police force. Although it returns to issues of sexual endangerment, first discussed in chapter 3, it focuses on the mid-1890s to the 1920s, a time when feminists, Progressive reformers, and social purity advocates launched their assault on urban vice and immorality. Arrest statistics confirm that the police did step up their campaign to rid Toronto of certain forms of illegal sexuality (notably prostitution and male homosexuality); however, these policing practices did not lay the foundation for working girls' increased security in the city.[35] In effect, the actions of the police and the decisions of the courts did more to uphold stereotypes of 'dangerous foreigners' and promiscuous 'good times girls' than to establish working girls' right to be free from sexual danger. Moreover, the stricter regulation of abortion, which often entailed the intimidation of women who had sought abortions, underlines the internal contradictions and conflicting goals of official campaigns to protect women from the perils of the city. By the early twentieth century, broad-based efforts to regulate single women's equality in the service of 'the race' were the most notable achievements of the anti-vice campaign.

The themes of work and leisure are reintroduced in chapter 7, which looks at state and private agencies' attempts to regulate wage-earning women's time on and off the job. By the 1910s and 1920s, as women from all classes entered a widening field of occupations, a range of regulatory strategies was devised to ensure their progress from paid work to marriage and child-rearing. Distinct programs of leisure management, tailored for different categories of working women, began to reinforce on a cultural level the structural inequalities between the poorest and best-paid workers.[36] Factory girls, for instance, were treated very differently from business women: the former were more likely to find themselves subjected to medical and psychiatric assessments of their moral inadequacies than the latter, who learned the behaviour expected of them through employee notice-boards and pep talks at sporting and social events. In spite of these class-based distinctions, both approaches to defining and imposing a discipline of work and play sprang from a broadly based concern that working women make a successful transition from singlehood and paid work to marriage and motherhood.

Two appendices shed further light on the changing fortunes and misfortunes of single women in the city. Appendix A presents census data that chart the growth of Toronto's economy and the contribution women workers made to the city's emergence as an industrial metropolis. Appendix B looks at arrest records to profile shifting police priorities in regard to women both as victims and as offenders. Viewed together, these appendices provide reference points for analysing turn-of-the-century debates about single women, work, and sexual morality.

Toronto's Girl Problem broaches new ground, certainly in the historiography of Toronto but also in women's, working-class and urban history. It does not ask whether city living oppressed or emancipated women. It focuses neither on women's workplace relations nor on their family life. The story of spinsters and professional independent women appears only in relation to their work with – and investigation of – working girls. Rather, it is the story of those women over whom so much ink was spilt in the late nineteenth and early twentieth centuries: young, single, predominantly working-class women who worked for wages. As Denise Riley notes, women 'suffer from an extraordinary weight of characterization,' but certain kinds of women, in particular historical contexts, attract even greater attention.[37] In the late nineteenth and early twentieth centuries, a period of unparalleled social and economic reorganization in Canadian life, debates over the morality of material progress consumed the nation. When Torontonians puzzled over the nature of progress in their city, they kept returning to the figure of the working girl. In the course of seeking answers about the prospects for life under industrial capitalism, they came up with the 'girl problem.' The working girl consequently evolved into an emblematic figure of the industrializing city: on the pages that follow, she assumes centre stage once again.

2

City Work, Moral Dilemmas

'Help wanted, female' was the call. Beginning in the 1880s, Toronto newspaper employment columns advertised not only for domestic help but for young women to work in small factories and shops. In 1895 the Toronto *News* carried the Leading Employment Exchange's advertisement for 'active and reliable girls and women' to work as salesladies, office help, dressmakers, and tailoresses; another ad, placed by the Universal Knitting Company, called for power knitting-machine operators. By the early 1900s ads for a host of garment industry operators dominated the 'Situations Vacant – Female' column in the *Star*: 'experienced paper boxmakers, also girls to learn,' 'strong, respectable girls' for Christie Brown's biscuit factory, and 'ten smart young girls; good wages; steady employment' for Knox Manufacturing Company were among the other workers wanted. Postings for domestics and factory operatives remained staples of the help-wanted columns well into the 1910s, but ads for stenographers, waitresses, counter-helpers, commissioned saleswomen, and switchboard operators offered competition. By the end of the First World War, employers in every sector of the city's economy clamoured for female help.

The majority of these wage-earners were young and single. Unlike their mothers and aunts, who provided unpaid household or farm labour, working girls, as they were called, represented a radical break from working women's past. At first it was Toronto 'society's' seemingly insatiable need for domestic servants that drew young women in greater numbers than their brothers, but the growing commercial and industrial city also provided an increasing range of non-domestic employment for women. The imbalance in the city's sex ratio in favour of women, evident as early as the mid-nineteenth century, skewed markedly when factory and sales work positions opened up for women in the 1880s and 1890s. By the early twentieth century waged labour for women had become virtually synonymous with city life, and increasingly it entailed work that was conducted beyond the domestic sphere.

From the standpoint of the late twentieth century, these characteristics of women's work seem unworthy of comment; at the turn of the century, however, they provoked great anxiety and prompted numerous inquiries into the causes and possible consequences of single women's entry into urban industrial life. Although the practice of young, single women working was hardly new, their working outside their own families' or their masters' homes was unprecedented in Canada. In Europe and the industrial cities of the United States, the impact of industrial capitalism and its effect on women workers had already inspired inquiries and led to the imposition of regulations governing the character and hours of women's work, but Canadians did not confront the social impact of industry and urbanization until the 1880s. Like other beneficiaries of industrialization, Canadians felt ambivalent about a brand of economic progress that wrenched traditionally homebound workers from the moorings of family life.

Concern about women 'adrift' in the industrial city was accompanied by fears about the disruption of family cohesion, the decline of rural life, and the growing militancy of the urban working class. In the 1880s the 'Labour Question' dominated debates about the costs and benefits of industrial capitalism, and most public discussions revolved around trade unions and male workers' rights to a family wage versus the industrialists' right to maximize their profits. Whenever talk turned specifically to the morality of industrial capitalism, however, the single woman worker rose to the top of the agenda. The male worker was a breadwinner, a potential source of unrest when he demanded his due, but an indispensable cog in the wheels of industry: the woman worker presented a moral problem, the solution for which would necessarily focus on morality.

The presence of single males in cities has traditionally raised concerns about disorderliness, yet the movement of young men into urban industrial work in late nineteenth century Toronto did not raise the same alarm as that inspired by female wage-earners. Male workers might go astray through the effects of drink or the influence of riotous fellows; at worst, they might turn to crime, particularly in periods of unemployment. Women, it was feared, might drift along similar courses and worse – towards prostitution. The issue of sexual morality loomed like a dark cloud over discussions of women's work in the industrializing city, casting waged labour as a test of chastity rather than an economic or political issue. While it is not surprising that philanthropists and evangelical reformers approached single women's waged work as a moral problem, their concerns about the erosion of protection for and restraints upon young single women were shared by unionists and feminists as well. Never before had women's work in Toronto placed young, single women at the forefront of economic and social change, and never before or since have they inspired such concern about the nature of 'modern' city life.

This chapter examines how government agencies 'discovered' the rise of single women workers in the late nineteenth and early twentieth centuries in the course of their investigations of industrialization and its costs and benefits. The evidence they gathered and the reports they produced document what came to be called 'the girl problem': the vulnerability and moral irresponsibility of young working women in the city. They do not mirror the reality of working girls' lives (although they do provide valuable information about working conditions); however, they are not merely ideological representations imposed on the experiences of working women. Rather, official investigations of wage-earning women trace the girl problem as it was constructed by men and a growing number of professional women vested with the authority to define it. Although they persistently portrayed working girls as a moral dilemma for industrial urban society, their picture of the girl problem changed over time; moreover, it was articulated differently by the various institutions, agencies, and individuals who wrote about it and attempted to offer solutions to it. The idea of the girl problem was informed by and responsive to the agencies that dealt with women wage-earners but also to single women workers, their struggles, their troubles, and their spirited search for pleasure in the dispiriting context of the industrializing city.

CITY WORK

Toronto, more than any other of Ontario's cities, attracted young single women eager to earn wages. Because it enjoyed a diverse economic base and was not dominated by heavy industry, it provided a relatively wide variety of economic opportunities for both women and men. Among urban migrants, young women stood out as prototypical city dwellers. The greater ratio of women to men in the city actually grew more pronounced as Toronto industrialized, then levelled off by the turn of the century. In 1851 there were 102.7 females for every 100 males in Toronto: by 1901 that figure had jumped to 112.5. The overrepresentation of females was even more dramatic among the city's unmarried adults. From 105.4 single women to every 100 single men in 1881, the ratio climbed as high as 120.9 to 100 in 1901. Toronto had transformed over the century from a male-dominated garrison town into a minor industrial metropolis and, not coincidentally, 'a place for young women.'[1]

Domestics dominated the city's female workforce until the mid-nineteenth century, when other forms of employment began to siphon off Toronto's servant pool. Until 1881 domestic service was the single greatest employer of women, yet its dominance of the female job market was already being challenged: more than half of Toronto's women workers had turned to work in city workshops, stores, and factories. As early as 1871, for instance, Henderson's straw-works employed 175 female employees and only 26 men and boys. This female-dominated firm was the city's single largest employer at the time. The garment industry, however, soon employed the greatest proportion of female workers, after domestic service. Tailors, dressmakers, furriers, corset manufacturers, and boot- and shoemakers employed almost 2,000 women out of a total female labour force of 6,000 in 1881. As the ready-to-wear market expanded over the 1880s, the number of female garment and shoe workers jumped to 4,500. There were no huge mills employing thousands of women as there were in New England, nor were there large tobacco factories such as Montreal's. In Toronto, wage-earning women worked in small workplaces and in over 1,000 factories by the 1890s.

Several industries, coddled by the National Policy, appeared to spring out of nowhere and at the same time to emerge with female-dominated labour forces. Before 1891, for instance, shirtmaking was not recorded in the census; by the beginning of the 1890s, over 500 women and only 53 men were listed as shirtmakers. By 1891 there were more women than men working in Toronto's corset, dressmaking, furrier, hosiery, and tailoring establishments, as well as in its book binderies and paper-bag factories. Women were also well represented in the city's bakeries and boot and shoe shops. The mechanization and 'de-skilling' of trades was almost invariably coincidental with the introduction of female labour. Once commercial bakeries, such as Christie Brown, and Robertson's candy manufacturers expanded their operations in the 1880s, their

·workforce was overwhelmingly female: while only 61 women worked in the city's bakeries in 1881, that number rose to 356 in a decade. The diversification of Toronto's secondary manufacturing sector, the feminization of several light industries, and the rapid growth of the city were simultaneous and mutually dependent.[2]

What stands out about the non-domestic jobs that women began to take up in the late nineteenth century is their economic marginality. Women book binders and corset makers might have hoped. for the independence that Toronto's few women scholars and doctors had begun to achieve, but their work offered no such possibilities; rather, they toiled to survive and to support themselves, their families, and in some cases their illegitimate offspring. To do so required good health, marketable skills, tenacity, and extremely good fortune. Because women were employed primarily at tasks associated with traditional female skills (such as sewing) or simple jobs that other workers could easily learn (such as folding paper boxes or inserting straw into brooms), employers could easily replace them with women eager to leave domestic service. Like male labourers who faced the down season of winter, women who worked in the clothing industry were let go in response to the fluctuating demands of fashion seasons; domestic servants were also vulnerable to seasonal layoffs, but downturns were felt most sharply by factory hands who worked in fragile, newly created sectors of secondary manufacturing. In short, the vast majority of wage-earning women in late nineteenth-century Toronto were neither dilettantes toiling for pin money nor bold career women: they were highly exploited workers for whom independence was more likely to be a burden than an opportunity.

Working conditions and pay were, of course, hardly better for the men who worked in the dangerous and backbreaking occupations that were closed to women. Yet even the poorest-paid labourer earned more than female women workers, and young men could fall back on a much wider range of semi-skilled occupations in hard times. The wage differential between male and female printing and bookbinding employees was typical: men earned an average of $448 annually, while women earned $185.[3] Domestic service and jobs associated with traditional female skills, including cooking, cleaning, knitting, and sewing, offered women their only alternative to sales or manufacturing work. Until the turn of the century, however, women's work was distinguishable from men's primarily because most female workers were poor. Even the city's several hundred teachers were paid substantially less than their male counterparts.[4] To be a self-supporting single working woman in late nineteenth-century Toronto was to live, in all but a few cases of doctors and professionals, a hand-to-mouth existence.

While the 1880s saw the mobilization of unionized workers as a political force, most workers organized along craft lines that marginalized or excluded female workers. The result was that women were much less likely than men to be unionized; indeed, for this reason, many trade unionists were hostile to female labour because manufacturers routinely replaced skilled male workers with young, inexperienced women. One exception to the general pattern of indifference and hostility was the support offered by the Wholesale Boot and Shoemakers' Union to female factory workers who struck in April 1882 to demand union recognition. After two years of protracted disputes that led to limited concessions over wages, the women joined the Toronto Trades and Labor Council, the first women's union in the city to do so. The Knights of Labor, drawn to Toronto in 1882 partly because of the success of the women operatives, helped to organize the city's first all-female local, composed of tailoresses and other garment workers, in 1886. Three years later, another women's local was formed after the Knights' general investigator of women's work and wages came to Toronto to drum up support. In spite of these early successes, the gains of Toronto's unionized women were not honoured consistently, and the decline in the 1890s of the Knights, the only labour organization that actively courted women workers, meant that women's activism tended to be sporadic, isolated, and often without lasting improvements in pay and conditions of labour.[5]

Over the following decades, few substantial improvements in the lot of women workers were made through the efforts of unions. Gender divisions and, to a lesser extent, ethnic tensions in the Toronto labour movement meant that employers could employ tactics to pit workers against one another. In an 1897 article in the *Daily Mail and Empire*, a clothing manufacturing openly admitted that he bought compliance from his male workers at the expense of his female employees: 'I don't treat the men bad, but I even up by taking advantage of the women.'[6] Men resented working girls for driving down wages and acting as strikebreakers, but working women became disenchanted when labour leaders settled strikes by agreeing that only men's wages were to be increased. Although the feminist movement, dominated by middle-class objectives, was a problematic vehicle for the improvement of working girls' lives, single wage-earning women could not count on their class allies to shield them from the exploitive practices of employers.[7]

MORAL DILEMMAS

In spite of the evident economic liabilities of women's labour, official pronouncements on wage-earning women fixed on the moral implications of women's work in the industrializing city. As members of the 1889 Royal Commission on Labour and Capital, the 1907 inquiry into the Bell Telephone operators' strike, and the 1916 Ontario Commission on Unemployment, state-appointed experts examined the conditions of female labour in emerging industrial occupations and submitted their recommendations for improvement. These three inquiries summarize information about the status of women workers; more significantly, they represent an official body of knowledge about working women. Expert investigators were implicated in power structures – the state, the medical profession, social welfare agencies, the law – and their findings therefore carried authority.[8] The images of single working women they produced were replicated and contested in a variety of other discourses and practices, from police constables' and reformatory reports about prostitutes to boarding-house and recreational programs for working girls. Although no single authoritative discourse on wage-earning women and the city emerged, official investigations of women in industrial life nevertheless played an important role in organizing working girls' struggles to survive and to explore the pleasures of the city into categories of respectability.

Between the 1880s, when the expansion of secondary manufacturing opened up employment opportunities for women, and the latter years of the First World War, when women's waged work was trumpeted as a patriotic duty, the single female woman worker attracted attention that far outweighed her supporting role in the city's economy. Seen in the 1880s as a curious and worrisome aberration from domestic femininity, by the 1910s, wage-earning women were viewed as temporary contributors to the wealth of the nation on their way to their more profound contribution as wives and mothers. Underlying this change in perception, however, was a persistent unease concerning the implications of women's non-domestic work. Avowedly scientific surveys were suffused with emotion over the migration of young single women to city jobs and the predicted threat their work posed to the moral stability of the nation. It was this fear above all else that animated studies of working women. Women who worked in factories and shops were not only adrift, but their flight from domesticity threatened to dislodge Canadians' anchoring in the comfort and security of the home and family. Once lucre drew young women into masculine workplaces, would they ever return to the hearth?

Although most women who composed the ranks of Canada's first industrial workers could hardly have afforded the luxury of a hearth in the first place, their unconventional labour and lifestyles none the less starkly contrasted the homebound existence of their mothers and aunts. Waged labour carried an aura of adventure and vulnerability for young women, and the city promised 'new attractions, new freedoms, and a veil of anonymity under which to pursue them.'[9] Concern about working girls' inability to make the right moral choices in a context of supposedly limitless temptations and dangers animated inquiries into the state of women's industrial work. In attempting to make sense of the single wage-earning woman's emergence, investigators of women and industrialization simultaneously exposed their deep suspicions about the morality of urban life and their anxieties about the future of 'the race.' Their ambivalence is evident in the unstable, almost chimerical image they constructed of the working girl: simultaneously a sacrifice to industrial growth, a potential source of urban vice, and the irresponsible guardian of future generations. Critical commentary on the sexual division of labour under industrial capitalism and the routine underpayment of wages in 'women's occupations' did not appear on their agenda. Instead, they were preoccupied with the moral meanings of the wage-earning woman. As later chapters will show, that preoccupation resonated in the policies of state agencies and the charitable and correctional organizations concerned with urban working women.

THE ROYAL COMMISSION ON THE RELATIONS OF LABOUR AND CAPITAL

The report of the Royal Commission on the Relations of Labour and Capital (1889) was the federal government's attempt to quell the labour unrest that had marked the 1880s and to reassure Canadians that the National Policy would bring prosperity to the young dominion without leading to social disharmony. At first glance, Canada's initial exploration of industrial life appears to have little to do with wage-earning women. Of approximately 1,800 witnesses who testified before the commissioners who visited Ontario, Quebec, New Brunswick, and Nova

Scotia, only 102 were women; a further 200 men offered opinions on the question of women's work under industrial capitalism. The men initially appointed to the commission in 1886 were faithful Tories, but pressure from the labour movement resulted in the appointment one year later of four men from the ranks of organized labour. In all, sixteen men, often at odds with each other on class issues, questioned witnesses and ultimately submitted two separate reports.

Historians have found the contrasting class biases in the commission's final recommendations more intriguing than its stance on working women. Like the commissioners, who were preoccupied with issues of men's work, historians have been inattentive to the 'muffled voices' of women and the testimony on women's work.[10] None the less, careful attention to the few words devoted to women workers and to the organization of those limited discussions in the text offers insight into the investigators' perception of working girls. Men from both political camps shared a conviction that women suffered a unique form of exploitation in industrial establishments, yet they disagreed in their assessment of the rise of the wage-earning woman. In short, the first (minority) report, penned by the pro-National Policy capitalist sympathizers, portrayed women workers as 'unfortunate girls' in need of charitable aid; the second (majority) report attempted to uphold the honour of wage-earning women as a matter of working-class pride. Both groups of men agreed, though, that the social costs of industrial capitalism were most aptly measured through its effects on wage-earning women's morality.

The employment of women in new industries rose as the employment of children declined. Child labour had fuelled Toronto's initial steps towards industrialization, particularly in light industries such as clothing and straw-making. The rise of the public school and moral reform movements in the 1870s and 1880s, however, placed great pressure on manufacturers to discontinue the hiring of children, who appeared to be the most exploited of industrial workers.[11] Skilled workers also objected to the low wages – usually one-quarter to one-third of men's wages – paid to children, because they drove down the wages offered by employers to adult males. In Ontario, lobbying from several quarters resulted in the passage of the 1886 Factory Act, a statute intended to prohibit the employment of males under twelve and females under fourteen years of age. Although the act was narrow in application and poorly enforced, its impact was observed in the increasing employment of women.

The royal commissioners upheld the view that industry's cheapest workers had quickly become its greatest victims and the most potent symbols of capitalist greed. Employers, prompted by prohibitions against child labour, had discovered that women would work for almost as little as children, as the majority report noted: 'To arrive at the greatest profit for the smallest expenditure the mills and factories are filled with women and children to the practical exclusion of adult males. The reason for this is obvious. Women and children may be counted on to work for small wages, to submit to petty and exasperating exactions and to work uncomplainingly for long hours.'[12] Employers' and employees' testimony about wages and conditions of labour amply supported their conclusions. While the employers all agreed to allow the publication of their names, many women workers requested anonymity before agreeing to testify. If employers' truthfulness is suspect, however, their ingenuous statements about fair wages for women are telling. They freely admitted that they paid inexperienced hands, such as errand girls, as little as $1.50 per week. In the garment industry, Toronto's biggest employer of women, it was customary for starting sewers to work without any pay while they apprenticed. Miss Helen Gurnett, a Toronto dressmaker, was apparently exasperated by the 'little girls' in her employ who '[thought] it dreadful if they have to serve 6 months' while earning nothing.[13] Seasonal unemployment was also a phenomenon that employers took for granted in trades geared to rapid changes in fashion. Toronto dry goods manufacturer R. Irving Walker remarked that his female employees rarely worked more than ten months out of the year. He believed that they preferred this practice since it allowed them to 'have a month's holidays and spend it in fixing up their clothing.' When questioned about his workers' ability to stretch their average weekly earnings of $4 over their 'holidays,' he responded that it depended upon the 'character of the hands': with 'ordinary care and industry,' he claimed, capable women who applied themselves to their work could save enough to survive.[14]

Essentialist notions of masculine and feminine abilities, coupled with the assumption that women did not expect to 'make something' of themselves allowed employers to justify their paying women one-third to one-half of the wages paid to men. Although business owners consistently claimed that competence and 'application to work' were the keys to their wage scales, they paid women less than men as a matter of course. Only one employer, a cigar manufacturer, declared that he paid his top women workers as much as the men.[15] Timothy Eaton, whose dry goods establishment would become the single largest employer of women in Toronto by the early twentieth century, followed the more common practice. He explained his philosophy of sex-based pay scales as follows: 'Girls are more apt when young. They take hold more rapidly at first than boys. But boys in time exert themselves more and aim at being something and to rise higher. But with girls it is different, and the wages they receive [depend] entirely on how much they apply themselves to business.'[16] On this basis, he justified paying up to $12 a week to 'average salesmen,' but a mere $6 to $8 to 'first-class saleswomen.'

Employers also testified that they had weathered the localized storms of women workers' resistance to their labour practices. Several employers admitted that their women workers had struck over long hours and paltry wages. When the women who worked for J.D. King and Company, a boot and shoe manufacturer, struck in 1882 and remained out for four weeks, they received no wage concessions. They returned to work on the promise of a 'uniform bill of wages' that applied only to certain types of piecework performed by girls and women. Others had achieved more success. The move of the Crompton Corset Company of Toronto to Berlin, a town west of the city, prompted the 'girls' to walk out en masse because their weekly rate of pay had been slashed almost in half. They forced the company to return to Toronto and to restore their previous wage rates.[17] In spite of their victory, however, they continued to live on as little as $3 per week. Some witnesses spoke as if it had never occurred to them that their female hands might require an adequate living wage. During her questioning, it dawned on Miss Burnett, a Toronto milliner, that if her workers 'depended on their own earnings while they [were] employed ... they must live very poorly indeed.' The state seemed equally unwilling to take seriously the issue of women's low wages. Factory inspector James Brown, when asked about the wages of women and children in the factories he had visited, replied: 'That is a matter we are not supposed to inquire into.'[18]

In contrast to their limited inquiries concerning unionization as a potential solution to women workers' problems, the investigators were keenly interested in the morality of the women who were swept up in the process of industrial capitalism. As feminist and labour historians have noted, capital and the state, as well as working-class organizations, have historically understood wage-earning women not as workers but as moral subjects. Overwrought fears about the consequences of women's paid labour were thus rooted in nineteenth-century observers' conviction that 'what women stood for was not simply domestic virtue and household skills but sexual ordering itself.'[19] In spite of their clear differences on class issues, the commission's pro-labour and pro-business factions could agree that the home was the cardinal point on the moral map of the social and economic changes fostered by the National Policy: the further from domesticity and family women workers seemed to drift, the more dear – and dangerous – seemed the cost of urban industrial capitalism.

It was difficult for the commissioners to consider women workers solely as victims, however, since they evidently were eager to escape the bonds of domesticity for the dangers of industrial work. They took for granted that men might be attracted to the prospect of work in factories, but they hounded witnesses for the answer to the vital question: why did increasing numbers of women prefer industrial over domestic work? 'They like to have their evenings to themselves,' Miss Burnett surmised; 'I suppose that is the real reason.' Labour sympathizers seemed to agree with employers that if young women were sensible, they would remain loyal to domestic work. Headstrong 'girls' were another matter. When Mr R. Meek, a Knights of Labour representative and journalist from Kingston, was asked whether shop women would not prefer to be domestic servants 'if they could reconcile their minds to it,' he responded that they would be better off financially. The problem, as he saw it, was that 'you cannot convince a young woman of that fact.' He sided with the milliner, Miss Burnett, in this instance: young women evidently wanted their 'evenings to themselves' without having to consult with their masters. John Armstrong, the commissioner who led the pro-labour camp, perceptively inquired whether women's emerging preference might not also be due to the demeaning nature of personal service. Miss Burnett dismissed his theory. She thought that, for most working women, 'it would be far more respectable to be in domestic service, if they only knew it.' The difficulty, she concluded, was 'to make them believe it.'[20]

Most of the commissioners and the employer witnesses, in contrast, had little difficulty 'believing' that there was something disreputable about factory and shop women. The respectability of the same forms of work for men was never raised, and in their discussions of mixed-sex workplaces, discussions of morality were restricted to questions about women. The largest of these enterprises, particularly tobacco factories and textile mills, inspired the commission's closest scrutiny of sexual propriety. Toilets obsessed the investigators, who seemed to equate bodily elimination in mixed-sex work places with all-out promiscuity. They asked virtually every employer of a mixed staff whether or not there were separate 'conveniences' for male and female workers and, if so, whether men ever tried to sneak into women's 'closets.' The degradation of feminine respectability, not the impropriety of male behaviour, was their overriding concern. Both factions of investigators, for instance, feared that women who worked in proximity to men would be corrupted by men's foul language, in spite of the fact that women workers did not report profanity as a major issue. One anonymous paper-box maker from Ottawa responded to a question about her male co-workers' use of 'violent language' by saying that she did not really mind: to her, it was 'just cursing; that is all.'[21]

What the commissioners saw in the persons of female bookbinders and cigar-rollers were young women whose work had displaced them from the supervision of families and allowed them to drift in the amoral city. Although less than 20 per cent of female wage-earners lived apart from their families, the investigators dwelt on the image of the 'homeless' girl, struggling alone in exploitive work shops. As Joanne Meyerowitz has observed in regard to single wage-earning women in Chicago, official investigators constructed the image of the woman adrift because she best symbolized 'the victimization of the innocent and weak in an urban world without moral standards.'[22] The other side of the commissioners' wariness about urban waged work was an uncritical stance towards traditional forms of female labour and rural life. Their enthusiasm for domestic service ignored the vulnerability of domestics – still the typical worker in the 1880s – to sexual harassment from male servants and household members within the confines of private households. Worse still, live-in domestics could neither escape their harassers at night nor count on their mistresses' support against errant masters. Perhaps it was working women's awareness of the gulf between the real dangers and humiliating practices of familiar forms of women's labour and the commissioners' misty, sentimental portrayal of domestic service that made it so difficult for them to 'believe' that they would be better off as servants.

'HELPLESS WORKWOMEN'

Both the majority and the minority reports of the royal commission reflected the investigators' disinclination to view working girls as 'workers.' When they addressed hours of work, rates of pay, conditions of labour, and workers' rights to organize, they spoke only of men. Discussions of women workers were shunted from the main body of the text to sections devoted exclusively to the moral ramifications of urban industrialization. The minority report, supported by the members who were more sympathetic to capital than to labour, adopted a paternalistic tone towards women workers, portraying them exclusively as victims. In their appendix on child and female labour they spoke of the 'evils' of exploitation without questioning factory owners' rights to determine labour practices. The solution, the minority group suggested, lay in uniform labour legislation throughout the dominion. They hoped that Ottawa would enact laws to prohibit the employment 'at severe or long-continued work' of girls 'approaching womanhood,' since women were apparently too ignorant to realize the dangers they courted. Swayed by medical testimony, the commissioners worried that the 'evil effects' of women's industrial labours would follow them throughout their lives. 'The miseries endured by this interesting class of workwomen,' they advised, were a subject for the country's legislators, not its unions.[23]

The minority report backers, however, did not shy away from criticizing capitalists for sacrificing their social responsibilities to Mammon. They were outraged by irresponsible manufacturers who allowed unscrupulous foremen to exploit 'unfortunate girls' by confiscating wages for petty infractions. They accused company directors who were members of the Society for the Protection of Women and Children of hypocrisy: the 'unfortunates' whom they rescued were quite possibly their own workers, 'rendered homeless' through their uncertain earnings.[24] Homelessness was a discreet allusion to prostitution, a topic that bubbled beneath the minority report. Toronto reform Mayor William Howland, a wealthy insurance executive turned moral campaigner, had brought up the subject in his evidence. He called women workers a 'helpless class' who, because they had 'no friends,' had to 'submit and take what they get.' Women in London's East End supplemented their earnings by working 'at something else,' he confided, and warned the commissioners that Canadian working women might also drift into immorality.

Where Howland might have offered an economic or political analysis of the problem, he turned instead to praise for respectable working women's ability to endure their exploitation. On the one hand, he could understand how 'unfortunate girls' might turn to prostitution; on the other, he assured the commissioners that 'a good woman will die first.'

He resolved this apparent contradiction by assuming that women who fell were 'young and careless,' pleasure-seekers who lacked proper moral training. Under the influence of 'possible starvation,' it was 'only too possible' that they would slip into working 'at something else' that presumably paid better. In simultaneously raising and discounting the economic rationale for prostitution, he declared his belief, typical of evangelical reformers, that working-class women's 'rooted laziness' was the real source of the problem. Prostitution, unlike the drudgery and limitless hours of domestic work, was a 'lazy life' that offered 'an easy living.' Leisure, it went without saying, was a privilege of class and a dangerous indulgence for working-class women. Once they tasted a life of ease, working girls soon became 'unfitted for industry' and unsuitable for moral rescue.

In his moral calculus of women's work, Howland considered a woman's willingness to work without complaint for meagre wages – the very economic preconditions for prostitution – to be the measure of her respectability. In Toronto, he told the commission, the police broke up brothels, but always told the women that they would be treated mercifully if they would take up 'decent work' or 'go to any home' supplied by the city. The Morality Department, Mayor Howland's brainchild, invariably recommended that women return either to their family home or to someone else's as a domestic servant. In neither case, though, did the 'possible starvation' of women workers assume great importance in the mayor's analysis of prostitution; rather, the test of 'industry' and endurance allowed Howland and his Morality Department to distinguish the respectable from the disreputable and to deal with them accordingly.[25]

The pro-labour faction rejected the patronizing stance of the minority group and boldly defended the honour of their sister workers against Howland's insinuations of promiscuity among the working class. Their majority report stuck to an economic analysis of prostitution as a difficult choice in the face of privation rather than an easy slide into a life of idle luxury. After reviewing the pay scales for women workers, they declared that it was virtually impossible for them to 'live respectably and clothe themselves decently' on their wages alone: 'Given these conditions, it is not a matter for surprise that one is occasionally driven in despair to a life of sin. But it is monstrous to condemn a whole class because of an occasional sinner, as has been done far too frequently in this matter.' Unconsciously, they shared Howland's belief that a respectable woman would sooner 'die' than market her sexuality, although they offered an alternative appraisal of working women's moral fortitude. For labour men, women workers' ability to live respectably in poverty was a badge of working-class honour. Factory operatives and shop girls rarely departed from the 'strict line of virtue' even though they worked hard over long hours 'for a very small allowance.' They taunted the pro-capital camp on the commission by pointing to the rising number of divorce cases among the country's wealthy and supposedly respectable families: while workers struggled heroically to maintain respectability, they jeered, immorality flourished in 'what are termed the "higher walks of life."'[26]

The majority report turned the tables on the minority group's picture of pathetic women workers by pointing to the exploitation of women in more traditional occupations, where bourgeois employers could exploit labour in private homes. Trade unionists and Knights of Labour delegates had testified to the commission that there was a great deal of abuse as well as exhausting labour involved in most domestic occupations. The Labour journalist R. Meek had claimed that some young women were too frail to work in service; moreover, employers often expected women to serve 'from daylight to dark, and even all night too.'[27] Domestics' hours were unregulated, their workplaces did not fall under the provisions of protective legislation, and they were subject to the potential physical and sexual abuses of their masters if they lived in. The majority report referred to evidence from Manchester, where almost 60 percent of prostitutes were reported to have been domestics, while only 16 percent had worked in factories prior to their 'fall.' Relying on a well-worn theory of upper-class libertinism, the majority report concluded that servants and industrial workers did sometimes turn to prostitution, but only when 'led astray' by lecherous ruling-class men. It was a testament to working-class respectability that most remained chaste: 'Those who assert to the contrary are common libellers of a class who are nobly striving to live upright, honourable lives.'[28]

Disagreements over whether women workers were driven to vice through the 'pinchings of poverty' or the 'temptation [of] an easy living' divided the two groups of commissioners. Significantly, though, men from both camps agreed that the female industrial worker, unlike her male counterpart, raised moral, not economic or political, concerns for Canadians. Indeed, it was the pro-labour commissioners who used 'Morals' as the title of the section of their report dealing with women.

The two reports foreshadowed subsequent surveys of women and industrialization, and hinted at the contrasting interpretations of urban
prostitution that emerged over the late nineteenth and early twentieth
centuries. In Toronto, as in most cities, the paternalism of the minority
report was put into practice by organizations such as the YWCA, Mayor
Howland's Morality Department, and juvenile and women's reformatories. Even after the influence of US Progressivism in the 1900s and its
emphasis on environmental rather than personal explanations of vice,
prostitution was discussed in all but labour organizations as a moral
failing rather than as an economic expedient. Labour leaders themselves
failed to recognize working-class men's sexual exploitation of working
women, preferring to sing the praises of 'poor, hardworking factory
operatives' as long as they managed nobly to uphold working-class
virtue. As class-based defenders of working women, male trade unionists were no less preoccupied by working girls' morality than their
capitalist opponents.

THE INDISCRIMINATE EMPLOYMENT OF WOMEN

The expansion of women's occupations in the 1890s and 1900s was as
clear an indicator as any that the character of Canadian life was changing in response to the expansion of industrial capitalism. Young wom-
en's preference for non-domestic work became particularly evident in
cities like Toronto. By 1891, forty-four different manufacturing firms
with ten or more workers employed a total of 7,000 women, or over
twice as many as had worked in secondary industry a decade earlier.
Equally apparent was the drop in the number of women who worked
as servants. While just under 3,000 domestics served the city's wealthy
homes in 1881, the domestic labour force did not keep pace with the
rapid increase in population over the following decades. Toronto quad-
rupled in size by 1911 to one-third of a million, but the number of
female servants only slightly more than doubled.[29] A dramatic shift had
occurred in the occupational makeup of the female labour force as it
mushroomed from approximately 6,400 wage earners in 1881 to more
than 42,000 by 1911. At the outset of the period, over half of Toronto's
female workers were employed as servants, whereas only one-quarter
worked in service by 1911.

Investigators who looked into the state of women's non-domestic
waged work were well aware of these economic and social transitions.
Their inquiries resonated with nostalgia and a determination to turn

back the clock so that women might return, if not to their own hearths, then, in Mayor Howland's words, 'to any home.' One of the early warnings about the flight from domestic service came from Jean Scott, a Toronto political scientist who reviewed 'the conditions of female labour in Ontario,' in 1892. The crux of the problem was that young women came to cities to take up domestic positions only to abandon them for jobs that offered 'higher wages and other advantages.'[30] As a result, servants' wages were inflated, ranging from $6 per month for inexperienced girls to $20 for experienced cooks. Throwing away this security, domestic servants carelessly sought out jobs in the city's shops and factories. Young women apparently preferred freedom from the round-the-clock demands of live-in service. The Ontario Bureau of Industry, a government agency launched in 1882 to monitor the development of urban industrialization, took up the question of young women's preference for manufacturing and retail jobs. In 1887 it had explored the reasons why women tolerated the long hours, hazardous working conditions, and meagre wages offered in manufacturing: 'Many work through necessity that they may live, others that they may help their parents, while no inconsiderable number are daughters of country farmers who prefer city life and fixed hours of work, even at low wages, rather than remain at home, on the farm.'[31] Scott agreed that the 'factory or shop girl' had an advantage over her domestic sisters because, as she observed, 'when her work is over her time is her own.'[32] Unbeholden to mistresses in their free time, working girls were free to explore all the city had to offer, or so she imagined.

On the surface, the servant 'crisis' referred to a labour shortage; at a deeper level, it represented the possibility that young women's non-domestic work would jeopardize their transition into wifehood and motherhood. The 'indiscriminate and extensive employment of women,' Scott warned, had endangered 'the life of the home.' Women who worked beyond domestic settings disrupted the fundamental ordering of the sexes: 'Man was intended by nature to be the bread-winner of the family; and if family life is to be maintained as such he must remain: so that the persistent usurpation of his place by unfair competition must mean eventually a danger to the continuance of the home.'[33] In the face of this menace, she called for labour laws that would restrict the hours and ages at which women could work. If young women could not be made to see the sense of domestic work, the state would have to intervene.

Conservatives like Scott rejected the economic logic of employing working girls and fought vainly against the young women's increasing-

ly evident distaste for domestic work. Wives of the captains of commerce and industry might have thrown up their hands at the servant
problem, but their husbands were happy to find a steady supply of
former domestics to work in their stores and factories. As child labour
and school attendance laws were more strictly enforced, employers
counted on young women workers as their chief source of cheap labour.
It is no exaggeration to conclude that Toronto's service and light manufacturing industries were built on the backs of working girls. To the
capitalists who profited handsomely, it would not do for academics like
Scott to advise the government to close off the employment of women
as they had done with children. The organization of women workers for
higher wages and greater control over the labour process was an
equally unpalatable alternative.

   In keeping with the spirit of Progressive inquiry, investigations of
working girls in the early twentieth century dropped an explicitly moral
approach and took on a social-scientific tone. As tens of thousands of
working girls joined Toronto's workforce, experts pondered how best
to manage that resource. Two state-sponsored investigations, one an
inquiry into a major strike and the other a study of unemployment,
reflected this new twist on the idea of the girl problem. The Royal
Commission into the Bell telephone operators' strike of 1907 and the
1915 Ontario Unemployment Commission both approached the employment of single women as something more than a necessary evil of
economic progress. The commissions acknowledged that low pay and
poor working conditions were problems that would require coordina-
tion of efforts between the benevolent state, enlightened employers, and
dedicated women workers. Above all, the work of young single women
was not to interfere with working girls' expected transformation into
healthy, respectable, married mothers. The conundrum investigators
confronted was the clash between economic and social goals: on the one
hand, the pace of economic development depended largely upon the
continued exploitation of women workers; on the other, it was essential
that waged labour preserve single women's characters and reproductive
capacities intact. Managing the girl problem was vital, then, for the
good of the economy *and* the race.

HOLDING THE LINE AGAINST BELL

No job action better dramatized the plight, and the spunk, of Toronto's
working girls than the strike of the Bell Telephone operators in Febru-

ary 1907. Not since the 1882 shoemakers' walkout had a strike by women workers attracted so much attention and public sympathy. The 'hello girls,' as they were dubbed by the press, walked off the job en masse to protest management's restructuring of hours and reduction of wages. The more than four hundred workers – all of them female and most of them single, between the ages of seventeen and twenty-two – were paid generously, according to Bell management. 'Learners' began at $18 per month and, after nine months, could go on to become regular staff at $20 per month.[34] The operators disagreed, claiming that similarly skilled women, such as typographers, could earn over $40 per month, while semi-skilled male hands were paid as much as $60.[35] In the eyes of the strikers, the work they performed was highly skilled and physically taxing; moreover, as providers of an essential public service, they believed that they deserved higher wages and greater control over their working conditions. When the manager of the Toronto Central Exchange, K.J. Dunstan, decreased hourly earnings, the operators hastily organized and voted to strike.[36] After less than a week out, the strikers agreed to submit their grievances to the federal Ministry of Labour, which promised to conduct an inquiry and make recommendations for improvements if the women called off their strike. For the operators a commission was a gamble; for the company it was a coup, for it brought the workers back on its own terms without requiring Bell to negotiate over matters of hours and wages.

Labour historians have dismissed the commission's report as a state-directed exercise in the diffusion of labour-management conflict and the reinforcement of workers' powerlessness.[37] The Bell Commission certainly did nothing more than chastise the company in suggesting that working conditions be improved. The report recommended that a conciliation board of management and workers be formed to negotiate disputes in the future, but it steered clear of the wage issue, stating that 'the question of wages [is] left to the market.'[38] In any case, the company refused to uphold the commission's recommendations once the report was presented in August 1907.

The Bell strike was more than a class issue in the minds of the hello girls, the Bell executives, and the commissioners. The strikers' youth and marital status 'structured their experience in particular ways and influenced the manner in which they understood it.'[39] For working girls, earning a living wage could enable them to fulfil daughterly duties, provide sufficient wages to buy the sorts of outfits that might attract a beau, or, particularly for those women approaching their thirties, allow a woman to support herself respectably. Similarly, employers looked upon these working girls not so much as workers as females in a transitional phase of a family life cycle. Manager Dunstan told the Toronto *Star* that his employees were young 'girls' who worked at Bell for 'pin money' or 'to earn a fur coat or something like that and leave to get married after two or three years.'[40] Although the commissioners pushed the company to admit that almost half of the workers were self-supporting and that most of the remainder supplemented household incomes with their earnings, Dunstan maintained that there was no cause to increase their wages, since the operators were 'ready to get married' after a short period of employment.[41] Their low wages could be justified on the basis of their age, their marital status, and their sex. In short, they were paid less than a living wage, while the company sat on a capital accumulation sum of $8,604,840, because they were 'girls.'

THE MEDICALIZATION OF WORKING GIRLS' GRIEVANCES

The commission criticized Bell's miserly wage rates without challenging the utility's right to control its profit-making schemes. Instead, the report, written by Deputy Minister of Labour (and future Prime Minister) William Lyon Mackenzie King and York County Court Judge John Winchester, saved its strongest criticism for the operators' working conditions. Although their work was undeniably dangerous and taxing, the women themselves had not walked out over this issue, which so exercised the investigators. Nor had they struck because they were concerned about their marital or maternal prospects. The commissioners, appalled by the predicted impact of operators' work on their childbearing capacities, castigated Bell for its cavalier attitude towards the long-term health of its employees. In their mismanagement of working girls on the job, employers such as Bell placed the next generation at risk. As the report ominously concluded, the 'working of women at high pressure' was 'a crime against Nature herself.'[42]

The commission marked a pivotal moment in the rise of medical experts as social managers who succeeded in constructing the strike, and the strikers, as a medical problem.[43] The structure of the report underlined the authority of the 33 medical witnesses: 'Opinions of Leading Physicians' filled a 14-page section, while the testimony of 21 women, including strikers, former employees, supervisors, and strikebreakers, was quoted intermittently in short extracts. The report published only a few complaints about workers' hours and wages. Hattie

Davis, an orphan who boarded with her aunt and uncle, was one of the strikers who told the commissioners she had to work overtime to afford her clothing and board. Other women testified that overtime work was often compulsory whenever the exchange was short-handed. As Mamie Breck stated, 'We simply had to take it whether we liked it or not.'[44]

The commissioners proved to be more interested in evidence of work-related injuries than in tight budgets. They brought in several women, such as Lily Rogers, who were not actually strikers but who could nevertheless substantiate the dangers of operators' work. Rogers stated that she had received a shock so severe while attending a long-distance line that she was struck unconscious and placed under a doctor's care for nervous strain. Laura MacBean went into convulsions and was 'totally incapacitated' for a month after receiving a severe shock. Emily Richmond permanently lost her hearing in her left ear and Hilda Watson tore the ligaments in her arm from the constant strain of reaching for high connection points.[45] Women reported that virtually every operator experienced fainting, 'hysterical fits,' blurred vision, and temporary hearing loss at some point in her employment. The report is filled with over twenty-two pages of such evidence. In contrast, the issue of wages, the precipitating factor in the strike, was confined to three pages.

Newly minted medical experts on women's work amassed sufficient evidence to conclude that switchboard work was harmful for working girls. Although electrocution was presumably inadvisable for workers of any age and either sex, the doctors repeatedly expressed concern about the effects of switchboard work on 'girls.' From work-related shocks and torn ligaments the doctors leapt to the matter of working girls' fitness for their true vocation: marriage and motherhood. Dr James Anderson, an ear, nose, and throat specialist who considered himself an expert on gynaecology, predicted that three or four years at the exchange would produce 'an exhausted womanhood ... unfit for any strenuous work and harmful upon the future motherhood.' Dr William Alexander prescribed an equally short work life. He predicted that girls who worked longer than three years 'would not be in a condition to perform the ordinary occupations of womanhood satisfactorily.'[46]

Dr Charles K. Clarke, the medical superintendent of the Toronto Asylum, an international authority on mental hygiene, and a founder of the Canadian eugenics movement, was a witness well accustomed to issuing warnings about racial decline. He was asked to explain how operators' work might affect their offspring and, ultimately, the nation. Since he theorized that there was always a physical cause for mental disease, he felt that the pressures of operating put the operators' future children at risk. The results of 'nervous strain between the ages of 17 and 25' were 'only too well known,' he concluded vaguely. Government authorities might safely leave the matter of the current generation's wages to the vicissitudes of the market, but the health of the next generation called for intervention. When asked if he thought it 'in the interests of the State' to prevent strain on the operators' nervous system, Clarke was adamant: it was 'the duty of the State' to intervene for the good of the race.[47]

In spite of the medical witnesses' assiduously itemized scientific qualifications, the doctors were as free with their moral pronouncements as Jean Scott or the royal commissioners had been. Dr Dwyer, the superintendent of St Michael's hospital, issued a blanket warning that operators who worked for five years would 'turn out badly in their future domestic relations.' Again, the impact of their overwork was far-reaching: 'They break down nervously and have nervous children and it is a loss to the community.' In view of women's position as child-bearers and child-rearers, Dwyer agreed with Clarke that operators' working conditions should be monitored as a natural resource. 'The women are an important factor in the welfare of the state,' he concluded, 'and ought to be protected.' Another general practitioner warned that without such careful management, operators would be 'disqualified' from becoming wives and mothers. Predictably, the doctors agreed that 'medical men' were 'in the best position to pronounce' on the appropriateness of operators' work.[48]

Medical testimony convinced Commissioners Winchester and King that the operators' problem was 'medical rather than economic.' Without legislative interference, Canada was in danger of becoming a nation of neurasthenics. All businesses under capitalism were geared toward profits, they conceded, but when money-making and 'the health of young girls and women' collided, the former should be 'compelled to make way.' The future wellbeing of the country was an issue 'of so grave concern' that it should not be left to the machinations of unregulated capital. Medical men would provide the answers: doctors would study the tolerance level of operators; doctors would determine work schedules; doctors would determine whether or not women would be allowed to work. The issue of operators' wages had, by the conclusion of the report, disappeared altogether.[49]

The investigators admitted that they could not envision how the state might implement and enforce medical recommendations, but they thought that Bell's 'self interest' would teach the company that better working conditions led to greater efficiency and, ultimately, to higher profits. 'Happily,' the state would not have to interfere with capital if businesses adhered to expert medical advice and restricted the hours of work for 'girls.'[50] In the absence of higher wages, of course, operators would continue to require overtime earnings to meet their living expenses. By leaving the matter of wages to the market, the investigators condemned the 'hello girls' to the exploitive labour practices that had precipitated the strike.

MANAGING TO BE RESPECTABLE

In the end, the report expressed greater confidence in the wisdom of employers than in their employees. 'Girls' did not seem to understand the burden of responsibility they bore for the next generation. The company had contended that the women were fatigued because they spent their evenings doing housework, sewing, or engaging in commercial amusements instead of resting.[51] The last diversion raised the familiar issue of working women's respectability. Surely employers would not be responsible for the shocks received by young women who came to work bleary-eyed after a night of dancing.

The commissioners set about to arrange work schedules so that the young women would have enough time to rest but not to play. King and Winchester suggested that operators be granted a two-hour meal break so that those who lived far from the exchange could go home instead of bringing their meals to work or buying them in restaurants. Since lengthening the meal hour would reduce each rest period from half an hour to twenty minutes, the women would have fewer opportunities to 'spend the time shopping or on the streets.'[52] In effect, the investigators recommended that the only appropriate place for working girls was work or home. Women who dissipated their time and earnings 'on the streets' were only asking for trouble.

Like earlier investigators who could not talk about working girls' wages and hours without stumbling onto the question of chastity, the Bell commissioners turned to the striking telephone operators' respectability. They were shocked to discover that young women who sounded so ladylike over the phone were paid a salary that could barely support a lady's maid. Winchester and King learned that 'the girl who had to make her own way in the world, to pay her own expenses, and who wished to live on a certain scale' could not survive on Bell's wages.

Dunstan had complained that the company had increased hours because the operators' starting salary of $4.50 per week attracted the 'down, down' types but not 'the class [they] wanted.' The commissioners saw his point when they asked: 'Any self-respecting woman wanting employment would naturally turn away from employment that would not give her a livelihood?' 'Most decidedly,' Dunstan responded without a hint of irony.[53]

For working girls, a living wage was calculated as an amount barely sufficient to support a life of respectability, their passport to marriage and motherhood. If women walked to work, brought their lunch, and steered clear of department stores by day and roller rinks by night, they could manage to live on next to nothing. But how many working girls, faced with the temptations of city life, could exercise such restraint? Judge Winchester, a man who had seen many prostitutes from the bench, must have known the answer. The phone company and other employers' wage rates were all too likely to push working girls to barter their sexuality. As the investigators on Toronto's Social Survey Commission would claim in 1915, and as Mayor Howland had earlier hinted, underpaid working girls often had to work 'at something else.'

In the aftermath of the strike, Bell workers and company management learned different lessons. Dunstan confirmed that the communications monopoly could endure the strike with ease, but he and his fellow managers also learned that tempering their drive for maximum efficiency with limited welfare measures could be more cost-effective in the long run. As part of its efforts to foster good will, the Main Exchange spruced up office decor and hired a matron to serve tea and coffee to the operators. It also introduced free medical examinations, as one executive disclosed to a manager, 'to save us trouble and expense inasmuch as we will avoid the training of useless operators who might be discharged because of unfitness.' Ultimately, these minor concessions helped to 'minimize dissatisfaction over wages, raise the prestige of the occupation, and discourage unionization.'[54]

The 'hello girls' discovered that favourable public opinion counted for nothing when unorganized workers struck against an unregulated monopoly. They also learned to distrust the power (and the will) of the state to regulate capital in their favour. But as young, single wage-earners they might also have realized that the state cared more about their future contribution as mothers than their current problems as workers. Because the report did not recommend a substantial wage hike, they saw that what counted was their respectability and their childbearing capacities, not their material woes. Once the company provided longer rest periods and pleasant lunchrooms, they would have no one but themselves to blame for their discontent. The operators learned that Bell could become friendlier but remain a giant all the same.

Inefficient Girls

By the onset of the First World War, the figure of the working girl had become a familiar, almost definitive, feature of the urban landscape. She no longer appeared as a woman adrift but as a creature of the city, at home in its streets, shops, and factories. Her seeming independence at work and play suggested that she could take care of herself, and few continued to use Howland's term, 'helpless workwomen' to describe the city's working women. None the less, poverty still characterized the experience of most workers, except for a handful of increasingly visible career women.

The first year of the war actually ushered in a severe economic slump, only one of many economic downturns that pushed marginal workers to desperate straights. For the most part, working girls' economic plight elicited less concern than the unemployment of men. But when women's chronic job insecurity was exposed during the investigation that led to the 1916 report of the Ontario Unemployment Commission, the trials of women workers were translated as a threat to the race. Moreover, the report blamed working girls' unemployment and low wages on their own inadequacies and predicted the ill effect of their chronic employment insecurity on their future families. The solution to the problem of female unemployment, as advice literature for working women would explore more fully in the post-war era, was to be a personal one rather than a challenge to the sexual division of labour under industrial capitalism.

In 1915 the Ontario government sponsored a commission to explore the impact of the 1914–15 depression that threw over 10 per cent of the total workforce out of work. The province was particularly anxious about the growing number of male tramps who migrated from city to city in search of work and charity. The commission report described full employment as an essential right of working men. Deprived of this right, men drifted into crime and pauperism; stripped of their role as breadwinners, they sank into intemperance and abandoned or terrorized their families. An earlier federal investigation into the high cost of living, the results of which were published in 1915, had painted a similar picture of unemployment: 'The unemployed man is injured by idleness, his skill deteriorates, his "zest of life" is weakened, and his habits of thrift are soon on the down grade.'[55]

Female unemployment was an entirely different matter, although one that received closer attention than female labour had received from the 1889 royal commission. The 1915 commission devoted most of its attention to unemployed men, yet the presence of female professionals among the investigators, including civil servants and prison and charity administrators, produced a fuller exploration of women workers.[56] One-fifth of the report discussed unemployment in 'women's occupations' and offered solutions tailored to women's peculiar position in the labour market as vital yet transitory workers. The co-secretary of the women's report, Miss Marjory MacMurchy, complained that 'the important position in paid employments now occupied by women is imperfectly appreciated,' and hoped that she and her fellow female professionals might educate the public through the commission. She echoed the medical experts from the Bell dispute when she elucidated the importance of women's work: 'The effect of this employment upon home life and the care of children is shown to be far reaching,' she claimed. MacMurchy set the tone for the Unemployment Commission's understanding of female unemployment; like earlier explorations of wage-earning women, it too would explore the repercussions of women's work – on the stability of the family and the future of the race, but also on the economic efficiency of the nation.[57]

The commissioners stated that unemployment stemmed from social rather than economic or political problems, and they were concerned less about the effect of unemployment on the unemployed than about its impact on 'the normal' in society. Their report thus melded a concern with environmental causes of social disharmony, typical of Progressives, and a focus on individual responsibility for social ills, reminiscent of evangelicalism but also linked to scientific eugenics. The commissioners explicitly rejected the notion of personal sin as the root of unemployment, but they did not abandon a theory of individual weaknesses as an explanation for poverty. In their formula, unemployment was attributable to 'economic tendencies' *and* 'personal causes.' Unemployment was a social problem only to the extent that it represented the accumulation of individual failures in an economic system where the state had not done enough to 'produce, protect and develop useful men and women.'[58]

The report traced the problem of female unemployment to working women's individual shortcomings. The effect of their unemployment, however, was not portrayed, like male unemployment, as a personal tragedy, or as a blow to 'feminine pride.' When approximately 10,000 women workers across the province were thrown out of work in the winter of 1914–15, the result was 'much harm to themselves *and* others.'[59] The commissioners assumed that women's wages were low (and even lower during the depression, when they were reduced by 10 to 30 per cent) because young, inexperienced girls flooded the market. A 'smaller or larger class of irresponsible workers' hurt more productive workers by driving down wages. 'Lack of training, indifference and inefficiency' were apparent in male workers as well, but the investigators thought that these 'defects exist[ed] so largely in women's employments' that inferior employees made life more difficult for 'efficient, skilled workers.' Inefficient workers also reduced their employers' profit margin. If all wage-earning women took their work seriously, what benefits 'might they not secure for their employers!'[60]

The Art of Living

The implications of working girls' inadequacies ran deeper than their drag on economic efficiency. The commissioners worried that the type of woman who was prone to unemployment was also inclined to be a poor manager of her life beyond the job. In a reversal of the 1889 royal commissioners' fears that waged labour would render young women unfit for marriage, the 1915 commissioners now warned that women's *un*employment would leave them ill prepared for their future role: 'If a girl is an unsatisfactory, indifferent saleswoman, stenographer, factory worker, teacher, nurse or other worker, the probability is that she will be an indifferent and unsatisfactory wife and mother.'[61] Again, the concern sprang from the investigators' domestic orientation. How was the working girl to care for a family if, like many 'office girls,' she ate the wrong food, wore the wrong clothing, and spent her money foolishly? Girls who did not learn at an early age 'the art of living' would be swayed by the influence of the 'modern advertiser' once they began to earn wages.[62] Instead of learning the values of thrift and 'making do,' working girls misspent their wages on 'matters of personal comfort such as dress, eating [and] laundry.' Advertisers preached the 'gospel of ease,' and the woman wage-earner proved a ready convert.[63]

Clubs for working girls were praised for their capacity to teach young working women self-management skills that would lead inevitably to individual success. Unlike unions, associations did not articulate or support workers' rights or challenge management's power to set hours and wages and to fire at will. Instead, clubs taught wage-earning women how to be contented, efficient workers. The report catalogued the virtues of workers' associations: 'Promoting comradeship and re-creation; studying and raising the standard of employment; training and fixing standards for trained workers; providing classes and lectures in general improvement; aiding to secure employment for the members of the association; helping newcomers and advising as to personal doubts and difficulties which beset workers in their various employments.'[64] The Canadian Business Women's Club, based in Toronto, where 11,500, or 40 per cent, of the province's stenographers worked, received the report's praise.[65] It provided members with 'opportunities for study and self-improvement, for outings and social enjoyment.' Clearly, the work ers' association offered a great deal to the employer who could only benefit from motivated, highly skilled workers committed to erasing each other's 'personal doubts.' Ideally, superior working women them-selves would weed out the 'misfits' who 'interfere[d] with [their] steady employment.'[66]

When it came to discussing material aid for unemployed women, the report had comparatively little to offer. The unemployed working girl seemed to be an afterthought in a patchwork of charitable organizations preoccupied with the danger of the 'unattached man' and the plight of widows and deserted wives. None of the witnesses quoted in the gen-eral evidence section of the report referred to relief programs for single women. The House of Industry and religious charities seemed to be the only institutions prepared to provide for unemployed working girls, although the bulk of their aid went to widows and families. Far more developed was the network of correctional institutions, which was equipped to incarcerate girls and women charged with vagrancy. The Superintendents of the Alexandra Industrial School for Girls, the Con-cord Industrial Farm for Women, and the Andrew Mercer Reformatory agreed that most of their inmates required domestic training 'to become decent citizens.'[67] Indeed, it was often a condition of a woman's release that she take on a position as a domestic servant.

Only those women willing to work as live-in servants received the limited aid offered to unemployed women. In Toronto, the Women's

Patriotic League, a recruitment centre for servants, was established during the 1914–15 depression.[68] The fact that their supply of potential workers outstripped the demand in the first months of the war points more to the desperation of unemployed applicants who normally worked in the city's factories, shops, and offices at $8 or $9 per week than it does to the desirability of the jobs themselves.[69] Most working girls regarded toiling for a mistress at an average of $18 per month, plus room and board, or for board alone in some cases, as a form of unemployment insurance. They eagerly anticipated returning to their more lucrative, less demeaning non-domestic work, as employers discovered once wartime industries began to compete for women workers in 1917.[70]

Only extraordinarily trying times produced a supply of servants in Toronto that exceeded the demand. The Unemployment Commission had been stymied by the same issue that had vexed the earlier surveys of women's work: why, if domestic service offered room, board, and respectable surroundings, did young women insist upon opting for work that entailed uncertain employment and the necessity to find alternative living arrangements? Closer attention to servants' complaints would have offered clues. Women who abandoned their jobs in service reflected bitterly on their subordinate status in wealthy households: 'I had to wear a cap, go in and out the back door,' one woman complained, no doubt speaking for many. The starched maid's aprons that signified the gentility of the family could feel like a 'badge of service' to the women forced to wear them.[71] Wealthy masters and mistresses, who saw their homes as embodiments of comfort, could not understand why women rejected service for factory jobs of 'monotonous toil and sordid degradation, relieved only by flirtation and dress,' as one of Toronto's leading intellectuals grumbled.[72] Women who railed at observing the 'rituals of deference,' relieved only with sleep in a stuffy attic, knew very well why they preferred non-domestic work.[73] 'I had a hard time to pay board and make ends meet when I started shopwork,' a former servant recalled in 1912, 'but I was much better used.'[74]

Not even the participation of professional women on the Unemployment Commission overcame experts' stubborn insistence that the girl problem would be solved if only working girls could be 'made to believe' that domestic service was their best option. Indeed it was career women like MacMurchy and the female superintendents of girls' and women's reformatories who were most enthusiastic about domestic training. These were independent working women who would hardly have considered donning a servant's bib themselves, even during lean times. Ironically, MacMurchy received her appointment as a commissioner as a result of the wartime depression.[75] The unemployment study exposed the gaps that had developed in the female workforce, once united in poverty and insecurity. By 1911, when one quarter of Toronto's female workforce was employed in the service sector and just over one third worked in the manufacturing sector, the number of 'professionals' had crept up to 13 per cent of the city's women workers.[76] In addition, the census counted 243 'government clerks and officials' among Toronto's female workforce of 43,000. Their numbers in the 1910s were not overwhelming, nor was every woman labelled professional well-paid or free from the threat of unemployment.[77] But the very category, first used in the 1911 census, signalled that a cadre of women had begun to train for professions which allowed them to support themselves with a measure of security and independence only dreamt of by the women adrift of the 1880s. This élite sector of women workers, including doctors, lawyers, social workers, and civil servants, pronounced upon the efficiency and morality of young, wage-earning women and consciously separated themselves from their working-class sisters for whom work remained a thin buffer from poverty. By the 1910s and 1920s new female professionals would make their careers out of judging working-class women: probation officers, reformatory superintendents, boarding-house supervisors, and the city's first women's court magistrate, Dr Margaret Patterson, joined the growing ranks of experts on the girl problem.

In the initial decades of industrialization, working girls' problems, voiced in the testimony of the country's first factory workers and the complaints of Bell telephone strikers, were barely heard over the din created by state appointees and 'expert' witnesses. Women workers consistently cited low wages and demeaning labour practices as their chief grievances, but the men and women appointed to study them saw not workers but moral subjects; their investigations not only discounted stark evidence of material grievances but constructed female wage-earners as a moral problem. In each of the major inquiries into industrial labour, the sexual respectability of working girls obsessed the expert witnesses and the professional investigators who wrote their reports. The girl problem, as they viewed it, called for a variety of solutions, including the restriction of women's work, the encouragement of employers to implement welfare schemes, and the training of working girls to optimize their efficiency. These scripts for social stability in the face of urban industrialization persistently ignored wage-earning women's right to a living wage. Even after authorities began to accept single women's waged work as a fact of modern urban life, they continued to dispense their prescription of domestic work to cure the girl problem. Investigators remained anxious about the prospect of combining new forms of women's work with the service they expected women to perform for the race.[78] Women who preferred factory, office, or sales work to domestic service lingered in the murky light of sexual suspicion.

3

Ruined Girls and Fallen Women

On 7 July 1888 the body of a twenty-year-old woman, an apparent suicide, was fished out of the Toronto Bay. The ensuing coroner's inquest disclosed that two weeks earlier Jennie Irving had gone to a widow's home on Mission Street in the poorest section of town to seek live-in employment as a dressmaker. Her employer, Mrs Glassey, soon found the woman incompetent and told her she must leave. With nowhere to turn, Irving implored that she be kept on until she found another situation. Mrs Glassey relented, but several days later she ordered her out after discovering the dressmaker on the sofa in the arms of the widow's brother-in-law. In order to secure a separation from her philandering husband, the man's wife tracked Irving down, demanding that she sign a statement about the affair. Irving protested in vain that the man had forced her to go with him: 'I am disgraced now and I will go and throw myself in the bay.' After her body was discovered, a search of her room in her previous lodgings in the Rossin Hotel revealed that she had had many suitors. Among them was Will Clendening, who had written to his 'darling Jennie' to say that he would never be happy until she was his. Another unposted letter, written by Irving to Harry Hewlett, declared that she could not 'resist the temptation of loving [him] more.'[1] The disclosure of her active love life raised doubts about Irving's claim of victimization. Was a woman who kept several suitors dangling credible as a seduced maiden?

Debates over the credibility of victims exposed the paradoxical nature of the girl problem. Authorities on the issue of working girls in the city recognized their vulnerability to economic privation and sexual exploitation, yet were equally convinced that a respectable woman would embrace death before compromising her character. Determining which working girls deserved aid, merited forgiveness, required reform, or were beyond redemption was a contentious issue in the late nineteenth century, when the police and charitable institutions first took on the girl problem. As the Toronto police devoted resources to combat vice and the YWCA established homes for working girls and 'fallen women,' the moral choices of young wage-earning women fell under greater scrutiny than ever before. In the same period the metropolitan press regularly served its readers stories of the procured girls, seduced and abandoned women, and 'unnatural mothers' who disposed of their unwanted off-spring. These melodrmatic images of working girls, alone and vulner-able, captured the doubts and fears of a city uneasy about its economic progress.

Until a working girl ended up in court as a complainant or a defend-ant, however, her status as a potential victim or source of immorality was indeterminate. Young women who could conform to the image of the woman adrift, a pitiable figure more sinned against than sinning, stood the best chance of convincing the courts that they were victims. Women who went on 'sprees' and made no apologies for their lifestyles were less credible, even when they appeared as complainants. Thus, extraordinary transformations took place in courtrooms: women who complained that they had been raped could end up painted as hardened and depraved; unmarried mothers who exposed newborn infants could be forgiven as victims of evil seducers. Not even murderers were be-yond redemption in the eyes of the jurymen and judges. The courts applied the moral distinctions elaborated by authorities on the girl problem and rendered them into fixed categories of guilt and innocence. In the process, the complexities of working girls' problems and the strategies they devised to overcome them were reduced to simple mor-ality tales.

Because the 'woman adrift' image dominated characterizations of wage-earning women in the early years of Toronto's industrial growth, working women in trouble risked losing their credibility if they could not play the part. Single women who turned to the criminal justice system to press sexual assault charges realized the cruel irony that women whose virginity had been violated failed to make believable victims. Popular portrayals of women as casualties of urban evil did not translate into the courts' readiness to punish real-life villains. When Clara Ford and Carrie Davies shot alleged sexual predators, they saved the criminal justice system the trouble. Their only hope of acquittal, however, lay in adopting the script of the ill-fated working girl. Their trials, along with lesser-known criminal cases, reveal the criminal law's critical role in conveying cultural notions of the single woman's vulnerability in the city. More than any other cases, however, Davies's and Ford's exemplify the mutability and contestability of working girls' moral status, and for that reason their stories are included in this chapter.

Legal contests over working girls' credibility as victims will be examined again in chapter 6, which focuses on the late 1890s to the 1920s. In that latter period of Progressive urban reform, voluntary agencies and the civic government committed unprecedented resources to establish moral order. For now, however, we concentrate on the 1880s and ealry 1890s, when reform-minded ladies and zealous Morality Department inspectors first mobilized to tackle Toronto's girl problem.

REACTING TO THE GIRL PROBLEM

To Anglo-Canadians, particularly those from rural Ontario, Toronto was 'the City' and consequently the embodiment of the social and economic ills associated with capitalist industrialization.[2] In Toronto, as in most industrializing cities, the establishment of a professional police force was the most visible response to those ills.[3] By the 1870s the force placed a 'distinct focus on curbing drunkenness, rowdyism, vagrancy and petty crime.'[4] The 'dangerous class,' not dangerous criminals, were their chief concern.[5] Although women were well represented among those arrested for being drunk or disorderly, the police spoke more often of their difficulties with drunken men and rowdy youths.[6] 'Respectable' Torontonians were sufficiently aroused that the city fathers granted the police an additional 100 men between 1875 and 1885. A larger force, they hoped, would achieve more success in imposing order on the unruly.

The mid-1880s also witnessed a reorientation of priorities in the Toronto police force, one that would turn increasing attention towards the young women of the dangerous class. In 1886, shortly after becoming mayor, William Howland established the city's first Morality Department, dubbed the Office of the Staff Inspector. Morality officers were to target infractions of public order that ranged beyond the usual public drunkenness offences; 'houses of ill fame, illicit liquor sales, gambling dens, and cruelty to children and animals as well as many other offences of a miscellaneous character fell under the new department's jurisdiction.[7] Although the number of prostitution-related charges did not jump immediately, the inauguration of the Morality Department marked the initiation of a police branch that made the suppression of the social evil and moral depredation of all varieties a priority.[8]

The stated policy of the Morality Department was to break up brothels and arrest street walkers with the intention of making prostitution unprofitable and convincing women to take up legitimate employment. The chief constable's report of 1892 declared that the Morality Department's repression of vice had left the city more free from dives and resorts of prostitution than it had been in the previous twenty-five years.[9] The charge of vagrancy was sufficiently broad to justify arrest on suspicion of prostitution. Young working-class women who strolled on the streets or in parks after dark or who boldly participated in the raucous culture of taverns risked arrest as vagrants. As early as 1871 Chief Constable Prince had complained that 'many young women, and mere girls, resort to [saloons and dancing rooms] unaccompanied by guardians or any one to protect them.' He went on to predict that 'the result must be detrimental to their educational and moral training, as well as to their health.'[10] Once imperilled, however, they threatened to spread moral and biological contagion to 'respectable' Torontonians. The endangered could transform quickly into the dangerous.

The emergence of the Morality Department did not signal a uniformly intolerant attitude on the part of the city police, however. Internal rivalries over the objectives of morals policing were most visible in relation to prostitution, as social purity reformers would complain by the turn of the century. The attitude of the rank-and-file constables seems to have been one of tacit tolerance, while the Morality Department was mandated to eradicate prostitution. Although Toronto (and Canada) never implemented the Contagious Diseases Acts, the city did tolerate commercial vice within certain confined areas until the 1890s. As Philippa Levine argues in regard to England, an apparent contradiction was evident in contrasting attitudes towards women's licit and illicit labour: while investigators called for restrictions on the nature and hours of women's factory labour, they regarded prostitution as a traditional, if unfortunate, women's trade.[11] In either case, however, these approaches to women's work upheld 'men's rights and abilities to contract, both as producers and consumers.'[12] The aims of the Morality Department threatened to challenge men's right to partake of heterosexual pleasures, as the half-heartedness of policing suggests. Whenever the police periodically did lean heavily on organized prostitution, they presented their work as a project of public health monitoring. Thus, for the police, prostitutes were simultaneously objects of pity, carriers of disease, and purveyors of necessary sexual services. Not surprisingly, the character of policing was marked by ambivalence.

This awkward blend of protectiveness and punitiveness was acted out countless times as police constables encountered young women at night on downtown streets. The Toronto *News*, the self-proclaimed voice of the people, recounted one such incident in which a 'copper' nabbed a seventeen-year-old 'night hawk' on Simcoe Street, in the city's informal red light district. Because her nervous demeanour and healthy appearance signalled that she had only recently 'commenced her downward path,' the policeman had been reluctant to arrest her. He told the reporter that he knew the 'poor thing' would feel the degradation keenly once thrown into a police cell with older prostitutes. The arrest, he explained, had been made in the interests of public safety: 'When I saw her go up to one young man, and button-hole him, and, when snubbed by him, tackle another, I thought my duty was very plain, and I took her in.' The distraught girl told the *News* reporter a heartrending story of having been brought up respectably in a village. Forced by circumstances, she took a job in Montreal as a nurse to support her ailing father. There she was tricked by a procuress into believing she could take a well-paying position in Toronto. The man sent to escort her turned out to be 'a perfect devil in sheep's clothing' who installed her in a brothel, where she had been a sexual slave ever since. Her tearful cries that she would reform at once if given a chance convinced the arresting officer that there was 'some hope for that girl,' but not if she were left to fend for herself.[13]

Stories such as this convinced leading Protestant ladies of Toronto to establish a chapter of the YWCA in 1878. For these women, preventing working girls' moral downfall and rescuing women adrift was a preferable alternative to arresting them. The city's young women workers were vulnerable, as one Y lady expressed, because so many lived 'independently, unsupported and unsupervised by family, community and church.'[14] Their solution was to establish supervised boarding-homes for Toronto's women adrift. Howland praised the Y's efforts: 'Now that women are reaching out to take part with men in the labour of the world, some form of protection is necessary, especially when young women gravitate toward the large cities.'[15] The founders of the YWCA, the daughters, wives, and mothers of Toronto's 'best families,' hoped that they might act in the place of boarders' own families and exert their feminine influence over vulnerable young women. 'Taking part in

the labour of *the world*,' eroded the home influence, the moral ground-
ing that protected young women from falling into temptation. As the
YWCA's annual report of 1879 explained in apocalyptic terms, single
women who worked in the industrializing city were no match for its
temptations: 'Never in the world's history was such a glamour thrown
around sin; never was vice presented in such a multitudinous variety
of forms, or in so fair a guise; and never before were the emissaries of
Satan so unwearied in their efforts to entrap unsuspecting victims.'[16]
The ladies pictured themselves as front-line soldiers in the war against
urban immorality. Their boarding-homes were not simply comfortable,
subsidized housing, but a means to ensure that working girls would not
succumb to the temptations of city life.

Only those wage-earning women who eschewed urban pleasures fit
the YWCA's bill for boarders whom they described as 'respectable
young women coming to the city for the purposes of engaging in employments.'[17] In practice, this profile excluded indigent women, older
workers, Catholics, women of colour, and those without certified spotless reputations.[18] Spokeswomen took great pains to stress that their
target clients fell into a very narrow category of self-supporting women.
'*This Home is NOT a charity*,' they trumpeted in describing one of their
boarding-homes. The privilege of living under the protection of the
YWCA was conferred not on the neediest, but on the noblest: 'It is
solely for those who are "nobly and independently" earning their own
living, and only such are allowed to remain there. Neither is it a Reformatory. Many a sad case has come to our notice and been looked after,
but *only respectable persons can be admitted* into the Home.'[19] YWCA
boarding-houses thereby rewarded young women who not only managed to survive on their meagre wages but also demonstrated their
adherence to the ladies' standards of feminine respectability.

Because new forms of waged labour drew women from home work
and thrust them into city life, Y leaders feared that economic progress
had weakened the moral foundation for the next generation. Blending
biblical allusions and banking logic, they justified their economic and
personal investment in the future of the city's working women: 'Innocent and trusting as many are, few know the dangers surrounding them
in a large city, and experience has taught us that nothing should be
neglected to protect these women whose "price is above rubies."'[20] Just
as shepherds protected their flocks from wolves and thorns, so the Y
women set out to tend the women who flocked to the city by providing

'good Christian homes.' The 'black sheep,' however, would have to struggle without their help.

Urban pleasures rather than economic pressures were the prime sources of imperilment, according to leaders of the YWCA. Women who in the country might be solicitous for their reputations were all too often drawn to the excitement of the street out of loneliness and alienation in a big city. In 1880 the YWCA described these women as if they were lambs innocently gambolling to the slaughter: '[They are] simple and credulous, ignorant alike of city ways and city dangers. [C]an we wonder that they soon learn that the street is brighter and more attractive than a cold, dark kitchen, or a colder and more comfortless room?'[21] Yonge Street, the major north–south thoroughfare and one of Toronto's most commercialized strips, was mentioned frequently as a popular spot for young women and the men who prowled in search of them. This street, along with Queen Street, displayed the city's dubious wares before innocent eyes. Shops, taverns, and cheap theatres dotted downtown streets, and passersby could spend their earnings consuming goods or entertainment or idly watching the crowds walk by. The common practice of dancing in the saloons along Toronto's commercial streets prompted special concern because it brought young women into close contact with twin dangers – alcohol and men.

YWCA women's anxieties that they might lose women adrift to city pleasures prompted the Toronto chapter to propose a special meeting in 1883 to discuss the importance of gaining an influence over 'the young women in the city ... [particularly regarding] the terrible evils arising from girls attending dance houses.'[22] Likewise, city parks were attractive to working women, who, if they lived away from home, could afford only tiny, airless quarters. Respectable Torontonians noted that hot summer evenings and Sunday afternoons were young people's favourite times to find respite from the dust and noise of the city. Observers were shocked to discover, however, that parks had become sites where men and women could associate casually in public. In the eyes of one YWCA woman, the potential for unchaperoned encounters resulted in 'terrible scenes of immorality in the parks.' The scandalized ladies consequently informed Inspector Archibald of the problem and requested that he instruct his officers to be more vigilant. Thus, they proposed a gendered scheme of supervision over the city's women adrift: the YWCA would cover the home front while the morals police would supervise 'the world.'

Fallen women demonstrated the moral impact of industrialization and city living.[23] That fall was to be avoided at all costs, but once a woman 'fell' she contributed to the immoral character of urban life. Working girls who had freely associated with men, indulged in public carousing, or, worst of all, become pregnant were ineligible for residence in a YWCA boarding-house. Y ladies believed that fallen women would contaminate 'respectable working women' unless they were isolated in another institution – the Haven.[24] This was a catch-all institution that accepted women of all ages and situations of moral endangerment and attempted to rescue them. Single mothers were one of the Y's most difficult rescue projects: attempts were made to restore the mother's reputation and preserve the infant from stigmatization at the same time. The YWCA projected that two-thirds of these women would become 'respectable members of society,' but if they were shunned and made to feel stigmatized 'they will sink down into vice and degradation, and in the end will become the most hardened and vicious of women.'[25] Unmarried mothers and women who had run afoul of the law were deemed to be in equal need of moral rescue. Restoring fallen women's characters required an intensive regime of prayer, religious instruction, and a strict work schedule designed to tow unfortunates back to the safe harbour of respectable society. Once the Prison Gate Mission was established in 1878, the Haven operated in part as a halfway house for recently discharged prisoners, most of whom, the ladies presumed, had been prostitutes. Their assumption was shared by the police. In 1870 (the last year when arrestees' 'occupations' were recorded) officers reported arresting over six hundred prostitutes even though they had made only fifty-one prostitution-related arrests that year.[26] Women who transgressed norms of public decency were, by definition, fallen women.

The key difference between a 'hardened and vicious' woman and one who might still be rescued from 'vice and degradation' was contrition. Like all good Christians, women of the Haven were expected to recognize their sins, humble themselves before God, and resolve to struggle along the steep and narrow path of righteousness. Unless she was willing to accept the ladies' maternal guidance, a woman could not remain in the Haven. The directors routinely refused to harbour women who were 'in any respect considered untrustworthy, or who by long continued evil habit [had] contracted vices difficult to eradicate.' The YWCA evidently preferred to rescue women who thought of their unfortunate experiences as the product of their own misjudgment rather than as a means of survival or as a fate thrust upon them. Those 'evil' women who stubbornly refused to atone for their sins were beyond the grasp of the rescuers, having 'drifted down the undercurrent of vice which rushes madly through every large centre of population.'[27] No home could save them, for they had passed from a state of imperilment to one of moral contagion.

In its efforts to protect respectable women and rescue fallen women, the YWCA perpetuated and rigidified the moral distinctions between single wage-earning women who had preserved themselves from urban immorality and those who had become the embodiment of 'the social evil.' The frequent references to women who had done nothing more than bear a child out of wedlock or wander about the streets at night the worse for drinking as 'hardened' and 'vicious' show how easily the image of the 'credulous, innocent' wage-earner could blur into the spectre of the abandoned woman, unfit even for the Haven. Strict codes of propriety established in boarding-homes helped to maintain this moral hierarchy, and simultaneously lent status to respectable working women while establishing lower castes for those who feel short of the mark.

Working women had to be ever vigilant if they were not to slip from the higher to the lower category of morality. If YWCA residents committed infractions against house rules, they were summarily dismissed as unfit for a respectable Christian home. In one Toronto house, for instance, a boarder was told to leave immediately after she was discovered chatting with two men on the front doorstep.[28] The Y's concern for the good name of the house and its residents ironically left the expelled boarder in greater danger of victimization by rendering her homeless. At best she might have been eligible for the Haven, although more rigorous standards of behaviour prevailed there. In spite of the YWCA's avowed intention to save women from moral stigmatization, then, its preoccupation with sexual virtue compromised its mission to make the city safer for working girls.

The YWCA and its wealthy supporters were more concerned with wage-earning women's ability to preserve their reputations, no matter how poorly they were paid, than with their limited earnings. YWCA matrons may not have known how little their husbands paid their female employees, but they certainly knew what domestic servants in their own households earned. Unwilling to recognize their complicity in the economic exploitation of working women, they described the sorry lot of working girls as an inevitable fact of life in the industrializing city: 'That working women occupy a very important place in this city is now a settled fact – our offices, factories, stores as well as our homes prove it. How hard many of them have to work; how tired and sick many of them become. Unless a woman is very competent, what a struggle she has to support herself.'[29] Although the spokeswomen of the Y recognized that young women faced a mighty task to support themselves and their families in many instances, women wage-earners' success came down to a question of individual competence and rectitude. They could forgive those who failed in the struggle of life while remaining assured that competent women would never fall.

ENTICED INTO DANGER

Narratives of sexual danger for young single women in the city abounded in the late nineteenth century. The melodramas that played on the stage of the Grand Theatre, the stories of seduction, betrayal, and abandonment picked up on the wire services and reported in city papers, and the arraignment of prostitutes regularly reported in police court columns taught Torontonians about the working girl's precarious hold on sexual respectability and safety.[30] The venues for the trial of offences that could not be tried summarily – the Court of General Sessions and the Assize Court – were also sources of knowledge about women's endangerment and the dangerousness of women.[31] In the case of prostitution offences, courtroom stories rarely conformed to the standard story of innocent young maidens ensnared by procurers. Most were portrayed as 'brazen courtezans' and hard-drinking 'pugnacious females.' On rare occasions when the facts of a prostitution case conformed to the myth of the victimized woman adrift, the court could be moved to recognize the woman as a victim. The following stories of sexual entrapment show that, like the ladies of the YWCA, the gentlemen of the jury were more inclined to look favourably on fallen women who could manage to appear contrite.

In 1885, the same year that W.T. Stead's infamous 'Maiden Tribute of Modern Babylon' launched the issue of procurement into an international controversy, Torontonians observed a local tale of sexual entrapment – not on stage at the Grand Theatre, but at the York County Assize Court. It featured four stock characters: the vengeful father, Joseph Kenney; his innocent, country-raised daughter, Eva; the villainous city seducer, George Tate; and the evil madam, Mrs Ellison. The story was that sixteen-year-old Eva had received a tempting offer to work in Toronto as an apprentice coat-maker under George Tate's supervision.

Since she had already worked for and boarded with Tate in the nearby village of Brampton, Eva's father consented.

The predictable fate of the country maiden befell Eva. Soon after her move to the city, Joseph Kenney received a disturbing letter from his daughter, prompting him to pay a visit. Tate, she admitted, had begun to have sex with her in his Brampton shop, and she had left home because she had been afraid to tell her family. 'I would have to leave home or tell,' she wrote to her father: '[Tate] advised me not to tell it would get him into trouble & me to [too].' She went to Toronto with her seducer because he had tricked her into believing that he would provide 'a nice situation.' Eva later testified that Tate first put her up at the Armoury Hotel but then he took her to a Mrs Ellison's at 109 Adelaide Street West six days later. 'It is a house of ill fame,' she testified at Tate's trial for 'enticing a female under twenty-one years to a house of ill fame.'[32] With $1.52 in her bag she left the brothel, only to be installed by Tate in another at 5 Gould Street.

Tate seemed to realize that he had to watch his step in a city where the winds of evangelical reform were gathering force. When he discovered that Eva had told her friends about her money-making venture, he warned her that 'there would be imprisonment for him and [her] both if [she] was found in a house of that kind.' In true villainous fashion, he assured the heroine that *her* reputation would suffer if she told the authorities about her predicament. Tate need not have worried. With friends as prominent as department store entrepreneur Timothy Eaton to put up his bail money and a 'victim' who had failed to raise the alarm immediately upon her seduction, Tate was acquitted in January 1886.[33]

Eva lacked the credibility of a bona fide heroine. Because her father was the official complainant, she was merely a Crown witness and one who had apparently complied with Tate's wishes without alerting the authorities herself. To a sixteen-year-old torn from her family, her father would have seemed to embody 'authority,' and she had written home to explain her predicament. Nevertheless, her account of her entry into commercial sex seemed too cool for the melodramatic seduced-maiden scenario. In her discussions of the sex trade with her friends, Eva may also have observed that sex for money paid better than apprentice cloak-making. In spite of the evidence of Eva's letter and testimony that connected her to Tate at Ellison's brothel, the courts rejected this apparent tale of urban villainy and the fall of an innocent maiden.

A contrite victim with claims to prior innocence made all the difference in an 1887 case in which a charge of 'enticing' led to the conviction and imprisonment of offenders. Ironically, the village of St Mary's, rather than the city, was the site of two teen-aged girls' entry into prostitution. One of them, seventeen-year-old Kate Whitehead, had answered a Toronto newspaper advertisement that called for a general servant to work in the mining town northwest of Toronto. Daniel Stewart, the advertiser, came to the Whitehead household in a working-class neighbourhood of Toronto's west end and asked Mrs Whitehead for permission to hire her daughter. The teenager was offered the generous wage of $8 per month and dutifully sent her mother $2 shortly after she began. After three weeks, however, she ran away from St Mary's, returning to the city with $8 and a complaint that her duties had stretched far beyond those of a servant.

At the trial of Stewart and his two female accomplices, Whitehead chastely remarked that she had begun to realize that she was in 'a bad place' when she heard other girls in the house 'singing bad songs.' Stewart had alternately threatened and enticed her by brandishing a gun and promising money, pretty clothes and 'no work to do for them.' Although she had been forced to service several customers in the St Mary's brothel, she had stoutly proclaimed: 'I would rather work honestly.' On the strength of Whitehead's and her mother's testimony and the evidence that she ran away, Stewart received two years less a day at the Central Prison, and his cohorts were sentenced to fifteen months at the Mercer Reformatory for Females.[34]

The myth of the innocent working woman, seduced into prostitution by a false promise of legitimate employment, was upheld in Whitehead's case. Only two years earlier the *News* had printed an expose about a procuress who masqueraded as a fortune-teller to lure young women.[35] Kate Whitehead's story lent credence to the widely held belief that working girls were no match for the city. Although she was a city-bred young woman who lived at home under the watchful eye of her mother, she had been a victim of a modern advertising medium that facilitated strange villains to prey upon the innocent even as it spun out stories in other columns of urban dangers. Ironically, Whitehead had proved to be a plucky heroine who, unlike Eva Kenney, had not feared her parent's wrath. Moreover, she had escaped with a total of $10 after only three weeks' work – $2 more than she would have earned in one month as a servant. The court confirmed that she had been a victim; yet Whitehead, once lured into prostitution, had at least managed to make it pay.[36]

For most of Toronto's working women, prostitution did not entail dramatic encounters with 'enticers,' and the Stewart case was the only incident that led to a conviction in the 1880s and early 1890s. The 'enticement' to prostitution, as Kenney and Whitehead likely recognized, was monetary. Unlike domestic service or cloak-making, it offered steady work, it required no apprenticeship, and it paid better. 'Ruined girls' like Kenney may reasonably have assumed that they would have been disowned by their families and resolved, consequently, to remain in the trade, at least until they found a preferable alternative. In the interim they tossed respectability aside rather than embrace poverty and shame – the stock ending to the seduced maiden's story.

INCREDIBLE VICTIMS

The courts' evaluation of feminine respectability was most evident in cases where working girls claimed that they had been sexually assaulted. In cases where charges ranged from indecent assault to rape, a capital offence, young wage-earning women were assumed to be either prostitutes or women with little concern for their reputations. Defence lawyers capitalized on the latitude granted them to probe the complainant's reputation, and pounced upon any evidence of drinking or associating with strange men – the same activities that so scandalized the ladies of the YWCA. In contrast, the reputation of accused men, particularly employers or professional men, could withstand the most damning evidence brought forward by the Crown. Against all odds, a small number of working girls nevertheless pressed charges.[37]

For servants raped by their employers, the inevitable class differences between themselves and their masters reduced their credibility: with only a servant girl's word, few jurymen were willing to convict a respectable gentleman of a capital crime. Masters and other men from the household were frequently left alone with young women workers, and their sense of control over their employees could inflate into a conviction that they had the right to exact sexual favours as well as labour. Attic servants' quarters, basements, kitchens – any room in the house could double as the hidden site for an assault. Fear of dismissal or violent reprisals kept most women from complaining, as fifteen-year-old Emily Greenhead's experience suggests.

Greenhead had worked in service for three years before being hired as a servant in the Jones household in 1892. Like most servants who complained of sexual assaults, she testified that her master had raped her while his wife was out. The defence counsel questioned why she had not screamed for help: 'I did not make a noise,' she responded under cross-examination. 'I did not cry out because I was afraid to.' Instead she had told her father, who laid a complaint. Not surprisingly, the jury preferred to believe the protestations of a wealthy master over those of a frightened girl.[38]

Servants in rooming-houses were equally vulnerable if left alone with male boarders. When servant Susannah Meyer ran downstairs crying that one of the boarders at 28 Simcoe Street had raped her, her employers advised her to lay charges. She claimed that Edward Gibson had pushed her into her third-floor room, pinned her to the floor, and covered her mouth so that she could not scream during the attack. The other boarders testified that they had heard nothing and the case was thrown out of court. While Meyer's employers' support was remarkable, it proved insufficient to lend credibility to her claims. The defence counsel discovered that she had laid a prior complaint against another male boarder and turned this discovery into evidence of her untruthfulness. The Crown offered no rebuttal.[39]

Women who worked in the sex trade or lived on the streets faced insurmountable odds as rape complainants. Once placed under relentless cross-examination, these alleged victims emerged as abandoned women who had provoked sexual encounters with strange men. Immodest behaviour at any point before, during, or after the alleged sexual assault gave defence lawyers the ammunition necessary to free their clients. Even the most tragic cases of victimization elicited scorn. When Elizabeth Griffiths wandered Toronto's downtown streets late one night in the winter of 1887, she sought nothing more than a warm place to sleep. A man led her to what she assumed to be a safe house on Adelaide Street. After she went up to bed, however, another man stormed into the room and raped her. The commotion alerted a neighbour, who corroborated Griffiths' story. The verdict was not guilty.[40] The men of the jury agreed with the defence lawyer that any young woman who walked along Adelaide Street (a noted thoroughfare in the red light district) at night, talking to strange men, was a prostitute looking for customers and, accordingly, a liar.

That the Crown prosecuted such cases is itself remarkable because the police were extremely reluctant to arrest men if the complainant was presumed to have a dubious reputation. Although prostitutes and brothel-keepers were especially vulnerable to attack because of their frequent contact with drunk or abusive men, the police rarely took their claims seriously. Jane Harding was a victim of three men on a drunken rampage as well as of the police and the courts. She reported that on the night of 22 July 1880 the assailants broke into her home at 381 Adelaide Street West, where she ran a brothel. She tried to escape through the window, but they grabbed her and forced her down to the floor until one of them had 'got his object accomplished.' After a great struggle she managed to escape to a nearby police station. 'It's a damned nice time in the morning to bother a person!' the duty officer complained when she flew in to report that the men had broken into her home and raped her. The availability of witnesses to corroborate the woman's story, however, prompted the Crown to take the case to court. But the trial added further insult to her injury. The defence lawyer's efforts to use Harding's past against her compounded the lacklustre response of the police. Because she had served time in the Toronto Gaol and the Kingston Penitentiary on prostitution charges and lately resided in a house where, by her own admission, 'girls frequently came in and out,' she had little hope of appearing as a credible rape victim. Ironically, the men were convicted of 'breaking and entering with intent to disturb the peace and assault' – a charge that expunged the sexual content from Harding's complaint. The verdict signalled the court's assumption that a prostitute or brothel-keeper, being a woman who had already lost her character, could not be raped, although as a house-holder she could be the victim of housebreaking.[41]

Women who worked in the city's sex trade had little to lose by press-ing sexual assault charges and appearing in open court, particularly if they had made earlier appearances on charges of prostitution, drunken-ness, or disorderliness. The ideals of feminine comportment and respect-ability were laughable to them, and their prior encounters with the police hardened them against the dismissive attitudes of men in author-ity. They bravely sat in court to tell their stories and to assert that they had been victimized, knowing that their chances of being believed were slim.

Working girls still jealous of their reputations after suffering sexual attacks may have hoped, vainly, that the criminal justice system would restore their characters. For these women, the discourse of fallen woman-hood provided an interpretive framework for their own misfortunes. They believed, along with moral authorities, that they lost their good name if they engaged in non-marital intercourse, whether or not the act took place with their consent, and looked to the courts as a means of redress. Most women preferred not to gamble on a justice system that required them to expose their most intimate fears before the public, and young single women may have been particularly keen to guard against further exposure of information that would shame their families or compromise their marriage prospects.

There were some, however, who bravely – and naively – hoped that the courts might accept the word of a previously chaste woman as a credible victim. Mary Bull claimed that her doctor had raped her out of a malicious desire to defile a virgin. As Dr William Graham led Bull into his office one day in 1886, he said he wished that he could marry 'a young girl as pure as [her].' The doctor then shut the door, threw her on the floor, and covered her mouth to keep her from screaming while he raped her. Bull tore out of the office as soon as the assault ended and ran to her boarding-house on Peter Street. Her fellow boarders testified that she was crying and terribly agitated when she entered the house. She told them that Graham was a 'dirty beast' and that he had 'torn her to pieces.'

Dr Archibald, the court physician, confirmed that her underclothes and dress were covered with blood after her doctor's visit and that her inner thighs and vulva were also bloodied. He ruled out the possibility that it was menstrual blood since she was midway through her menstrual cycle. His explanation for her 'torn' state, however, made a mockery of Bull's story. 'The bleeding might have been caused by the forcible insertion of a finger,' he offered, even though Dr Graham had been treating his patient for rheumatism. Archibald further demonstrated his willingness to uphold professional and male solidarity in the face of contradictory physical evidence and the complainant's word by questioning Bull's sanity. Dr Archibald speculated that she had imagined the whole scene: 'Women might have strange ideas after an examination ... I can hardly see how a man could overpower a woman and have connection with her against her will while he had one hand over her mouth.' Dr Archibald's damning testimony and the absence of witnesses to the attack won Dr Graham an acquittal. In contrast, Mary Bull, an out-of-work servant who had been engaged to be married, lost much more than her case: 'I lost my character.'[42]

The most despondent women acted as their own judges and juries. Jennie Irving, alias Brown, had claimed that she had not gone willingly with her seducer, the married man who had 'forced [her] to have connections with him.' At the coroner's inquest, the man was not even called as a witness. The widow who had taken her in, however, judged that the young dressmaker had acted according to her own moral script: 'She often remarked to me that bad girls come to a bad ending.'[43] The despondent woman may have realized that she was more likely to be recognized as a victim in death than she had been in life.

Jennie Irving's self-imposed death sentence was an extreme example of the guilt that could consume sexual assault victims. Although the maligned seamstress's suicide fulfilled moralists' predictions about the fate of women adrift, single wage-earning women were generally more resourceful than either the judicial system or their self-appointed rescuers gave them credit for. Like domestics who spirited away their master's silverware, fallen women sometimes turned to illegal means to gain leverage in untenable situations. Unfortunately, since evidence of their improvisations comes from criminal trials and coroners' records, it is their failed schemes and not their triumphs that can be recovered.

One of single wage-earning women's greatest risks was pregnancy. Involuntary motherhood was a burden that any woman might endure; for single women, though, it could spell disaster. Like widows and deserted wives, they could not easily explain an unexpected pregnancy. Single women who continued to live at home faced the unenviable prospect of bringing shame to their families, while those who boarded risked eviction if their landlord discovered their condition. In either case the birth of a child could keep a woman from waged work for weeks, and the subsequent pressure to feed, clothe and house a child overtaxed the trifling earnings of self-supporting women. Those without the support of their families or the men who had impregnated them turned to their friends and co-workers as well as to midwives, abortionists, druggists, baby-farmers, and, in some cases, to their own hands.

Abortion and baby-farming were the final options for single women who wished to escape the consequences of their 'fall.' They were dependent on traditional women's advice networks that operated in rural areas, yet they also took advantage of a wide range of urban services for women 'in trouble.'[44] In Toronto, druggists supplied abortifacients and sometimes freelanced in their backrooms as abortionists. More commonly, they acted as drug agents. Midwives were also in the business of providing urban neighbourhoods with medical aid for women's troubles. In the poorest parts of town, clients were as likely to seek a midwife's help in aborting a fetus as delivering a child. Finally, women who could scrape together extortionate sums of money purchased the services of amateur and professionally trained doctors.

The extent of the abortion trade in Toronto in the late nineteenth century is impossible to determine. Evidence in coroners' and court records indicates that the women who survived abortions did so at great personal risk. Unwilling mothers were clearly prepared to accept physical dangers rather than face the prospect of bringing a pregnancy to term. Cases that upheld popular beliefs about the fate of women adrift in the city prompted juries to convict – not the women, but those who had performed the operations. In a classic tale of a young maiden's desertion, betrayal, and eventual death at the hands of her cowardly suitor, Torontonians learned of Elizabeth Bray's untimely end. The 'SAD CASE,' as the *News* called it, was the story of a working girl who, orphaned at thirteen, came to Toronto to live with her aunt, who ran a boarding house on Walton Street. By the age of fifteen she worked with her sister as an operative at the Crompton Corset Company, among the city's largest employers of women and one of the large factories investigated by the Royal Commission on Capital and Labour. Gamble, one of the male boarders who was a piano-factory worker, took a shine to the young woman. Her aunt knew that her niece and Gamble 'were in the habit of going out walking' but she suspected nothing because he was a married man. After receiving an anonymous letter warning that her niece had 'got into trouble,' she reconsidered. '[Gamble] seemed to have power over her,' Bray's aunt later testified, even though he had assured her that 'he would not wrong an orphan girl.' Out of loyalty to her lover or out of fear, Bray supported Gamble's story that he had had nothing to do with her.

Desperately improvising a scenario reminiscent of YWCA predictions of city evils, Elizabeth searched for an alternative explanation for her pregnancy. She drew on familiar melodramatic renderings of 'poor, orphan girls' to claim that she had been attacked by a strange man who had dragged her away from a picnic to a 'lonesome place' in High Park where he had forced himself upon her. In offering this clichéd story of imperilment, she refashioned her ill-advised affair with a married man into an unsolicited assault so that she might save her lover and preserve her status as a victim of anonymous male villainy.

She might have succeeded had she not died of puerperal peritonitis several weeks after her pregnancy was discovered. The ensuing coroner's inquest disclosed that Gamble had moved to a rooming-house with Bray and arranged to procure an abortion. Gamble appropriated his own melodramatic plot conventions by posing as Bray's brother, and fibbing to their landlady that he was trying to save his 'sister's' reputation because her fictitious fiancé had 'abandoned' her. After unsuccessful attempts to tap into the underground female network of abortion contacts, Gamble turned to what he assumed was his last option: he performed the abortion himself. His clumsy efforts resulted in the eighteen-year-old's death and earned him a conviction on a charge of murder.

In spite of both Bray's and Gamble's attempts to elevate their predicament to the level of myth, their plight was depressingly familiar. It was not Bray's story of a picnicking heroine violated by a villain, nor was it Gamble's tale of a cold-hearted fiancé who had abandoned his bride-to-be. It was simply the ignoble end of a young single working woman, killed by her paramour in his misguided attempt to save them both from disgrace. She died. He received a 'strong recommendation of mercy' and his death sentence was quietly commuted.[45]

In general, the police preferred to prosecute men and women who operated extensive abortion services through abortion laws designed to punish abortionists, not their clients.[46] It was not uncommon, however, for women to be threatened with criminal charges to coerce them into testifying against apprehended abortionists. In 1886 the trial of Dr Ransom J. Andrews on a charge of 'attempting to procure an abortion' drew crowds at the January assizes in Toronto. For some time he had run a booming abortion business out of a house in the city's west end. When police officers, acting on a tip from the newly instituted Morality Department, raided Andrews' 'clinic,' they found their star witness in one Jennie Leslie, a young woman recovering from an abortion. Staff Inspector Archibald was doubly rewarded, for his officers found hundreds of letters in the clinic written by women pleading for relief from their unintended pregnancies. Had every one of the correspondents paid Andrews the $50 fee he had charged Leslie, the doctor would have been sitting on a fortune. He was sufficiently wealthy to hire one of Canada's premier criminal lawyers, Britain Bath Osler, to defend him. The great Osler's skills proved wanting, however, and the abortionist was convicted and sentenced to five years in the Kingston penitentiary.[47]

The Andrews case stands out from the bulk of abortion trials in which juries demonstrated great reluctance to punish abortionists for their work, even if they had endangered women's lives. In spite of the Morality Department's stated objective to close down the abortion trade in Toronto, it appears from the small number of cases prosecuted in the 1880s and early 1890s and the high proportion of acquittals that most Torontonians lent tacit approval to the underground business that discretely saved women and their families from disgrace. Unless a woman died as the result of a botched abortion, an abortionist was relatively immune from prosecution.[48]

The same leniency was apparent in regard to women charged with killing newborns. The vast majority of mothers who faced infanticide charges were single, young, and poor, and it appears that the courts were willing to take these mitigating factors into account.[49] At the same time, baby-farmers, who were often older married women or widows, were also treated leniently. Of eleven cases that came before the High Court of Justice in the period from 1880 to 1893, only one woman was convicted on a charge of manslaughter. In the remaining ten cases, mothers and baby-farmers were acquitted of charges ranging from 'maternal neglect' to murder.

Historians who have found similar evidence elsewhere have puzzled over this evidence. Most explain judicial leniency as an expression of 'compassion' and sympathy towards women who were clearly in dire straits. Constance Backhouse explains that judges could afford to be lenient because infanticide 'ensure[d] the proper continuation of male blood lines.'[50] More compelling, perhaps, is a class-based explanation. If destitute single women disposed of their infants, city fathers would see a corresponding reduction in the number of destitute persons seeking relief and the 'dangerous class' would have fewer potential recruits. The guilty secret of more than a few respectable households was the paternity of a child born to a servant. If she disposed of the child, everyone involved might escape shame. Unlike civil actions for seduction, infanticide cases rarely exposed the identity of the father – to the great relief, no doubt, of men who knowingly or unknowingly abrogated their paternal obligations. Finally, judicial indulgence should be linked to the fragility of infant life in a city still without treated drinking water or pasteurized milk. When the babies of the wealthy died of diseases in infancy, the lives of poor undernourished infants could seem cheap indeed. The child-saving movement in Canada did not arise until the mid-1890s, and its mission to save and nurture neglected and abandoned children met with limited support. The courts were not so much disposed to consider unwilling single mothers as victims, then, as they were to regard their crimes as minor offences requiring great discretion.[51]

Infanticide was usually the final act in a series of attempts to terminate pregnancy.[52] It appears that there were no more than a handful of professional abortionists, including Andrews, in Toronto before to the turn of the century. For the most part, commercial abortifacients and home remedies, passed on in secret by female friends and relatives, were the first choice of poor unmarried women. The reliability of abortifacients was dubious at best, and women were driven to mechanical means if they were still determined to induce a miscarriage.[53] After the second trimester, however, pregnant women were more likely to die than to survive an abortion.[54] When women turned to infanticide, then, they pursued what they believed to be their final option short of suicide.

Single women were not the only unwilling mothers who sought a grisly solution to their trials, but they were more likely than married women or widows to face disgrace if they brought a child into the world. Self-supporting poor women were in the most precarious position. Those who could barely feed themselves could not feed another. The stories of women who were caught provide vivid glimpses into the gloomy prospects that faced poverty-stricken unwed mothers. Yet even these most tragic figures were not entirely victims. In disposing of their infants they rid themselves of a burden that severely handicapped their chances at legitimate marriage and brought shame to their entire families, a stigma which they understood would stain the character of the newborn as well.

Infanticide was a cruel but common fact in early industrial Toronto. The annual number of infants found dead in rubbish heaps, privies, and vacant lots often exceeded thirty.[55] Of the few women actually charged with infanticide, not one woman received the death sentence.[56] Apart from the Burnside Hospital for unwed mothers there were no state-run institutions for single women with newborns in Toronto. There was a patchwork of private alternatives, the foremost of which were baby-farms, which were licensed under city bylaws. The city provided minimal supervision over the operation of these private homes, usually run by a widow, which undertook the care of infants and young children for a fee. If a client, typically the baby's mother, wished to give up the child for adoption, or if a client refused to pay for the child's maintenance, the baby-farmer acted as a negotiator in the adoption of the child. Other than the House of Industry, no institution would accept a single mother and her newborn. Without the money to pay a baby-farmer, unable to solicit support from her family, deprived of connections to a sympathetic church or synagogue, and unwilling to darken the doorsteps of the poorhouse, a single working mother might very well have panicked at the arrival of an unwanted child.

The stories uncovered in infanticide cases starkly illustrate the extremes to which single working women went to avoid becoming single mothers and, as the YWCA had described, 'feeling under the ban of society.'[57] Moving to the city from a small town was the first step in leaving their shame behind. Unlike small towns or villages, cities tolerated strangers and eccentric behaviour that would stir the curiosity of home-town relatives and neighbours. Since it had become common for young women to leave their families and villages in Ontario for job prospects in Toronto, unmarried pregnant women could apply for a job and rent a room with few questions asked. Such was the story of Mary Meharg, who in 1891 left the town of Orangeville, forty miles north of Toronto, soon after she discovered she was pregnant. Meharg managed to find a job as an operator at Shea's knitting factory, a prominent employer of working girls. She might have remained one of the city's anonymous working girls had her landlady not discovered a dead infant wrapped in papers and rags on an ash-heap in a rear shed. In spite of the substantial evidence against Meharg, including the presence of blood-soaked bedding in her room, the coroner's jury concluded that an 'unknown person or persons' was responsible for the baby's death.[58] Meharg may have returned to Orangeville without anyone in her home town the wiser about her deed, or she might have moved to another city where it would have been possible to make a fresh start. In either case, her problem was disposed of at the morgue.

Cheap lodging-houses provided emergency shelters for pregnant women who resorted to killing their newborns. Single expectant mothers, desperate for their earnings, kept their pregnancies secret virtually until the last minute, then proceeded to lodging-houses where nobody knew or cared who they were. The murder or desertion of a newborn was, in these cases, the dreadful conclusion to a nine-month ordeal of concealment. In July 1884 Lizzie Smith chose this option. Shortly before giving birth she quit her job as a servant but placed her name on a job registry list, fully prepared to work as soon as she delivered. She rented a room in the Ward, saying that she had come to town to look for a situation. Passing off her labour pains as diarrhea, she went to the backyard privy several times during the night. A faint cry and a loud splash in the privy alerted women in the densely crowded neighbourhood, who called for the police to investigate. Smith feebly denied the accusation that she had dispatched an infant into the pit, even though a trail of blood led from her bed to the privy. The Crown had enough evidence to press charges for manslaughter, yet the jury refused to return a verdict of guilty.[59] Most transients, however, were never traced, and landlords in the city's most squalid quarter rarely knew the names of working girls who handed over the coins for a night's lodging and then moved on. The ill-contrived concealment schemes of the women who were eventually traced suggest how easily farsighted women might have disposed of their infants successfully and avoided detection altogether.[60]

A form of passive infanticide was to abandon newborns with baby-farmers. The level of health and safety standards in these privately run institutions varied greatly. Clients received service that corresponded to the rate they were able to pay, and the wages of working women translated into grossly inadequate care. Babies invariably suffered and even died if mothers refused or were unable to pay for minimal standards of health and nutrition.[61] Matilda Berry was responsible for more than her share of infant deaths. In 1881, at her third trial for manslaughter, she testified that the latest child who had died in her care was the 'illegitimate child of Annie Marshall who [was] employed at [the] Russell Hotel on Adelaide Street E.' One week after giving birth at the Burnside maternity hospital, Annie Marshall went to Berry's Cabbagetown address to drop off her baby. Berry charged two dollars per week, but in the two months that the Marshall baby spent at her home she received only the initial two-dollar payment. Berry elicited sympathy when she revealed that she often had to cope with cash shortfalls in her business. She testified that five other babies had been abandoned under similar circumstances and that each had died because their single working mothers had deserted them. The jury, perhaps sensitive to Berry's financial constraints or to the fact the mother had since disappeared, decided not to convict the baby-farmer and not to recommend that her licence be revoked.[62]

Baby-farmers were relatively immune from prosecution because the untimely death of infants who, after all, were bastards was seen as nothing more than unfortunate. However, Torontonians were terribly concerned about the sexual indiscretion of fallen women and their downward path to 'unnatural motherhood.' Thus, when Sarah Fox was charged with the murder of her five-week-old baby in 1891, her trial was covered as a story of moral rather than financial bankruptcy. The Toronto *World* drew on popular notions of the rural maiden 'adrift' in a sea of urban temptations when it ran a front-page story entitled, 'A Woman's Awful Plight.' The 'self-confessed murderess['s]' misdeed unfolded after Detective Black 'unearthed the Story of Sarah Fox's Shame and Crime.' The story revealed that Fox had admitted to having killed the child, who died as a result of strangulation and a skull fracture. The young unmarried mother had started to care for her child, as many others in her situation did, by paying a baby-farmer to take it in. After four weeks she ran out of money and took her child from a baby-farm in the Ward to another near the garment district. Realizing that she could no longer pay for the baby's upkeep, she gave the second baby-farmer a false address. The enterprising woman nevertheless traced Fox through the Burnside to the League Coffee House where she worked, and demanded that she pay or take the baby back. Sounding like a 'hardened and vicious' woman, she told the baby-farmer to '[t]hrow it out as she did not want it.' When the woman 'spoke to her reprovingly of the duties and feelings of a mother,' she seemed to convince Fox to care for the infant by urging her to place it in the care of its grandparents.

After walking only a few blocks from the coffee house, however, Fox rid herself of her burden. The *World* explained how she had strangled the infant with the strings of its cape: 'Satisfied that it was dead she flung it over the first wall she came to.'[63] Luckily for Fox, there was enough of the seduced and abandoned maiden in her story to elicit the jury's sympathy. Although she had confessed to wilful murder, she was convicted on the lesser charge of manslaughter and granted a 'recommendation to mercy' from the jury. The twenty-year-old had come to the city from a village just north of Toronto to find work. In 1890 she had met a brickyard labourer and began to have sexual intercourse with him under the mistaken belief that he would marry her. The man reneged on his promise when she announced that she was pregnant. Apparently unwilling to confess her predicament to her parents, she had the baby at the Burnside and left a week later to search for the employment she needed to support both herself and her baby. Hers was a true story that became a cautionary tale about the fate that awaited young single women who turned to the city for employment. Sarah Fox had managed to find a job but, unguided by her parents and unguarded in a home without the supervision provided by a YWCA boarding-house, she drifted into the currents of temptation that ran through the city.

In the course of Fox's trial a murderer had been transformed into an unfortunate woman who merited a recommendation to mercy. Absent from her trial and the newspaper discussions of her case were any remarks about the culpability of her baby's father, or the fact that the wages at the League Coffee House rendered the two-dollar-per-week baby-farm fee out of reach. Instead, the criminal justice system, like the official investigations of wage-earning women, reduced the compromise and craft demanded of unmarried mothers and exploited workers into morality tales of imperilled women adrift.

PUGNACIOUS FEMALES

Women who fought back presented a challenge for those who believed that cities made victims of working girls. Readers of Toronto daily newspapers knew well that working-class women did not shrink from a fight. Until the turn of the century, the charges most likely to land a woman before the courts were drunkenness and disorderliness. Working-class life was played out and fought out on the street, largely on account of the cramped and unhealthy housing that meagre wages could purchase. In the poorest families, where the contribution of young children was essential to sustain the family economy, girls learned that the city was to be their territory as well as their brothers'. They were people of the street, not the boulevard, and their lives revolved around the struggle to survive and to strike out if pushed too far.[64] When women fought in the streets, entire neighbourhoods witnessed the physical and verbal abuse they inflicted upon children, men, and other women. Jealous Lilly Kelly tried to break up an affair between Jane Harding and Jim Daly ('a regular 'masher' among York Street girls) by 'banging' Harding with her baby. 'The pugnacious female,' the *News* reported, was sent to jail for a month for the assault. An unmarried seventeen-year-old mother was convicted of disorderliness for throwing stones at the father who refused to support his offspring.[65] Although women more commonly appeared as victims of men's assaults, there were many who evidently were prepared to fight back.[66] In their own neighbourhoods and on the stages of cheap theatres where melodramas were staged, working-class girls learned very early that waiting for a hero to save them could prove fatal, and that men were as likely to be threats to their safety as insurers of it. In short, they believed they had a right to self-preservation.

Throwing punches in a drunken brawl was one thing: murdering an upper-class man was quite another.[67] As Mary Hartman and Ruth Harris have argued in their studies of Victorian and fin-de-siècle murderesses, women who killed husbands or paramours underwent astonishing courtroom transitions, entering as killers and emerging as sympathetic victims. For Hartman, this form of exculpation was a product of class privilege, since middle-class women were the most likely to be freed; for Harris, melodramatic conventions of the seduced and abandoned woman, along with emerging notions of female hysteria, inspired leniency towards murderous vitriol-throwers and lady assassins. These historians agree that women were not granted clemency unless they convincingly displayed traits of feminine frailty or irresponsibility. Faced with the gallows or the guillotine, most women on trial for muder threw themselves wholeheartedly into the role.[68]

The trials of the two women tried for murder in turn-of-the century Toronto offer dramatic proof that chivalric justice was not merely a privilege of class or race. In many respects, they were typical working girls - poor, young, and single.[69] When, in separate incidents, they shot and killed men they accused of sexual assaults, their ordinary lives exploded into media events. Long after the Lilly Kellys of the city were forgotten, the stories of Clara Ford and Carrie Davies lived on. Their extraordinary acts and trials attracted intensive attention as newspaper writers scrambled to make sense of their crimes for the reading public. Explaining their acquittals provided a further challenge. Could a murderess be a victim?

WOUNDED WOMAN, DEAD MAN

Clara Ford, a 'mulatto' seamstress in her early thirties, lived alone above Mrs Dorsay's 'negro restaurant' on York Street, one of the main thoroughfares of 'the Ward' and the heart of Toronto's small black community.[70] On 20 November 1894 two detectives visited the unlikely suspect's tiny apartment and arrested her for the murder of Frank Westwood, a white, well-to-do Methodist lad.

On his deathbed Westwood had claimed that he had not recognized his assailant. A man with a dark complexion, a moustache, and a fedora had rung his doorbell and shot him at close range, he told the police. Enigmatically, he had ended his ante-mortem statement with, 'mum's the word.' For six weeks the Toronto police force searched in vain for the killer whom the dead man had failed to identify.[71] Midway through November, the cold trail warmed up when detectives received a tip from a pickpocket, Gus Clarke, who informed them that a black woman who had once lived in the rear of the Westwood home had a penchant for dressing in men's clothes; moreover, he and several other petty criminals had overheard her threaten to do in young Westwood if she found him with another woman.

A search of Ford's humble rooms uncovered incriminating circumstantial evidence: a suit of men's clothes, a fedora, and a pistol of the same calibre as the murder weapon. Detective Reburn and Inspector Stark of the Toronto police force questioned Ford at the station for several hours until she broke down and gave a detailed confession of her activities on the night of the murder. She told the police that she had visited a friend in the garment district near Spadina and Adelaide Streets. To provide herself with an alibi, she told the woman that she was going to attend the Toronto Opera House, a popular venue for melodramas, to see 'The Black Crook.' Instead, she donned men's clothing and proceeded along the lakeshore until she reached Jameson Avenue in fashionable Parkdale. Under cover of darkness she stood by the bushes in front of Lakeside Hall, the Westwoods' palatial home, and rang the bell. When eighteen-year-old Frank came to the door, she shot him twice and then fled the scene, retracing her steps to her quarters in the Ward.

When asked her motive, Ford resorted to a story of wounded womanhood, a convention of melodrama and the excuse commonly offered by 'Society ladies' who sought retribution for infidelity, abandonment, or injury to their reputation.[72] She told the police that Westwood had knocked her down one night and taken 'improper liberties' with her. He had, as she put it, 'insulted' her.[73] When asked why she had not reported the 'insult,' she betrayed a cynical awareness of racism: there was 'no use for a woman of my colour going to the police for justice.'[74]

In some respects, Ford possessed the qualities of a blameless woman adrift. She had been exposed to a sexual assault on the street and she could not retreat to the protection of a parental home, nor did she have a husband or father to protect her. Furthermore, the black seamstress was a member of Toronto's least powerful community.[75] Not surprisingly, the woman had felt compelled to take justice into her own hands. Most of the Toronto daily newspapers rationalized her crime as the act of a wounded woman. In explaining her motives for the murder, the dailies constructed narratives that closely resembled the melodramas of the day, which featured the perpetually embattled heroine, the embodiment of virtue, versus the villain, the personification of evil.[76] When heroes were otherwise detained, heroines were forced to come to their own defence. As a Toronto theatre critic and journalist reflected in 1925, 'the heroine often dressed in boy's clothes and shot the villain.'[77] When the *Globe* printed Ford's confession, suggesting that it offered 'at least a more reasonable explanation of the crime' than earlier theories, the paper addressed an audience accustomed to such bizarre tales of good and evil.[78]

To be credible as a heroine or, more to the point, a victim of male lust, Ford had to follow character conventions as convincingly as she had scripted her melodramatic explanation for the shooting. The heroine no less than the hero, or indeed the villain, was judged by her character; in contrast to the male characters, though, chastity was the measure of her character. Where heroes battled to restore lost honour, heroines struggled against all odds to preserve feminine honour, for, once lost, it could never be regained. Ford asked that she be understood as a wounded heroine: 'I thought Westwood did not treat me respectfully,' she had confessed.[79] The question in the minds of Torontonians was this: was Clara Ford a woman worthy of a gentleman's respect?

Pre-trial speculation focused on Ford's reputation, since she did not give the impression of a woman unused to fighting back. Several of the dailies were less willing to cast the defendant as a wounded woman and the otherwise respectable victim as a villain. 'She is a woman who at times has exhibited terrible ebullitions of temper, and it transpires that she has threatened the lives of at least two persons,' claimed the *Empire*. It refused to believe that 'the supposed insult offered by Frank Westwood' was anything more than 'a passing remark.' Ford had been miscast as a fragile maiden: she was a tough habitué of the Ward who 'took pride in exhibiting her fearlessness of everything earthly.'[80]

If Ford could not earn a role as wounded woman, she seemed more credible as typically eccentric 'Negro.' In consideration of her 'African blood' she could still be portrayed as a pitiful animal, in the opinion of the *World*: 'Ushered into a world by whom she knew not, she had been buffeted about with no more comprehension of cause or reason than has a dog; nay, not so much, for she knew not friends from foes. As she grew older she realized that it was to the presence of African blood in her veins that many of the rebuffs she received were due. She brooded over this fact, and the untold, untellable suffering and misery which people of her colour had suffered in the past.'[81] The *World* discredited Ford's claims of threatened modesty, but it did grant that her racial characteristics may have been the source of a 'wild impulse' to strike out against a rich white man. Thus she might still be considered a victim, albeit on the basis of her racial rather than her sexual character.

Whether Ford was a cross-dressing pugilist or an unfortunate product of miscegenation, she strained Torontonians' capacity to think of her as an innocent heroine who might be forgiven for having defended her honour. She could not defend, after all, something she did not possess.[82] The *World* spelled out the formula of wounded womanhood: 'It must first be established that Clara Ford was a virtuous young woman, so virtuous, in fact, that she was shocked at the approaches of a boy four-teen years younger than herself; that she led a moral life and was extremely sensitive of her reputation for morality.'[83] Even before her trial, then, the plot conventions had been laid out. For five months the city waited for the leading lady to take the stage in a most demanding role.

Clara Ford's trial opened to critical acclaim, but she did not appear as a wounded woman. Instead, she played a character part in a racist drama orchestrated by a white man posing as a chivalrous protector. The Crown was represented by the venerable B.B. Osler, the man who had success-fully prosecuted Louis Riel.[84] His opponent, E.F.B. 'Blackie' Johnston, was a fiery orator and a criminal lawyer noted for his wily defence tactics. In view of Ford's poverty, he accepted the case without fees. Filling out the male roles were Justice Sir John Boyd, knighted for his service as the chancellor of Ontario, and twelve men, mainly farmers and artisans, who represented the accused's peers. The lone woman in the cast represented the life to be lost or saved in this real-life melodrama.

The Crown contended that Ford had the motive, the means, and the opportunity to kill Frank Westwood. She had lived for several years in a lean-to near the Westwood estate; she possessed a gun; she was known to dress in men's clothes; and she was overheard threatening Westwood's life. If there was insufficient circumstantial evidence, then Ford's confession to the detectives sealed the Crown's case. Osler admit-ted that there was 'evidence of a certain relationship of an improper kind' between the deceased and the accused, but he stopped short of lending credence to Ford's claim that she had been wronged. 'West-wood's story is the old one of love and passion, condemned by the law of God and man': 'It is the story of a mulatto girl who had been the plaything of an apparently respectable young man. Discarded by him for another, she deliberately shot him to death.'[85] After three and a half days of damning evidence and testimony, the prosecution rested its apparently solid case.

Johnston's only hope was to persuade the jury that his client had been a victim, a woman adrift on whom they might bestow a merciful verdict. Ford herself had offered a confession that painted her as an 'insulted' heroine, but Johnston decided against the defence. As the *World* had earlier advised, he would first have had to establish that she had jealously guarded a spotless reputation that Westwood had besmirched. Johnston had asked himself whether a poor black seamstress who lived alone in the Ward, sported men's clothes, carried a revolver, and knocked over annoying men could play the part of the modest victim. His answer was no.

In a brilliant defensive move, Johnston managed simultaneously to present his client as a credible victim, resuscitate Westwood's character, and position himself as a champion of honour. Asking the jury to believe that Ford could have been 'insulted' by a young gentleman was too risky a gamble, so he suggested that they consider how Ford might have been victimized in another way: as a female with 'African blood' who had been an easy target for big-city detectives who had given her 'the third degree' and badgered her into a false confession. 'Was it any wonder,' Johnston demanded, 'that she, womanlike, would say anything to get out of the clutches of those vultures?' The detectives had exploited her ignorance for their own gain, while Johnston, in contrast, had defended the innocent woman without charge because she had 'not a dollar.' By rescripting his client's confession, he tacitly sided with those who dismissed the possibility that an immodest woman, particularly one of 'mixed' blood, could be sexually assaulted by a respectable white man.

The jury's verdict of not guilty, delivered after less than half an hour of deliberation, was met with tumultuous applause from the large gathering at the courthouse. The jurors told a *World* reporter that they had deemed Ford to be 'a defenceless woman who was bluffed and coddled by turns ... the only evidence against her was the admissions that had been scared out of her.' The *World* rejected both versions of Ford's explanation, and wryly observed that justice could never be done when women were on trial: 'There are few men so little touched by sentiment as not to shrink from the idea of hanging a woman.' Men, after all, looked to women as 'embodying the best and highest virtues.' The paper astutely concluded that Ford had gone free because she had been indulged by men who had the power of life and death over her. Indeed, Ford herself recognized that her acquittal was a testimony to chivalry when she announced to the largely male crowd at her victory celebration, 'I thank you for the way you stood by me ... This does the boys of Toronto credit.'[86]

Clara Ford's acquittal saved her neck, but it hardly did the 'girls' of Toronto credit. Like most of the working girls who claimed that they had been sexually assaulted by socially superior men, she failed to convince men that she could be a credible victim. Luckily for Ford, her skilful lawyer came up with an alternative story that hinged on the jurymen's readiness to believe that single working women, particularly those of 'lower races,' were no match for overzealous, villainous detectives. Ford's story of wounded womanhood had more dramatic appeal, but Johnston realized that a woman with her reputation could not play the part once the drama opened.

THE 'BRUTE' AND THE 'LITTLE GIRL'

A woman more aptly cast to play the innocent heroine was Carrie Davies. Like Ford, she confessed to shooting a wealthy white man on account of his unsolicited sexual advances. And like Ford, she was acquitted after a sensational trial. Although Davies was a more credible victim, her 1915 trial none the less confirmed the limited terms on which working girls could be considered wounded women. Her valiant defence of her medically certified chastity provided her credibility and allowed men in authority to come to her rescue. Her defence proceeded, then, in the manner that Ford's might have had Ford been considered suitable for the role of the embattled maiden. Race was a factor in both acquittals; however, in Davies's case, vaunted notions of Britishness, rather than racist interpretations of 'mongrels,' made her a sympathetic figure in the dock. The wartime context of Davies's trial allowed her supporters to resuscitate an image of helplessness and vulnerability that had become anachronistic by the 1910s. Finally, in both cases, the nature of their crimes was, paradoxically, the key to their acquittals: extraordinary effort was expended to erase these women's motives, their volition, and their power to seek revenge for wrongs.

Carrie Davies was an eighteen-year-old maid who at sixteen had emigrated from Bedfordshire, England. The death of her father, a pensioner who had been wounded in the Boer War, left her mother struggling to support three daughters, of whom Carrie was the eldest. The family decided that Carrie would work in service in Toronto, where her married sister lived. By the time she joined the dwindling ranks of Toronto's maids, most single wage-earning women had turned to alternative employment. In the 1910s young women such as Davies upheld an increasingly old-fashioned ideal of service and self-sacrifice.

Davies earned a position at the home of Charles Massey, where she worked as a general servant in 1913. By scrimping and living modestly, she began to repay her sister and brother-in-law for her passage, and she regularly sent her mother a substantial portion of her monthly wage of sixteen dollars. All seemed well until 9 February 1915, when the British, church going, dutiful daughter shot and killed her master. Davies appeared before Magistrate Denison in Toronto Police Court the following morning. From the prisoner's dock she told the court why she had shot 'Bert' Massey. On the weekend before to the murder, Massey had become drunk and made lewd remarks to her. While she attempted to go about her chores, he tackled her on the bed and suggested she try on his wife's undergarments. When Davies went to see her sister and brother-in-law to seek their advice they recommended that she return, as she had promised Mrs Massey she would not leave the house, but maintain caution. Davies brooded until, overcome with fear, she shot her master on his doorstep as he returned from work. She made no attempt to escape or deny her responsibility. When asked by the police why she had killed him, her reply was straightforward: 'I really shot him in self defence ... he took advantage of me yesterday and I thought he was going to do the same today.'[87]

The young maid's confession of murder in self-defence vied with war news as the all-absorbing topic of the day. Davies described her deed as an attempt to preserve her character. Her extraordinary effort to defend her chastity and remain at her post reassured Torontonians that there were still young wage-earning women who cared more about their reputations than their pleasures. As comfortingly anachronistic as Davies's dowdy dress and sense of duty made her appear, her crime was not excused on the basis of its conformity to melodramatic conventions. Rather, Torontonians connected the British 'girl's' plight to the cause of Britain itself as it struggled against the 'Hun.' Through her trial, Davies came to stand for the 'civilized' values for which Canadian soldiers were prepared to die, and kill. No longer could the 'seduced maiden' scenario on its own establish the working girl as a credible victim.

Campaigns to raise money for Davies's defence produced several scripts for her acquittal. The first was provided by the Toronto Local Council of Women, an umbrella organization that represented the city's women's organizations. The case inspired a special TLCW meeting on 17 February. The day before, many of the members had attended Davies's Police Court hearing, where their appearance shocked several reporters. A headline in the *Daily News* described the 'Disgusting Scene When Women Mobbed Corridors and Courtroom to satisfy Curiosity.'[88] The ladies, however, believed that their concern for women and for the city's moral standard justified their involvement in cases such as this. They determined that they would mobilize their considerable fund-raising talents to secure 'the services of one of Toronto's prominent K.C.'s as counsel.' Their efforts were an attempt to present the Davies case as a women's issue – a lesson for Torontonians that masters ought not to think of their servants as sexual pawns.

It was a fraternal organization, however, that became Davies's chief spokesman by defining her case as a class issue, a matter of British patriotism, and, above all, a test of male honour. When the Masseys hired an alienist to test Davies's sanity, many from Toronto's British working class interpreted the move as a rotten trick devised by a wealthy family trying to avoid publicity. The Bedfordshire Fraternal Association, a group of Englishmen who had emigrated from Davies's home, was particularly stirred by her trouble. The day before the TLCW meeting, the BFA had placed $25 in trust as a defence fund for Davies and her family. Once the TLCW learned that the family had already secured a lawyer and that the BFA had launched a defence appeal, the ladies tactfully retreated from the front lines. Their withdrawal virtually closed off discussion of the sexual exploitation of maids. Instead, the men of the BFA framed her crime in working-class masculinist terms and reaffirmed their wage-earning sisters' dependence on male protectors.

Working girls also came forward as individual advocates who identified with the young servant and her troubles. They numbered among the hundreds of men and women who sent letters of support and contributions to the defence fund through the *Telegram*. Contributors chose pen names, including 'British working girl,' 'Funny-looking English Girl,' 'Another English Carrie,' 'Good-looking English Girl,' 'Girl who feels proud to be English with an ideal soldier lover,' and 'One Who Knows.' They sent in humble donations ranging from 25 cents to $3.00. Some working women pooled their resources to make larger contributions. Sixteen operators from the Toronto Hat Factory on Adelaide Street West sent 'two blooming lasses' to the Telegram office shortly before the trial began to submit the $6.25 they had collected for Davies.[89]

Hartley Dewart, the man hired by the BFA to defend Davies, was in the best position to spin a plausible narrative that might excuse his client. The unenviable task of prosecuting the case fell to an esteemed member of the Toronto bar, Edward DuVernet. The Crown counsel had often appeared before the High Court in capital cases and was well used to the pressures both of defending the unsavory and prosecuting the weak. It was the latter scenario that he faced in the Davies case. 'I have never had a more unpleasant duty than to prosecute such a young girl on such a serious charge,' he opened. The defendant's spotless reputation and loyalty to her mistress was commendable, but he doubted that Massey's advances met common law requirements of provocation: 'It is for you,' he informed the jury, 'to determine if there was sudden provocation. You must judge whether this girl was insulted.'[90]

Hartley Dewart, in contrast, gloried in his role. He deftly ennobled his position as Davies's lawyer by linking the case to the greatest issues of the day: the defence of the British empire and the danger of barbarism. Under Dewart's rhetorical direction, Davies's reputation as a dutiful, chaste young woman became not only what British soldiers were fighting to protect but a symbol of the countries under attack by the German army. Like the Hun, Massey had tried 'to accomplish the ruin of the girl.' If the jury members could not, as men, put themselves 'in the position of an innocent and honourable girl of eighteen,' he asked them to imagine how Davies's father might have felt about a threat to his daughter's chastity had he been alive.

Dewart called only three witnesses. The first was Dr Arthur Harrington, who testified that the defendant was a virgin. His statement appeared on the surface to weaken her case because it confirmed that Davies had not been raped and had therefore claimed a life for a minor physical encounter to which she alone had been a witness. In accordance with rescue and reform agencies' measurements of feminine respectability, though, her virginity also established her character. Dewart argued that she was a modest girl – so modest, in fact, that she was driven to guard what exceeded the 'price of rubies.'

Finally, after calling her brother-in-law to the stand, Dewart had Davies recount the circumstances of her move to Canada, her commitment to support her mother and sisters in the old country, and her devotion to her soldier sweetheart who had recently been sent overseas. He then came to the question of her motive: 'I thought he'd do me harm,' she demurely replied.[91] Hers was the story of a 'little girl,' as Dewart insisted on calling her, torn between duty and fear and driven by the advances of a brute. Davies was not a murderer but a victim of her extraordinary loyalty to her mistress and her unshakeable sense of propriety.

The defence tactic simultaneously established that Davies would have been a candidate for the YWCA Haven if she had actually been raped. 'If she did not defend herself against this man,' Dewart said in his closing remarks, 'she would have been a fallen woman, an outcast, one more sacrifice to brutish lust. Let that sink into your mind.' It was not difficult, in time of war, to remind men whose sons might have been earning medals for killing Germans that civilized communities sometimes excused and even praised killers. Davies was as heroic in her capacity as a guardian of virtue as British soldiers who likewise killed without malice in their hearts. Facing 'a fate that she felt would be worse than death,' Dewart concluded, she merely resolved to protect herself.[92] The defence strategy had clearly touched a sensitive nerve: Davies was acquitted to great cheers from the crowd of spectators, who had expected nothing less.

Unlike the women who killed, however, most women adrift who sought recourse through the courts did not attain the status of heroic victims. No defence funds were established on their behalf; throngs of well-wishers did not follow them from the courtroom or throw victory parties; and publicity-hungry lawyers did not pad their reputations by saving them from the gallows. The dismal prospects of women who pressed charges of indecent assault or rape may very well have crept into Clara Ford's and Carrie Davies's consciousness before they pulled the trigger. The notoriety of their crimes elevated these otherwise ordinary wage-earning women to mythic proportions, leaving Torontonians with the false impression that the criminal justice system was soft on working girls.

In fact, the status of victim was conferred on wage-earning women only grudgingly and with compensatory drama. The rare stories of 'Unnatural Mothers,' 'Ruined Girls,' and 'Wounded Women' made front-page news, while the everyday tales of young women picked up for vagrancy and sent to prison failed to excite comparable public sympathy. Similarly, the courts were reluctant to support victims of sexual violence who directly challenged the assumption that being raped was somehow shameful. Men in the criminal justice system preferred to address sexual coercion tangentially, as a factor in the forgiveness of abortionists and unwed mothers guilty of ridding themselves of their infants. Bestowing victim status on women who killed allegedly dangerous men or threw themselves into the bay to hide their shame spared the courts the unpleasant task of trying men for sexual offences.

Finally, the translation of working girls' tragic experiences into stories of victims may have exculpated certain notorious offenders, but it came with a price. Women who 'fell' into crime or immorality could be reintegrated into respectable society only if they were abject and prepared to rely on the mercy of moral and social superiors. Focusing on the wrongs done to them and the culpability of their exploiters was viewed with considerably less favour. That the criminal justice system was more sympathetic towards murderers than it was towards sexual assault complainants suggests that single women who exposed men's crimes faced greater risks than those who killed them or their illegitimate offspring.

'Fallen women' learn the virtues of domesticity at the Andrew Mercer Ontario Reformatory for Females in 1903. Strict time-management in prison instilled regular work habits, while uniforms reinforced the deference that mistresses expected of domestic servants.

Girl workers toil in factory-like conditions in the mail department of the Robert Simpson Company, c. 1909. Employers preferred them for routine tasks that required attention to detail. They also preferred young women because they could be paid less than any other workers.

TORONTO VIGILANCE COMMITTEE

DEPARTMENT OF INVESTIGATION
AND LAW ENFORCEMENT

ALL CREEDS - - - **ALL RACES**

THE WORK OF THIS DEPARTMENT INCLUDES:

Prevention of Crime.

"1. Efforts to prevent real white slavery; i.e., the holding of girls in involuntary servitude for immoral purposes. A number of such cases have come to light in Toronto.

"2. The prevention, by educational and other means, of young girls entering upon immoral careers. Our representatives have followed a number of young girls, who were in the company of young men whom we suspected of being desirous of ruining the girls. We are always ready to step in and prevent any overt act.

"3. The suppression of unduly obnoxious behaviour on the part of immoral women, and their elimination from districts where young children are being brought up. Children must not be confronted with vice. The Vigilance Committee came to the aid, none too soon, of the little children of St. Patrick Square, Hagerman, Mutual, and other streets.

Alluring Advertisements.

"4. The investigation of advertisements appearing in the daily papers. Recently a number of persons have been advertising for lady stenographers, waitresses, etc., and when the applicants called, they would be rudely treated by being asked such questions as: 'Do you wish to have a good time, and make big money?' 'Do you smoke, play cards, dance, stand on your head?' 'Do you desire to go to wine suppers?' 'What are your measurements from your hips down?" One villain of a man induced one of the young girls to go to an establishment he operated on Bathurst Street, and there accomplished, possibly, the ruin of the girl. OUR SISTERS AND DAUGHTERS MUST NOT BE SUBJECTED TO THESE GROSS AFFRONTS!

"5. The meeting of trains and boats, so far as possible, and arranging for suitable boarding-places for the girls who are coming to our city from Canada, the Old Country, the United States, and other parts of the world.

"6. The elimination of improper post-cards, indecent literature, etc.

"7. Efforts to aid in preventing boys being led astray by moral perverts.

After the "Cadets" and Chinese.

"8. The punishing of that class of 'men' who live off the avails of prostitution, causing women and girls to live a life of shame in order that these so-called cadets may be supported in idleness.

"9. Strenuous efforts to break up Chinese dens of infamy, kept for the purpose of ruining young Canadian girls.

Better Wages.

"10. Agitation in favour of better pay for the girl employees in stores, factories and offices, and of having the scarlet man punished as severely as the scarlet woman. An endeavour to have the police authorized to escort young girls and boys, under 16 years of age, to their homes, if they are found out at a late hour wandering about the streets.

HELP US TO USHER IN "A BETTER TORONTO"

Those Desiring to Financially aid will please forward checques to REV. R. B. ST. CLAIR, Treas. of Dept. 181 Argyle St., TORONTO.

Any Information Received, treated with Strictest Confidence. Address;
Supt., Vigilance Committee, Toronto, Ont.

LEFT: Social purity groups stressed the vulnerability of young women to the depredations of modern life. Attacking white slavery was the key to the Vigilance Committee's assault on urban vice in 1912. Once young women began 'immoral careers,' however, they became part of the problem.

ABOVE: As the journalist C.S. Clark claimed, winter sports offered as many opportunities as summer outings for young women to excite men's passions. Here a group of young women, c. 1909, sit happily sandwiched between young men on a toboggan.

LEFT: A 'good times girl'? An occasional prostitute? A victim of a white slaver? By the turn of the century, experts claimed that they alone could distinguish between the working girl as victim and the working girl as 'moral menace.'

ABOVE: Young women congregate on the boardwalk at Scarboro Beach Amusement Park, trying to decide between the Shooting Gallery and the Snake Show, 1907.

Eaton's switchboard operators at their posts under the scrutiny of female supervisors, 1923. By the turn of the century, white-collar work began to offer ambitious young women limited advancement possibilities. Higher positions usually entailed monitoring younger, less-skilled women.

In the foreground, working girls adorned in the latest fashions spare a glance for the camera as they wait in line to apply for waitressing jobs at the 1920 Canadian National Exhibition. At $1.25 per day, they would depend heavily on tips, but what might they do to attract them?

Shift change at Eaton's mail-order building on Louisa Street, 1908: working girls stream towards Yonge Street and its prospects of pleasures and perils.

In the wake of the recommendations flowing from the Bell Telephone strike settlement, employers began to recognize the value of after-hours facilities that kept employees away from commercial amusements. Here, contented working girls relax in the quarters of the Eaton's Junior Girls' Recreation Club, 1919.

The Main Entrance

Sherbourne House Club—

is a Residence and Club for business women and girls living away from home. It aims especially at conducting a pleasant and inexpensive home on a co-operative basis without profit, for the accommodation of self-supporting women who must board, and supplies its members with a commodious, safe and sanitary residence and club house. The desire is that each resident shall enjoy many of the comforts, much of the liberty and always the sympathy and inspiration of home life.

MARY LOUISE BOLLERT, M.A.
Superintendent of Sherbourne House Club and Director of Education Department of The Robert Simpson Co., Limited.

The well-educated Miss Bollert administered Toronto's single largest residence for 'business women and girls' according to democratic principles of self-management. The facility was so popular that some residents remained for more than a decade.

Pamphlet No. V.D. 5.
10M-Nov.-1928

ONTARIO
PROVINCIAL DEPARTMENT OF HEALTH

FACTS
ON
SEX HYGIENE
FOR
Girls and Young Women

Toronto:
Printed and Published by the Printer to the
King's Most Excellent Majesty
1928

FREE

Facts For Girls

During the late war many young girls who previously had never expected to work in a factory, store or an office were drawn into such work from a sense of duty and patriotism. These girls were naturally thrown into a new world and in a very short time began to realize that there were a good many things happening which previously had been outside their lives, but which under their new conditions had to be taken into account.

Luckily most of these young girls, accustomed to self-control, were equal to the new conditions and no harm resulted. But it is not good policy to send unprotected girls out to work away from home where they would be rubbing against all kinds of persons, unless these girls have been previously informed as to the dangers of their new position.

Since the war many young girls are taking advantage of the increased wages and also many are forced by the high cost of living to help in the upkeep of the home. This pamphlet is written to be a help to such girls in order that they may not endanger their own health and future life by love of excitement or ignorance of certain of the fundamental facts concerning sex laws.

In the wake of wartime reports about the extent of venereal disease in troops, efforts to educate the public about 'sex hygiene' redoubled. Young women were cautioned against promiscuity but discouraged from avoiding men altogether lest they neglect their duty to 'the race.'

A working-class entertainment district at the corner of Queen and Bay Streets, c. 1920. To the left, movie posters at the Colonial theatre offer adventure and romance films; to the right, wall posters advertise 'classy burlesque' at the Gayety Theatre.

Two winners of the Sherbourne House Club's annual Hallowe'en costume contest ham it up for the camera. The carnival atmosphere allowed respectable businesswomen to mimic and mock heterosexual conventions of romance.

4

The Social Evil in the Queen City

Prior to the publication of his notorious exposé of immorality in Toronto, Montreal journalist Christopher St George Clark thought it wise to ascertain whether the controversial subject-matter might expose him to prosecution on obscenity charges. On 24 April 1898 he wrote Deputy Attorney General J.R. Cartwright a provocative letter, warning that he intended to uncover the sexual depravity that festered underneath the nose of the Morality Department. He claimed that the policy of raiding brothels had led to the spread of immorality. The result was that apparently respectable working girls had taken over sexual services previously provided by professionals: 'Young men tell me that girls employed by the T. Eaton Co. are many of them prostitutes. That is to say, a young man must first get well acquainted with them, so that they know who he is, and then the result follows.' In his book, published later that year, he supplied many more such examples of Toronto working girls who willingly catered to the sexual cravings of the city's young men; this version of the social evil, not the organized vice industry, called for suppression.[1]

Clark stood alone in the early 1890s as a public figure who openly advocated the regulation of brothels as a means to localize and circumscribe vice. He was not alone, however, when it came to criticizing the police policy of periodic brothel raids. From the 1890s to the 1910s, women's organizations, leaders of the social purity movement, and city administrators devoted unprecedented energy to the study of prostitution in all its guises. Although they proposed different solutions to the problem, they agreed that the time had come for proactive approaches to the urban sex trade. Whether they advocated licensing, more consistent and thorough policing, or the implementation of new laws designed to trap those who profited from prostitution, they shared a conviction that commercialized sex, more than any other problem, was the root of all evils.

Prostitution was the leitmotif in surveys of urban problems conducted at the turn of the century. Although reform organizations pointed to a host of evils in the industrial city – gambling dens, slums, impure water, intemperance, crime – they could agree that prostitution was *the* social evil. Images of victimized women forced to provide sexual services persisted, although, in keeping with the earlier ambivalence concerning fallen women, prostitutes could also appear as temptresses who led pure young men astray. By the early twentieth century, however, surveyors of the social evil were more inclined to assume that working girls made their way into prostitution voluntarily through the casual bartering of sexuality. The line between the noble workwoman and the fallen woman had become blurred by the emergence of a shadowy figure known as the occasional prostitute – a working girl who supplemented her earnings by doling out sexual favours. There were some, notably in the social purity movement, who continued to think in terms of urban villains and innocent maidens, but the men and women who observed working girls' easy way with men, their taste for finery, and their growing preference for work that left their evenings and weekends free suspected that young women in the city, not their customers or procurers, might be the source of the problem.[2] In either case, working girls required stricter moral regulation.

Prostitution and working girls were hardly the sole issues to consume reform lobby groups in this period, as other studies have shown. Historians of the social purity movement, for instance, have looked at its impact on temperance, sabbatarianism, and censorship, while more recent works have stressed its efforts to construct moral subjects. Similarly, the work of organizations such as the National Council of Women of Canada have been seen as laying the groundwork for the first wave of feminism and the campaign for woman suffrage. Lastly, Progressivism has been portrayed as a rational effort to manage the problems of urban industrialization by imposing order and increasing efficiency in economic and social life. Yet each of these movements and organizations was also a key player in a discursive process that magnified the girl problem. Studying them in this light is not an artificial exercise, for in their pronouncements about what was wrong with city life and what should be done to remedy it, the working girl was invariably front and centre.

As overblown and alarmist as white slavery narratives and stories of occasional prostitutes may seem in our cynical view of 'Victorian' excesses, the state was remarkably responsive to alarmist claims that vice had taken over the cities. In Toronto, the home base of the Canadian social purity movement and a leading centre of first wave feminism and Progressivism, a flurry of institution-building took place in response to demands that governments deploy a wider range of weapons to fight the social evil. The Children's Aid Society (CAS), two industrial schools for girls, a children's court, and a women's court were all established between the mid-1890s and the 1910s. Although the CAS and the children's court also dealt with neglected or troublesome boys, the municipal and provincial governments were clearly prepared to devote resources to the detection and correction of girls and young women who ran into trouble or who themselves presented a moral danger to civil society. At the same time, the expanded activities of the YWCA in concert with other organizations devoted exclusively or in part to young women, including the Women's Christian Temperance Union (WCTU), the Big Sisters, and settlement houses, confirmed that responding to the girl problem would play an important part in establishing Toronto as a city upon a hill.

THE SCATTERING OF LOOSE WOMEN

Ever since the Morality Department was established in 1886, the official policy of the Toronto police toward prostitution had been one of intolerance. Indeed, Toronto had earned its nickname, 'Toronto the Good,' on account of the Department's posturing on all matters moral. Annual Police reports, however, reveal disunity on this contentious policy matter. From the policeman on the beat to the chief constable, the force was avowedly in favour of maintaining an informally regulated red light district segregated from the 'respectable' part of the city. In his annual report of 1894, the chief constable flatly stated that 'a policy of repression, in too severe a form, may lower rather than improve the moral tone of the people.' He warned advocates of the war against the social evil that it had backfired because it prompted 'women of the town to seek the shelter of private lodgings in respectable localities instead of confining themselves to places where their presence is not objected to.'[3] The spread of prostitution in middle-class, commercial and residential areas, however, presented an even greater problem for the police who faced the wrath of powerful ratepayers. Shutting down brothels also threatened to reduce police officers' opportunities to extort money from the vice industry. In either case, the Toronto police were uncomfortable with the prospect of challenging the prevailing system of tacitly tolerated and informally regulated brothels.

In alluding to 'respectable' citizens' fears of encroaching immorality, the chief touched on a common worry among bourgeois urbanites in the late nineteenth century. In short, it had become difficult to distinguish between the respectable and the disreputable in large cities. On downtown streets the city's diverse characters met as strangers united only by a commercial transaction, a shared seat on a crowded tram, or a momentary glance outside a theatre. Toronto's diversity did not encompass a great range of ethnic or racial groups as did the cosmopolitan cultures of New York or Chicago, but its demographic homogeneity was not in itself a great comfort to anxious citizens. Class was the prime signifier of character in a city where the vast majority of citizens came from the same British stock. Italians, European Jews, the tiny black and Chinese communities, and the very poor – in short, the inhabitants of 'the Ward' – could be easily identified by the majority of white, native-born, and British Torontonians who readily identified such people as morally suspect. But the residents of St John's Ward lived in the confines of a well-defined downtown district and rarely ventured into the finer neighbourhoods to the north. It was much more difficult for 'respectable' Torontonians to assess the moral character of the working-class people they encountered outside the city's most depressed areas. Might the labourer down the block be a thief? Could the seamstress who lived above the store be a prostitute?

The police could offer no assurances. In fact, the chief constable believed that middle-class Torontonians had cause to increase their suspicions of working-class people, and of single wage-earning women in particular. He reported in 1896 that brothel raids had opened the floodgates on a previously contained vice district and allowed a foul stream of immorality to pollute the entire city. He firmly opposed the city's official policy of brothel raids as a means to stamp out vice. The number of 'regularly established houses of prostitution' had admittedly dropped as a result of the raids, and the number of brothel-related charges did sink from 174 in 1894 to 46 in 1895. Yet these apparently encouraging statistics offered cold comfort to the chief, who believed that raids were not the only reason that houses of ill fame had become less numerous: 'Competition from women living singly so as not to come within the scope of the law may be one explanation of the cause.'

In addition to these single women installed in private quarters, others plied their trade, like the proverbial whore, 'at every corner': 'Solicitation on the street is not rife, though loose women are to be seen on the thoroughfares after nightfall.'[4] In the minds of the police, the prostitute was no longer a victimized woman adrift; rather, she might be any 'apparently respectable' working girl who lived on her own or who walked without an escort on the street at night.

AN IMMENSE HOUSE OF ILL FAME

The journalist C.S. Clark took greater liberty than leaders of the police force in criticizing the activities of the Morality Department. His famous tract *Of Toronto the Good* (1898) was a collection of personal observations that exposed the supposedly lurid underside of 'the Queen City.'[5] He recounted his adventures as an 'urban spectator' and revelled in the 'fact and fantasy of urban exploration.'[6] As a cosmopolitan urbanite, wise to secrets of the city, he attempted to shock his readers with true, or possibly true, tales of vice. But his pornographic peeks at urban immorality were laced with puritanical homilies. The information he disclosed may have come from bellboys and the young men he met on the streets, but the message was clearly intended for respectable men and women: 'The price at which I place the book (50c) will keep it out of the hands of all except those who can reason and discuss the theories I advocate,' he reassured the deputy attorney general.[7]

Clark distinguished himself from the majority of people writing about the social evil by his straight talking and scientific detachment. 'I have never done anything to promote public morals,' he proudly declared: 'I simply say I advocate what I do from the independent standpoint of the logician.' Like the chief constable, he believed that the suppression of vice and harmless pastimes, such as ball-playing, had fostered the spread of immorality. While young men's appetite for disreputable pleasures had increased in the face of the crackdown against innocent fun, Howland's war against brothels had forced immoral women into freelance vice. The cosmetic cleanup of vice districts merely masked the fact that 'loose women [had] scattered themselves about' in private rooms where they plied their trade without police interference.[8]

Of Toronto the Good countered the discourse of fallen womanhood by stressing the agency of working women who determined their own paths to vice. In many ways the tract anticipated the sentiment shared by social welfare agencies, the courts, and penologists by the 1910s.

None of them was entirely unsympathetic to the plight of self-supporting women: girls might 'go astray in an effort to keep themselves on the small salaries paid to them.'[9] Nevertheless, Clark maintained that most girls were lured into prostitution through moral weakness and cupidity. Clark's Toronto was a city of deception and allure, where working girls had moved front and centre into the ranks of the deceivers. The 'scattering' of loose women from raided brothels meant that it had become difficult to distinguish respectable young women from the lewd entrepreneurs who had taken to the streets to ensnare customers. In Montreal, where brothels were tolerated by the police, he had never been solicited, but in 'Toronto the Good' solicitation was a nightly occurrence. Only the urbane observer could discern this new type of prostitute's intent, for words and gestures were unnecessary to her craft. 'I do not mean to say that women stop me on the street,' he admitted, 'but every man or boy knows that soliciting can be done without a word being spoken, and that is the way I have been solicited in Toronto.' He described how women let men know that they were prostitutes: 'You meet a girl on the street and a flash from her eyes will tell you *what* she is. You look back after passing her, and she does the same. If you desire to follow her, do so and the probabilities are ninety-nine to one that you have a street walker.' To Clark, a 'girl's' flirting was not so much an expression of interest as a declaratory act of self-definition: a glance told men 'what' she was. Thus, he equated a wink or a nod with outright haranguing of customers. The only difference, he wryly concluded, was that 'in the case of respectable girls such a course is called flirting [whereas] in prostitutes it is called soliciting.'[10]

If flirting and soliciting were essentially the same acts, how was a man to distinguish an apparently respectable young woman from a truly chaste one? Clark believed that disreputable women manipulated popular perceptions of innocent femininity in their ploys to trap the *real* victims: men. When such women were not confined to brothels they became a much greater danger to men precisely because they were 'presumably respectable but ... not really virtuous.' Clark asserted that these deceptive tactics proved that 'girls [were] more to blame than boys.' He worried that young men, unwise to the wiles of women, would be unable to escape their clutches.

Male readers who were concerned lest they mistake a respectable young woman for a prostitute were reassured that no virtuous female would allow herself to be seduced. Clark effectively denied charges from women's organizations and social purity advocates that women were victims of men who pressed them into having sex. At the time he wrote *Of Toronto the Good*, for instance, members of the WCTU complained that a number of young women who visited the Toronto Islands had been 'ruined' by men who gave them boat rides. 'I don't believe any such nonsense,' Clark scoffed. He countered that 90 per cent of 'girls go over to the island for that very express purpose.' In his estimation, the islands were an open-air sex market and the city 'an immense house of ill-fame, the roof of which is the blue canopy of heaven during the summer months.'[11]

Clark's famous contention appeared in the context of his general warning to respectable young men to be wary of loose women scattered throughout the city. He quoted from Proverbs to add biblical weight to his admonition:

> In the twilight, in the evening, in the black and dark night ...
> Now is she without, now in the streets, and lieth in wait at every corner ...
> Let not thine heart decline to her ways, go not astray in her paths.
> For she hath cast down many wounded: yea, many strong men have been slain by her.
> Her house is the way of hell going down to the chambers of death.[12]

The verses were well suited to Clark's interpretation of freelance prostitution in turn-of-the-century Toronto: men are the ones in danger in the city because women lie in wait on 'black and dark' street corners. Men would be safer visiting prostitutes than exposing themselves to the designs of these unregulated urban entrepreneurs.

Clark essentially mouthed what police officers outside the Morality Department believed: working girls were inherently worthy of suspicion as morals offenders. The chief's interchangeable references to 'lewd women,' 'women of the town,' and 'women living singly' are noteworthy as indices of ambivalence about the presence of working girls in the public spaces of the city. Renting rooms, for instance, was something working men had done for years, yet when working girls began to rent their own quarters they were instantly objects of suspicion. Clark alleged that prostitutes were free to rent rooms from unsuspecting landlords because they installed sewing machines and pretended to be seamstresses. Rejecting the possibility that women with sewing machines in their rooms might indeed be seamstresses, Clark painted all working women 'living singly' with the same brush of immorality.

'They take men there at night and no one is any the wiser,' he claimed, without divulging the source of his knowledge.[13]

By granting women a greater degree of self-direction in their decision to engage in prostitution, Clark further departed from the evangelical conception of fallen womanhood in his conviction that women who had traded in their respectability could never, not even through contrition, earn it back.[14] He wrote as if illicit sexual activity amounted to stepping off a precipice and into a bottomless pit: 'There is only one means of safety, and that is to avoid the first step. Once place your foot on the downward path, and you are lost forever.' To illustrate his point he recounted a tragic tale of a boating accident on the Detroit River, where a young man and woman had met their deaths. A search for background information on the woman led the reporter to the details of her 'downfall, disgrace, and subsequent death.' She had made the fateful decision to move to Toronto from her family's southwestern Ontario farm because she had 'tir[ed] of her home in the country.' In the city she took up work as a 'typewriter' for a law firm. Before long she 'fell into fast company' and 'her downfall soon followed.' There was apparently no moral observation to make concerning the 'downfall' of the man who died with her, for the story mentions only that he was a hotel-keeper. The reporter's exclusive focus on the young working woman's reckless course to ruin ably suited Clark's interpretation of the growth of freelance prostitution. The 'professionally unchaste' had been replaced by 'girls who are presumably respectable, but who are not really so.'[15]

THE WAR AGAINST 'WHITE SLAVERY'

Had a social purity advocate told the story of the unfortunate 'typewriter,' different conclusions might have been drawn. As defenders of a single standard of sexual morality for both sexes and supporters of a strict policy of vice suppression, they were disinclined to excuse men from their role in perpetuating the social evil. They were also more apt to see young single women as passive participants in matters of sexual morality. Moreover, social purity compaigners breathed new life into the old image of the embattled working girl by introducing a new urban villan: the 'white slaver.' Their tales dramatized their belief that an organized traffic in women, and not merely the practice of isolated procurers, threatened the moral foundation of city life.

As the 'war on the white slave trade' developed on the local, national, and international fronts, Torontonians heard salacious reports of seduction, sexual enslavement, and breathtaking rescues by the forces of morality. Although the authors of anti-'white slavery' tracts and novels broke new ground in their frank calls for improved sexual education of the nation's youth, their literature reproduced the myth of the woman adrift. Their message was essentially reactionary: young women ought not to move away from the safety of their homes to seek work because they were no match for the inevitable evils of the city.

Social purity advocates were no more convinced than the police or Clark that existing approaches to the problem of urban immorality worked. Rejecting Clark's libertarian position and disgusted by the lackadaisical policing of prostitution, they demanded that a wider net of legal regulation be cast over sexual vice. Maintaining an isolated red light district or conducting periodic brothel raids did nothing to stop the organized trade in innocent women, they pointed out. The city would not be safe for working girls until the police and the courts exercised their power to stamp out vice.

News of an international 'white slave' ring first reached Canadians in 1885 with reports of William Stead's investigations of child prostitution in London's East End. His sleuthing 'proved' the existence of a market in young women that served the brothels of Europe. Although many who supported his cause objected to his methods (which involved purchasing a virgin from an impoverished family and coercing a former madam to pose as a procuress), his undercover work brought speedy results in Parliament, which passed the Criminal Law Amendment Act in the same year. This sweeping piece of morals legislation imposed stiff penalties on brothel operators and those who seduced or inveigled women into prostitution.[16]

The Canadian Parliament was equally receptive to lobbyists' demands for a legislative response to organized immorality. The Criminal Code of 1892 reflected much of the Criminal Law Amendment Act's concern for the sexual exploitation of women and girls.[17] The code made it an offence to procure chaste women under the age of twenty-one for 'unlawful carnal connection' both within Canada and beyond its borders. In addition, it was unlawful to force a woman to become a prostitute or to lure her to a bawdy-house, whether through verbal or physical threats or by the use of drugs or alcohol.[18] The penalties for such offences ranged from two years' to fourteen years' imprisonment in the case of guardians or householders who permitted the defilement of a girl under sixteen and in the event of abduction of a girl or woman for the purpose of marriage or carnal knowledge.[19] Canadian legislators were clearly committed to suppressing exploitive practices that could be linked to an organized system of white slavery.

Canadian campaigns against the traffic in women did not begin until the turn of the century and did not reach their zenith until the 1910s. Churches and women's groups translated international cries for a response to the 'white slave' trade for local and national audiences whom they attempted to convince of the operation of the trade in Canadian cities. The Canadian contribution to the international war was coordinated by newly established departments of Protestant churches. In 1902 the Temperance, Prohibition, and Moral Reform Department of the Methodist Church of Canada was formed, and the Reverend S.D. Chown was made its general secretary. Five years later the Presbyterian Church added its own watchdog on moral issues – the Board of Moral and Social Reform headed by the Reverend Dr John Shearer. Shortly afterward, Shearer and another Toronto cleric, the Methodist T.A. Moore, set up an umbrella organization to coordinate the Protestant churches' efforts to uplift the moral tone of Canadian society. The Moral and Social Reform Council of Canada became the premier organization in the social purity movement's strategy to rid Canada of the scourge of white slavery. An offshoot of the council, the National Committee for the Suppression of the White Slave Traffic, formed in 1912, was responsible for successfully lobbying the federal government to introduce measures to suppress the alleged trade.

Aside from the well-organized activities of the Protestant churches, the country's women's groups were also on the front lines of the war. As early as 1905 the delegates to the convention of the International Council of Women brought back to Canadian local councils the warning that the traffic in women was not exclusively a European problem but a Canadian one as well. Local efforts began in the area of public education in the hope that women and parents might be warned of the dangers that lay around them. Those in greatest danger, council women advised, were pure country girls: 'Men and women who make it [their] practice to deal in human flesh, go to small towns and through misrepresentations and a sum of money from ten to twenty dollars, induce unsophisticated girls to go to the city. The girls are nearly all under twenty.'[20] At a time when thousands of Canadian women left their rural homes each year for waged work in cities, such allegations might have alarmed parents already anxious about the safety of their working daughters.

NCWC women were spurred to take a more proactive approach after the 1909 Quinquennial Convention of the International Council met in Toronto. Topping the agenda was the traffic in young women. The delegates, many of whom were from Toronto, heard their sisters' pleas to act in every country against the white slave trade. Canadians apparently felt guilty that they had been so slow to join the international battle: 'While we have been doubting, speculating and discussing, the nefarious traffic has reached tremendous proportions,' a member of the NCWC's Committee on the White Slave Trade reported in 1910. That their revised plan of action was to shape anti-prostitution legislation was made clear in her concluding call to battle: 'Shoulder to shoulder, let us attack this evil, and attack it at a vital point – the law.'[21] By 1912 the committee was able to reflect upon the groundswell of nationwide support for the suppression of organized vice: 'We rejoice in the fact that there is a general movement throughout Canada to suppress the business of social vice, including the white slave traffic, for purity is the very foundation of national life.'[22] The report added that Canada was losing 1,500 girls per annum to the international trade and that many of them disappeared into the dens of American red light districts. Would a Christian nation allow such an abomination to continue?

Just how this traffic in women was carried out was the subject of white-slavery literature that mobilized popular fears and whipped Canadians into a moral panic over a practice that was nowhere conclusively established. 'The day had passed for proving the existence of a traffic in girls for immoral purposes,' Rev. Shearer wrote in the popular 1911 treatise, *The War on the White Slave Trade* (1911), a text that became the bible of the anti-white slavers in Canada and the United States.[23] He opened his contribution with a reference to the dangers Canadian working women faced by crossing the border to seek success. 'Writers, nurses, teachers, stenographers, ladies' companions, seamstresses and domestic helpers' had moved south to find higher-paying jobs and greater advancement possibilities, but with disastrous consequences. Shearer claimed that procurers offered false promises of lucrative jobs in deceptive newspaper advertisements. 'Let women accept these jobs '[and] the innocent lambs go blindly to slaughter.'[24] White slavers were diabolical trappers who 'baited' their prey 'in the rural village or town' and swapped them, like latter-day fur traders, for money in cities where prostitution flourished.

Shearer continued this metaphoric representation of young women as naïve quarry in a story about a rural domestic servant who answered a tempting newspaper advertisement for a position in Ottawa. The first hint of trouble was that the work was to be light and the wages liberal. As Shearer put it, now depicting the victim as a fish, '[the] unsuspecting country girl saw and took the gilded bait.' Had a (male) railway official not recognized that her destination was a brothel, she might not have been so lucky. Shearer concluded the story with a further invocation of the working-girl-as-dumb-animal theme: 'One trembles to think how many similar lambs may not have thus escaped the slaughter.'[25]

The lamb metaphor, of course, touched on biblical symbols of innocence and sacrifice. Although the white slavers in his stories were predominantly men, and Chinese, black, Jewish, and other 'foreigners' in particular, the saviours of the victims were also men. As women of the YWCA had earlier observed, young lambs evidently needed shepherds to free them from the brambles of urban temptation and danger. In another story Shearer showed his readers 'how the purest and most innocent girls may be entrapped and enslaved.' He opened with a familiar saw: 'A winsome young lady from a rural village that might be named [but wasn't], was on her way to visit a girl friend in a well-known city.' In this case a 'respectable looking' woman intercepted the girl on the train and invited her to her home, whereupon she was locked in a room. A man presently entered but did not accomplish her ruin; instead, he altered the familiar scenario as soon as he recognized the young woman as the daughter of a business associate. The rapacious seducer suddenly transformed into a hero by shepherding her out of the brothel and back to the safety of her friend's home.[26] She would not to be one more sacrifice for the sins of the city; but how many country lasses could expect to be so fortunate?

'Unsuspecting girl[s],' fresh from the security of the family circle, might avoid the traps of white slavers on their perilous journey to the city, but their trials had only begun. By coyly omitting the names of cities and villages, Shearer maintained the mythic poles of 'country' and 'city' as signifiers of good and evil. Country girls unwise to the codes that allowed seasoned urbanites such as Clark or social purity crusaders to distinguish between the 'apparently respectable' and the truly pure were likely to fall victim to white slavers. Their substitute homes in the city offered no protection because cheap boarding-houses were full of strangers. Without a family-based home life they were likely to turn to the street and its commercial amusement for diversion from their dreary jobs. If hunters did not manage to trap their prey on trains or at public amusements they could track them at work, where employers and work-mates were both in a position to offer working girls 'various insidious temptations.'[27] To Shearer there was neither a single place nor a moment in a working girl's life when she could feel safe from exploitation or temptation in the city. At home, work, and play, young women were forced or tempted to a 'fate worse than death.' Nor could they turn with assurance to anyone for help: a friendly woman who offered directions at a railway station, a boarding-house keeper, an ice cream vendor, or a co-worker might all be undercover agents in the white slave trade. Innocent lambs were easy prey for city wolves in sheep's clothing.

The persuasiveness of white slavery narratives lay in the simultaneous references to specific cases and archetypal situations. Stories of country girls, big cities, boarding-houses or encounters with strangers at train stations were familiar to any urbanite and easily imagined by rural readers. When general stories were followed by specific cases, it was difficult to place the incidents in anything other than the interpretive framework already provided. When Shearer cited the case of Max Chbofsky, a Russian Jew who was charged with bringing 'pretty' nineteen-year-old 'Ella F—' into the United States from Toronto and sentenced to a year in prison, it is clear that the reader is to assume that the 'foreigner' is a white slaver and that 'Ella F—' is a pure, Anglo-Canadian girl. Shearer reported another case of a Toronto 'Hebrew' who forced seventeen year-old 'Annie K—' to marry him and 'turned her over to the White Slave Traffic' as soon as they wed.[28] In reality, the man had been sentenced to six months at the Central Prison for abduction, and his trial brought out no evidence of an organized traffic in women. Fears, not fact, were the building-blocks of white slavery narratives and the movement that mobilized Canadians into a war against the supposed traffic in women. The time for proof was over, Shearer claimed; the time to act was at hand.

The National Council of Women and the Moral and Social Reform Council of Canada spearheaded an assault on Parliament, hoping to turn legislators into allies. The government was inundated with briefs and reform proposals throughout 1912, and the message was consistent: amend the Criminal Code to bring the traffickers in women to justice. The government responded by introducing a set of amendments to the Criminal Code, adding the penalty of whipping for repeat offenders convicted of procuring and removing the age restriction for victims of procurement.[29] New offences and reduced requirements for evidence against suspected offenders were also introduced. Accusations of a white slavery trade inspired the creation of the new offences, including concealment in a bawdy-house, abducting an immigrant woman to a brothel, and exerting control over a woman or girl for the purposes of prostitution. Indeed, Justice Minister Doherty successfully argued for the passage of these amendments on the grounds that they would permit the police and the courts to combat white slavery.[30] The amended Criminal Code of 1913 was a significant victory in the social purity movement's war against vice.

INVESTIGATING VICE

Not only was Toronto chosen as the headquarters for Canadian social purity groups, it was the Canadian city most influenced by American Progressivism. Elsewhere in English Canada, particularly in the west, attempts to humanize progress were cast in explicitly Christian tones; the 'social gospel' is a more appropriate term for that version of reform and social criticism.[31] In Toronto, however, the civic administration looked for guidance to US cities where Progressives had introduced a social scientific discourse to discussions of city problems.[32] Unlike evangelical reformers or social purity advocates who considered the 'evils' of industrial urbanization as inevitable, urban Progressives saw the city as a social problem to be alleviated through rational management and social action. They actively sought the cooperation of the state, both to support their private welfare schemes and to enhance the effectiveness of reform and correctional agencies. Vice was at the top of Toronto's Progressive agenda, as it was in US cities such as Chicago, New York, and Minneapolis. Beyond improving drinking water, regulating utilities, clearing slums, and instituting similar municipal reforms, urban Progressives urged civic leaders to set their sights on the creation of a moral city. Christianity and science met in their hopes for a New Jerusalem. As Mayor Robert Flemming stated in his inaugural address in 1897, Toronto had 'an enviable and well-deserved reputation for business stability [and] high moral character ... that set it upon a hill among civic organizations.'[33]

Vice was not simply one of many areas in need of regulation; rather, it was the key to the Progressives' sense that the city was out of moral order. To overlook their concern with vice and the state of working girls' morality is to miss the essence of their search for order.[34] In Chicago and New York, vice commissions had revealed that the social evil was in fact a much graver problem than had ever been imagined.

Unlike social purity narratives that recounted incidents of white slavery in anecdotal form, the commissions 'proved' their stories of the white slave trade with statistics that set out the number of saloons, brothels, prostitutes, and pimps they discovered in the Stygian quarters of the city. In this updated version of urban spectatorship, teams of researchers, acting as undercover anthropologists in their own cities, gathered data on the social evil and prepared reports that were widely publicized. When Torontonians caught wind of the New York and Chicago surveys, they puzzled over the vice question in their own rapidly growing city. Should they conduct a scientific study of the social evil?

In 1902 an exhaustive survey of the 'social evil' in New York City was published by a 'Committee of Fifteen' prominent businessmen, philanthropists, and clerics who believed that the problem of vice was 'intimately connected with that of the movement of population toward the city.' The economic pressures of self-support and the allure of city life meant that young women were drawn to the 'border-land of vice and virtue.'[35] The New York report was the definitive survey of urban vice until 1911, when the Chicago Vice Commission published its shocking findings. The exhaustive study of 'The Social Evil in Chicago' was extremely influential, appearing as it did during the height of social purity agitation in the United States. Between 1911 and 1913, eleven US cities followed Chicago's example and launched similar investigations into organized vice.[36] Their impact on the course of the Toronto campaign against urban immorality was to be profound.

The aim of the Chicago commissioners was to 'map out such a course, as in its judgement, [would] bring about some relief from the frightful conditions that surround[ed] them.'[37] The 'conditions' they referred to amounted to 'vice as a disease of society.' A chapter entitled 'Sources of Supply' dealt specifically with the issue of white slavery. The commission's report provided a blueprint for subsequent vice surveys, which 'mapped out' the geography of immorality in various cities across North America. The Chicago commission concurred with New York's Committee of Fifteen that both vice and white slavery operated unabated in the city: 'Trafficking in the bodies of women does exist, and is carried on by individuals, acting for their own individual benefit ... [T]hese persons are known to each other, and are more or less informally associated.'[38] The profitable trade in girls and women depended on an intricate network of economic and social relations in the same way that any other of the city's big businesses operated. The 'profit-sharers in vice' included property owners, midwives, the police, doctors, employers, saloon-keepers and amusement vendors. Hence, it was not the procurer alone who shouldered the blame but the economic and social relations of the city that allowed vice to flourish. It seemed, according to meticulous surveys of the 'social evil,' that the preconditions for vice were woven into the very fabric of urban life.

The report of the Chicago Vice Commission sent shock waves through North American cities. Its impact was still felt in the year after it was published and it quickly became the reference text of urban moral reformers. Among organizations predisposed to believe in the existence of white slavery, the conviction that vice might flourish in their own cities grew dramatically. The report's liberal use of field notes and complicated data on prostitutes' backgrounds convinced local reformers that only a thorough scientific survey could adequately assess the problem. It was a sober statistical foil for the melodramatic narratives of *The War on the White Slave Trade*, and thus convinced many sceptics that the problem of urban vice did not exist only in the minds of social purity fanatics. Accordingly, local Progressive reformers clamoured to bring a Chicago-style survey to their own cities, both to expose the problem of organized vice and to report results in a format that legislators would find credible.

THE ROOT OF ALL EVILS

In Toronto, the group that spearheaded efforts to implement a vice survey of the city was the Toronto Local Council of Women. The TLCW had long addressed the problems of immorality through its 'Protection of Women and Girls' and 'White Slavery Traffic' committees, but its efforts had been restricted to specific projects such as the establishment of a juveniles' court.[39] By the 1910s, however, the council women in Toronto had developed lobbying skills that allowed them direct access to the ear of civic government. Their continuing concern over the morality and safety of young women and their growing political acumen earned the TLCW a leadership position among those who felt that Toronto merited a vice survey.

The council's agitation for an exploration of urban vice stemmed as well from its growing preoccupation with the city's working girls. In December 1912 Miss Neufeld, a settlement house social worker who had trained in New York and Chicago, addressed the council's regular monthly meeting on the issue of the city's young single women. As the minutes recorded, she spoke on a topic that was 'close to her heart': 'What is being done in Toronto for the working girl? How is it done? Who does it? How many girls are reached?'[40] Although she doubted that Toronto's girls were in as much danger as New York's or Chicago's, she believed that the TLCW was the organization best suited to the task of investigating the moral state of the city's working girls. A special committee to 'make a survey of conditions as they exist in Toronto' was struck immediately, and the TLCW embarked on its investigation of urban vice in their city.

The girl problem seemed all the more urgent in the context of the white slavery panic that swept Toronto in the early 1910s. Tales of enforcement of the Mann Act in the United States and the enactment of stiff anti-prostitution laws in many American cities increased Canadians' fears that white slavers might target Canada as a preferred hunting-ground. In a highly charged meeting of the TLCW on 19 March 1913, Dr Margaret Paterson, the active moral reform campaigner who later became Toronto's first Women's Court magistrate, told her fellow members that 'Canada was fast becoming a hotbed' of vice. She told her stunned listeners that a gambler had recently bargained for his release from police custody on the promise that he would divulge the names of one hundred people 'in Toronto alone who were traders of the white slave.' Those who continued to call the allegations of a traffic in women 'a "Pipe Dream"' were deplorably ignorant.

At Dr Patterson's behest, the TLCW resolved to 'approach the City council for the establishment of a Vice Commission ... to investigate the moral conditions in this city.' In the few short months since they began to study the girl problem, the TLCW had cast their sights toward the much broader terrain of urban morality. Although their immediate concern was the safety of working girls in the 'hotbed' of city dangers, they contended that the problem of white slavery was virtually synonymous with the larger issue of urban vice. The TLCW accordingly recommended that Toronto sponsor a 'vice commission such as they have in Chicago to get right down to the root of all evils.'[41]

The TLCW's political sophistication prepared it for the inevitable foot-dragging of politicians faced with a request for fiscal resources. Council members attacked on two fronts. While the Citizenship Committee stormed the Board of Control in May 1913, the newly formed 'Survey Committee' launched its own investigation to prepare for the possibility that an official, city-sponsored survey might not materialize. Even after the city approved the commission on 27 October 1913, the council women continued their makeshift investigation until February 1914. 'The work was not only too large but of too complicated a nature for the amateur,' they freely admitted.[42] The task they had in mind required the funding, facilities, and expertise of the state.

The city's assumption of the cost and administration of the TLCW's investigation of 'moral conditions' was hardly a hostile takeover. The council women clearly recognized that white slavery, the girl problem, and urban immorality had become so complex that they could not hope to undertake a scientific investigation along the lines of Chicago's vice report. Nor was this a case of naïve women's blind deference to experts. The TLCW understood that it had neither the time nor the skills to examine the city's underside, but it maintained the conviction that women brought unique sensitivities to social issues. Miss Neufeld and TLCW president Florence Heustis might have used such an argument to secure their spots on the twenty-two-member commission.[43] They undoubtedly informed the chairman, George Warburton of the YMCA, that their primary concern in participating was the moral welfare of the city's single working women. Miss Neufeld would have her chance to see if Toronto had a girl problem after all.

THE TORONTO SOCIAL SURVEY

The membership of the Social Survey Commission reflected the balance between government officials, experts, and volunteer reformers that City Council sought for a topnotch investigative team. In addition to four elected politicians six clergymen, four representatives of social reform organizations, three doctors, two lawyers, two businessmen, and an academic served on the Commission. Together they hoped to expose 'actually existing conditions' and to recommend the appropriate action that the city should take to improve the urban environment.[44]

With the optimism and assurance that characterized Progressive enterprises, the investigators proclaimed that theirs was a fact-finding mission, in distinct contrast to Shearer's fables and Clark's diatribes. They proceeded in the tradition of the Chicago vice commissioners, who had attested that their conclusions were based on 'incontrovertible facts.'[45] Like most Progressives, the members of the Toronto commission considered themselves to be objective scientific investigators who methodically explored social phenomena. For them the city was a laboratory full of troubling specimens of urban life. In their descriptions of encounters with the city's underclass they mimicked anthropologists reporting discoveries of exotic tribes. When they mapped the locations where vice flourished they became social geographers, sketching what the mayor called a 'moral survey of the City.' Although clergymen had a strong presence on the commission, the members did not think that religious or any other sentiments would impair their assessment of the truth – 'statements of fact that fairly represented existing conditions.' To reassure the sceptics who might dismiss the Toronto Social Survey as another hysterical tale of white slavery, they pledged that they would not 'play the alarmist and paint the conditions existing in the City in lurid colours.'[46] Instead, they would prepare the investigative equivalent of a photograph – a modern tool for the presentation of fact.

The content of the report, published two years after the survey was launched, was more imaginative than the commissioners cared to admit. It may not have been as lurid as social purity anecdotes, but it was far from a snapshot of vice. In spite of the investigators' commitment to accuracy, they unconsciously brought to their work a jumble of preconceptions about both big-city living and the troubling freedoms of single working women. Remarkably, they dismissed 'the problem of the white slave traffic,' the issue they were empanelled to investigate, in only three pages. The remainder of the seventy-two-page report was an exposé of problems, including 'feeble-mindedness,' 'the foreigner,' and, above all, a new breed of working women they dubbed 'occasional prostitutes.' The report's publication in 1915 marked a significant turning point in debates over single women's moral statues. Confirming C.S. Clark's earlier observations, the report presented the working girl as an agent rather than an object of urban vice. This characterization was most notable in discussions of the urban leisure scene, a topic so troublesome to the commissioners that it is reserved for the next chapter, which looks directly of the pleasures of the city.

The investigators were not at all discouraged to find an absence of evidence that a white slave traffic supplied a network of brothels. After exhaustive interviews with prostitutes, social workers, and refuge-home matrons, the commissioners decided that there was insufficient evidence 'of a system of obtaining and retaining involuntary victims for the business of vice.' Nevertheless, the investigators dropped their evidentiary standards and slipped into the familiar genre of the white slavery narrative to show that isolated incidents of abduction and entrapment *probably* took place. According to the surveyors, two reported cases in

Toronto were not, 'strictly speaking, white slavery,' but they were 'in principle not very far removed.' Even in these cases, there was no evidence that the young women had been drugged, beaten, or otherwise coerced into sexual slavery; furthermore, investigators failed to establish that the men and women who lured them into their service were members of a white slavery 'vice trust.'[47]

Undeterred, the surveyors proceeded to spin out narratives of the cases that were cut from the same rhetorical cloth as Rev. John Shearer's dramatizations of the dangers that young women courted when they worked in the city. In the first story that had apparently been 'ventilated in the courts,' a fourteen-year-old 'foreign' girl met her downfall a few days after she was engaged as a waitress in an ice cream parlour. Her employer locked her in her bedroom and a man 'accomplished her ruin.' Even though she had been with a wide range of men, 'including numerous Chinamen,' she was not entirely a victim, since 'on subsequent occasions she … certainly acted voluntarily.' In the second case, another ice cream parlour trap was set for a young domestic, also 'of foreign birth.' The 'young girl' had worked as a servant but decided to leave her situation for this new line of work that would lead, she hoped, to better pay, presents, and '"good times" generally.' Her benevolent master tried to convince her that she was in danger, but she did not heed his warning, assuming that he was actually trying to retain her services. Several days after she left, the inevitable happened: the prodigal servant scurried back to her master's door in the middle of the night after having narrowly escaped a strange man's attempt to violate her.[48]

In both of these tales the innocence of the women was amplified by their youth and their recent immigrant status. On both counts they could not have expected to be wise to the wickedness of the city, nor would they be aware of the voluntary agencies that might have assisted them. Underlying their apparent innocence, however, was their wilful pursuit of immoral pleasures. The first 'young girl' did not seek her parents' aid immediately, but rather continued to have sexual relations with 'all sorts of men.' That Chinese men numbered among her customers confirmed her degraded state in the eyes of the readers, who identified Asians as the most mysterious of races.[49] In the case of the second woman, a servant's abandonment of a respectable occupation for one that promised 'good times' branded her as morally suspect. No one had forced her to abandon honest labour for a job in the ice cream parlour. The lure of pleasure and an easier life brought out her defiance, just as it had drawn the first woman into voluntary vice.

The social survey commissioners may have borrowed narrative strategies from the social purity movement, but they differed in placing a greater responsibility for prostitution on the shoulders of the prostitutes themselves. In fact, as their tales of spurious white slavery suggest, prostitution was linked to working girls' taste for the pleasures of city living. They examined other social and economic problems that contributed to prostitution in Toronto, including inadequate housing, poor health care, the difficulties faced by foreign immigrants, insufficient recreation, and poverty, but concluded that economic and social injustice was morally significant only to the extent that it created the preconditions for vice. Similarly, the investigators discounted working girls' low wages as an explanation for prostitution, since many wage-earning women seemed able to retain their respectability on next to nothing. The commissioners may have deviated from their mandate to study white slavery, but they did not stray from their original focus on prostitution as *the* social evil.

SEEKING THE ROOTS OF PROSTITUTION

Progressives prided themselves on their attention to the environmental factors behind social problems, so it was not surprising that the social survey included a section on the question of 'poverty as a cause of prostitution.' It began with a complicated formula to account for the ongoing existence of prostitution, which it defined as 'the outcome of a complex social condition, which, through artificial stimulation, multiplies both the supply and demand.'[50] One of those conditions was working girls' economic marginality, a factor that constituted the supply side of the vice equation. In the surveyors' estimation it was inappropriate to look at prostitution solely as a product of female depravity, since poverty seemed to exist wherever they observed the social evil. They quoted labour organizer Reginald Wright Kaufman's statement that 'a chief cause of ... immorality as exists among the working girls ... is their insufficient wages.'[51]

Data from their Toronto investigation certainly upheld Kaufman's research on prostitution in US and European cities, which showed how poorly prostitutes had been paid in jobs they had held before entering the sex trade. The commission had 'an experienced woman investigator' look into the wages of women who worked in retail stores, telephone exchanges, laundries, and factories, and found that the average working girl earned from six to nine dollars per week. Women's meagre wages meant that the seasonal layoffs in many enterprises were difficult to weather. Although they discovered that the majority of working girls lived at home, it was 'the girl who is alone in the city and has to depend entirely on herself' who captured their attention, because she was most likely to feel the effects of poverty and to suffer the possibility of homelessness. Layoffs, unemployment, and sickness could spell disaster for the independent working girl who was unable to save her wages for anything except the barest necessities. Poverty was such a defining feature of young women's work experience that the social surveyors concluded that all working girls experienced the 'pressure of economic conditions' that drove some of them 'into a life of vice.' But they were left with the question of why some women struggled nobly while others gave in to poverty.[52]

The commissioners' social scientific appreciation of prostitution was compromised by their abiding conviction that only immorally disposed women would sell their sexual services, no matter how desperate. Having dispensed with the hard facts of women's wages, they turned to the technique of moral evaluations. Immediately after the labour organizer's argument about the economic roots of prostitution, the report quoted a 'prominent social worker' who believed that wages were not 'to any considerable extent' a factor in women's decision to work as prostitutes. The commissioners were clearly not averse to incorporating impressionistic evidence, particularly when it was couched in statistical terms. A Toronto rescue mission director, for instance, confidently stated that in treating hundreds of prostitutes annually for seven years, the mission had not found a single woman who had been driven by low pay 'to her misdeeds.'

These expert opinions were given more weight in the report than the statements of other experts – prostitutes. Nineteen of thirty-seven prostitutes surveyed had claimed that low wages in other legitimate lines of women's work had led them to consider prostitution. Six of those nineteen had earned six dollars or less per week, putting them at the bottom of the scale of women wage-earners. In spite of Kaufman's testimony and their own data on working girls' wages, the commissioners decided to weigh very heavily the impressions of social workers and moral rescuers who turned to the more familiar discourse of fallen womanhood. Their cursory attention to women's wages and their vulnerability to seasonal unemployment failed to shake their prior assumptions about the social evil as a product of individual depravity: 'It is obvious,' they decided, 'that insufficient wages is not the only nor indeed the chief cause' of prostitution.[53]

Accounting for the social evil entailed analysing not the fact that greater value was placed on women's sexuality than on their work, but the moral shortcomings of women who resolved to make that economic logic pay. Thus, the commissioners nodded towards economic explanations of prostitution without considering wage-earning women's poverty as a causal factor because they resorted to syllogistic reasoning: working girls are paid low wages; not all working girls become prostitutes; therefore, poor pay is not a cause of prostitution. They pointed out that girls who struggled to survive on five or six dollars per week and managed to 'retain their virtue' proved, first, that it could be done, and, second, that something other than poverty – namely, moral weakness – accounted for women's downfall. The report further challenged the economic theory with evidence that domestics, women who supposedly never worried about food and shelter, were consistently overrepresented among women arrested on prostitution-related charges in Toronto and in most cities. Accordingly, the commissioners speculated that 'something other than the pressure of want' accounted for women's entry into prostitution.[34]

Coming up with an estimate of a living wage for working girls in Toronto, a task that would later occupy the bureaucrats on the Ontario Minimum Wage Board, seemed beyond the commissioners. Instead of tabulating the costs of room and board, transportation, clothing, entertainment, and incidentals, they merely observed that 'the vast majority of working girls in the city' were able to live respectably on the lowest wages. Making do on next to nothing clearly called for extraordinary abilities, which some working girls unfortunately did not possess. Because poorly trained women could never hope to manage their finances wisely, the commissioners refused to estimate a living wage: 'No sum can be specified which is just sufficient to avoid dangerous pressure.' When prostitutes confessed that insufficient wages had driven them to vice, the investigators contradicted them, suggesting that their pay at honest labour had merely been insufficient to allow them to indulge their taste for fun and finery. It was not that they were about to starve, but that their 'desire[s] for good clothes, amusement etc.' had become 'inducements to immorality.'

Young women's low wages permitted them enough to survive as long as they forswore the city pleasures that were beyond their means. Working girls no longer 'fell' as a result of poverty, enticers, or white slavers. In the up-to-date analysis of the social survey, working women slid: 'a girl debarred by poverty from reasonable and wholesome pleasures and indulgences, makes up for them by "good times" of a ques-

tionable character, thus lowering her moral tone and incidentally placing herself under obligation to her male associates, and thus comes,
gradually and by a process, the significance of which she may not
herself clearly apprehend, closer and closer to the danger line.'[55] Imper-
ceptibly, wage-earning women were swept into a cycle of poverty,
desire, and degradation. With every turn of the cycle – another new
dress purchased, another evening out with a man, another favour
granted to him in return – the working girl spun farther from the
bounds of decency.

In the burgeoning city, where vaudeville houses, nickelodeons, and
dancehalls had actively begun to court the working-girl customer, the
temptations of urban living had multiplied considerably. Women who
toiled for nine or ten hours a day, or longer in the case of domestics,
were hardpressed to resist. Once working girls developed a taste for
good times, they ran the risk of wanting more than they could afford
and turning to men to pay their way. When a young working woman
took this step, she descended on an 'easy and rapid' 'downward
course.'[56] In other words, a moral slide still led to a fall from respectability. In this respect at least the social surveyors maintained the evangelical tradition of moral reckoning; but, significantly, they did not
adopt the social purity movement's castigation of immoral men. Nowhere, for instance, did the social surveyors chastise the 'gentlemen' to
whom the working girls became indebted; apparently they did not tra-
verse a 'line' when they demanded sexual favours in return for money
and material goods. The moral decision remained the woman's alone.

Presenting the Toronto Social Survey as a study solely of working girls'
role in the social evil would do a disservice to the complexity of the
analysis. Prostitution was *the* social evil because it brought a range of
social problems into focus. As Mariana Valverde has shown, white
Anglo-Celtic Canadians who had dominated national life for more than
a century grew increasingly anxious that 'the race' was in danger of
decline.[57] As in other western countries, the fear of degeneration of the
racial stock inspired concern about the deviant, the criminal, and the
subnormal.[58] The only way to combat this process of degeneration was
to strive towards racial purity, a goal antithetical to the existence of the
social evil. Commercialized sex not only permitted the spread of syphilis, a degenerative disease, but it allowed the commingling of the races
because it flourished in the poverty stricken neighbourhoods populated
by 'foreigners.' The products of such doubtful unions, bred in an en-

vironment of crime and despair, could only be inferior. Propelled by such concerns, the social surveyors turned their sights on the problems of feeble-mindedness and foreigners.

Although the immigration of non-Anglo-Celtics to Canada rose significantly as the federal government strove to populate the recently opened west, it was not so much their numbers as what they represented in the eyes of the dominant majority that accounts for the hysterical tone of writings about immigrants. In Toronto the 'foreign born' had barely crested 10 per cent of the population by the 1910s, but the social surveyors none the less used a diluvian metaphor to capture their sense of being overwhelmed: 'The great tide of immigration that has of late years been flowing into this country has presented serious problems to our Canadian communities, especially the larger cities; and among these problems not the least is the complication of the social evil.' These alien people, racially distinct from 'true' Canadians, were predisposed towards vice because many came from parts of the world where 'the standard of sexual morality as well as the general standard of living are not those of Canada.' In cities such as Toronto they lived in cramped, unhealthy housing, where boys, girls, and adults slept in the same rooms. Under such conditions, girls lost their modesty – their protection from the temptations to which working girls were inevitably exposed in the course of city life.[59]

Foreign women – European Jews, Italians, Slavs – were actually underrepresented among those charged with morals offences. In fact, it was 'old country girls,' or British women, who were overrepresented. This disturbing fact could not, according to the hierarchy that placed Anglo-Celtics at the peak of the racial pyramid, be attributed to the low moral standards of the British; rather, some young British women who immigrated to Canada must not be 'of the best class,' since most were 'of a rather superior type.'[60] Unscrupulous commercial immigration firms did not exercise proper care in the selection of 'girls,' nor did they ensure their supervision upon their landing in Canadian cities. Whereas the 'fall' of young 'foreign' women seemed almost inevitable in the eyes of the commissioners, 'girls from the old country' did not drift into immorality unless they were inferior and inadequately supervised. Foreign-born women, after all, were more likely to be in contact with male foreigners, – the 'Chinamen,' Jews, and Italians whom the surveyors linked to 'what might almost be called a vice trust.'[61]

No matter what their ethnicity, however, the working girls most likely to go astray were the 'subnormal,' young women who themselves were likely products of degenerate unions and a depraved environment. The surveyors adopted the discourse of eugenicists, who in the 1910s were working out scales of intelligence as a means of measuring individuals' potential contribution, or cost, to society. Those whom medical and psychiatric experts deemed to be mentally and morally deficient were labelled 'feeble-minded.' One of the foremost experts in the assessment and treatment of subnormals, Dr Helen MacMurchy, provided the commissioners with most of their evidence.[62] Her evidence linked mental inefficiency to vice through evidence that feeble-minded women were prone to moral laxity. She quoted prison and psychiatric studies which declared that most prostitutes were feeble-minded (information about the mental or moral state of their customers was not provided). The report explained that the feeble-minded were a menace because mental deficiency often produced 'abnormal sensual propensities and lack of moral perception.' Even those 'defectives' who did not display 'immoral tendencies' posed a danger because they were 'incapable of resisting suggestion, and [were therefore] easily led astray.' Feeble-mindedness was not confined to women, but its long-term impact on the race manifested itself most alarmingly in subnormal women's breeding propensities. In fact, Dr MacMurchy spoke as if procreation were exclusively a female function that placed an unwarranted burden on social services. Responsibility for the seemingly endless cycle of degeneration could be traced to unwed mothers: 'From the Infants' Home, full of the offspring of feeble-minded girls, round in a dreadful circle of vice to the Refuge or Haven, ... the feeble-minded daughter of a feeble-minded mother returns to give birth to another generation of the feeble-minded.'[63] Canada needed new citizens to take up the challenges of nation-building, but the children of single feeble-minded mothers threatened, along with foreigners, to subsume the 'normal.' Mindful of the human toll already mounting after one year of war, the social surveyors were even more convinced that sexual immorality was leading Toronto, the nation, and the race towards tragedy.

In the final analysis, there was little to distinguish the typical working girl, discussed earlier in the report, from the feeble-minded woman. As the 1916 Unemployment Commission had observed, working girls seemed unable to stick out jobs for more than a few months, and many were so frivolous and irresponsible that they were justifiably dismissed. Frustrated that they could not afford material pleasures, they were easily 'led astray' by persuasive gentlemen willing to pay. The convergence of the categories of working girl and 'occasional prostitute'

was matched by a similar collapsing of the concepts of unwed motherhood and feeble-mindedness. The social surveyors were not alone in
their assumptions. The federal government possessed the power to
screen potentially troublesome immigrants, and Barbara Roberts has
shown that by the early twentieth century the immigration department
began to label single mother deportees feeble-minded.[64] MacMurchy, the
medical expert who, along with Dr C.K. Clarke, was instrumental in
introducing the concept of feeble-mindedness to Canadians, recommended that subnormal women be incarcerated so that those who could
benefit from intensive training might be distinguished from women
requiring 'permanent custody.' Hers was an extreme solution that
would have required authorities to lock up tens of thousands of working girls, for it had become increasingly difficult, at least for commissioned surveyors, to distinguish between the city's respectable wage-
earning women, occasional prostitutes, and the feeble-minded. In the
decade after the Social Survey Report's release, calls for the medical and
psychiatric evaluation of morally suspect workng girls only increased.

By the 1910s the social evil had become considerably more complex
than it had seemed to C.S. Clark. In the hands of Progressives, it had
changed from a relatively straightforward picture of sexual slavery and
an international traffic in women to an all-encompassing scourge on
urban industrial society. For all their pretensions to scientific detachment, the Toronto social surveyors were not averse to borrowing the
rhetorical techniques of the social purity movement. Stories of country
girls beset by villainous white slavers added spice to the otherwise
restrained recitation of data. Moreover, the themes of the report replicated C.S. Clark's barbs concerning the indiscretions of 'apparently
respectable' young women, such as those who worked at Eaton's, and
Shearer's warnings about foreign procurers. Students of the social evil
differed in the responsibility they attached to the purveyors and clients
of commercialized sex but they could agree that the continued migration of young, single women to the cities in search of work ensured that
there would be a steady supply of recruits – voluntary or otherwise –
to the ranks of the fallen. The social evil was more than the accumulation of working girls' immoral compromises and acts: it had become a
national calamity.

5

Good Times and Bad Girls

Disguised as a working girl, journalist Maud Petit infiltrated a Toronto biscuit factory, not in search of secret recipes but to uncover the secrets of working women's ability to survive on meagre wages. Under the pen name of 'Videre,' a name that implied omniscient powers of observation, Maud Petit wrote about her attempt to find decent housing and nourishment on her salary of five dollars per week as a jam-dolloper.[1] What intrigued her most, however, was the question of leisure. How could working girls manage to amuse themselves in their time off when they lived on next to nothing?[2] Videre reported that her fellow biscuit-workers did find ways to make do on extraordinarily low pay. She discovered that 'girl workers' were remarkably resilient, irrepressible creatures. In fact, working girls seemed a little too irrepressible for their own good. Their cramped quarters and monotonous work generated a great deal of restlessness and left them eager for amusement in a city willing to provide it. Unfortunately, the diversions available to down-town workers were hardly those that promised healthful exercise or spiritual renewal. Videre thought that working girls would do better if they performed daily gymnastic drills to dissipate nervous energy and sublimate their eagerness for good times. She could not, however, imagine how wage-earning women could be lured away from an increasing array of commercial pleasures.

Even Videre, for all her didactic cheeriness, experienced brief moments of identification with the jam dollopers' yearnings for pleasure. Fashion was her weak spot. Assuming that factory operatives dressed poorly, she began her masquerade in a $1.25 shirtwaist and a worn hat, authentic sartorial touches for the working girl, she imagined. After only a week on the jam line she noticed that her co-workers wore flashy outfits. Videre admitted to her readers that she soon decided to skip one-third of her meals in order to afford similar finery.[3] Only the most self-denying of the city's young wage-earners – anomalous women, such as the dowdy Carrie Davies – seemed able to resist such temptation. And if Videre, a middle-class professional woman, was willing to give up a meal, what might the city's factory operatives and shop girls sacrifice on the altar of their pleasures?

Since the discovery of the woman adrift in the 1880s, single wage-earning women's time away from work consistently inspired more concern than their lives on the job. New organizations concerned with single women's leisure began to join the YWCA in devising means to steer working girls away from disreputable pleasures. Social workers, journalists, feminists, and religious conservatives, as well as medical and penal professionals, offered their differing views on the problem of working girls and urban amusements. They swam against the tide of change, however, as the growth and diversification of the commercial amusement industry altered wage-earning women's relation to city life. Realizing the huge untapped market represented by working girls, entertainment entrepreneurs began to woo female clientele by lowering or waiving admission prices, establishing special seating sections for spectator events, and featuring 'clean' sketches in theatres. The number of 'places of amusement' in Toronto shot from 9 in 1900 to 112 by 1915.[4] Not only were there were more places to seek fun, but novel ways for women and men to have fun together. By the early twentieth century a wide assortment of commercial amusements, including nickelodeons, amusement parks, vaudeville houses, and public dancehalls, eagerly opened their doors to working girls.

These new venues for wage-earning women's pleasures were simultaneously targeted as prime sites of urban moral regulation. As the Toronto Social Survey report confirms, the Progressives' search for environmental hazards in urban life granted a prominent role to commercial amusements. The police, the courts, and correctional personnel also equated commercial pleasures with illicit sex; their response, in concert with similar campaigns in US cities, was to regulate young women's urban amusements to protect both working girls and the race. Thus Progressive lobbyists, not content merely to document the problem of questionable leisure pursuits, needled legislatures to criminalize working women's pleasures and the penal system to correct their irresponsible behaviour.

By the early twentieth century, Toronto's girl problem was bound up in a broader contest over working-class urban entertainments. In the course of debating the roots and possible solutions to the amusement problem, moral reform organizations and state agencies articulated a new discipline of leisure tailored for single women who worked and played amid the temptations of city life. Toronto's reformatories and industrial schools would enforce that discipline in an attempt to turn 'good times girls' into good girls. The stakes were high, eugenicists warned. Without the strict monitoring of working girls' amusements, they predicted, young women would not find husbands and establish families; instead, they would succumb to moral and biological contagion, passing on their afflictions not only to their sexual partners but to the next generation.

THE PLEASURES OF THE CITY

Before the turn of the century, commercial leisure in Toronto, as in most industrializing cities, catered to working-class males at one level, and to high-class 'Society' on the other. Controversy over the Morality Department's efforts to police such diversions as crap-shooting, gambling, and playing stickball on the streets were resented as an assault on working men's rightful pleasures.[5] Aside from the 'strumpets' who drank and danced in saloons, working-class women were excluded from the masculine diversions that the Morality Department suppressed.[6] During the streetcar debates of the 1890s, for instance, the right of the urban working class to affordable leisure was articulated in masculinist terms. The question of working girls' right to amusement was scarcely raised.

The victory of the Sunday streetcar lobby did, however, open up discussion about the proper role of recreation for Toronto's working class. Working men had a right to secular amusement on their day of rest, but that right would be narrowly confined within the bounds of masculine sports and family outings. Supporters of Sunday streetcars claimed that the right kind of fun would do much to foster a healthy, morally upright working class while curbing workers' tastes for more salacious diversions.[7] The same logic was later applied by middle-class reformers who tackled the girl problem.

The pioneers of leisure reform for working girls were the ladies of the YWCA. As early as 1883 they had announced that they would strive to provide 'legitimate amusements' that would prevent working girls 'from attending questionable places of amusement.'[8] Their clumsy early attempts were decided flops. The Y's first offering, the Girls' Friendly

Society, offered lessons in practical bookkeeping, sewing, and house-keeping – activities which, not surprisingly, failed to strike their clients as amusing.

Most single wage-earners preferred to spend their slim earnings on a glass of beer and songs around a piano. Many were partial to an afternoon of melodrama at the Grand, where they could find sociability and entertainment. One reporter caricatured the working women who frequented cheap theatres as 'matinee girls who, with tears streaming down their faces and with jaws working convulsively on the masticated gum, follow ... the fortunes of the suffering and persecuted heroine.'[9] The admission price to matinees in the 1880s was generally 25 cents, a substantial chunk of a seamstress' or domestic's earnings and thus a telling indication of the value working girls placed on their diversions. Those who could not part with 25 cents could find tawdry entertainment in Monteford's Museum at Bay and Adelaide where, for 10 cents, they might take in lectures on wild men from Borneo, displays of living and no-longer-living curiosities, minstrel shows, and wax renderings of arch-criminals or royalty, all in one visit. In the summer, the parks that ringed the city beckoned. Steamers that dotted the wharfs along the lakeshore chugged city-dwellers to the cool respite offered in Victoria and Lorne Parks, and for 15 cents, passengers were treated not only to a fresh breeze off the lake but to brass bands that provided music for the voyage. Even greater pleasures were in store for passengers bound for Hanlan's Point on the Toronto Islands. Until the construction of Scarboro Beach Park in 1907, it was unrivalled as 'the playground of the people.' While well-heeled citizens took tea on the verandah of the clubhouse of the Royal Canadian Yacht Club, more humble Torontonians scrambled off the ferries and headed for Dotty's Hippodrome for a dizzying ride on the carousel or a spin on the switchback railway. Young women could be sure to find cocky young men if they sidled over to the shooting gallery. Even the chill of winter did not preclude working girls' taking part in ice or roller skating. For 10 cents a girl could go skating, partake in refreshments, or simply cling to the side-boards and wonder at the talents of professionals, such as Professor Franks, 'the Great Stilt Skater.'[10]

Because these leisure activities threw men and women together indiscriminately, many observers assumed that intimate heterosexual contact was the very object of commercial amusements. C.S. Clark believed that single women sought these pleasures not to escape the drudgery of their work lives, as the Y ladies believed, but simply to consort with men. He described the Toronto Islands as the hunting-grounds of young women intent on making 'hap-hazard acquaintances with gentlemen they know nothing at all about.' On Saturday nights, he claimed, it was not unusual to find couples 'en flagrante delecto [sic].' In the city itself, he observed that unsupervised women were drawn to 'any event that draws a crowd.'[11] Women's sporting enthusiasms were equally suspect. Girls did not skate from a love for the outdoors, he charged, but to 'bump' into strange men. He described one rink where a seventeen-year-old 'young miss' repeatedly skated into a young man. When her friend admonished her for risking her reputation, she allegedly replied: 'My reputation ... I don't give a damn for that, I lost it years ago!' Young women took up cycling with similar moral recklessness, for bicycles allowed girls 'to go to all the places where boys are.' Wherever young men engaged in outdoor sport, he observed, 'the streets are thronged with girls in their teens – a nightly occurrence.' Clark assumed that the male cyclists, skaters, and visitors to the Islands were entirely innocent. For the priggish journalist, the boldness of young women who flouted middle-class conventions of courtship called for comment: 'I can remember when it was considered necessary for those of opposite sexes to be introduced before they considered themselves acquainted,' he grumbled.[12] Now, it seemed, there were no rules.

SURVEYING THE GIRL PROBLEM

By the turn of the century, as the range of city pleasures available to women multiplied, a wider range of participants entered into debates over the girl problem in Toronto. Aside from the YMCA and YWCA, the city's settlement houses took on the task of leisure reform. Although their efforts were devoted largely to the young men of the Ward, for whom rational recreation was prescribed as an antidote to criminal tendencies, the head worker of Central Neighbourhood House (CNH) threw her energies into the problem of young working girls' leisure tastes. In 1913 Elizabeth Neufeld enlisted the aid of four students from the school of social work, recently established at the University of Toronto, to search out the local vice scene.[13] Their findings indicated that working women's poverty, the availability of doubtful amusements, and the lack of wholesome alternatives were the preconditions of prostitution.

Neufeld's concerns about working girls' pleasures had initially prompted the TLCW to lobby for the Social Survey, and the survey report ultimately reflected her concerns. The commissioners frowned on the influence of unsavory pleasures on the city's young people who, deprived of rigorous moral training, were only too keen to partake of commercial amusements. Believing that the search for pleasure was a natural yearning of youth, they called not only for the suppression of 'injurious' amusements, but for the 'fuller provision of the beneficial and wholesome.'[14]

Despite the surveyors' recognition of urban temptations and their compassion for the yearnings of youth, they focused on young *women's* inappropriate leisure choices as the primary source of vice. Their report offered a gendered script for the definition and analysis of immorality. When the surveyors proposed novel recreational programs as the foundation for virtuous communities, they referred to young men's and women's leisure; when they addressed the causes of the social evil, in contrast, they spoke exclusively about working girls' troubling taste for good times. Working girls were not expected to forswear fun, yet they were admonished to restrict their amusement to activities that neither inflamed passions nor threw them into company with strange men. To describe women who seemed to care, like Clark's clumsy skater, more for their pleasures than their reputations, the surveyors created the new category of 'occasional prostitute.'

The report defined occasionals as working girls who supplemented their income and spiced up their nightlife by doling out sexual favours to men.[15] To the ranks of regulars or professionals had lately been added women who worked by day 'as a blind to avoid arrest as a vagrant' and bona fide working girls who merely 'sport[ed] on the side.' These 'semi-professionals' had told interviewers that they went out '"for fun" or "for a good time."' The surveyors thought they knew better, translating occasionals' motives as sexual passion, a desire for fast company, and the 'suppers, shows and drinks paid for them by their male associates, which are the only remuneration they accept.'[16] The fact that the young women did not view their activities as prostitution made little difference to the university students and church workers who interviewed them. Women who accepted presents of jewellery or clothing while '"out for a good time"' were declared as guilty as the professionals who dealt in currency.

At the core of the surveyors' unease with sexual bartering was a class-based suspicion of working girls who seemed to have it easy. What little public credibility the working girl had enjoyed had been earned by the image – and the reality – of the noble workwoman who placed respectability above temptations of easier money. As Laura Hapke argues, bourgeois sympathy for the working girl's plight rested on a romanticization of her economic marginality and an identification with her ladylike devotion to feminine propriety. But exposés like Videre's undercover report assured middle-class readers that working-class women were inevitably too coarse to achieve true gentility. Part of the admiration for wage-earning women, then, lay in the assurance that their aspirations for mobility would be confined to marriage and motherhood, not the economic independence enjoyed by the journalists who wrote about them.[17] Similarly, the city's social surveyors felt that working girls had no right to yearn for pleasures that workers who were paid a pittance could not afford. Accordingly, the report scolded working girls who were 'actuated by the desire for more comfortable or luxurious living than they can earn.'[18]

New forms of commercial amusement and their proliferation in Toronto multiplied familiar worries about working girls' inappropriate use of their time away from work. Adding to the assortment of entertainments available at the end of the nineteenth century was a year-round panoply of cheap diversions. While dime museums and theatres had earlier attracted female patrons, vaudeville and burlesque houses began to compete for paying customers. From the 1890s to the 1920s, these two forms of live musical variety were all the rage. The diversity of their programs catered to all tastes – minstrel shows, comedy sketches, trapeze artistry, instrumental and vocal music, and magicians' acts could all be enjoyed at a matinée for as little as 15 cents. Ticket prices actually decreased as competition in the entertainment industry grew fierce. The Majestic Theatre advertised its lowest ticket prices at 5 and 10 cents in 1910 for 'Six Big Vaudeville Acts' and the 'Latest Moving Pictures.' The Gayety Burlesque and Vaudeville Theatre expressly invited women by offering daily ladies' matinees at 10 cents a seat, while the Star Burlesque House ('SMOKE IF YOU LIKE') courted a rougher crowd for its girlie shows. By the 1910s Shea's Theatre, the premier vaudeville house in the city, also offered 'photo-plays' as part of the standard fare in addition to live performances. Scattered throughout the downtown were scores of nickelodeons owned by small-time amusement operators. By mid-decade, larger theatres such as the Hippodrome at City Hall Square were edging out these smaller moving-picture venues and swallowing up customers. Aside from short films, many of which featured working-girl heroines who faced the designs of white slavers, early movie serials such as *The Hazards of Helen* starred

young working women who could more than hold their own against
the perils of city life. Thrilled at images of themselves, transformed into
vivacious urban adventurers flickering across the screen in darkened
theatres, working girls swarmed to movie-houses by the thousands.[19]

Several earlier forms of entertainment had survived and expanded.
The Canadian National Exhibition, operating annually since 1879, had
introduced various amusement devices, including a Ferris wheel, in the
1890s, and by the early 1900s its midway, packed with rides, games,
and exotic foods such as Coney Island hotdogs and ice cream cones,
drew tens of thousands of visitors each day. In 1907 Scarboro Beach
Park, a combination open-air circus and amusement park, opened to
great fanfare as the 'The City of Illusions.' Lit by thousands of electric
bulbs, its image shimmered on the lake and was visible from the roller
coaster and merry-go-round at Hanlan's Point. The 'surf bathing' at
Scarboro Beach, unlike most of the city's beaches reserved for men and
boys only, allowed youth of both sexes to cavort in the waves while
wearing scanty outfits. While dance parlours expected patrons to wear
more discreet clothing, they too depended upon both male and female
patronage. As hotels had done for years, the dance parlours that
popped up on entertainment strips along Yonge Street offered patrons
a cheerful, exciting outing, enlivened by music and the energy of bodies
in motion.[20]

The Toronto social surveyors, echoing C.S. Clark's earlier claims
about working girls' morality, stated that women who frequented these
and updated commercial amusements 'for a good time' were, in reality,
simply out 'to pick up men.'[21] Dance halls were prime sites for 'occasional prostitution' because 'there was no supervision and the practice
of men accosting and dancing with girls whom they did not know was
general.' The women patrons hardly seemed to mind this practice;
indeed, they admitted to undercover investigators that they 'proposed
"making dates"' with their dance partners. These respondents were
duly recorded as 'occasionals.' Rinks offered similarly favourable conditions for 'semi-professional' prostitutes to 'ply their trade,' since
unescorted women were seen to allow 'unknown men to accost and
skate with them.' The inadequate policing of city parks and amusement
resorts caused men's 'scraping acquaintance with girls and paying their
way to various booths.'[22] Although in each of these cases it was men
who initiated verbal or physical contact, they were not defined as
'occasional mashers' or 'good times boys.' On women alone lay the
moral responsibility for offers of sexual favours in exchange for a

kewpie doll, an ice cream cone, or a show. Every treat could be seen as an act of prostitution when commercial amusements were conflated with commercial sex.

MANAGING THE GIRL PROBLEM

The rise of the commercial amusement industry and working girls' patronage of it inspired a multi-pronged response. Toronto's reform agencies, influenced by American Progressives such as Jane Addams, turned to the merits of recreation as an antidote to improper amusements. More conservative agencies, such as the Methodists, continued to preach restraint as the preferred policy for young women who faced temptations.[23] Medical and penal experts prescribed professional treatment, including incarceration and sterilization, for single women who were unwilling or unable to resist the allures of commercial amusements. No one, however, disputed the belief that working girls' leisure required stricter regulation if young single women were to make a successful transition to marriage and motherhood. The twin spectres of feeble-mindedness and venereal disease haunted the imaginations of the social workers, feminists, social purity advocates, and medical professionals who made the girl problem their special project. Convinced of the reality of those threats, state agencies readily added muscle to less coercive efforts to wean bad girls from good times.

The articulation of a discipline of pleasure specifically for working girls began in earnest in Toronto during the Progressive era. Social workers and leaders of the playground movement breathed new life into the YWCA's earlier schemes to substitute improving diversions for commercial amusements.[24] Arguing that the provision of recreational facilities for the children of the Ward would act as a moral prophylactic against crime and vice, the TLCW and the Toronto Playground Association successfully lobbied the city government for supervised playgrounds and expanded green space.[25]

Central Neighborhood House head worker Elizabeth Neufeld led the effort to apply the lessons of reformative recreation to the girl problem. She was well versed in the tenets of the Progressive recreation movement and, like Jane Addams, was particularly struck by the unique temptations and dangers working girls faced in city life. In 1911, shortly after CNH was founded, she launched her campaign to reform local wage-earning women's taste for 'good times.' Her first step was to establish a 'working girls Club.' Instead of sewing lessons dictated by lady volunteers, the 'girls' themselves helped to choose their activities. In November 1912, for instance, fifty working girls and their guests attended a show put on by local musicians, singers, and actors. A related scheme involved helping some of the neighbourhood's young women, 'all girls working in factories,' to meet with an organizer of inexpensive holidays. 'As a result of this,' she reported in 1912, 'the girls are planning to start a fund for the purpose of purchasing land and starting a vacation for working girls.' She anticipated correctly that the idealistic scheme would probably fail, but she supported the girls none the less: 'It is very much worth while to give people a chance to see things that are better and finer.'[26] Neufeld tried to reroute working girls towards rational pastimes and to suppress injurious forms of amusement. Her approach to dancehalls typified this two-fronted assault. In the fall of 1913 the CNH board discussed opening a commercial dancehall to counter a popular hall on Elm Street 'not conducted in a most desirable manner.' Rumours of inadequate supervision of a dancehall on University Avenue prompted a similar response: 'We shall ... want to start a weekly dance there so that we may be able to supplant the undesirable management.'[27] Several weeks later the CNH established a weekly dance at a hall at the corner of Elm and Teraulay Streets in the heart of the Ward.[28] By charging girls 5 cents admission and boys 10 cents, they hoped to monitor the 'heterosocial' pleasures of local youth.[29]

Neufeld's preoccupation with factory operatives' free time revised the discourse of improving leisure that emerged in the context of the streetcar debates of the 1890s. First, she took seriously the need and right of young women workers to have fun; second, she recognized that healthy recreation was beyond the means of poorly paid women workers; third, she believed that it was necessary for working girls to learn that there were loftier uses of free time than the reckless pursuit of commercial pleasures that would lead not to drinking, gambling and crime, as it did with men, but to prostitution. What she proposed was a new pleasure discipline tailored exclusively for the city's working girls.

The TLCW threw its hat into the recreation ring by sponsoring the Big Sisters Association (BSA) in 1914. The organization arose out of the TLCW's work with the juvenile court, which it had lobbied the city to establish.[30] 'Lady' volunteers sat in court to hear cases involving girls and acted as lay probation officers for young women under sixteen. Their work consisted of 'rehabilitative and preventative' programs for young women in trouble with the law. Significantly, the Big Sisters did not force their clients to follow a Spartan regime that ruled out fun; rather, their project was to teach young women 'the art of having a good time in a wise and safe way.' As informal parole officers, the Big Sisters supervised the free time of young women who had appeared in court, including those who had been victims of morals crimes or family disputes. The BSA executive stressed at every meeting their concern about the need for 'safe, supervised recreation for girls.' Big Sisters evaluated moral status through recreational habits: good girls attended Sunday school regularly, stayed home with their parents at night, and went to none but church socials; bad girls consorted with strange men and went out with friends of whom their parents did not approve.[31]

The Big Sisters' brand of pleasure discipline did not sit well with more conservative Protestant groups, which continued to value reservation over recreation. Before to the First World War, Protestant reformers were inclined to view recreation more as a potential danger than as a possible avenue of salvation. Accordingly, a young woman's desire to have fun was to be suppressed if she was to retain her reputation. Rev. T.A. Moore, the secretary of the Temperance and Moral Reform Department of the Methodist church, wrote in 1912 that the solution to the girl problem was to increase the home influence. His goal was rather impractical, considering that an estimated 15,000 of Toronto's 40,000 single working women lived away from home at the time.[32] Nevertheless, he expressed a certain naïve hope that working girls might simply turn their backs on city life.

Still, Protestant reformers were not uniformly intent on suppressing the yearning for pleasure. As Mariana Valverde has argued, social purity advocates pioneered the field of sex education in Canada, believing that ignorance left youth without the fortitude to resist the temptations of urban life.[33] Beatrice Brigden, for instance, one of the most popular speakers in the Department of Temperance and Moral Reform of the Methodist church, specialized in 'The Girl and Her Problems.' In the interest of 'pure living and upright citizenship' for young women, she delivered optimistic pep talks on overcoming 'the difficult and perplexing Problems which constantly confront[ed] them.'[34]

Attempts to purify young women's yearnings did not, however, win social purity advocates the clientele of chaste working women they hoped to save from the allures of amusement. Like the apathetic recruits in the Girls' Friendly Society in the 1880s, Toronto's working girls of the 1910s were impatient with tedious lessons of restraint when more appealing diversions beckoned. As the commercial amusement industry expanded, the battle against worldly fun grew even more difficult for those Christians who were unwilling to compromise with the changing scene of city amusements. When the WCTU tried to form a club in 1912 for working women who would disavow 'undesirable dress, deportment and conversation,' for instance, they failed: where the WCTU ladies called for sacrifice, commercial amusements pandered to self-gratification.[35] At their most indulgent, the advocates of social purity adopted an embattled posture towards the problem of working girls and urban pleasures. Without the means to enforce their evangelical pleasure discipline, they lost ground to irrepressible working girls and the city's vigorous commercial amusement industry.

THE MEDICALIZATION OF THE GIRL PROBLEM

Medical and psychiatric experts played a pivotal role in turning single working women's leisure habits into a social problem. As Foucault observed, the turn of the century witnessed the rise of social and biological managers who deployed the 'juridical and medical control of perversions, for the sake of a general protection of society and the race.'[36] Doctors argued that social issues, under their management, could be investigated, diagnosed, treated, and, it was hoped, cured. As men, and women, of science, they balanced the Progressive emphasis on environmental causes of immorality by stressing the physiological and psychological abnormalities of criminal and deviant individuals. Thus, where the Big Sisters, for example, blamed the girl problem on the temptations of urban life, medical professionals were inclined to trace the problem to biological anomalies and dysfunctional personalities.

In the early twentieth century, a growing number of doctors and psychiatrists were in the business of diagnosing working girls who seemed unable or disinclined to adhere to the discipline of pleasure. The labels they invented – 'feeble-minded,' 'delinquent,' 'morally degenerate,' 'psychopathic,' and 'sex-crazed' – were reserved for young working-class women who were, in Elizabeth Lunbeck's words, 'willfully passionate.'[37] Young women who seemed inordinately fond of pleasures that threw them into contact with men were diagnosed as hypersexuals who could be cured only through medical treatment. There was no male corollary to the female sex delinquent, just as evangelical reformers had not troubled themselves about 'fallen men.'[38] Sexual delinquency was female delinquency.

Urban amusements were growth mediums for sexual delinquency, and to many doctors and psychiatrists the particular province of the feeble-minded woman. Dancehalls, ice cream parlours, and movie theatres, where young men and women mingled without supervision, were just the thing to inflame 'abnormal desires.' Rev. J. Edward Starr, Toronto's first Juvenile Court judge, relied on medical and psychiatric terminology to explain how young women fell into delinquency. He observed in 1913 that 'thoughtless young girl[s] of nervous temperament' were frequently too weak to resist the 'strangely alluring' temptation of a 'joyride' with men who turned out, so often, to be 'scoundrels.' As a result, they contracted venereal disease or otherwise suffered the 'irretrievable consequences' of their folly.[39] Starr's offhand use of the psychiatric term 'neurotic' signalled a shift in perspective on the girl problem. Miss M.J. Clarke, one of the first social workers to graduate from the University of Toronto and the daughter of the psychiatrist C.K. Clarke, also adopted a psychiatric model of female deviance: 'We often find that those who used to be considered "incorrigible," "bad," and "immoral," are, as matter of fact, feeble-minded, and not responsible for their actions.'[40]

The psychiatric outpatient clinic at the Toronto General Hospital was established to probe the causes of sexual delinquency.[41] The clinic, located in the Ward, was opened in 1909 by Dr Clarke, and its primary purpose was to allow psychiatrists to collect scientific data on the links between feeble-mindedness, illicit sexuality, and venereal disease. Both male and female patients were analysed, but the young women merited extra attention, according to reports of the clinic's practice. Many were referred by the Juvenile Court and the Children's Aid Society. This transfer of authority from child-rescuers and the judiciary to psychiatrists points to medical professionals' success in appropriating the girl problem as their area of expertise and bringing a psychiatric discourse to debates about working girls and their inappropriate pleasures.

Clarke summarized over a decade of his work in 'A Study of 5,600 Cases Passing Through the Psychiatric Clinic.'[42] Every one of the cases he cited in detail involved working girls whose scores on intelligence tests and confessions of illicit sexual activity provided him with the psychological evidence he sought.[43] Sure enough, each of the women who had acquired venereal diseases or who shamelessly recounted their sexual adventures to interviewers was categorized as mentally subnormal. Those who passed the intelligence tests could still be categorized as 'high grade morons' if they failed 'to recognize the most obvious moral obligations.'[44] Not surprisingly, none of the women who came to the clinic was deemed to be normal. Moreover, psychiatric and medical experts were apparently the only diagnosticians qualified to spot the subnormal. They issued repeated warnings that 'morons' were dangerous precisely because they were notoriously adept at masking their subnormality until it was too late.

Unconcerned about experts' assessments of their responses, many young women made no attempt to pass inspection. Spirited subjects expressed outright contempt for the testing process. One can only imagine how sexually active or knowledgeable working girls delighted in shocking the doctors who diagnosed young women's lack of shame as a symptom of feeble-mindedness. In clinical detail, Clarke recounted a session with a saucy 'high grade moron': 'During her whole conversation [she] was chewing gum, and did not show the slightest hesitation in telling her story. This girl's good looks make it difficult to save her from herself, and society from her evil influence as a distributor of venereal disease.' Having given herself over to pleasure, she was also a failure as a worker. The closest she came to leading a disciplined life was in frequenting dancehalls 'with great regularity.'[45]

While psychiatrists were busy toting up figures on the magnitude of sexual delinquency, the state seemed to be hiding its head in the sand. Rev. Starr provided valuable support for medical proposals when he complained in 1913 that greater resources were needed for the detection and control of the subnormal. In Toronto alone, he estimated, there were already 5,000 prostitutes 'from which come born prostitutes.' With rising rates of venereal disease and the growing threat of race degeneration, when would the state finally intervene?[46]

INVENTING DELINQUENCY

By the 1910s a broader, tighter net was thrown around the leisure activities of young working women who freely partook of city pleasures. In Foucault's terms, a carceral continuum, rationalized through a therapeutic idiom, extended to the whole social body in this period. Although the continuum encompassed a widening range of actors and disciplinary techniques, it was marked by a driving energy to identify and treat deviants. Coercive responses and normalizing processes were deployed simultaneously.[47] In dealing with Toronto's 'deviant' young women, the carceral archipelago included a range of responses from arranging supervised dances and conducting clubs for working girls to

arresting and incarcerating young women who spurned the new pleasure discipline. By defining certain pleasurable activities and the women
who engaged in them as criminal or deviant, the police, social workers,
penal officials, doctors, and psychiatrists employed similar disciplinary
techniques to reform working girls' leisure.

The Toronto Morality Department's anti-vice policy, long under attack
even from high-ranking police officers, met with harsh criticism from
the Social Survey Commission. Raiding brothels from time to time and
arresting keepers and inmates, most of whom escaped with fines, was
not only an inadequate response to the social evil but a means of perpetuating vice. Over the period covered by the survey, 1913–15, the
investigators found that only 233 of 418 prostitution-related arrests had
resulted in convictions; the rest ended in withdrawals, remands, or
discharges. Of women convicted and sentenced, only one-third were
incarcerated for an average of fifty days, hardly sufficient to change
their immoral ways, in the opinion of the commissioners. By fining
rather than 'reclaiming' prostitutes, the state acted as the supreme pimp
by making 'the public treasury a sharer in the proceeds of a disgraceful
business.'[48]

Of all the 'traffikers [sic] in vice,' it was the prostitute – professional
and occasional alike – who required the strictest response from the
police, the courts, and the correctional system. The commissioners
recommended that a 'more correct public attitude toward [vice]' would
be encouraged if all first offenders were imprisoned without the option
of their paying a fine. They regarded this policy as wise, humane, and
ultimately in the best interest both of the female morals offender and
the race. Incarceration was 'a necessary first step' in reclaiming women
from dissipated lives. The ideal setting for the moral reclamation of
'dissolute women' was, accordingly, a reformatory where inmates
would serve sentences of indeterminate length and, after release, com-
ply with the regulations of a parole officer.[49] This highly coercive appa-
ratus, envisioned for any young woman guilty of as minor an offence
as skating arm-in-arm with a strange man, would also be a gendered
one: the social surveyors did not call for punitive responses for young
men who, apparently, did not sink into depravity by treating a woman
to a sundae or asking her to dance. Although the surveyors complained
about a lack of cooperation from state agencies empowered to enforce
their vision of a 'City upon a Hill,' arrest statistics, sentencing practices,
and psychiatric assessments in the early twentieth century confirm that
single wage-earning women who participated in dubious pleasures

could find themselves behind bars. In extreme cases, where recalcitrant working girls refused to renounce good times, experts recommended sterilization and life imprisonment.

The legal framework for the regulation of young women's leisure was erected by all three levels of government. Pressure from the child-saving movement to respond to the problems of neglected and erring children prompted the federal government to pass the Juvenile Delinquents Act (1908). The legislation was based on the same sentiments that guided the playground movement. As the preamble declared, the act's intent was 'to check [delinquents'] evil tendencies and to strengthen their better instincts.'[50] Allen Aylesworth, the Liberal minister of justice who introduced the bill, explained that his ministry had been moved by 'a mass of literature' from various child welfare advocates. Canada, they had claimed, was one of the few 'civilized nations' not to have made adequate provision for the reclamation of its youthful offenders.[51] The government hoped, therefore, that the Juvenile Delinquents Act might introduce a more enlightened and humane approach to the troubling reality of youth crime and immorality.

In Ontario, most of the act's provisions were already in place as a result of the Industrial Schools Act of 1877 and the Act for the Prevention of Cruelty to and better Protection of Children (1893). Mayor William Howland had been the driving force behind the industrial schools movement in the 1880s, while J.J. Kelso had launched the Canadian child welfare movement from Toronto. Their lobbying efforts had placed Ontario, and Toronto in particular, at the forefront of international efforts to nip minors' 'evil tendencies' in the bud by removing them from immoral or abusive environments and placing them in the care of the state. The Industrial Schools Act had empowered municipalities to erect juvenile reformatories in which children under sixteen would serve sentences designed to reroute them toward moral, industrious lives. In keeping with Torontonians' preoccupation with male criminality in the late nineteenth century, the first institution to be built was the Victoria Industrial School for Boys in 1886.[52]

The Children's Aid Society, established through Kelso's lobbying in 1893, was also empowered to take custody of minors in need of 'care and control.' Agents of the CAS exercised the same powers as police officers to arrest offenders without warrant. Although much of their work touched the lives of prepubescent children, their state-sanctioned authority could apply to any minor under the age of twenty-one. The

Acts/Agents,

CAS was authorized to intervene in the trial of minors deemed to be neglected or delinquent and to suggest appropriate responses for the magistrate's consideration. Although CAS agents could suggest parental supervision or placement in a foster home as a non-punitive alternative, they could also recommend that the court impose a reformatory sentence in the case of 'willfully wayward and unmanageable children.'[53] By 1893, then, many of the corrective and protective mechanisms that the 1908 Juvenile Delinquents Act called for were already in place in Toronto, the nation's leader in child welfare and correctional reform.[54]

In Ontario, as in most North American jurisdictions, a separate correctional system for females was also established in the early decades of industrialization.[55] The province led the way in erecting the first women's reformatory in the country in 1878. The Andrew Mercer Ontario Reformatory for Females was touted as innovative and humane in that it was administered by a female superintendent and designed to be 'governed by kindness.' A Refuge for Girls was incorporated into the building, and girls as young as five were sent there to serve sentences for petty crimes.[56] In 1893 the refuge was replaced by the Alexandra Industrial School for Girls, a reformatory institution for females up to the age of sixteen, although in practice young women sometimes remained into their early twenties. The final separate correctional facilities for females were the St Mary's Industrial School (for Catholics) and the Concord Industrial Farm for Women located just north of the city. By the turn of the century, Toronto led the country in its network of institutions and agencies for the monitoring, apprehension, and incarceration of young women.[57]

Working girls who could not give a good account of themselves if apprehended on city streets had always been vulnerable to arrest on the catchall charge of vagrancy, but the Juvenile Delinquents Act significantly widened the scope of surveillance over their behaviour. Just as psychiatrists defined 'sexually precocious' behaviour in young women (but not men) as delinquency, so legal actors were granted even greater latitude to determine the response to their moral transgression. The act provided no legal definition for delinquency, an offence that had no basis in the Criminal Code or at common law, nor did it compel magistrates to impose sentences of specified duration.[58] Young women who freely – or wilfully – sampled the city's pleasures could find themselves summarily tried and convicted of delinquency and incarcerated until they reached the age of twenty-one. The penalty for adults who contributed to the delinquency of minors, in contrast, was set at a maximum of one year's imprisonment. Thus, police officers, CAS agents, parents, or private citizens could set a punitive mechanism into motion when they alleged that young women engaged in dubious pleasures.

THE MAKING OF BAD GIRLS

By the early twentieth century, as the carceral continuum expanded, it was not only fallen women but girls thought *likely* to go astray who ended up in reform institutions. In the Mercer Reformatory and the Alexandra and St Mary's reform schools the overwhelming majority of inmates served sentences for victimless crimes. Vague labels such as 'incorrigibility,' 'delinquency,' and the time-honoured 'vagrancy' were attached to these girls and women once they left the docks of Toronto's juvenile or police courts. Their terms ranged from a few months to a decade in the case of some juvenile offenders. Although inmates who were older, married, or convicted of crimes against persons or property did not disappear from correctional institutions, the composition of inmate populations underwent a radical shift towards younger women and first offenders convicted of morals offences.

At the Mercer Reformatory, for instance, the prison register indicates that before the introduction of indeterminate sentencing in 1913, more than 40 per cent of inmates were over thirty years old and only 17 per cent were under twenty.[59] From 1914 to the end of Superintendent O'Sullivan's tenure in 1927, the age breakdown shifted significantly: almost 43 per cent of the inmates were under twenty and the proportion of women over thirty had sunk to 17 per cent. Similarly, the prisoners who were committed in the latter half of O'Sullivan's tenure were more likely to serve time for minor morals offences than were their earlier counterparts. The proportion of 'vagrants,' for instance, rose from just over 20 per cent in the period from 1901 to 1913 to approximately 36 per cent over the following fourteen years. The rate of women charged specifically with prostitution offences doubled from 12 to 24 per cent. In contrast, thieves dwindled from 25 per cent of the reformatory's population to only 15 per cent by the period from 1914 to 1927. The number of women serving time for public order offences, primarily drunkenness and disorderliness, underwent an identical transition.[60] By the second half of her superintendency, then, O'Sullivan oversaw an inmate population of extremely young women, two-thirds of whom were under twenty-five; an equally large proportion were serving sentences for ill-defined morals offences.[61]

In 1913 the Ontario government empowered the Mercer Reformatory to accept women serving indeterminate sentences that would expire only after they convinced their keepers that they had reformed. Magistrates were thereafter permitted to sentence women to indeterminate sentences of up to two years less a day for any offence, no matter how trivial.[62] This provision meant that women charged with offences such as vagrancy could now serve two years for crimes that under the Criminal Code carried a maximum sentence of six months to one year.[63] Magistrates' readiness to take advantage of new sentencing provisions was evident almost immediately. The proportion of Mercer inmates who received sentences of more than one year jumped from 17 per cent in 1901–13, to 58 per cent between 1914 and 1917. Accordingly, the average period of confinement rose as well: from 1901–13, Superintendent O'Sullivan had, on average, 201 days to reform each inmate, a period she considered inadequate. In the four years following the introduction of indeterminate sentencing, the average period of confinement rose by more than 50 per cent to 328 days. Those serving indeterminate sentences – and between 1914 and 1917 over half of Mercer inmates did so – had to convince prison staff that they had overcome their 'evil tendencies' if they hoped to shorten their maximum sentence.

Although virtually all inmates had been committed after a brief summary trial and only a small fraction were charged with specified sexual offences, O'Sullivan felt qualified to state in 1919 that 'with few exceptions, all [Mercer inmates] were sex offenders.' In her sweeping, unsubstantiated statement O'Sullivan reflected an attitude shared by most arresting officers, judges, and social workers by the 1910s: young women in conflict with the law must, in some way, have engaged in immoral activities. For these women, eligibility for early release would depend on their readiness to 'throw off the bonds of bad habits and to displace evil ways with good healthy manners.'[64]

Behind the walls of Toronto's two industrial schools were girls and young women – most of them working girls – who were unable, or disinclined, to live up to the discipline of pleasure. Parents were as likely as arresting officers to drag them before the Police or Juvenile Court. In either case, a working girl's power to defend herself was extremely limited: most were minors and few could afford lawyers or anticipate help from their families, especially when their parents had laid 'incorrigibility' complaints in the first place. Contemporary newspapers tended not to grant such cases much space in their columns, and few aside from Toronto's poor realized that young women could be arrested and incarcerated on suspicion of sexual delinquency. Unlucky working girls discovered at first hand that their pursuit of pleasure could, in certain circumstances, lead to years of imprisonment and post-release supervision by medical and moral overseers.

Although the state provided the mechanisms for the reformation of 'good times girls,' committal records of juvenile institutions indicate that in the majority of cases a girl's guardians were the ones who initiated the punitive response to their daughter's misbehaviour.[65] Invariably the families were poor and, in many cases, destitute. The refusal of a teen-aged girl to assume domestic burdens in favour of her own pleasures could set off a crisis, particularly in families with many children or absent fathers. Parents, driven by the frustration of a recalcitrant daughter and the desperation that arose from the burden of feeding and clothing a non-contributing family member, turned to the sergeant's desk at their local police stations.

Charges such as 'incorrigibility' or 'difficult to control' were the most common complaints laid by parents against their daughters. At Toronto's first training school for girls, these phrases appeared consistently on the standard complaint forms, suggesting that recording clerks supplied parents with the official discourse of delinquency. One of the first inmates of the Alexandra Industrial School, Agnes Neale, was sent by her mother. Mrs Neale's complaint read as follows:

I am the mother of this girl. I reside no. 13 Soho Ave. I with the girl have resided in Toronto since her birth. She has become incorrigible. I am unable to control her. She runs away from home and sleeps out at night frequently. She recently has formed the acquaintance and associates with girls whom I believe to be prostitutes. I am of the opinion that if she is not put under restraint she will grow up to lead an idle and dissolute life. She is fourteen years old. I would like to have her sent to the Alexandra Industrial School for four years.[66]

In a few brief sentences the committal form linked Agnes's incorrigibility and association with suspected prostitutes to a projected life of idleness. For her part, Mrs Neale may have been more concerned about Agnes's current unreliability as a worker. Her mark, indicating her illiteracy, and her address on the western fringe of the Ward confirms the family's poverty. Mrs Neale's reticence about 'Mr Neale' also suggests that Agnes's father had died or abandoned the family and that the daughter's earnings were all the more vital to the survival of the household. 'Idle and dissolute' daughters were burdens, and parents like Mrs

Neale, who had younger children to rear, readily availed themselves of state agencies that pledged to bring their daughters under control.[67]

Parental claims of female delinquency invariably turned on the question of a young woman's unwillingness to balance her personal pleasures with her domestic duties. Evidence that would have been dismissed as hearsay in an adult court could trigger the Juvenile Court judge to sentence delinquents to lengthy terms in industrial schools. Allegations of idleness and suspicions of prostitution were sufficient to define fourteen-year-old Louise Dupont's offence as 'general delinquency.' Mrs Dupont had become exasperated with her daughter's behaviour: 'I cannot manage her. She is out until all hours of the night with company.' Louise's mother and the court suspected that the company her daughter sought was not that of a girlfriend but of men willing to pay for sexual favours. Louise admitted only that she had gone to Hamilton with a girlfriend for four or five days.[68]

Since working daughters' earnings were vital to the household economy, the costs of their commercial amusements could be dear in both moral and economic terms. When young women spent their money on their own pleasures, they doubly violated parental authority.[69] The 'exhibits' brought forward to prove Louise guilty of delinquency included a new hat, a 'very obscene picture,' unaccounted-for money, and 'a broken package of cigarettes in [her] pockets.' These articles raised two equally compelling questions for the court: how had Louise acquired these goods, and why, if she had earned money, had she not turned her wages over to her mother? Louise clearly spent her money, however earned, on her own vanities and indulgences. Had she acquired a sensible hat for her mother or an extra quart of milk for the family with her inexplicable earnings, one may speculate that Louise might not have ended up in court.

What propelled young women like Louise to take to the streets when the majority of working daughters fulfilled parental expectations of obedience can never be determined. Historians have debated the meaning of working girls' risky behaviour, but most agree that not every 'good times' girl was a carefree pleasure-seeker in search of autonomy. Linda Gordon suggests that staying out late or 'picking up' strange men at amusement resorts expressed working-class teenaged women's rejection of their subservience in the home and their consequent vulnerability to violence and abuse. Behaviour labelled as sauciness or coarseness by parents, the police, and social workers actually expressed 'rejection of an obedience that had been self-destructive and that the girls knew to be self-destructive.'[70] The problem, as police, prison, and court records reveal, was that sexual rebellion could entail trading one form of victimization for another.

In Hortense Flambeau's case, allegations of incest lurked behind the events that led eventually to her conviction as a delinquent. Mrs Flambeau found herself torn, like many mothers, between dependence upon her husband and concern for her daughter who ran away from home in 1917. When a constable tried to retrieve the runaway, a family crisis erupted. Hortense refused to return, alleging that a 'serious charge' should be laid, not against her but her father. Both parents categorically denied what amounted to Hortense's complaint of incest and simply wanted to see an end to the sordid affair.

In the eyes of the Catholic Children's Aid worker assigned to the Flambeau case, it had only begun. The case worker, Mr O'Connor, asked that the fourteen-year-old be given an indefinite sentence – that is, up to seven years – at St Mary's because the seed of immorality had been planted in her thoughts. Whether or not Hortense's claim was true, O'Connor judged that she now had 'a perverted mind and should be given a longer time so that she may be allowed to forget the occurrence that led to her commitment to the school.'[71] He supported this supposition with evidence of what the social surveyors would have labelled 'occasional prostitution.' Hortense had apparently admitted that during her two-week absence from home she had stayed at a boarding-house in the Ward. A Mr Thibideau not only paid her admission to several 'picture shows,' but also loaned her thirteen dollars to pay her board: 'I do not think [the] girl is so innocent as she and her mother try to make [her] appear,' the Catholic CAS report concluded. The only player to be exonerated in this family drama constructed in juvenile court was the father, who had most likely precipitated Hortense's flight from home. She and her mother were equally censured and silenced, although it fell to the daughter to serve an indefinite period of incarceration on a charge of 'delinquency.'

Female runaways did not automatically receive reformatory sentences. Most parental complaints went no further than the local police station. As long as the young woman seemed willing to submit herself to parental authority, the matter was dropped. Only when a teenager was a repeat offender or suspected of sexual delinquency did the courts intervene. Both parents and young women encountered unexpected consequences if the police were notified of suspected delinquency. The penetration of penality into civil life in these cases led to the policing not only of deviant girls but of deviant families.[72]

Widowed or abandoned mothers who laid complaints of delinquency were tried alongside their daughters for their inability to instill the values demanded of respectable working girls. The CAS and the juvenile court exercised their power to enforce these standards of motherly and daughterly behaviour. In Eve Lavallée's case, child welfare experts inferred that the fifteen-year-old's mother had provided inadequate supervision for her daughter in her after-work hours. Ironically, Mrs Lavallée had, initiated the complaint, saying that Eve 'was not under proper control.'

The 'evidence' was manifold. Mrs Lavallée, forced to provide for several children by working as an office cleaner, allowed Eve and one of her sisters to become waitresses at the British Restaurant, which a 'Chinaman' operated, according to a CAS report. Asked by the court if there was further evidence of Eve's delinquency, Mrs Lavallée responded: 'Yes, she goes out in autos with young men.'[73] Car rides and Chinese restaurants were codes that stood for the girl problem and the dangers of foreigners in the minds of Progressive reformers.[74] Mrs Lavallée must have made these links herself when she decided to forbid her daughters to work at the Chinese restaurant. Eve's sister complied, but Eve continued in defiance of her mother's and the Catholic CAS's wishes.

When she was finally apprehended, case workers were more concerned about how and with whom Eve had spent her free time than with her ability to support herself on the wages of a waitress. The CAS report to the juvenile court sealed Eve's fate with damning evidence of her dissolute behaviour and lack of shame: 'When asked where she spent her evenings after work she said in the shows. Eve's face was much painted and made up. She assumed a defiant attitude and used very bad language.'[75] In other words, Eve had displayed the characteristics of a potentially feeble-minded sexual delinquent. Another social worker neatly summarized Eve's low moral state: 'This girl is utterly wrong.' The corroborating evidence in this instance was that 'she goes out in autos with older girls than herself.' Her suspected sexual delinquency prompted a referral to the Toronto General Hospital Psychiatric Clinic. There, Dr C.N. Hincks diagnosed the psychological underpinnings of her taste for 'good times': 'She is a psychopath,' he declared, 'very stubborn, hardened against society, given to violent fits of temper, etc.' Not surprisingly, given Hincks' expertise, the courts imposed an indefinite sentence for 'petty crime.'[76]

The aims of the state and the parent in this case were evidently at odds. Mrs Lavallée had merely wanted help in gaining control over her daughter and hoped that she might be taught a lesson; medical and correctional officials, in contrast, were warding off the degeneration of the race. After only one year of Eve's possible six-year sentence had expired, Mrs Lavallée vainly petitioned for her daughter's release, now claiming that 'the girl ... had not really done anything wrong.' Since Mrs Lavallée was still working to support her five children, CAS worker Mr O'Connor advised against Eve's release, and the sexual 'psychopath' remained behind locked doors.[77]

REGULATION ON RELEASE

Despite girls' allegations of physical and sexual abuse at the hands of their families, not to mention correctional authorities' own suspicions of inadequate parental supervision as the cause of sexual delinquency, faith in 'the home' as the answer to young single women's problems remained unshaken. Just as domestic work was persistently presented as an anchor for working girls who would otherwise drift into city temptations, so prison and parole officials assumed that home life would restore bad girls to respectable ways. Most adolescent women released from juvenile or adult reformatories were released into family custody, and parents were legally bound to impose control over their daughters' free time if they managed to earn an early release. When guardians accepted young women released from industrial schools, the women were expected to perform not merely as caregivers and supervisors but as de facto parole officers. Standard release forms at St Mary's read as follows:

I, ——, hereby agree to accept the care of my daughter, ——, from the St. Mary's Industrial School, and I further agree that if she shows any inclination of getting beyond my control that I will notify the Children's Aid Society and ask them to replace her in the school.[78]

The release agreement clearly expressed the assumption that a delinquent's family would, in concert with official overseers, police her behaviour more effectively than they had done prior to her arrest.

Parental supervision did not, however, preclude continuing surveillance from state and quasi-state agents. If a girl's parents were unwilling or unable to supervise their daughter's leisure time, a range of experts was ready to step in. In 1916 the establishment of the Ontario Board of Parole meant that early release requests would be assessed by a group of appointees who would apply formal standards to determine an inmate's eligibility for parole.[79] J.J. Kelso, for instance, used his position as the director of the CAS to coordinate professionals' efforts to monitor parolees. In July 1919 Kelso asked Miss Husband, a public health nurse, to visit sixteen-year-old Madelaine Chisholm to ensure that she was not consorting with an Italian girl who was 'not considered a desirable companion for Madelaine.' After serving a two-year sentence at St Mary's for vagrancy, Madelaine had returned to her family home in the Junction, a neighbourhood another CAS worker described as 'a wretched locality ... the worst part of Toronto that I have ever visited.'[80] She worked at Gunn's meat-packing house for $3.50 per week, an outrageously small sum, particularly in the inflationary post-war period. Nurse Husband duly reported in September that trouble was brewing at the Chisholms'. Although a sixteen-year-old who had just spent two years in a reformatory and who now toiled five or six days a week in a meat-packing house might understandably have yearned for nights to herself, spending her evenings away from home was unacceptable to her official overseers. Miss Husband informed Madelaine's parents that if they did not know where and with whom their daughter amused herself, she would have to return to St Mary's in compliance with the release agreement.

This time, the Chisholms refused to cooperate. To the consternation of the public health nurse and the CAS worker, they had struck a compromise with their daughter: as long as she worked steadily, contributed her pitiful earnings to the family budget, and helped with the housework they would tolerate her nocturnal wanderings. Madelaine's parents imposed their own brand of the pleasure discipline, one that asked merely that her pleasures not interfere with her duties. The Chisholms' uneasy truce was likely negotiated in many poor, working-class households where, for a few dollars per week, a wage-earning daughter might bargain for several precious hours' respite from a crowded home, a 'wretched locality,' and the watchful eyes of her elders.

As long as discharged inmates maintained a respectable, home-based existence in their time off, correctional officials seemed only mildly concerned with their material wellbeing. The CAS worker who described Madelaine's wage as 'a disgrace for any respectable firm' did not suggest finding her a better-paying job. Release supervisors, like other observers of the labour force, tended to look at working girls' jobs as moral tests, the failure of which earned more than verbal chastisement.

Parole officer O'Connor admitted in 1907 that the jobs he secured for Gretta Norton, first at a paper-box factory and then at the Watson Candy factory, allowed her to earn 'only small wages.'[81] Unlike other working girls, however, Gretta did not enjoy the luxury of quitting without risking re-arrest.

Young women were not truly reclaimed unless they faithfully performed their work, no matter how menial or poorly paid, and eschewed good times. Jean Nolan was one of St Mary's success stories. After her release in 1907 the sixteen-year-old worked at the Toronto Plate Glass Company and gave her family no cause for uneasiness in her time off. Jean's mother felt that her daughter had been 'radically improved' by her 'stay' at St Mary's. As O'Connor reported, '[Jean] evidently tries to select good company for herself and seems to have no desire to go any place without her mother's knowledge and permission.'[82] Where formerly she did whatever she pleased in her spare time, she now circumscribed her pleasures to suit her mother's and the Children's Aid worker's standards of propriety. During her 'stay' she had imbibed the tonic of self-restraint that fortified her against temptation and braced her to be a productive worker, a dutiful daughter, and a marriageable young woman.

Mercer Reformatory inmates were technically adults, yet all but a few of the inmates were still young enough, it was hoped, to reform their deviant ways. Superintendent O'Sullivan looked upon incarceration as 'an opportunity for breaking away from bad habits and evil companions.'[83] It was also an opportunity for the staff to inculcate the values of proper attitudes towards work and leisure. Inmates who did not learn how to work hard and play properly were invariably made to serve their full terms.

Medical evidence of feeble-mindedness virtually guaranteed that a Mercer inmate would remain in prison as long as the law allowed. Indeed, Mercer's medical officer, Dr King, recommended that feeble-minded young women, such as Amanda Fergus, required perpetual supervision. The young inmate's great flaw appears to have been her unapologetic pursuit of good times. 'She admits leading a loose life,' King began, '[yet] she is very sharp in her defence of herself and of her every statement.' Although she had 'a mind evidently her own,' King diagnosed Fergus as 'weak-minded' because she consorted with 'designing young men.' Her work habits suffered as a result: 'She leaves a place when not satisfied and has no fear of her mistress.'

Although she asserted her independence on several fronts, it was Fergus's unashamed pursuit of pleasure that sealed her fate before her expert assessors.

Amanda bore all the traits of sex delinquency and thus carried the threat of race degeneration. Her inability to resist 'good times' and unwillingness to suppress her desire for amusement led Dr King to predict that unless she were kept away from temptation 'she will most certainly find her way back here and possibly bring with her a baby child. A permanent home under constant supervision is to my mind the only salvation for girls of this class.'[84] Amanda, the 'girl' who testily defended her right to pleasure and rejected her mistress's demands for obedience, operated according to her own alternative set of pleasure priorities. Although King's recommendation for her lifelong supervision was eventually rejected, Amanda did not earn an early release.

Women who were less sharp in defending their former lifestyles were in a better position to avoid serving their full sentences. Released women were expected to be morally circumspect in their play and diligent in their work, for a young woman who abandoned her struggle to support herself respectably soon discovered easier means of subsistence. Unmarried inmates were expected to take up useful employment on their release, but only if they stuck to work that left them with little free time. Although inmates who learned on Mercer's power sewing machines how to be skilled factory operatives could earn as much as $7 to $9 per week in 1916, the post-release field officer, Margaret Howe, preferred to arrange for domestic situations.[85] She alleged that maids, who earned approximately half the wages of experienced operatives, did not have to pay board, lodging, carfare, and other incidentals, and thus they were at least as well off as their blue-collar counterparts. The critical advantage of domestic work, however, was 'the added satisfaction to those interested in their welfare of knowing where they are at night.'[86]

Mistresses were eager to report infractions of parole agreements that required released women to maintain the standards of discipline that had been imposed upon them in prison. O'Sullivan learned that Fannie Cook had broken her parole after her mistress complained that the young maid had abandoned her post. The superintendent counselled the discomfited mistress that she should have suspected Fannie's backsliding once she began to spend her evenings out: 'Let me tell you that no girl from the Reformatory can be trusted who remains out late at night. Any girl who fails to come in at a decent hour is not doing what she ought to do.'[87] Fannie's inappropriate use of her free time was thus the key to her inadequacy as a worker. If the local police could locate the young woman, O'Sullivan vowed, she would be returned to Mercer, where she would have another opportunity to learn how to lead a disciplined, regular life.

The case files of Toronto's juvenile and adult women's reformatories reveal stories of women whose self-directed pleasures and forthright defence of their right to do as they pleased in their free time rendered them vulnerable to the enforcers of the pleasure discipline. For every Amanda Fergus or Eve Lavallée there were many others who, like Madelaine Chisholm, managed to reach agreements with their parents over the extent and nature of their pleasures. However, the stories of young women like Jean Nolan, the sixteen-year-old who had 'no desire to go any place,' were not common. Had Toronto's working girls quietly stayed at home after work, the city's amusement industry would not have boomed in the early twentieth century. Opulent vaudeville houses that put on clean sketches and movie houses that ran serials and films featuring intrepid girl heroines eagerly courted the working-girl patron. Neither could Toronto's many amusement parks have reaped profits for their backers if tens of thousands of young wage-earning women had not traded their nickels and dimes for hours of thrills and merriment.

Observers of working girls' unprecedented foray into the city's commercial amusement scene worried that young women were trading more than coins, however. Bound up in their own middle-class courtship conventions, journalists and members of the Toronto Social Survey Commission looked at the leisure pursuits of an alien class and discovered 'occasional' prostitution – the only term that could adequately describe their impression of the casual acquaintanceships working girls struck up with strange men in dancehalls, ice cream parlours, and skating-rinks. While some Progressives, such as the social worker Elizabeth Neufeld, promoted alternative forms of amusement for working girls, others, motivated in part by medical experts' dire warnings about feeble-mindedness and race degeneration, felt that more coercive responses were warranted. Gazing at working girls' amusements across a divide of class, as well as of age and sex in many instances, investigative voyeurs viewed wage-earning women's taste for commercial amusements with a kind of horrid fascination. Only women like Videre, a middle-class professional woman who stepped into the work place of working girls, could begin to appreciate how hard-won those transitory pleasures felt after a day of menial toil at minuscule pay. The jam-dollopers who returned to the biscuit factory on Monday morning certainly understood.

6

Temptations, Crimes, and Follies

As working girls' visibility both as workers and as participants in the urban leisure scene increased, tales of women adrift in the city seemed less credible. In the columns of Toronto daily newspapers, dramatic accounts of white slavery and sympathetic sketches of 'fallen angels' appeared alongside grittier tales of 'peroxide blondes who chew gum while their lawyers dwell on their virtues ... females with cream puff intellects and ice cream hearts.' Police court reporter Harry Wodson thought that 'lady scribes' and their soft-hearted readers had the picture of vice and immorality all wrong. Pathetic stories of frail and erring women were all very well for those who 'wallowed in maudlin sentimentality,' he brayed, but realists recognized that the supposed victims of vice were in fact dangerous.[1]

Although the social purity movement's impact on the federal and municipal governments in the early 1900s was profound, their deadly serious narratives of white slavery were simultaneously transformed into entertaining and titillating plays and films, such as the wildly popular *Traffic in Souls*. Toronto theatregoers who attended *Queen of the White Slaves*, for instance, were promised 'love, intrigue, laughter and tears.' The notable inclusion of 'laughter' among the anticipated range of emotions signalled a playful approach to the theme of sexual endangerment. In fact, dire warnings about the perils of the city for working girls had become the stuff of satire. The 1910 broadway hit tune, 'Heaven Will Protect the Working Girl,' likely sung in Shea's Theatre on a vaudeville bill, mocked sentimental ballads about country lasses and their moral ruin in the city. A mother sings this warning to her daughter 'Neuralgia':

The city is a wicked place as anyone can see,
And cruel dangers 'round your path may hurl;
So ev'ry week you'd better send your wages back to me
For Heaven will protect a working girl.[2]

Sure enough, Neuralgia is set upon by a villain who 'treat[s] her respectful as those villains always do' until he takes her to dine and spins his web of seduction. Forewarned of his wiles, the young maiden spurns his advances, declaring: 'You may tempt the upper classes with your villainous demitasses / But Heaven will protect the working girl.' As the titles of other popular songs, such as 'Tessie, Stop Teasing Me' and 'Mainstreet Wasn't Big Enough for Mary' suggest, Harry Wodson was not the only one who had trouble believing that cheeky, pleasure-loving working girls could be victims.[3]

Similar contests were fought out in the course of morals policing. In the early twentieth century, unprecedented assaults were launched on the organized sex trade in North American cities and, in most cases, young women, more than clients or brothel operators, were the targets of police sweeps. In contrast to the period discsussed in chapter 3, Toronto feminists and social purity advocates had gained sufficient political clout to pressure the police into targeting men as well as women in anti-vice campaigns. In fact, as US and Canadian urban historians have shown, arrests for morals offences escalated sharply from the late nineteenth century, and men comprised the majority of arrestees. The urban reform project to create cleaner, healthier, and safer cities may have led to the imposition of new restraints on male sexual licence, but it certainly failed to supplant long-held suspicions about working girls' moral laxity. Even in this era uniquely intolerant of masculine pleasures, women who found themselves endangered could not rely on unqualified support in the criminal justice system. Indeed, it is surprising that the dramatic acquittals of Ford and Davies did not inspire more women to take the law into their own hands.

What did these various debates about urban morals regulation mean for the working girl and her safety in the city? Although women's historians have explored the impact of anti-prostitution measures on working-class women, the breakup of the vice industry in the early twentieth century occurred in a wider context of related changes in the regulation of abortion, sexual assault, and consensual sex, both hetero- and homosexual.[4] Similarly, the stricter policing of male morals offenders took place during an upsurge in racist sentiment against non-Anglo-Celtic immigrants. Sterner measures against sexual violence were based more on xenophobic reactions to 'strangers' than on a growing conviction that working girls had a right to safety as well as freedom. Rising rates of arrest for homosexual offences and (heterosexual) 'carnal knowledge' confirm that non-marital, non-procreative sex rather than sexual aggression per se preoccupied the police and the courts. The campaign against abortion can be seen in a similar light. Although the prosecution of incompetent practitioners may have saved some women's lives, the underlying aim was to halt a practice that allowed women sexual freedom and threatened the future of the race. Finally, the hoary tactic of impeaching the character of sexual assault complainants demonstrates that the image of the helpless workwoman may have dimmed in theatres, but that of the fallen woman still shone brightly in courtrooms.

POLICING TORONTO THE GOOD

Given the high profile of the social evil on the political agenda at the turn of the century, it is not surprising that contemporaries and historians have considered the attack on organized prostitution the sine qua non of morals regulation. Toronto's efforts in that regard were certainly notable. In contrast to Montreal and Winnipeg, where scandals made the police tolerance of vice an open secret, the city's police tried to uphold the appellation 'Toronto the Good.' Arrest statistics show that Toronto escalated its campaign against prostitution as pressure from the social purity movement mounted; however, the Toronto police were more willing than other Canadian forces to punish male clients.[5] In spite of these impressive statistics, critics, particularly the social survey commissioners, complained about official complacency. Even the police called for a different approach to vice, one that would target occasional prostitution. The regulation of dancehalls and the introduction of policewomen, along with the time-honoured tactic of vagrancy arrests, became critical components of the force's efforts to keep up with the changing face of urban vice.

The gendered character of morals regulation is well documented by arrest statistics, which show that the police battle against prostitution in Toronto was waged disproportionately at the expense of women who offered sexual services for sale. In all but one year at the zenith of the white slavery panic, the police were inclined to consider male customers less culpable participants in heterosexual commerce. The absence of male 'magdalene' homes or houses of refuge underscored the prevailing assumption that prostitutes, not their clients, posed a moral danger. Those men who were arrested, moreover, usually escaped with a fine in the rare instances when they were found guilty, as social purity advocates complained.

Brothel arrests do not tell the whole story of vice regulation, however. From the 1890s to the 1920s, the annual reports of the police chief reveal that the Toronto police no longer concentrated on houses of ill fame in their campaign against illicit sex. Chief Constable Grasset reported that vice policing had broadened because the nature of commercialized sex had modernized in conjunction with other sectors of the urban economy. In his reports he noted that freelance prostitutes had taken over the sex trade. The chief admitted in 1897 that the police 'find it no easy matter to deal effectively with this class of persons. Enticing men from windows and doorways, being safer than solicitation on the streets, has been resorted to in some localities.' Changes in the urban landscape, particularly the expansion of rental housing, made it possible, the police admitted, for young women to sell sexual services without having to operate either in a brothel or on the street, where they could more readily be apprehended. According to Chief Grasset, 'the trend seem[ed] to be in the direction of separate apartments, where women living alone [could] render it very difficult for the police to proceed against them successfully.'[6]

Feminists and leaders of Toronto's social purity campaign were impatient with such excuses. Still convinced that 'villains' led working girls into 'temptations, crimes and follies,' they called on the police to shut down every house of ill fame in the city.[7] To quell the clamour, the police stepped up their campaign against prostitution; not surprisingly, the number of brothel arrests, peaked as the social purity campaign gained steam. In the year after Rev St Clair publicly attacked the force in 1912, for instance, the number of arrests for being found in a house of ill fame skyrocketed from 103 (of which 90 were of women) to 411 arrests of women and 243 of men. The social survey commissioners were nevertheless convinced that the police could do better. Writing in 1916, a few months after their critical survey report was released, Chief Grasset snapped: 'The allegations made in some quarters that the police were inclined to be tolerant with sexual vice, are as fantastic as they are untrue.'[8] To prove that the commissioners' attacks were unwarranted, the police swept down on the city's brothels once again and brought unprecedented numbers of women and men before the police magistrate. In 1915 arrests of frequenters and keepers of houses of ill fame shot to the highest level in Toronto's history to that point.[9] In that year alone there were 528 prostitution arrests, with men accounting for two-thirds of those apprehended by the police. This startling rise in male arrests was clearly intended to appease feminists and social purists who advocated a 'white life for two.'

Both men and women paid a price for the force's reactionary measures; however, they did not bear the burden equally. Although the numbers of women arrested as inmates or keepers of brothels had never been very great in comparison to the numbers in major categories of drunkenness or, later, bylaw infractions, they were at their highest levels during the white slavery panic. In 1915, the year the police made the greatest number of brothel arrests, the two offences of frequenting and keeping a house of ill fame comprised 13.9 per cent of all female arrests. For men, who actually comprised the bulk of arrestees that year, these same charges accounted for a mere 1.2 per cent of their arrests. Since brothel offences averaged only 5.7 per cent of women's arrests throughout the period from 1893 to 1930, the social purity movement's influence over the policing of prostitution in the 1910s and its disproportionate impact on young women was evidently profound.

If vagrancy charges are added to brothel-related arrests, it becomes even clearer that young women were the principal victims in the battle against the social evil. For men and women, vagrancy could cover minor infractions of public decorum, such as sleeping on the streets, begging, or having no visible means of support. However, it carried a distinctly sexual meaning when applied to young women. 'Streetwalkers,' or women suspected of street solicitation, were routinely charged with vagrancy, and women who did not seem to have legitimate means of support could be arrested as vagrants on suspicion of prostitution.[10] Inmate case files from juvenile and adult women's reformatories show that teenaged women who stayed out without their parents' permission, women who lived with men out of wedlock, and unmarried women who were found in bed with men were routinely arrested as vagrants. A host of ill-defined infractions of sexual delinquency were cloaked beneath female vagrancy arrests.[11]

The absence of arrestee profiles renders it impossible to sift aged, widowed, or married women vagrants from the young unmarried women who were more likely to have been arrested as suspected prostitutes, but changes in female vagrancy arrests over time confirm that the 'tramp' label had a double meaning. From 1893 to 1930, 7.6 per cent of all women arrested in Toronto were charged with vagrancy; during the height of moral reform lobbying in Toronto (1912 to 1916) that rate almost doubled to 13.3 per cent. The bulk of morals policing in the city is thus hidden in the omnibus charge of vagrancy. In the 1920s, even after anti-white-slavery campaigns subsided and the suppression of brothels spawned novel patterns of freelance and pimp-controlled prostitution, the number of female vagrancy charges remained high.[12] When Chief Grasset declared in 1915 that 'the social evil, in so far as the law can be applied, has received the energetic attention of the Police,' he might very well have credited the force's use of female vagrancy arrests as the rear guard attack on urban immorality.[13]

Attempts to regulate sexual behaviour were also waged through more subtle forms of control. After 1896, when the police were granted the power to devise their own bylaws, a great deal of day-to-day policing occurred through the enforcement of those regulations. The bylaws that most affected young women focused on their sexual behaviour in public. The regulation of dancehalls in particular is a case study in the 'moralization' of delinquent subjects.[14] Bylaws concerning the licensing of dancehalls empowered the police to regulate every aspect of operations, from the age of persons admitted to the prohibition of alcohol and the determination of closing hours. Whereas saloons had long been a concern of the police, dancehalls became priorities by the 1910s. It was not the police force, however, that initiated this shift, but the Toronto Local Council of Women. In 1913 the group successfully lobbied the force to hire two female officers to patrol the city's dancehalls. Chief Constable Grasset reluctantly admitted that women could bring unique skills of observation and supervision to the job.[15] By 1915 he reported that the policewomen's 'visitations' to dance halls had produced such 'a good effect' that they had come to 'justify their appointment.' Two more policewomen were hired by the force in 1919 to patrol all forms of commercial recreation with an eye toward protecting and supervising young female patrons.[16] By 1924 Grasset's successor, Chief Dickson, announced that the 'absence of complaints [concerning dancehalls] would indicate that such places are now conducted properly.'[17]

Although both men and women attended dancehalls, police regulated their behaviour differently, scrutinizing men's drinking and women's flirting. This gendered form of supervision was, in practice, evocative of the policing of morality. Chief Dickson reported in 1924 that since the enactment of 'the by-law regulating the hours and prohibition of females entering such places without an escort, very little difficulty ha[d] been experienced.' As a result of police vigilance, many small dancehalls had been closed.[18] This one bylaw demonstrates how the police could impose gender scripts for public behaviour through the enforcement of licensing regulations. It was up to individual officers to determine whether or not a young woman had been 'escorted' to a dance hall or had attended with the aim of picking up a man. In the latter case she was likely to find herself under suspicion of 'occasional prostitution.' Moreover, there was no provision in the bylaw for the apprehension of 'unescorted' males or men who picked up dates in dancehalls, even though controlling male sexual behaviour would presumably have been a more effective way to protect young women from harm.

The arguments for and uses of policewomen exemplify the role of policing in creating new categories of gender-specific offences. The TLCW and the Equal Franchise League (EFL) first called for the hiring of policewomen to help make the city safer for women. Female officers would enhance the male force's effectiveness by supervising public parks and the urban playgrounds of the city's poor.[19] The clubwomen were supported in their bid by Alice Stebbin Wells, a pioneer policewoman from Los Angeles, who toured North America to promote the hiring of women officers for the control of vice. Her speeches gave the TLCW, the EFL, and the city's social purity advocates reason to believe that female officers might succeed where male officers had failed in their duty to eradicate urban immorality.[20] Ideally, their sex would allow policewomen access to sensitive areas, such as washrooms and changerooms, and, more important, permit women officers to gain the trust of the young women they were assigned to police.

The first women hired by the Toronto police force were assigned, fittingly, to the Morality Department. The civic administration confined female enforcers of the law, like the female subjects they were assigned to police, in moral categories. They were not granted the power to arrest, even by the 1920s when they began to perform a greater degree of public patrolling duties; instead, they were expected to exert powers of moral suasion over young women. They turned up in all the places where working girls were thought to be at risk, so that dancehalls, ice rinks, amusement parks, theatres, and public parks became their 'beats' rather than the regular patrol routes of male officers. But their professional marginality did not place them beyond the carceral continuum. They did much the same work as Big Sisters, for instance, attending the juvenile and women's courts, acting as liaisons with probation and parole officers, and counselling women thought to be in moral danger. As one clubwoman warmly reported in 1914, the impact of female law enforcement agents was already visible in the police force's increased willingness to bring a wider range of moral offences to the attention of the courts.

The urban moral reform campaign was clearly an effective means for the production of female delinquents, but its impact on women's sexual safety in the city is more difficult to evaluate. Men were not immune from prosecution, since the Toronto police did arrest a growing number of men whom they charged with sexual offences.[21] Historians of policing have been too eager to equate rising arrest rates with a growing intolerance for the victimization of women, however. A similar elevation took place in arrests of men accused of consensual homosexual sex as well as of men who may or may not have used threats or violence to have 'carnal knowledge' of young women.[22] More important, court transcripts and news coverage indicate that complainants continued to face stiff odds in attempting to convince the courts that they had been forced to have sex, particularly when defence lawyers invoked the image of the 'good times' girl in cross-examinations.

Like prostitution-related arrests, sexual offence charges peaked at the height of Toronto's Progressive reform era: sexual crimes against women accounted for a higher proportion of men's arrests in that period than either before or after. From 1893 to 1909 the number of arrests for rape, attempted rape, seduction, procuring, carnal knowledge, and indecent assault averaged only 34.9 per annum. Over the following six years that rate almost tripled to 96.8, then levelled off over the following fifteen years to 73.9 per annum. This trend seems to suggest that the police had come to consider women's complaints more seriously.[23]

The sharp decline in arrests for rape points to a different conclusion, however. Although the rate of arrests for men's sexual crimes against women was lowest at the turn of the century, rape, a capital offence, actually accounted for 29.2 per cent of all sexual offences, compared to a mere 6.4 per cent and 8 per cent in the 1910s and 1920s. Although Roger Lane and others quote such statistics as evidence that the city grew safer for women as the police imposed stricter controls over male sexual aggression, evidence from trial transcripts and victims' complaints suggests that working women were no better protected from random attacks or assaults from known men in the midst or in the aftermath of Toronto's urban reform era.[24] Furthermore, the high rate of acquittals and short sentences routinely meted out to offenders indicates that the criminal justice system had not suddenly come to consider violent crimes against women as grave offences. The readiness of the police to lay charges against male sexual offenders was more than balanced by the underlying assumption that working girls who ran into trouble had foolishly or even purposely courted danger. Only when women had been attacked by dangerous strangers or 'interfered with' by abortionists were the courts inspired to take a sterner attitude toward male offenders.

THE THREAT OF THE STRANGER

The master narrative that had framed the interpretation of sexual assault trials in the late nineteenth century invoked images of helpless women adrift, poor and friendless in the big city and vulnerable to the designs of villains. Clara Ford's and Carrie Davies' defenders had successfully manipulated these images, though notably in murder trials, not in rape trials. As defendants rather than complainants, their stories of victimization could not be countered by the men they had accused of sexual assault. By the early twentieth century, competing narratives disrupted those earlier portrayals of sexual danger, which in any case had never established the credibility of fallen women who had tried to press charges. As the number of non-British immigrants climbed quickly in the 1890s and 1900s, the appearance of 'foreigners' was discursively linked to poverty, crime, and vice.[25] Elizabeth Neufeld noted that Anglo-Celtic Torontonians were fearful of the Ward, where most of the city's foreigners lived: 'Perhaps it is the dagger of an Italian desperado of which they dream – perhaps the bearded faces of the 'Sheenies' are sufficient in themselves to inspire terror.' Neufeld aptly concluded that their anxieties could be attributed to 'Fear of the Unknown.'[26] The threat of foreign men, conjured up by the Toronto social surveyors, police court reporters, and the yellow press, aroused fear in both men and women. J.S. Woodsworth's *The Strangers within Our Gates* (1909) added a more sober warning that foreigners had infiltrated cities and begun to threaten the Canadian way of life. From the press to the pulpit, the apprehensions of Anglo-Celtic Canadians were mobilized and magnified.[27]

The image of the pleasure-seeking working girl competed with that of the dangerous stranger. As Harry Wodson had jibed, working girls were not as innocent as 'lady scribes' portrayed them or as they tried to appear before the magistrate when they were hauled up on morals charges. He had observed firsthand how many of them traipsed into court, laughing and chatting with the 'profligate rakes' who were charged with sexual offences.[28] Like the discoverers of 'occasional prostitutes,' Wodson believed that attending dancehalls and riding in motor cars – not white slavers or foreigners – led carefree working girls into vice. Whatever Torontonians may have feared from the denizens of the Ward and their ilk, they were equally aware of the 'good times' girl, not only from her image on screen and stage, but from observing thousands of young women who nightly poured out of factories and shops and into the world of city pleasures.

Sexual assault trials often dredged up these presumptions about dangerous foreigners and concupiscent working girls. Unlike the early decades of industrialization, when villains had been anonymous strangers, these new predators had identifiable faces, often dark-skinned and somehow mysterious, that signified 'otherness' to the dominant community. For that reason, the possibilities for conviction on sexual assault charges opened up in the early twentieth century as the police, prosecutors, and courts recognized that a few men (who were not at all like themselves) presented a threat to working girls.

The most dramatic trial in this period was that of David Hawes, who was convicted for the rape of Louisa LeBar. Hawes, a middle-aged black porter, lived in Ottawa but frequently passed through Toronto in the course of his work. The Clara Ford case had exposed Torontonians' readiness to believe that blacks were inclined to outrageous behaviour – behaviour that, in whites, might be labelled insanity. Academics and scientists upheld popular racist notions with theories that 'proved' that blacks and native Americans retained animal characteristics that their white counterparts had overcome. Leading Torontonians, such as long-reigning Police Magistrate Denison, openly referred to blacks as child-like savages.[29] Minstrel shows, a staple of vaudeville entertainment and musical review, portrayed blacks as better suited to slavery than to freedom. But blacks were not always harmless fools, as the almost daily reports of lynchings in the US south reminded Canadians. While the entertainment page presented black men as buffoons, the front page showed them as archetypal rapists.

The alleged victim was, in dramatic contrast, the very picture of innocence and the perfect candidate for travellers' aid. Louisa LeBar was a seventeen-year-old servant who travelled by train from Manitoba to rural Ontario, where she was to meet her sister. During the trip she became acquainted with the porter who, she claimed, enticed her into the Government Palace Car when she had to switch trains at Toronto's Union Station. Although several passengers and railway employees, including Crown witnesses, reported seeing the pair together, no one could corroborate her story that she had been raped, and the examining physician reported finding no bruises or marks of any type on her body. Although Hawes was defended by E.F.B. Johnston and rising star T.C. Robinette, two of the foremost criminal lawyers in the province, he was found guilty. The judge, who threatened to exercise his option to impose the death penalty, predicted that subsequent trials of 'cases of this kind' would soon provoke other judges to pass such a sentence.[31] 'You dogged the girl all the way from Winnipeg, with mean, despicable and evil intent,' Justice Fergusson spat at the convicted man.[32] The stiff sentence of ten years was meant to reduce the number of rapes, which comprised, he grossly exaggerated, half the cases coming before the country's assize courts. The *News* menaced that Hawes was lucky: had he not enjoyed the benefits of British justice, he would have been tried 'very summarily and suffered immediate death at the hands of an angry mob.'[33]

In an even more remarkable case, an apparent 'good times' girl was given the benefit of doubt over two foreigners she accused of raping her – Yovan Yockock and Yako Toshilik. The sixteen-year-old had gone down to their ice cream parlour one evening in 1919 in search of work as a waitress. When she found that they were not hiring, she stayed in the parlour, accepting ice cream from the proprietors as well as chocolates and cups of tea from men who came into the shop. After closing time, she told the police, the two foreigners raped her. Again, the medical examination showed no signs that her hymen had been ruptured, and her body bore no marks of violence. Furthermore, the police had been unable to find any witnesses to corroborate her story.

Amazingly, the Crown attorney's office decided to prosecute the case. Kirkland hardly presented the image of a credible victim to those for whom downtown ice cream parlours were houses of assignation and acceptance of treats from strangers constituted occasional prostitution. Scores of other young women who behaved as Kirkland did were behind bars and locked doors in reformatories on charges of delinquency and vagrancy. None the less, the case went to trial, and the men were convicted and sentenced to seven years for attempted rape. As startling as the conviction may have appeared, the *Star*'s headline the day after sentencing was even more shocking: 'GIRL RETRACTS STORY WHICH JAILED TWO MEN.' In tears, the young woman had gone to the men's lawyer to admit that her original story had been 'a dream.' Whether her original complaint or her later retraction represented the 'truth' of the matter, the ice cream parlour operators had clearly been the victims of xenophobia.[34]

Perhaps the most openly racist comments were reserved for the city's largely bachelor population of Chinese. Their unfamiliar food and dress inspired racist fantasies of their mysterious powers over white women. *Jack Canuck*, a populist weekly that claimed to speak for the working man, was the most obnoxious exponent of anti-Asian racism. Its 1911 series on 'The Yellow Peril in Toronto,' for instance, made direct links between the sexual vulnerability of young (white) women to the 'Chinese pitfall.' Chinese laundrymen were apparently able to ensnare young women by showing them Oriental treasures and offering them cups of (drugged) Chinese tea: 'A drowsy feeling [ensues], and when she returns to her senses the evil deed has been consummated.'[35] Morality Department Inspector Kennedy thought the young women were more to blame. The 'lure of the Chinaman' had only developed because young women had 'too much liberty to roam the streets ... to their utter demoralization.'[36]

Remarkably, no charges of sexual assault were filed against Chinese men in the late nineteenth or early twentieth century in Toronto. The myth of Chinese men drugging and seducing white women into sexual slavery was fuelled by scandal-mongering journalism, not by court reports. In one case of procurement, however, the image of the dangerous foreigner was portrayed alongside that of the frivolous working girl. The case of Fooke Lee, a laundryman who allegedly attempted to procure two hired women for sexual purposes, demonstrates that even racist notions of Chinese sexual procurement did not supplant the growing sense that modern working girls should know how to avoid city dangers.

Olive and Ruth Crawford, new to the city in 1913 from the rural outskirts of York County, were happy to find a temporary cleaning job at Fooke Lee's Chinese laundry. The sisters, aged 21 and 18, might not have questioned Lee's intentions had they not told their landlady about him. Olive later stated that he had asked the women if they would like another job: 'My sister asked what kind of job and he replied, Oh, you know what kind of job and said he would give us a dollar each for it and it would only take a minute and for us to get right down on the floor.' Their landlady, warned by the metropolitan press of the 'yellow peril,' cautioned her tenants to be wary of the 'Chinaman' and to take care that he did not touch them. Ruth, in contrast, claimed that she harboured no such fears of 'Chinamen': 'It was only when he made motions for us to lie on the floor that I became frightened and remembered what [my landlady] had said.' Both sisters averred under cross-examination that they were perfectly chaste, but the men of the jury had their doubts. Lee was acquitted.[37]

This ambivalence about taking a working girl's word against a foreigner's was even more apparent when both parties were 'foreigners.' In a case involving Jewish men, a young single woman faced even greater odds in convincing the courts she had been raped, because she appeared to be a 'good times' girl. Although tailors Jake Greenfield and John Austin were convicted of indecently assaulting Nancy Jordon and were subsequently sentenced to three and four months each in jail, the story she had told was of a gang rape. On 6 February 1910 she and the men went out on Toronto Bay for a ride in an ice boat. Back in the city, they took her to 'Bernstein's place' on York Street in the predominantly Jewish section of the Ward. Greenfield asked for a room for himself and his 'sister.' Jordon described how they had proceeded to force her onto the bed and undress her: 'I was afraid of them. Greenfield got on top of me. The light was turned out. He took his privates out and got into me some while Austin held me. Then Austin did the same.'[38] Although the indictment against the pair was initially for rape, it was reduced, as were most cases that came before the courts, to 'indecent assault' by the time of their trial. Jordon's apparent consent probably influenced the plea-bargaining. She had, after all, willingly gone on an unchaperoned date with the men, repaired to a rooming-house, refrained from telling the hotel clerk that she was not Greenfield's sister, and made no attempt to escape or shout for help during the incident. The story might well have come from Clark's *Toronto the Good* or the social survey report. Jordon's taste for fast times meant that Greenfield and Austin escaped a possible life sentence.[39]

Although foreign men were vulnerable to arrest and, in several cases, convicted for sexual offences, the conviction of foreigners was by no means assured. Racism clearly motivated the Toronto police's force's keen attention to the sexual depredations of Asian, black, and Jewish men, just as they closely monitored their gambling and (Christian) Sabbath-breaking proclivities. The conviction of David Hawes and the ice cream parlour operators were exceptional. As cases such as the

Crawford sisters' suggest, the courts were still cautious when it came to accepting the word of a working girl. Neither the outworn myth of the woman adrift nor fears of dangerous 'others' could augment their credibility.

CHARACTER ON TRIAL

In reform-minded Toronto, victims of sexual assault were assisted by official posturing against sexual immorality of all sorts. Decades of lobbying against the evils of drink and more recent moves to introduce censorship and restrict all forms of public entertainment through licensing had borne fruit by the 1910s. The temperance movement and the campaign to clean up dancehalls, for instance, lent credibility to women who complained that they had been attacked by drunken men and dance hall patrons. At the same time, increasing vigilance against minor moral infractions may have led to a civil libertarian backlash in Toronto. Skilful defence lawyers, and T.C. Robinette in particular, capitalized on new statutory definitions of chastity and the image of the 'good times' girl to challenge complainants' credibility. Most succeeded. Torontonians were occasionally prepared to believe sexual assault claims if apparently respectable young women had been led into danger through doubtful amusements. The dance hall was arguably the most contentious site of alleged immorality, and it was the most strictly regulated commercial amusement. The police were proud of their efforts to suppress potentially illicit relations between the city's young women and men, as the annual reports of the chief constable confirm. And so it was particularly vexing when, in spite of official overseers' policing of urban recreations, women were none the less victimized by rapists whom they had encountered in dancehalls.

One of the few men to be convicted on the capital charge of rape fit the caricature of the dance hall rapist. Although the offence did not occur in the dancehall, the facility had fostered an atmosphere of heterosexual familiarity that brought together two strangers, Keith Gordon and Caroline Monteith, on a hot summer's night in 1923. As both of the dancehall acquaintances learned, the line between consent and coercion could blur in such heady settings.

On a Saturday night in July, Monteith donned a special dress, bid her mother good night, promised to be home by 12:30, and set out for the Hillcrest Dance Hall on Yonge Street at the northwestern fringe of the fashionable Rosedale district. Keith Gordon also happened to attend that night, popping out from time to time to drive downtown for a glass of bootlegged beer. He met Monteith and asked her to dance, then left for more beer. When he returned at 11:30 the dance was ending, in compliance with city bylaws, and Monteith was still on the stairs, perhaps hoping that the man she had danced with would return. She accepted a ride home from Gordon; he suggested they take a detour to the country since she did not have to be home for another hour.

After driving several miles they reached farmers' fields on the outskirts of the city. Gordon pulled over, urging Monteith to get out and 'have a bit of fun,' in his words. In his matter-of-fact statement to Toronto Detective Silverthorn, he detailed their negotiation: 'She replied she was afraid I would do her harm as she had never done it before. She then lay back with her own free will and told me I could do it if I did not get her in the family way and I said I wouldn't. We then had connection.'[40] After brushing dirt off the woman's dress, he drove her home by 12:30. Trouble ensued when Monteith's mother noticed her rushing in to wash her bloodied undergarments.

Monteith was a thirty-year old tailoress whose background suggested that she was a proper young woman. Still living at home, she abided by her mother's curfew, knowing that Mrs Monteith would be waiting up for her. The accused rapist himself confirmed that she was no 'good times girl' when he recounted to the police that 'she had never done it before.' The mother's prompt report to the police and the damning evidence of blood stains further contributed to the respectability of the Monteith family. Had the alleged victim laid the complaint, the character of the case would have taken on a different tone. Mrs Monteith, the instigator of the legal process, was unusually committed to seeing justice served, even at the expense of exposing her daughter to the publicity and trauma of a trial.

Left to her own devices, Monteith probably would have preferred to keep the incident a secret, particularly from her mother. In the course of the trial, Gordon testified that when he dropped Monteith home, she had agreed to meet him for another date; moreover, unlike most men accused of rape, he had freely related his version of the events to the police before he was officially charged. Unfortunately, for Gordon, his openness proved to be his undoing. By confirming that she was a virgin, he cast himself in the role of a seducer, and a drunken one at that. With a righteous mother at Monteith's side, the Crown was able to convince the jury that a respectable thirty-year-old, still chaste, was an easy target for a dancehall Lothario. Gordon paid for his naïveté with a six-year sentence at the Kingston Penitentiary, not simply because the jury believed Monteith's story but because the incident confirmed suspicions that dancehalls inflamed passions. Whether or not the evidence established that Monteith's and Gordon's sexual contact was non-consensual, the *story* of a chance encounter between a beer-swilling man and a previously chaste woman resonated with concerns over inadequately regulated amusements.[41]

When sexual adventures in public places turned into perilous encounters, the police were open to criticism that they had not fulfilled their mission to regulate urban morality. YWCA women themselves patrolled the preferred gathering-places of young people for a short while in 1918, and the professional police professed to keep the city clear of sexual miscreants once policewomen took over.[42] The police force and the women of the Local Council and the YWCA all agreed that more intensive policing of casual sex would raise the level both of public morality and of public safety. It did not occur to them that young women might be safer in the arms of their dates than in the hands of the law.

Young women eager to escape the scrutiny of their families and neighbours knew to keep an eye out for the police. The embarrassment of being escorted home by an officer who might reveal dalliances was a frightening prospect to working girls who lived under their parents' roofs. These thoughts may have run through Jean Argent's mind when she and her boyfriend were caught kissing in Rosedale Ravine on a warm September night in 1918. Two men who identified themselves as detectives informed the pair that they were under arrest and separated the young couple. Once the boyfriend was dragged off, Argent found herself alone with 'Detective' O'Hara. The police later described the terror he inflicted: 'O'Hara pulled the girl down and got on top of her and said 'are you going to give me it' she refused when he put his hand over her mouth she screamed for help and he told her if she did not open her legs he would cut them open with a knife, she says he has connections with her and tore her under-clothes. O'Hara told her if she screamed he would let the other man do the same.'[43] The battered and confused seventeen-year-old, unsure that the assailant was an imposter, bravely reported the crime at a nearby police station.

O'Hara's ploy worked because he co-opted the moral authority of the police. The young couple, no doubt aware that their petting in the park would be construed as immoral, were easy prey for the malfeasant 'detective.' The crime itself dramatically undercut respect for the police:

why should delinquents and criminals heed the word of men who might themselves be dangerous? And what reason would young women have to trust those who claimed to protect them? By the 1910s, when the Toronto police force numbered over 500, the patrolling cop was likely to be just another stranger to the citizens he watched over. Tragically, there was no reason for Jean Argent to doubt the veracity of O'Hara's claim.

O'Hara's trial was largely a secret to Torontonians because the court decided to close the proceedings to the public.[44] In this unusual move, both Argent and the police were spared the embarrassment of having the public know the details of the attack. O'Hara had no chance against the conclusive evidence against him, and although he had only been convicted of several minor offences prior to the rape, he received a life sentence, the stiffest penalty handed down in decades. But he did not spend the remainder of his days in the Kingston Penitentiary. After serving eight years he was paroled and returned to Toronto. After his release in 1928 he struck again on his own, using the identical ruse in the same park. This time a domestic servant was the victim.[45]

In spite of the police force's public commitment to protect young women from danger, the cases of Keith Gordon and Michael O'Hara stand out from the vast majority of trials where men were acquitted and women were made to feel somehow culpable.[46] Many were acquitted, thanks to the skill of their lawyers. In Toronto several members of the bar earned their reputations as leading criminal lawyers by taking on, and winning, such cases. Their clients could observe them shift responsibility during cross-examination from their own shoulders to those of alleged victims. As the following cases illustrate, defence lawyers conscripted social-purity-inspired definitions of chastity in the cause of defending male civil liberties.

T.C. Robinette was particularly skilled in this art although his ploys did not go unchallenged. Crown attorneys, judges, and, most notably, complainants themselves took issue with his deft attacks on women's sexual respectability. He very nearly met his match in Gertrude Kerr, a stenographer who alleged that William White had sexually assaulted her in his car. Robinette began by quizzing her about her intentions when she accepted a ride from the defendant after purchasing sheet music from him. Kerr testily responded that she had seen no reason to consider his offer as anything but a courtesy: 'Well, he had his car there and I did not think anything of it. I did not care about standing in the street doing business with him and I thought he was a perfect gentleman and I never dreamt anything would happen getting in.' White had other things in mind when she accepted. Instead of driving her to the music conservatory, as he had offered, he drove off to a northern section of the city where he proceeded to kiss and fondle her. Kerr told Robinette that she had not screamed because she thought 'the quietest way was the best way out.' Nor did she hit him: 'I was going to,' she recounted, 'but I thought I had better keep my hands off him; I was ascared.' Leaping out of the car was not a viable option either, because she did not know where she was. After a ten-minute struggle, he agreed to drive her back downtown.

Gertrude Kerr felt too 'frightened and excited' during the drive to stop White from assaulting her, but once she was on familiar ground she resolved to make him pay for his effrontery. As a country girl fresh from Collingwood, a small town north of Toronto, she had learned that the local justice of the peace was the authority to notify in case of crime, so she phoned the Toronto JP rather than the police. He advised her to call the Crown attorney, who accepted her testimony and advised the police to arrest White. Robinette argued that this unusual chain of events smacked of political interference, but he found it difficult to shake Kerr on cross-examination. He wondered, for example, why she had kept the sheet music White had sold her on the night of the alleged attack. The following sharp exchange occurred:

[Kerr]: [A]s I had laid a warrant against him I had to have something.
Robinette: You are pretty cute – that is a good answer. How do you know so much about these matters, laying warrants?
[Kerr]: If I went out in the car if I did not have the songs to show I had done business with Mr White, they would naturally think I went out for a good time.

Robinette was suspicious of a savvy working girl who was clearly far from a helpless maiden. For her part, Kerr astutely realized that a young woman who accepted a ride from a relative stranger could be branded as a 'good times' girl and therefore as an implausible victim. Robinette further berated her for phoning the JP instead of telling her mother about the incident, as any modest daughter would be expected to do. The Crown attorney intervened on Kerr's behalf, saying that at eighteen years old 'her judgement would not be mature.' Neither the crown nor the defence, then, quite knew how to accommodate a young woman's clearheaded attempt to see justice done within a narrative of sexual victimization.

Kerr's translation of country wisdom into city smarts reduced her credibility. 'You are pretty wise,' Robinette taunted. Fed up with his insinuations, Kerr shot back: 'You need to be in this city.' She believed that working girls in Toronto had to become 'wise,' since they lived in a city where businessmen apparently went about assaulting unsuspecting victims. For Kerr, pressing charges was, more than anything, a vindication of her character: 'I did not come here for notoriety but I do not want Mr White to go about saying to everybody he can do what he likes to me and get away with it.' The brand of justice Kerr sought was not served. 'White is just as innocent as you or I,' Robinette protested at the end of his bail hearing. The grand jury concurred by determining that there was no cause for the case to be tried.[47]

Robinette managed to confuse judges and juries alike about the admissibility of evidence concerning a victim's sexual history. Amendments to the Criminal Code in 1913 that introduced new offences against 'previously chaste' girls and women did not overturn existing sexual assault statutes, which required no test of complainants' chastity. The wily lawyer none the less manipulated people's confusion on this matter, and proceeded as if every complainant had to meet a legally prescribed examination of chastity. In many cases he successfully argued that men charged with having either consensual or non-consensual sex with minors could not be convicted because the young woman had been unchaste at the time of the incident.[48] In a case in which his client was charged with 'conspiracy to induce a woman to commit fornication,' Robinette argued that Robert Ewers should not be convicted on the word of Mary Allison, a seventeen-year-old servant of 'known immoral character.' An older woman, Laura Payne, had apparently arranged for Ewers to meet Allison at the Clyde Hotel in February 1910. Both adults were convicted; Payne was sentenced to two years at the Mercer and Ewers, initially, to Kingston for four years. Robinette first persuaded County Court Judge Winchester to reduce his client's sentence to two years at the Central Prison, and then set about, with the dominion minister of justice Allen Aylesworth's support, to clear Ewers's name. As it transpired, Payne and Ewers had arranged for a previous assignation that resulted in Allison's becoming pregnant. This evidence, Aylesworth wrote Winchester, 'would constitute her in February a girl of known immoral character.'[49] Judge Winchester replied that the indictment mentioned nothing about the chastity of the female, 'so that the question of moral or immoral character [did] not require consideration'; furthermore one 'case of immorality' did not render a woman of 'known immoral character.'[50] Although he refused to budge from this literal reading of the charge, he did reduce Ewers's sentence and recommended that he be paroled after serving only five months. Laura Payne and Mary Allison paid a stiffer price for the incident at the Clyde Hotel: Payne, not a wealthy client, served her full sentence, while Allison bore the stigma of the trial and the burden of single motherhood.

The Toronto Morality Department was often at odds with Robinette in its campaign against illicit sex. He apparently felt as strongly as C.S. Clark that the city's moral watchdogs snapped at innocent parties when they arrested men for what he argued to be consensual sexual encounters. The case of Marshall Ferris gave him a golden opportunity to take aim at the excesses of the moral reform movement in Toronto. In the process, Dorothy French became an unwitting pawn in the civil libertarian battle against the Morality Department.

A detective discovered that the seventeen-year-old had been having sex with a wealthy widower, fifty-two-year-old Marshall Ferris, in an office in the posh King Edward Hotel. The Morality Department threatened to arrest French as a vagrant and prostitute unless she testified against Ferris on the charge of 'permitting defilement of a girl under eighteen.' With prison as a frightening alternative, French told the court that she had met the older man while having tea at the hotel. She told Ferris that she had just moved from the country to Toronto to look for a position, and he replied that he would help her. They met at the tearoom several times, and she eventually agreed to have sex with him. Magistrate Stark wanted to know if she had ever before had sexual relations with a man; when she conceded that she had had connections with a boyfriend, he peppered her with questions: Who was it? Where did it occur? How many times? Was he the only one? Sobbing uncontrollably, French answered each of his questions and meekly added, 'It doesn't bear on this case.'

Robinette took up where the magistrate left off. In his attempt to brand French as an occasional prostitute he questioned her motives for taking tea alone in the hotel: 'We have nice places downtown to eat; the tea rooms are perfectly safe,' he teased the already cowed witness. By the time he extracted French's admission that she accepted a total of five dollars from Ferris, he had turned her into an occasional prostitute, more eager to accept a prone 'position' than a bona fide job. Crown Attorney Hughes interrupted several times to point out that Robinette was unjustly dragging out highly prejudicial evidence about French's chastity. The charge, he pointed out, applied simply to 'a girl under eighteen' and not to a 'previously chaste' woman. His final protest might have been raised at almost every sexual assault trial: 'We are trying the girl here instead of Ferris.'[51]

Had the Morality Department not intervened in Ferris's affair with Dorothy French, how might she have negotiated her way through this unequal relationship? Ferris was almost old enough to be her grandfather, and he was independently wealthy. French was a single woman in her late teens, newly arrived from the country and unemployed. He was a stranger in a big city who had listened to her problems and taken her to tea in one of the city's poshest hotels. How well had she known that her youth and sexual favours gave her power to bargain over the terms of the relationship? Evidently, she was no designing 'Sister Carrie': she had been cajoled into permitting the older man to gratify his lust for a mere five dollars. Her own account of the affair was a feeble attempt to stress her powerlessness: 'It was just merely conversation, just led from one thing to another ... until something happened.' When asked what that 'something' was, she sobbed, 'immorality.'[52] This was hardly the testimony of a hardhearted golddigger or a 'good times' girl of the social surveyors' rendering; rather, it reflected a working girl's capitulation to a narrative of occasional prostitution concocted by her moral overseers.

Marshall Ferris did not need to slip knockout drops into French's demitasse to achieve his purpose. Nor was he a seductive Chinaman bent on entrapping a white woman. Liaisons such as theirs were not the stuff of ballads or photoplays; instead, they showed that coercive and consensual encounters could both lead to trouble in a climate of urban moral reform. Working girls intent on sexual adventure bargained with little more than their youth and vivaciousness, and the craftiest women figured out how to make their charms pay. Unlucky ones, like Dorothy French, learned that the campaign against sexual immorality could erode their characters, even when they were not technically on trial.

SEXUAL FREEDOM AND THE RACE

Working girls who had abortions also fit uneasily into the victim paradigm. Although, as was the case in the late nineteenth century, abortionists were more likely than their clients to be tried and convicted, single women were tried informally for their sexual indiscretions and their threats to the race. By the turn of the century the Toronto Morality Department stepped up its efforts to stamp out all methods of contraception and birth control in the name of preserving the race rather than reducing the risk of unwanted pregnancy. Still, women (to say nothing of the entrepreneurs of birth control) had their own agendas. The stigma of single motherhood had not disappeared, and working girls were not paid enough to support a child; they continued to seek out contraceptives and, when other options failed, abortionists.[53]

In Canada, as in virtually every industrializing nation at the turn of the century, the sinking rate of fertility was perceived as a major threat to national interests: the annual number of live births per 1,000 adult Canadian women plummeted from 189 in 1871 to 94 by 1931. In Ontario the decline was even more precipitous: the rate sank from 191 to 79 over the same period.[54] Despite the drop in the birth rate, the population of the country doubled solely on account of immigration and the higher fertility rates of recent immigrants. Nativists brought these demographic trends to public light and openly accused native-born women of committing race suicide while foreigners and the feeble-minded overpopulated the nation's cities. Rising demands for the suppression of contraception and abortion were products of this wider effort to control fertility in the interest of the nation and the race.[55]

Birth control and abortion meant something quite different to working girls in trouble, however. For single women, motherhood was shameful no matter how they disposed of their children. If a working woman wished to avoid that fate, she might turn to her mother, her boyfriend, or female friends. Factory work and other occupations that brought working girls together also permitted contact with co-workers who could offer advice for those 'in trouble.'[56] Women used a variety of aids, from traditional home remedies to sophisticated medical techniques. Also available were commercial products, including pessaries, spermicidal agents, condoms, cervical caps, and abortifacient pills, typically advertised as 'rubber goods,' 'marital aids,' or 'female regulators.' As C.S. Clark alleged, Criminal Code restrictions against the advertisement and sale of contraceptive devices were easily and regularly violated: 'I saw a druggist's advertisement ... in a Toronto paper with this significant line: *Rubber Goods of ALL KINDS for Sale.* There is not a boy in Toronto, I dare say, who does not know what that means.'[57] The girls of Toronto apparently knew about such products as well. They were more likely, however, to seek out a drugstore on an anonymous street corner for abortifacient pills or, if those failed, to obtain a discreet reference to a doctor who might help them out. While some druggists made arrangements with doctors and abortionists who provided this service, more enterprising sorts performed the operation in their own quarters at the back of drug stores. Coroners' and criminal court records of these improvised solutions affirm that the possibility of failure and the spectre of death continued to undercut women's exercise of their sexual autonomy in spite of popular assumptions about working girls' untrammelled liberties.

Toronto offered women everything from an array of back-alley quacks to professionally trained doctors willing to perform abortions. In 1908 Judge Winchester, the same man who had acted as a commissioner in the inquiry into the Bell operators' strike, demanded that the Canadian Medical Association take action against their criminal brethren, who he believed performed at least one abortion per week in Toronto alone. A medical journal editor admitted that at least six doctors in the city regularly performed abortions, but that the profession did not have the power to prosecute them.[58] The tragedy, as Winchester saw it, was that the police were powerless until the illness or death of a woman led them to the door of an abortionist.[59]

As Toronto's anti-vice campaign took aim against illicit pleasures and non-procreative sex, the police stepped up their attempts to catch both successful and incompetent abortionists. While the police's vigilance undoubtedly sprang in part from a desire to ensure women's safety, most of the men and women prosecuted were professionally trained or medically expert practitioners whose records of service were generally good. In the 1910s juries and judges began to demonstrate greater willingness to convict abortionists who, in the nineteenth century, had frequently escaped penalty for their mistakes or demonstrated incompetence.[60] In addition, the War fanned the flames of anti-abortionist sentiment. Many Canadians asked themselves if abortionists should be allowed to help women sacrifice the next generation in their ignoble pursuit of pleasure when so many had died in a noble cause.

As methods of crime prevention and detection grew more sophisticated with the introduction of photography, fingerprinting, and undercover detection, the policing of abortion also became more refined.[61] No longer were coroner's inquests, deathbed statements, and tips from doctors the only routes for the apprehension of abortionists. In the 1910s the police formalized the older practice of doctor-snitching by monitoring suspicious hospital records. When a woman entered a hospital for treatment of abortion-related complications, her medical chart became police property. In practice, this elaborate system of abortion surveillance, like the police patrol of dancehalls, was highly discretionary and ultimately served more to expose women's profligacy than to root out incompetent abortionists.

In cases such as Annie Sweet's, the Morality Department was able to trace an abortionist through hospital records. Hers was a textbook case of a 'good times' girl gone wrong. She was an eighteen-year-old 'general office worker' whose furtive sexual encounters with a Mr Good in the Globe Theatre left her in trouble. Good offered to pay for abortifacients, and when they failed to work he gave her twenty dollars for an abortion. Hemorrhaging, a typical side effect of a sloppy operation, followed the procedure, and Sweet decided to seek help at the emergency department of the Toronto Western Hospital. Stamped on her hospital identification card was an instruction: 'N.B. Notify Staff Inspector's Office, City Hall, before this patient is discharged.' Her doctor's warning to keep silent prompted her to deny that she had had an abortion, but the medical evidence was conclusive. Threatened by the police with a charge of contempt of court, she eventually agreed to testify against her doctor. For all her pain and humiliation the court acquitted the abortionist but exposed her shame to the world.[62]

Evidence of the prosecution of abortionists rather than of women seeking abortions does not diminish the punitive effect of abortion trials on the women who testified. Skilful defence lawyers who borrowed their arguments from rape defences managed to shift suspicions of moral turpitude from abortionists to their clients. Although abortion patients were Crown witnesses and technically not on trial, they often ended up portrayed in court, much like rape complainants, as the real criminals.

In 1912 a high-profile case placed the word of a working girl against the reputation of two wealthy Jewish lads defended by Hartley Dewart, the man who later defended Carrie Davies. In this case he set out to raise doubts about the chastity of Maud McComb, a young working girl who claimed that she had been seduced by Julius Backrack, a twenty-year-old travelling salesman employed in his father's wholesale jobbing business. Backrack sent McComb to Ottawa for abortifacients, but, as was often the case, they failed to work. On returning to Toronto, the young man's older brother Emmanuel introduced McComb to another woman who had 'been through the same mill herself'; but, again, she was unable to help. After being refused by a doctor in Toronto,

McComb and the brothers decided to drive across the border where, four refusals later, they finally found a doctor in Rochester who would perform an abortion. Had McComb not become so ill as to require hospitalization, the trio's desperate measures would never have been exposed in court.

As was invariably the case in abortion trials, the Backracks' case revolved around the issue of McComb's character. Dewart managed to find several other men willing to testify that they had also had sex with McComb during the period in which she had seen Julius Backrack. Crown Attorney Greer objected to the use of evidence introduced to paint McComb as unchaste. In words reminiscent of the Crown counsel's objections to Robinette's grilling of Dorothy French, Greer complained, 'The girl's virtue is not in question at all before this Jury.' Dewart countered that if the Crown could enter evidence to establish that McComb's liaison with Backrack resulted in her pregnancy and subsequent abortion, the defence should surely have the right to show that a number of other men might have been responsible. Dewart wished to admit their testimony as evidence that she was 'a girl of loose or immoral character.' The other men's testimony should be admitted, he argued, 'as evidence of the girl's credibility.'[63] Judge Denton laboured over Dewart's argument, saying that he would normally admit such testimony in cases where it *was* 'necessary to show ... that the girl is of chaste character.'[64] In the end, Denton decided to admit testimony from McComb's alleged sexual partners, since, 'on her own evidence this girl's record [was] not too enviable.'

Widely held assumptions about sexually designing Jews outweighed suspicions that the victim in this case was far from innocent. Jewish business leaders evidently interpreted the Backrack trial as a stain on their community's reputation. After the young men were convicted, the case went to appeal along with the supportive signatures of thirty-five Jews – all men – including some of the city's wealthiest entrepreneurs.[65] In spite of their impressive array of defenders, the Backrack brothers lost their appeal. Their sentences – eighteen months for Julius at the Central Prison and three months for Emmanuel – were extraordinarily long in view of McComb's 'unenviable' reputation and the frequent acquittal of abortionists. The racial component of the case had been difficult for jurymen to ignore: here were two Jews who had helped an Anglo-Celtic woman to do away with her child. But McComb paid a price too: first by narrowly escaping death at the hands of a backroom abortionist, and second by enduring the public excoriation of her character in court. In the end, the trial condemned the supposed abortion victim for transgressing the norms of respectable femininity while it simultaneously upheld prohibitions against interethnic sexual contact.[66]

Cases where working girls died as a result of an abortion were predictably the most likely to incite condemnation. Not only was the life of a potential citizen cut short, but the woman herself did not survive to face the consequences of her shame, to testify against the abortionist or to redeem herself through marriage. The emotion such tragedies inspired was most intense if racially 'pure' Canadian girls died. Death, however, could absolve fallen women of their sins, as women who tried to expunge their shame by throwing themselves into the bay hoped. In such instances the hackneyed narratives of villains and wronged heroines could be redeployed even as they were given a modern slant. The villains by this point could be a smooth society man and a respected doctor, while the victim could be played by a new breed of working woman: the business girl.

Ruth Dembner was a beautiful young woman who came from an affluent, solidly Anglo-Celtic section of High Park. Twenty years earlier a daughter of wealthy parents would not have become a working girl, but by the mid-1920s it had become common for single women of every class but the proto-aristocracy to work for wages. Many who attended university went on to careers in social service, business, law, or medicine but the twenty-two year-old Dembner pursued a less stellar course and became a private secretary to an insurance company manager. Still, her salary of thirty dollars per week was almost twice as high as the average female wage-earner's at the time.[67] Dembner's prospects for a continued life of comfort seemed rosy; she was engaged to marry the dashing young Bartlett Brooks, a junior executive working his way up through his father's business. The young couple seemed to dwell more on the pleasures of the day than on the responsibilities of tomorrow, however; they led a fast-paced life of amusement, to the Dembner family's consternation. As her father later reflected, 'she was practically independent in her conduct ... She generally did as she liked and she was fond of entertainment, motoring, dancing and so on.'[68]

These words, of course, were spoken in the aftermath of Dembner's tragic death as the result of a sloppy abortion. In its coverage of the subsequent trial of her fiancé and Dr O.C.J. Withrow, the abortionist, the *Globe* recounted Dembner's history of indulging in fast times. Her parents had noticed that she seemed run-down, and had sent her to the family doctor for a checkup. His diagnosis was that the business girl had been 'burning her candle at both ends' and was consequently risking her health. Warned that she might require 'an operation,' she toned down her nightlife for a while, only to 'resume her round of gaiety.' The doctor had been most critical of Dembner's having shown 'pluck in working during her period of delicate health,' and spoke reprovingly of her future role as a wife and mother. Heedless of these dangers, the lively business girl continued her life of frivolity.[69]

In consequence of her pursuit of pleasure, Dembner became pregnant. Since Brooks was not yet of age, the couple apparently decided that an abortion would spare them and their families a great deal of embarrassment. Of utmost importance, then, was a competent doctor who would act discreetly. Unlike most working girls, for whom price might have been a greater concern, Dembner, funded by her lover, enjoyed the luxury of shopping around for the best surgeon. As Dembner later recounted in the hours before her death, she went to see Dr Withrow in January 1927 without telling her parents about her predicament. He agreed to perform an abortion at the Strathcona Hospital for seventy-five dollars. After the operation he sent her, ill and vomiting, to recover at the Muskoka Sanitorium north of Toronto in the company of a nurse. Her fever rose, and she collapsed in agony as she disembarked from the train. Harrowing images of the beautiful young woman, dying in the snow, cut off from her family, and dispatched to her death by an abortionist, filled front-page accounts of the case. Her statement led the police to Withrow and Brooks, both of whom were charged with manslaughter after she died of peritonitis on 19 February.

The police stumbled upon a case that allowed the state to prosecute an abortionist and his accomplice and strike a blow to the birth control movement in the province at the same time. The arrest of Withrow was a major coup because he was the president of the Ontario Birth Control League, which he had formed after attending the Sixth International Malthusian League Conference in 1925.[70] Like many eugenicists, he supported rational population-planning for all social groups, but was most concerned about the overpopulation of the feeble-minded. As a gynecologist, he was well situated not only to dispense advice but to offer devices and services to women who wanted to prevent or terminate pregnancy. And, as the Dembner case revealed, he could be persuaded to provide abortions for the 'fit' as well as the 'subnormal.'

Even before the investigation into Ruth Dembner's death, Withrow's practice had raised suspicions among medical personnel that he performed abortions disguised as dilation and curettage operations.[71] Nurse Ethridge of the Cottage Hospital in downtown Toronto testified at his trial that Withrow had stopped practising there 'on account of the nature of the cases he used to bring in. So many D and C and appendix cases that the Hospital became suspicious of the real cause.'[72] Withrow had been denied surgery privileges at the Toronto Western Hospital, and so, by 1927, he performed D and Cs exclusively at the Strathcona Hospital, another private institution located not far from Dembner's home.[73] This testimony, combined with damning physical evidence from the autopsy, secured Withrow's conviction for manslaughter.

Had Dembner lived, she might have been subjected to the humiliation of an examination into her sexual indiscretions; as a dead victim, her innocence was restored, cleansed, in a quintessentially Canadian manner, by her suffering in the snows of Muskoka. In contrast, the men who survived her were painted by the Crown and the press as unmanly scoundrels. The headline in the *Star* on the final day of the coroner's inquest read: 'Jury Brands Brooks as Cold-Blooded and Inhuman in their Verdict.' The coroner interpreted Dembner's death as a tragedy of male irresponsibility and female vulnerability: 'The whole story is sordid. A young girl, 22 years of age, whose life in some way has been sacrificed. Can you conscientiously and honestly say that anybody is at fault? Should this life have been sacrificed if she had been properly advised and properly taken care of, and probably not interfered with?'[74] Justice Logie, in sentencing Brooks, castigated the young man for abandoning his fiancée and directing her into the hands of an abortionist rather than a minister: 'To put the blame on the girl was a cowardly defence,' he upbraided Brooks. Moreover, the judge reversed the usual practice in sexual assault trials of castigating women's characters and exonerating men's. He contrasted the 'dainty, well-brought up girl' to the irresponsible seducer: 'I believe that she was a good and innocent girl and that you ruined her and led her to make desperate efforts to avoid the results of indiscretion.'[75] In condemning Brooks and depicting Dembner as a victim of male villainy, Justice Logie reassured Torontonians that working daughters of the 'best families' ought not to be confused with the Maud McCombs of the working class. Rewriting the script of Dembner's pleasure-driven life, he declared that respectable young women could be counted on to relinquish their work and pleasure for domesticity as long as they were not 'interfered with.'[76]

As the man who had performed the operation and dispatched the dainty Dembner to her death, Withrow received sterner condemnation than young Brooks. The aging, arthritic doctor was sentenced to seven years at the Kingston Penitentiary, not for Dembner's death alone but for his well-documented and extensive abortion practice. Justice Logie stated in his sentencing remarks that 'every one of the 'D. and C.' operations performed by Dr Withrow was an abortion.' A stiff sentence would be a lesson to all doctors who covertly provided abortion services to their patients: 'The crime of abortion is all too common,' Logie proclaimed to justify the exemplary intent of the seven-year sentence.

Withrow's well-placed associates in the Birth Control League and the eugenics movement none the less viewed the doctor as a martyr to the cause of race betterment and rallied to his aid. Dr Clarence Hinks, President of the Canadian National Committee for Mental Hygiene and a former colleague of Withrow's from the Social Services Clinic, petitioned Attorney General William Price for clemency. Price, who had spearheaded the campaign against Withrow, was unwilling to pardon the doctor who had heartlessly sent an ill patient to her death to cover his crime.[77] Not until three years later, after persistent calls for Withrow's release on account of his physical deterioration, did the ministry retreat from its uncompromising stance against the abortionist and grant him his freedom.[78] Again, in spite of both the abortionist's and the fiancé's misfortunes, it was the young woman who payed the highest price.

PLEASURE AND REGRET

Had Ruth Dembner lived, she might have told a different version of her story, for women did not need to be 'interfered with' to decide to have an abortion. Nor did their reasons for pursuing that option have anything to do with a design to commit race suicide; rather, single women followed personal agendas unrelated to the tenets of the social hygiene movement. Judgmental parents or reluctant fathers could influence pregnant women's decisions, but women themselves ultimately wielded the power to choose whether to attempt the termination of their pregnancy.

Court evidence and coroner's records expose not only the nature of abortion and its regulation but also the contentiousness of heterosexual negotiations about women's sexual autonomy and men's sexual responsibility. One of the most common considerations on which women based their decision to abort was the reluctance of their sexual partners to accept their roles as fathers. Unsuccessful abortions or regrets after the termination of pregnancies could move single women to charge their welshing partners with abortion. In this type of abortion case, the trials of men accused of assisting in or counselling their girlfriends to have abortions show how bitter single working women could capitalize on the state's crackdown against abortion for their own ends.

Working girls who reluctantly delivered babies after unsuccessful abortions faced the shame of giving birth without the sanctity of marriage and the respectability of a husband. Although both sexual partners often agreed that the termination of pregnancy would be the best choice, failed attempts weighed more heavily on the woman. Added to the physical dangers of abortifacients, sepsis, and, ultimately, childbirth was the incalculable cost to the woman's reputation. Men faced no such burdens, to the consternation of their estranged lovers.

One disgruntled woman, seventeen-year-old Mary Jane McNally, complained to the police about her married lover's assistance in her abortion only after they broke up. Since her lover, William Bustard, was a police constable, she decided she would retaliate by informing Bustard's superior officer of his criminal actions. At Bustard's trial, 'Blackie' Johnston, the man who had defended Clara Ford, suggested that the McNally family had fabricated the charge because they were upset at her going out with men. 'No, I never went with men,' she saucily replied: 'I went out with one; that was plenty.' He persisted in accusing her of being a prostitute, since Bustard had occasionally given her money. 'I never asked for it,' was her matter-of-fact response. Her flippancy, fatal in rape victims' self-presentation, failed to deter the court from convicting Constable Bustard of attempting to commit an abortion. If, in the era of urban moral reform, the police were expected to be credible enforcers of propriety, the force could hardly afford to have an amateur abortionist on staff.[79]

For women left with unwanted babies, avowals of love mattered little unless their partners were willing to marry and support them. Vengeful women could turn to the courts for redress even if their partners had attempted to conduct themselves honourably. Through no fault of his own, William Brechin was forced to abandon his sweetheart, Marie Goodchild, when he was conscripted into the Canadian Expeditionary Force in 1917. He wrote to Goodchild, promising to see her on his last leave before going overseas: 'I will not leave you in the lurch so don't worry about my leaving you in the hole.' Apparently Goodchild was worried because their initial attempts at inducing a miscarriage with abortifacients had failed. 'How did those p— work,' he demurely inquired. 'Are you feeling alright now. Write at once dearie it is nice to know one girl cares for you.' Because Canada was at war, Brechin's letters from boot camp were intercepted as part of a routine security measure, and his abortion scheme was discovered. The CEF discharged

Brechin, and Goodchild charged him with supplying abortifacients, including pennyroyal, cotton root, and tansy pills.

In a rare glimpse at a man's resentment over his girlfriend's charges of seduction, Brechin wrote to remind Goodchild that she had been a willing participant in what he had regarded as loving encounters: 'I was kind of mad at you Sunday night you keep trying to rub it into me that I'm a scamp and am totally to blame for your wildness. Now I have heard it pretty straight that you were not green to things absolutely when you met me. I am sorry that we carried on as we did but really we did have some lovely times together I look back on them with a feeling of both pleasure and regret Still what has been can't be helped now I always had and still have a big cozy feeling in my heart for you.' For all his fondness, Brechin was likelier than his unmarried pregnant sweetheart to recall his sexual encounters with pleasure. His 'cozy feeling' undoubtedly changed when he found himself before the court. Already discharged by the CEF, he did not stand much chance of impressing the jury. Goodchild failed to secure a husband and provider by laying her complaint, but she did gain the satisfaction of seeing him sentenced to three months at the Guelph Reformatory for Men.[80]

The campaign to bring about a City upon a Hill created new victims and villains in the drama of urban life. Most important, attempts to introduce stricter morals regulation meant that the police were less tolerant of men who seemed, as prostitution clients, rapists, or abortionists, to pose a moral danger. As the disposition of criminal trials showed, however, the courts were willing to convict only when men appeared to represent a moral danger to the wider community: frequenters of brothels created the demand for the social evil; foreign rapists stood for the threat to Anglo-Celtic purity; abortionists threatened the viability of the race. Working girls were only incidental beneficiaries of the moral reform agenda in the early twentieth century. When these modern contests over immorality pitted women against men who enjoyed claims to respectability, working girls rarely escaped with their characters intact, even when men were on trial. The increasing regulation of public amusement sites, such as dancehalls and parks, failed to protect working girls from sexual danger and left them more vulnerable to charges of sexual delinquency. At the same time, prostitutes continued to face a greater burden than their clients as the city tried to sweep away organized prostitution. 'Heaven' may have protected some working girls from peril, but most enjoyed no greater safety in Toronto the Good.

7

Citizens, Workers, and Mothers of the Race

The working girl of the early-twentieth century was hard to miss. She was still closeted behind the walls of impressive homes and stuck behind power sewing machines in the city's garment factories, but she was also the person who gathered moviegoers' tickets, answered the phone in law offices, and served up luncheon specials in restaurants. Tens of thousands of young single women took up jobs as stenographers, typists, clerks, and bookkeepers as the city became a centre of commerce and communications. For young women hoping to find well-paying jobs, knowing the ropes of the business world helped a great deal. As one commerce school gushed to potential female students: 'In business, the possibilities are unlimited.'[1] From the Art Deco façade of Eaton's College Street store to the towering headquarters of the Canadian Imperial Bank of Commerce, retail and office buildings literally and figuratively overshadowed Toronto's factories as the largest employers of women by the 1920s. As the city began to flaunt the trappings of a metropolis, the women who strode into work in trim suits and high heels took on a new air of sophistication as well.

The rise of this new breed of working girl – the businesswoman – did not, however, convince contemporaries that the girl problem had disappeared. Who could say whether the confidently striding business woman might not kick up her heels after work to jazz music at a dance club? What were the chances that she might switch to sensible shoes and decide to make a career of her work rather than marriage? Ironically, as the female workforce expanded and a growing proportion of working girls held jobs that no longer spelled poverty, efforts to manage the girl problem increased. The post-War era was a reactionary period dominated by a desire to return to 'normalcy,' an idyllic state in which individuals would assume their appointed roles. For working girls who had become a vital source of cheap labour, their mission was to work while they were single (in sectors that men had either abandoned or rejected), and then leave the paid workforce to marry and raise children.

By the 1920s, working for pay for at least several years was something that virtually all women shared, although their experiences as wage-earning women could vary dramatically. The fifteen-year-old paper box maker who lived with her family in Cabbagetown and the twenty-five-year-old private secretary who shared a flat with a fellow businesswoman in Rosedale might have taken the same streetcar to work, but the destinations they reached and the pay packets they received set them apart. For decades middle-class observers had worried that the daughters of the poor drifted into prostitution or became the prey of white slavers; now, when they pondered the fate of the working girl, they were talking about their own daughters too.

The changing class composition of the female workforce and the rise of the businesswoman inspired new solutions for the girl problem, responses that were considered appropriate for middle-class, well-educated young women. A host of new female professionals, including social workers, girls' club organizers, boarding-house mistresses, YWCA secretaries, and educators, were paid to come up with advice and programs to smooth the way for Toronto's unmarried, wage-earning women. Despite the presumed respectability of this new audience of working women, the schemes they implemented, from recreation to subsidized housing projects, borrowed heavily from strategies originally devised to deal with sexual delinquents and female lawbreakers. Advice literature for business women, for instance, set out the same guidelines for behaviour that had first been dictated for inefficient workers and incarcerated women. Like parolees, working women who had never run afoul of the law were now admonished to be dutiful, efficient workers and to prepare themselves for respectable marriages. Not surprisingly, the translation of advice across the divide of class and respectability altered the script: advisers believed that businesswomen, unlike working-class delinquents, were capable of mastering the art of self-management. While the range of non-coercive responses to the girl problem multiplied, however, the assumption remained that working women of all classes were ephemeral workers who would eventually fulfil a higher destiny. Even the Minimum Wage Act for women, passed in 1920, was promoted not to ensure working girls' right to a living wage but to steer them towards 'the proper conduct of life.'

Working girls of all sorts eagerly availed themselves of the benefits offered them, whether it meant sitting down to tea and biscuits in a company restroom or going for a swim at the Y. What they derived from sex hygiene lectures or films about inefficient workers is more difficult to assess. Partaking in programs provided by employers or educators certainly failed to suppress every woman's taste for the spicier pleasures of the city, as worn-out working girls admitted. Similarly, young women did not passively accept the uplifting advice of professionals who lectured them on the technique of living or the noble purpose of sexuality. As the scribblings of boarding-house clients and the 'confessions' of businesswomen suggest, working girls imbibed the advice that seemed to help them through their working lives, but they also came up with their own compromises between pleasure and responsibility.

HOMES FOR WORKING GIRLS

Young women could not be convinced that they would be better off working in homes as domestic servants, but they were easily convinced of the advantages of living in homes for working girls. In addition to Toronto's YWCA houses (which numbered five by the 1910s), the city offered over thirteen supervised and subsidized homes for single wage-earning women and provided room registries to match respectable women and respectable boarding-homes. In part, these efforts were intended to meet Toronto's housing crisis; more important, as housing literature proclaimed, they aimed to ensure that working girls would be given every opportunity to live respectably, neither working too hard nor playing too carelessly.

Most supervised boarding-homes were operated by philanthropic clubwomen or women who worked through Protestant and Catholic Churches. Georgina House (GH), an Anglican home opened in 1909, was founded by Georgina Broughall, who proclaimed that her scheme would 'meet in some measure the much talked about "Boarding House Problem."'[1] For five dollars per week, GH residents could find 'a real home, with refined surroundings, good food and all that makes for that end.'[2] As in most homes, women were offered private bedrooms and rooms shared with one other woman, while transients were more likely to sleep in dormitory facilities.

The largest single boarding facility for single working women was the non-denominational Sherbourne House, built by the Simpson's department store magnate H.H. Fudger in 1917 at a cost of half a million dollars. Intended for the 'feminine staff' of Simpson's and other businesswomen, it provided 150 bedrooms in a four-story building behind a mansion that was converted into a clubhouse. Together with the YWCA houses, these institutions and others like them aimed not only to house working women but to 'promote the best type of womanhood.'[3]

Boarding-houses were designed to meet the needs of both capital and working girls. Mindful of their corporate sponsors' investment in an efficient female workforce, boarding-house operators supervised residents with an eye towards conserving their energy for their work duties. Miss Bollert, the professionally trained supervisor of Sherbourne House, explained her challenge: 'Seventy-two per cent of the business girl's life is spent in "home life" and on this depends her health and fitness for business.' Provided with housekeeping services, prepared meals, and laundry facilities, the business girl was more likely to arrive at work tidy, refreshed, and well nourished. Many of the Bell commissioners' concerns about working women's use of leisure time were addressed by boarding-houses. Club facilities, including reading rooms, gymnasia, tennis courts, and ice rinks, in the case of Sherbourne House, were provided to encourage working women to spend their spare time in recreation instead of 'walk[ing] the streets or go[ing] to the picture shows.' Exercise was not so much invigorating as a means to restore energy drained in dull days on the factory line or at the typewriter. Both sports teams and club activities were accordingly promoted as beneficial to both working women and their employers. Supervised boarding-houses, in Bollert's words, kept women 'good,' not in 'a moral sense alone, but ... efficient so that they may go forth with health of body and spirit to do good useful work.'[4]

Fostering ideals of citizenship, particularly after women were granted the vote in 1918, also became a boarding-home priority. The working women's club, an idea promoted by Marjory MacMurchy in her contribution to the report of the Unemployment Commission, was considered a great boon in this regard. Although all boarding-homes governed residents' freedoms and responsibilities, they also provided meeting-spaces for clubs where working women governed themselves. 'Knowing that "all work and no play makes Jack a dull boy,"' the staff at Georgina House established a 'Business Women's Club' in 1910 to fortify residents 'physically, mentally, morally and spiritually for the great battle of life.' At YWCA houses, both residents and outside members enjoyed the facilities. Sherbourne House sponsored 'dramatic, reading and glee clubs' and offered its meeting-rooms for the Imperial Order Daughters of the Empire (IODE) and the TLCW, among other groups. Unlike the other boarding-homes, however, Sherbourne House was also managed by the residents, who were responsible for making and enforcing 'only those [rules] necessary to the well-being of group life.' Miss Bollert remained the superintendent, but she relied upon the residents to formulate regulations that maximized each resident's comfort and liberty without sacrificing either the rights of other residents or 'the reputation of the house.'[5] The women who served in the various offices of Sherbourne House's 'Self-government Committee' learned practical lessons of citizenship and community leadership.

To the leaders of the boarding-house movement, good citizenship and good business were complimentary products of supervised homes. Boarding-home operators hoped that the 'refined atmosphere of a happy home' would steer their residents towards civic service. Lectures on such topics as 'The Penny Bank,' 'Responsibility and Influence,' and 'Hygiene' were held regularly at women's boarding-homes. Observers praised supervised homes for treating wage-earning women 'as human beings and not as mere working machines.' The *Globe* declared that Canadians had for too long taken the working girl's contributions for granted: 'It would seem to be but our duty, from an economic as well as a humanitarian stand-point, to see that she lives under conditions which tend to make her efficient, as well as a worthy citizen. It is not too much to say that the future of the country lies in the hands of these girls.'[6]

In spite of the lofty ideals of supervised homes, single women did not sign on as residents with lessons in efficiency or citizenship in mind. Working women looked to boarding-homes for security, convenience, comfort, and companionship. A daily breakfast and dinner ensured that residents could be relatively well nourished, even if they skipped lunch, like Videre, to buy a piece of finery. Facilities as basic as laundry basins were often absent in private rooms, but in subsidized homes women could enjoy the use of a full range of amenities for everything from personal hygiene to skills upgrading. Boarding-house women were also less likely to suffer the loneliness and isolation endured by many women who lived in rooming-houses. With scores of other young, single women about, often engaged in similar employments or studies, residents could gain a sense of camaraderie. Regular socials, dress-up parties, and seasonal bashes added variety to the monotony of women's workaday lives. Young women who appreciated and responded to the boarding-house regime found a home life as happy as or happier than their own families could offer.

The keys to happiness in a supervised house were peer cooperation and a willingness to heed rules. All houses had provisions for the expulsion of recalcitrant residents who challenged or defied regulations. At Georgina House, one of the most straitlaced homes, residents were required to make their own beds and keep their rooms tidy, return home by 10:30 p.m. (and remain silent thereafter), attend daily prayer, request the superintendent's permission to entertain guests, and refrain from talking to friends at the front gate. The management justified GH rules as 'only such as prevail in any refined Christian family.' In some cases, fines were imposed for infractions, and repeated flouting of house rules resulted in expulsion. In 1922, for instance, one of the YWCA homes instituted a new system of late fines which restricted women to a maximum of two late passes per week. 'At first the feeling was one of complaint,' the Home Department of the Y heard, 'but gradually the girls are expressing their approval.'[7] Not even at Sherbourne House were women allowed to come and go as they pleased, despite the fact that many were over thirty. No matter how democratically framed, boarding houses replicated a quasi-familial brand of control over residents.

It would be incorrect to assume, however, that women who were economically independent simply acquiesced to boarding-house regulations. Some voted with their feet and sought alternative forms of accommodation. Six women reportedly left Georgina House in its first year to board 'where they [could] keep later hours.'[8] The demand for subsidized boarding spots in Toronto nevertheless persistently outstripped the number of rooms available. In its first eight months of operation, Sherbourne House had to turn down more than three thousand applicants.[9] The accommodation shortage became even more acute over the following decade, in part because residents who entered as teenagers often remained into their late twenties. In Georgina House, where limits on the duration of boarders' tenure were lax, women stayed for a decade or more. The YWCA imposed a limit of two years because it felt obligated to meet the demand for housing from the steady stream of new arrivals to the city. Working women clearly made boarding-houses their homes, not just a way station. Long-term living arrangements demanded compromise on the part of management, particularly in the matter of women's pleasures.

The vexed questions of male visitors and mixed dancing frequently exposed differences between fun-minded women and boarding-house supervisors concerned about the reputation of their houses. Managers were loath to provide resorts for 'good times' girls; after all, their homes were there to provide 'healthful, happy and high principled alternatives' to dubious forms of amusement.[10] Residents who cared less for boarding-house ideals than heterosexual romance none the less persisted in pushing the boundaries of acceptable pleasures. The YWCA, for instance, had long frowned upon the presence of men in boarding-houses. On rare occasions, such as Christmas celebrations, escorts were allowed to accompany boarders as long as both parties adhered to chaperons' standards of decorum. At the turn of the century management began to allow women-only dances, but it was not until the 1920s that the YWCA finally relented and sponsored mixed dances.

This hotly debated issue was referred to the executive board at the request of women at the West Toronto Y. On the advice of its 'special committee re dancing,' the Y executive offered its tentative acceptance, with the proviso that it did 'not approve of promoting dancing.' Only as an aspect of recreation did the committee feel that dancing would be permitted, as long as it did not interfere with the regular activities. To reassure those who feared that the Y had abdicated its supervisory role, the committee established strict limits over the frequency and form such dances would take. 'Mixed parties' offering 'social dancing' were permitted, provided that the house secretary and another secretary or board member was there to supervise.[11] In other words, YWCA homes were not about to become dancehalls where working girls could pick up strange men. Still, the decision was a victory for boarders who successfully exerted pressure on the Y executive.

No matter how many prayer sessions or improving lectures on penny banks boarders attended, they seemed far more interested in men. In boarding-house scrapbooks, residents dwelled on the triumphs and tragedies of romance, displaying self-mockery over their frantic attempts to win beaux. In the close quarters of boarding-houses it was futile for a woman to hide a budding love affair from her housemates. Lingering on the street and waiting for a goodnight kiss left a resident vulnerable to a writeup in the Georgina House 'Girls' Club Journal': 'Wouldn't it be nice if we all had an extra nickel in order to park outside a half hour longer as Miss Leaham did the other night.' Such tongue-in-cheek reports were published to amuse boarders and to keep everyone in the house apprised of the progress of romantic unions. Apparently, in the 'cozy niches' of Georgina House, 'many a lover's tale' were whispered. As one gossip columnist bubbled in 1921: 'Many of us wonder how many more "showers" will be given during the year 1922? We predict several!' Jokes constantly referred to the boarders' keenness to become engaged. Perhaps to console herself that she had not been one of the lucky ones, one boarder quipped: 'With all the diamonds flashing around on left hands, I should be getting a new room soon!'[12]

If any of the residents who swooned over 'strong, husky men' were ever sexually assaulted by them or left pregnant out of wedlock, house journals and management reports provide no clues. Boarders discussed heterosexual contact as a burning desire, not a potential tragedy. Aside from a cryptic YWCA report about a young woman who had 'been unfortunate as the result of a motor ride,' the potential perils of hetero-sexual pleasures were never mentioned.[13] In fact, women were more often portrayed as sexual aggressors in love games. A woman who admitted to being 'crazy about men' wrote to the Georgina House journal advice columnist 'Annie Laurie' to ask how a woman could vamp a man: 'To vamp a man, roll your eyes, and smile sweetly.'[14] Not long before, C.S. Clark and the social surveyors had regarded this sort of behaviour as a technique of freelance prostitution; now, on the pages of an Anglican boarders' journal, picking up men had become a topic for good-natured ribbing.

Eminently respectable residents used the GH journal to fantasize about leading racier lives than their well-monitored boarding-houses allowed for. 'Miss Rita Cowle' was written up after she spent an even-ing at the fashionable King Edward Hotel: 'We wonder if she carried a flask in her jazz garter as we hear many of the girls are dancing now.'[15] 'Vamps' and 'flappers' would never have made it through the door of a supervised boarding-home, nor would they likely have been interested in houses that imposed curfews and restraints on residents' freedoms. Residents' respectability, confirmed both by the boarding-house regime and the character references they were required to provide, allowed them the security to explore fast living in the pages of their journals rather than on city streets.

The physical security and peer surveillance that characterized board-ing-house life also gave women the comfort to mock female fears of sexual danger. In their romanticized world of heterosexual passions, women were willing, even desperate, participants in physical intimacy. Riding alone in a car with a young man meant thrills, not 'unfortunate experiences' as a joke in the GH journal suggested: 'One Girl: Do you ever get pinched when you are driving fast? Another: No, but I often get squeezed when we're driving slow.'[16] The distinction a woman might make between a pinch and a squeeze could spell the difference between a sexual assault complaint and a 'lover's tale.' The playful expression of heterosexual desire in these journals suggests that wage-earning women who were considered perfectly respectable could, by the 1920s, openly express a taste for good times without risking their reputations.

Sherbourne House had from its inception offered residents a greater degree of freedom than had boarding-houses with a religious mission. The rules, rooted neither in Protestant philanthropy nor in executive control, were more liberal in regard to boarders' freedom to indulge in pleasures that brought men and women together. The standard time for women to return to the house was 10:30 p.m., but residents could stay out as long as they wished provided that they signed up the night before. A 1926 party announcement, issued in the same year that the Y grudgingly debated mixed dancing, expressed the superintendent's enthusiastic acceptance of male guests: 'There will be Dancing in the Dining Room, Cards in the Sun Room and Games in the Drawing Room ... Everybody may invite *one man*! Please do not ask any girls.' The transition to mixed socializing under the auspices of a boarding-home was not as jarring as it had been at YWCA houses, however. From its inauguration, Sherbourne House's superintendent had stressed that 'callers, both men and women, will always be cordially welcome in the evenings in the club parlours and lounge rooms.'[17]

Inviting respectable men for supervised socials was one way that supervisors tried to encourage respectable unions between men and women. As Carroll Smith-Rosenberg and others have argued for the United States, psychiatrists and other health care professionals pathologized independent working women by the 1920s, particularly those who lived, studied, and worked in female institutions, because they seemed unwilling or unable to forge heterosexual bonds.[18] The 'cozy niches' where some residents traded stories of antics with their boyfriends probably also allowed other women to exchange intimacies of their own. Boarders formed intense and enduring unions after years or even decades of cohabitation; whether or not they included sexual love, their partnerships certainly obviated marriage and motherhood. A poem reprinted in the Georgina House 'Girls' Club Journal' suggests that some of the residents questioned their fellow boarders' enthusiasm for marriage:

Love's Warning

Oh, girls, before you risk a kiss,
and hitch up for your lives,
Recall if singleness is bliss,
'Tis folly to be *wives!*[19]

There is no explicit mention of lesbianism in Toronto boarding-house records, but the relaxing of policies towards heterosexual socializing in the mid-1920s may well have been aimed at aloof women who failed to show sufficient interest in men. Pictures from the annual Hallowe'en dress-up ball at Sherbourne House show that women masqueraded both as flappers and as mannish lesbians. Residents satirized themselves as transitional figures between old-fashioned Victorian women and independent New Women, but most chose characters that conveyed their distinctly modern identities and, perhaps, their ambivalent sexual tastes. Of the 121 women pictured in the 1925 Hallowe'en photograph, 16 were dressed as men. Women often competed as couples who posed with the 'wife' demurely at her 'husband's' side.[20] The prize-winners that year were two women who posed in vampish attire and two who dressed as men – one a Charlie Chaplin lookalike and the other a sporty society type. In the carnival atmosphere of Hallowe'en, their intimate poses and costumes simultaneously subverted heterosexual norms while reinforcing the normality of affection between women and men, or at least those who could pass as men.[21]

By 1927 men were invited to the Sherbourne House Hallowe'en ball, yet residents continued to appear as mock couples alongside heterosexual couples. Party announcements issued at the end of the decade invited every woman to bring a 'boyfriend' for the usual round of dancing, cards, and games.[22] If the superintendent cheerily tried to steer boarders towards 'normal' interests, Hallowe'en provided at least one remaining opportunity for those who rejected normality to challenge gender conventions and invert the imagery of heterosexual romance.

Although thousands of young women passed through the doors of YWCA homes, Georgina House, and Sherbourne House, the majority of Toronto's single female workforce either chose or were forced to find alternative accommodations. Monitors of young women's housing consistently estimated that from 20 to 30 per cent of working girls (totalling almost 20,000 women by the mid 1920s) lived apart from their families.[23]

To assist single women seeking 'suitable and congenial homes,' the TLCW and the YWCA sponsored two programs. The Aberdeen Club, a brainchild of the TLCW, was a housing complex for working women, leased in 1914 from the Toronto Housing Company and funded through rental payments and bequests from philanthropists. The TLCW noted the 'very great' demand of 'business women for small apartments,' and pointed out that over the duration of its five-year lease the club had been continuously occupied. Mounting expenses prompted an end to the project in 1919, but the ladies felt that the scheme had proved that business-women and girls could conduct their financial affairs responsibly. By offering tenants lessons in budgeting, they felt they had provided lessons in citizenship and 'given a definite practical service to the community.'[24]

The YWCA room-registry system proved to be a more enduring success. Like the Aberdeen Club, it was launched so that single women who came to the city to look for work would find respectable housing. Registry volunteers visited advertised rooming-houses to determine their 'class,' and referred applicants to suitable quarters. In January 1920, two months after its inauguration, 74 houses had been visited, 45 landladies registered, and 64 of 117 applicants placed. The registry had come to rival the newspapers after only one year in operation as working women's chief source of housing information. It also meant that landladies did not have to advertise with a card and thus announce the transient status of their residents. The net effect of this scheme, the YWCA hoped, was to be a kind of eugenics of housing: 'better class applicants,' placed in 'more desirable houses,' would ultimately foster a higher grade of community life.[25]

The registry was one of several programs launched in the 1910s and 1920s to monitor wage-earning women's home lives in a rational, systematic manner. Torontonians were no longer prepared to leave the home environment of working girls and business women to fate. Attempting to mould efficient workers and responsible citizens made organizers feel that they were making a great contribution to the economy and the nation; clients cooperated only to the extent that they benefited from the material and social benefits of living with their fellow wage-earning women.

KEEPING LIFE NORMAL

If a captive audience of boarding-house residents was not easy to reach with messages of community service and efficiency, the floating population of women wage-earners presented an even greater challenge. In searching for new ways to manage the girl problem, philanthropists and professionals seized upon the idea of recreation, a mainstay of YWCA programs for years and a centrepiece of Progressive penology. As the social surveyors had urged, young women could be weaned from good times only if more wholesome amusements were available. Similarly, penologists used recreation to channel deviant impulses into productive, non-delinquent pursuits. The idea of recreation for working girls was not new; however, it was invested with new meanings. Above all, healthy amusements were promoted as a means to shape young women into productive workers who would also be fit to take on the physical and moral burdens of marriage and motherhood.

The YWCA, like many other Protestant evangelical organizations, began to relax its stiff stance towards amusement in the 1910s. Encouraging young people to play, Christian reformers argued, was an effective way to get them to pray. Sects as dour as the Presbyterians and the Methodists began to sponsor picnics, socials, and even movie nights that were intended to compete directly with the ever more numerous commercial amusements of the city. As more university-trained social workers headed programs in Christian service organizations, they blended the secular tenets of the recreation movement with the more traditional aims of instilling spiritual values. In a post-war brochure on the national work of the Dominion YWCA, the organizations' aims for 'the girls in industry' were summarized as 'recreation-education-self-expression-service and citizenship.'[26] Recreation was no longer a frivolous pasttime of good-time girls or society women, but an essential element in working girls' welfare: 'All girls need fun,' the brochure trumpeted. Recreation had become nothing less that a tonic prescribed to 'keep life normal.'[27]

Just as boarding-house residents had their own reasons for wanting to live in a supervised home, so the city's working girls happily took advantage of the free or inexpensive recreational facilities provided by the Y and, in the case of companies like Eaton's, their employers. Swimming and indoor sports seem to have been extremely popular. The YWCA general secretary's report for March 1922 indicated that of 3,060 women who had visited the Elm Street Y, 867 had used the swimming-pool and 752 had made use of the gym. An additional 544 women attended club meetings in the building.[28] Their use of the facilities was organized by trained physical education specialists, most of whom were graduates of the University of Toronto. 'This is the day of the expert,'

Y ladies proclaimed in praising the professional qualifications of their staff. In their vision of wholesome recreation, having fun had been reduced to a science.

YWCA clients had less rarefied notions of play than experts might have wished. Sports offered a pleasurable release for the physical and emotional tensions of life on the factory line or behind the sales counter. In winter months women who lived at home or boarded downtown were only a short walk or streetcar ride from a warm pool. Domestics and other isolated workers could relieve their loneliness in organized group activities that allowed them to meet other working girls. Clients' changing tastes prompted the Y to drop compulsory religious sessions in 1918; instead, secretaries were encouraged to take extra courses in games and recreations.[29] Working girls' demand, not recreational philosophy alone, prompted the YWCA to provide Toronto's young working women with an extensive range of 'wholesome amusements' by the 1920s. In fact, by the post-war decade, it would be fair to argue that the 'C' in YWCA had come to stand foremost for citizenship and only incidentally for Christian.

The state, which conferred the formal rights of citizenship on women in 1918 with the granting of the vote, was equally concerned to manage female citizenship for the national good. Government ministries and professional experts on the girl problem joined the Y after the war in counselling young women about the importance of leisure self-management. Advisers urged women to manage their leisure pursuits as a means to enhance their job performance and preserve their health. Businesswomen were reputed to be as notorious as factory girls for their inefficiency and poor use of free time. Educators and new government ministries in the emerging welfare state encouraged women workers to change their image from that of carefree pleasure-seekers to one of temperate workers who used their spare time judiciously. The proliferation of advice literature for young women after the war constituted a significant shift in authoritative discourses on working women. Where commissions and investigative surveys had approached single women's non-domestic work as a social problem, post-war advice literature considered working away from home to be a normal and desirable step on a young woman's road to adulthood. Ironically, the girl who did *not* want to play and the single woman who did *not* work prior to marriage became problems. Finally, advice literature differed from other sources of knowledge about working women, such as investigative exposés: it was directed at wage-earning women and, in most cases, it was written by female experts, including women workers themselves.

By the 1920s the principles of scientific management were introduced not only on factory lines but in offices, department stores, and government bureaus.[30] By the end of the war, as the white-collar sector rapidly feminized, young women were increasingly the recipients of such directives. If the administrative revolution was to occur, wage-earning women would have to cooperate.[31] As important as it was for workers to perform their tasks effectively at work, it was equally vital that they use their leisure time efficiently. Indeed, workers' efficient use of free time was crucial to their ability to operate at peak capacity on the job, as Frederick Winslow Taylor, the 'father' of scientific management, believed.[32] While managers and 'efficiency experts' were to oversee the behaviour of employees on the job, it was up to the workers to regulate their time off the job. Experts on working women took their cues from this emerging managerial discourse when they stepped in to advise working girls and businesswomen on ways to utilize their free time for their own and their employers' benefit.

Whereas investigations of working women in the late nineteenth century had looked with trepidation at the rise of the working girl, advice literature in the post-war era praised the contributions that wage-earning women could make. The war had awakened Canadians to the economic and social contributions of working women and inspired writers to determine the best ways to tap that precious resource in the post-war world. One of those writers was Marjory MacMurchy, who during the war had headed the women's department of the Canadian Reconstruction Association (CRA). The department had recruited women into industry after 1916, and worked toward the smooth reintroduction of male workers by encouraging women to take up white-collar work. MacMurchy's government-sponsored study, *The Canadian Girl at Work* (1919), appeared in the same year as Ellen Knox's commercially published *The Girl of the New Day*. Knox, the principal of the élite Havergal College for Girls, reviewed the various occupations appropriate for females and offered vocational guidance for young women. Over the following few years, both books were widely circulated throughout the province and heralded as important advances in the training of young women for work and citizenship.[33]

The Division of Industrial Hygiene (DIH), part of the reorganized Ontario Board of Health as of 1920, was responsible for two other important works in this genre. Among its first projects was the production of a film intended to detail women's 'personal hygiene and such measures for health protection as rest with the workers themselves.' Called *Her Own Fault*, the film was shown in Toronto movie theatres and intended for the edification of factory workers. *Health Confessions of Business Women*, in contrast, was directed toward white-collar workers. It was published following a DIH contest announced in daily newspapers in 1922. A prize of fifteen dollars was to be awarded to the businesswoman who wrote the best letter about her 'technique of living.' *Health Confessions* was an edited collection of more than two hundred letters arranged, along with editorial comments, into a compendium of tips for business women's self-management.[34] Both *Her Own Fault* and *Health Confessions* were hailed as 'distinctly original' efforts in the post-war campaign to teach wage-earning women how best to balance their leisure needs and work duties.[35]

Similar surveys of businesswomen's attitudes towards their work and leisure were carried out in the United States. In 1929, for instance, a study of white-collar women in Chicago catalogued their difficulties in meeting their employers' demands that they be both decorative and serious, competent but not ambitious, efficient yet affable. No matter what her occupation, the businesswoman's attire symbolized this continuing struggle: 'the clerical worker was supposed to be attractive, but not too sexy. She was not supposed to dress drably, but she also had to avoid flashiness.' As Sharon Hartman Strom advises, historians should also take working women's sartorial dilemmas seriously, since they offer insight into feminine work culture and subjectivity. Some of the best-educated white-collar women made careers out of their work and managed to forge new identities as self-made individuals; others, particularly younger women and those from working-class backgrounds, looked at their jobs as an opportunity to dress up and to meet male bosses. Serious-minded women rejected this brand of flightiness, and they were only too happy to set the record straight about the responsible businesswoman's trials and triumphs.[36]

The organizers of the Health Confessions contest solicited contributions from women who could counter the popular image of office workers as 'frivolous, vain and pleasure-loving.' The editorial introduction to the contestants' published letters opened with a recitation of commonly held assumptions about white-collar women: 'Business girls only wake up at 5 p.m. Their main object is to get through their work somehow and then enjoy themselves ... Business girls commonly dance all night.' Instead of dismissing these charges, the editors claimed that they understood that the 'monotony' and 'self-repression' of office work drove some women to overtax their minds and bodies 'in an unconscious attempt to make the pleasures of sixteen hours outweigh the miseries of eight.'[37] The solution lay in the 'technique of living.'

Working from the premise that young women were supplied with a finite amount of energy, a theory that had never been seriously considered in relation to domestics, experts advised them not to waste that resource on pleasures. Ellen Knox believed that the 'girl of today' who 'dash[ed] along like an express train' was apt to rob her employer and future family of vital energy. 'You cannot, you dare not fling away the health which might be yours,' she pleaded. Knox cautioned that a young women who 'burn[ed] her candle at both ends' while single would be 'forever a drag upon her husband, forever a strain upon her children.' Others, like Ruth Dembner, suffered even worse fates. The best advice Knox could offer was to avoid 'having too good a time generally.'[38]

The judicious use of free time was meant to complement the efficient use of time at work, according to experts. Knox suggested a list of dos and don'ts for working girls. Dos included an active outdoor life of sports and gymnastics, regular hours, balanced meals, sensible, well-ventilated clothes, and low heels. The don'ts were dancing and movies, 'dainties' such as cream puffs and sundaes, and fancy blouses and high heels. The trick was to learn how to make the proper decisions on one's own.

Knowing where to draw the line in leisure time was the most difficult task for single women, tempted as they were by free nights and fast times in the city. Many of the women in the Health Confessions contest, such as a contestant who called herself 'C.A. Nada,' admitted that they learned this lesson through 'failures in personal maintenance.' 'Live and Learn' was so thoroughly seduced by the pleasures and pace of city living that her standards of personal hygiene slipped. She confessed that as an eighteen-year-old girl arriving in the city 'from an old-fashioned home' to work in a downtown office, she succumbed to excitement and fashion: 'Seeing girls wearing what looked to me like lovely evening dresses at work went to my head ... I got the lowest-necked georgette blouse and the shortest skirt I could find and high heels and silk stocking[s] with roses on them and hennaed my hair and somehow I looked so different I began to act different and dropped all my good old habits.'[39] She fell into a life of nightly parties and 'never got to bed before twelve,' and was reduced to wearing soiled clothes. When her co-workers began to ostracize her in the 'dirty corner' of the office, she resolved to make a change: 'I decided I'd have to go slower ... I cut out lots of parties, went to bed earlier, got up earlier, and I guess now my hobby is pretty clothes and washing.'

'Live and Learn' struggled to achieve the standard of cleanliness required of businesswomen and saw in her 'clean and dainty' clothing a symbol of her achievement: 'I know that all it stands for makes you lead a saner quieter sort of life and that certainly tells on health.' Her decision to sacrifice fast-paced city pleasures for the mundane tasks of washing and mending was echoed in other businesswomen's advice. 'Rita' observed, no doubt correctly, that 'a business girl['s] appearance had a great deal to do with her success and happiness.' She and the other businesswomen who offered their advice on personal maintenance also acknowledged that attractiveness, a requisite of office work, could not be purchased on the average salary of white-collar workers; rather, cleanliness and daintiness were the fruits of careful planning and hard work during single women's free time.[40]

Businesswomen's wise management and efficient use of their leisure time was an index of their responsibility as workers and their respectability as women. Dedicated employees did not fall prey to the temptations of city living. They did not dance the night away only to arrive at work bleary-eyed and cross. Such folly was clearly a woman's 'own fault,' as the eponymous film dramatized. 'Mamie,' a factory operative character who squanders her energy on frantic, late-night fox-trotting and lunchtime department store jaunts, becomes too tired to perform at top speed on the factory line.[41] Ellen Knox reiterated the film's message in her advice book: '[It is impossible to] rack yourself to pieces by night, and then work yourself to pieces by day.' At the same time, leisure was not to be a period of unstructured rest or relaxation. In an apparent contradiction of her own plea for restraint, Knox commanded, 'Do everything at the double, play at the double, work at the double.'[42] What, then, did advice writers mean when they called upon young, single working women to play?

If women could expect to be worked 'to pieces' during the day, then they would have to pull themselves back together during their leisure time. As Chris Rojek has argued, sociologists have often confused leisure with 'free time' and have thereby overlooked the material and psychic constraints on workers' time off the job. The pressures on women to contain their leisure activities within the bounds of moderation and sexual respectability underline his insight that 'leisure is not free time, but an effect of systems of legitimation.'[43] In the context of post-war Canada, advice writers praised women workers who struck a balance between the demands of work, the necessity of personal maintenance, and the duty to re-create themselves through play.

In a chapter of *The Canadian Girl at Work* entitled 'What Every Girl Needs to Know,' MacMurchy elucidated the necessity of play, claiming that 'rest and recreation' were as vital to a girl's health and happiness as food and congenial work: 'The ideal girl is healthy and happy, she sleeps 8 hours or more at night, and plays a reasonable part of her time.' Without a supervisor to tell her how to spend her leisure time, however, it was up to a businesswoman herself to police her activities. 'The girl must learn to be her own captain, her own commanding officer,' MacMurchy explained in military terms: 'She should give herself orders.' In case her readers might not know which orders to give, she specified that 'good times' were essential to health provided that they were 'planned with good sense and restricted to suitable times and places.'[44] The readers of *Health Confessions* received time-management charts to help plan their free time.[45] It was up to young working women to manage the only part of the day beyond their employers' control.

Single women's ability to choose healthy leisure pursuits was increasingly touted as the hallmark of feminine citizenship. By the 1920s advisers suggested that it was respectable businesswomen's civic duty to pass on the message of wholesome amusements to their still morally suspect working-class sisters. Knox reminded readers who aspired to become YWCA secretaries that they would have to convince 'little factory girls' of the value of outdoor play and indoor gymnastics. The inability to make appropriate use of leisure time had become a signifier of class and status, rather than a weakness of working women per se: Factory operatives 'will wander off with their comrades into the streets, irresistibly attracted by the lure of the glare outside, by the excitement of movie and dance hall, and, once wandering, who can prophesy their fate?'[46] Refined businesswomen who were presumed to recognize the nobler aims of free time were encouraged to devote themselves to helping working-class women appreciate 'wholesome amusements.' 'Great things can be done by busy women during their so-called hours of leisure,' glowed an article about a working girls' camp run by businesswomen.[47] The growing economic gap between female factory operatives and white-collar women who made a career out of their better-paying work was measured in terms not only of wages but of leisure tastes.

Advisers learned from the decline of the social purity movement that fiery predictions of doom without positive inducements for compliance usually failed to convince young people to mend their ways. When they discussed wage-earning women's leisure, then, they seasoned their warnings with the rhetoric of success. Recreationists, advice writers, and ambitious businesswomen speculated that a well-rested, physically fit worker would provide her employers with the best service, and that, accordingly, she would be rewarded for her performance on the job. 'Eileen,' the temperate counterpart to the frivolous 'Mamie' in *Her Own Fault*, was a case in point. The film shows how Eileen's regime of healthy meals, a daily exercise program and regular sleep keeps her in fighting trim for work. Her cheeriness and productivity attract the attention of a male supervisor, who asks her out for a canoe ride and picnic in High Park; a short while later she is promoted to forelady. The dissipated Mamie, meanwhile, loses her job as a result of her shoddy work and ill health. The message is clear: women who master the 'technique of life' can expect success in the workplace and anticipate the attention of male overseers and the inevitable promise of marriage.

Working girls who went to see *Her Own Fault* at one of the Kum See movie theatres may have shared a few giggles over the film. In many ways, Mamie is the more appealing character. While Eileen does everything right (and at the double too, if the fast-motion sequence of her rubber heel-trimming skills is any indication), Mamie gives in to her urges and scoffs at Eileen's suggestion that she take better care of herself. The Georgina House 'girls' also poked fun at calisthenics programs designed to keep wage-earning women in fine trim. They drew up a list of satirical 'Exercises for Reducing, Specially Suited for the Business Girl' and mimicked the directions they would have heard in YWCA classes or in company recreation programs. The 'Lumbago Dip' was a typical example:

Stand erect, bend slowly from the waist, touch tips of shoes with extended fingers. At your first attempt you will probably bring on a stroke of apoplexy. If you succeed, however (in touching the floor, not in bringing on the stroke) repeat until you are blue in the face. You will be amazed to discover how far the floor is from the human chin.

Other exercises called for bending backwards from the waist 'until your head hits the floor,' or rolling down a steep hill towards a railroad crossing. On one level, these absurd exercises mocked the seriousness of recreation advocates but their jokes also reveal how deeply the message of improving leisure pursuits had penetrated the consciousness of wage-earning women. Even those women who preferred to spend their breaks bargain-hunting and their nights fox-trotting knew how they were *supposed* to behave.[48]

Businesswomen who participated in the Health Confessions contest indicated that healthy recreation could be turned to personal advantage; inattention to exercise and rest could spell disaster. Their recommendations for the pursuit of health were framed in the discourse of finance administration. 'Jasmine' wrote as if she were a stock broker: 'During my stenographic career, I have found that nothing gives better return for careful treatment than does the human body, and that a good business girl and late nights do not harmonize.' Health Confessions contestants wrote that women who did not perfect the 'technique of life' would never advance: 'The girl who makes a practice of jazzing till midnight, every night, getting up late in the morning, rushing through an insufficient breakfast, and hustling down to the office at the last minute will never get beyond the stenographer's chair,' 'Common Sense' smugly predicted.[49] Businesswomen's advisers cautioned that investing in commercial amusements would yield only a meagre return of transitory pleasure while bankrupting their health and careers.

The mark of the 'good business girl' was efficiency and compliance on the job, combined with self-discipline and self-management off the job. A private in the office chain of command by day, the young woman worker was promoted each night to 'captain' of her leisure. But advice writers generally considered a career in business to be, like military service, a temporary training period for future civic service. Only a handful of single women would go on to become career soldiers in the business world. Most would move on to their civilian duties as wives and mothers. Once married, women would work under the gentle command of their husbands and in the service of their children and community. At play no less than at work, then, 'the good business girl' devoted herself to her employer, her future family and, ultimately, her nation.

WORKING TOWARDS THE NEW DAY

Success for the woman worker was more than a matter of efficiency: it required the right attitude. In order to restore the world to normality after the carnage of the First World War, working girls would have to play their part not only by working and playing the right way but by thinking and feeling the right way. Young women were encouraged to consider their work as a pleasurable duty to their employer rather than as a route to self-fulfilment or economic independence. The war's terrible toll added patriotic colours to these calls for self-sacrifice. Aside from convincing women who had worked in high-paying industrial jobs during the war that staying on would be selfish, advice writers and agencies such as the CRA tried to persuade working girls of the enormous debts they owed to the brothers and fathers who had been killed and to the nation they had died to defend. Attempts to shape the attitudes of young women workers, much like social purity education, took aim not only at individuals' behaviour but at their subjectivity. The technique of moral suasion, emblematic of new managerial responses to the girl problem, was subtler than demands to go back home or even to play properly; the actual messages, however, were far from subtle.

Post-war advice advanced the premise that young women's paid work paralleled men's military contribution to the nation. Forty per cent of Canadian fatalities were Ontario men, and Toronto alone had sacrificed over 3,100 to make the world safe for democracy.[50] Men of honour had not shirked their duty, nor must young women, now that the soldiers had returned and women had been granted the vote. Marjory MacMurchy reminded high-school girls that women's work had taken on greater significance since they had joined men 'in copartnership, laying the foundation of a new earth.'[51] Ellen Knox imagined that the white crosses over fallen soldiers' graves were 'so many question marks, asking how far you intend to live and sacrifice yourself for Canada.' If young women would not respond to calls from the dead, then surely the figures of wounded veterans hobbling home from battlefields would provide a ghastly reminder of their duties: 'Every tap of a soldier's crutch on the pavement is the record of a choice, a challenge to know how far you in your turn are living, giving, sacrificing for Canada.'[52] Working for pay was no longer a dangerous departure from domesticity or a contributing factor in the social evil; in short, it had become a patriotic duty.

In contrast to earlier investigations of women's work, a wage-earning woman's attitude towards her work, rather than the sort of work she performed, had become a moral problem. Above all, businesswomen and working girls were to keep their minds squarely on their imminent obligations as wives and mothers. The urgency of this message was underscored by demographic and economic changes. The sex ratio, for years slanted towards a preponderance of young women, tipped even further after the death of thousands of young men in the war. Moreover, growing numbers of businesswomen, and not just professionals, could now afford to support themselves, particularly if they shared expenses with other women, without having to marry. As the number of boarding-house residents in their thirties and beyond suggests, many self-supporting women preferred single life which, in the minds of working girls' advisers, spelled selfishness.

Writers earnestly exhorted women to reject the masculine world of business for feminine self-fulfilment in the home. Ellen Knox, herself a single working woman, painted a bleak picture of the hollow lives that businesswomen would lead if they lived only for their careers: 'Think of the wretchedness of being so absorbed in turning your life into dollars and cents that, Scrooge-like, you favour your melancholy dinner … of an evening by your bank-book … Think of deciding that for you, at any rate, there will be no home life of your own!'[53] Completely oblivious to the gregarious housing arrangements women found in boarding-homes and shared apartments, Knox updated the caricature of the old maid to fit the 'career woman' of the post-war era – the unloved, unloving woman who existed solely to make money.

Any concern on a woman worker's part for her wages was branded as selfish materialism. 'We should remember that while what we earn is important there are other considerations as important,' MacMurchy clucked.[54] The perceived independence of wage-earning women was clearly still an issue, although it was no longer tied to the social evil. Instead, in post-war advice literature, the economic independence that had opened up for the wage-earning elite imperilled the future of the race and the nation.

The ideal of service to others was to guide young women's choices in their work and social lives. Women who were self-supporting were encouraged to be 'useful citizen[s], doing [their] part in the development of Canada.' Their usefulness was defined largely in terms of the demands of an economy built in part on the super-exploitation of young workers who, in the vast majority of cases, never joined unions or remained in the paid workforce for more than a few years. Hence, MacMurchy could consider calling for working girls to be 'generous, unselfish [and] efficient' as good advice.[55]

By the post-war period, the greatest challenge for advisers of working women lay in achieving a balance between the masculine skills demanded in the workplace and the feminine attributes called for in marriage. Overly ambitious businesswomen excelled at the former but failed at the latter; dance-mad, fashion-crazed working girls presented the opposite problem. Magazines for women stressed that self-presentation ought to be of great concern to working women, especially those who worked in offices for male bosses. Hairstyle and the choice of dress, makeup and heel height all signified grades of respectability. In a *Chatelaine* magazine story, the 'good girl, bad girl' scenario was dramatized by two working women with contrasting attitudes to fashion. The plain woman fills in for her popular twin sister, who is too exhausted from late-night dancing to attend a job interview. Although initially reluctant to hire a dowdy woman, the male interviewer is so impressed by her no-nonsense 'cotton stockings' that he hires and later marries her; the silk-stockinged sister, meanwhile, is left unemployed and unmarried.[56] In another romantic parable directed at business-women, an ordinary-looking secretary catches her boss's attention: 'She's not like the rest of those senseless hussies, forever titivating before a mirror.' Because she 'takes an interest in her work instead of calculating the effect she is having on the man she's taking dictation from,' her boss asks her to marry him.[57] The editors of *Health Confessions* added that employers who normally dismissed frivolous women invariably made exceptions for the businesswoman who '"has a head," [and] "could run the office alone."'[58] The message was that good work, rather than good looks, was rewarded – not with pay raises but, if women were lucky, with marriage proposals.

This combination of efficiency and femininity was a goal towards which participants in the Health Confessions contest worked. The announcement for the contest had described the ideal businesswoman as 'something of a machine, cheerful and serene and on the spot,' and thereby encouraged contestants to write in with their successes and failures in meeting those apparently paradoxical demands.[59] If 'cheerful machines' ever existed, they did so in ambitious yet nurturing secretaries who, like wives or mothers, discreetly established the conditions for 'their man's' success. White-collar women's association with high-status male bosses may have offset the demeaning nature of secretarial work, as Health Confessions contestants' pride over their indispensability suggests.[60] They knew that they could 'run the office alone' even if their bosses never told them so. 'Brownie' shared her motto with her fellow office workers: 'I must not think I am "merely a business girl"; I am an important cog in the world's machinery, and it is up to me to help keep it going.' The key to happiness, another woman added, was devotion and loyalty: 'We must love our work and not be working simply for money, but for the good we get from it and the help we are to our employer.'[61]

The Health Confessions contestants seem to have been remarkably eager to fulfil the ideals of selflessness promoted in educational films and guidance books; however, their emphasis on self-effacement was buoyed by a strong sense of self-interest. The hundreds of letters proclaiming the need for cheerfulness on the job also explicitly described businesswomen's work as uninteresting and unfulfiling. For 'Toppy' and many other office workers, 'work [was] largely made up of small detail, monotonous routine and little fussings and *hurry*.' She derived no pleasure from such toil; rather, she found it 'wearing and rather dispiriting.' 'Patricia' agreed that dwelling on the actual tasks businesswomen performed could be debilitating: 'I think everyone should learn not to think too seriously of the humdrum monotony of doing the same thing each and every day.' Women could achieve happiness only through wilful transcendence of their material circumstances. Through sheer force of will, 'Gratitude' had managed to think of her work as a privilege: 'I have come to look upon [work] as the good fairy who gives me clothes and food and all I have, and I have been well repaid by endeavouring to give it something in return.'[62] As a result, she found that her job had ceased to be 'a drag.' Successful businesswomen may have given their bosses the impression that they lived to file and type, but they were well aware that being treated like a cog in a wheel did not mean that one had to feel like a machine.

The winner of the Health Confessions contest, 'A Plodder,' suggested that psychological management was as important to contentment as the wise use of leisure time. 'Forget your work and revel in doing what you please,' she wrote. She prescribed a full roster of entertainments, including boating, swimming, motoring – even dancing – as long as women were left 'in good trim' for work. The best tonic, however, was a brisk walk to work, when a businesswoman could stride confidently, 'as if [she] meant it.'[63] 'A Plodder's' apparent subservience to employers' interests was compromised by her self-conscious manipulation of recreationists' ideals, reflecting what Chris Weedon might term a 'contradictory and precarious' sense of self.[64] The prizewinner's 'technique of life' was nothing more than a game played to fool herself and others in order to get ahead. She recognized that the sprightly walk and the morning smile did not manifest themselves naturally but had to be consciously constructed – *as if* she meant it.

Still, some women could not bring themselves to play this game of self-effacement. Talented women whose goals were blocked in businesses that did not value their female employees were liable to give up 'and become *just* a shopgirl, or *just* an office girl.' Those who could not resign themselves to the sexist impediments to material progress suffered the most. One contestant put her case bluntly: 'The business girl has to crush her individuality – many a hard battle has to be fought, and the victory when gained, often leaves a bitter flavour.'[65] For businesswomen, unlike their professional advisers, the problem involved more than simply balancing femininity and efficiency; for them, it entailed struggling to maintain a sense of self while performing as a machine.

WOMEN, WORK, AND WELFARE

Although wage-earning women's poverty had long been recognized as a social problem, primarily in regard to the social evil, it was not until the 1910s that efforts to improve their material existence were launched. In addition to housing and recreational schemes, women's wages and working conditions were finally addressed as a focus for reform. The limited scale of improvements and the terms on which they were implemented, however, reproduced working girls' marginal status as workers. Like advice literature that encouraged young women to consider their work a noble sacrifice, welfare programs were instituted with the economic interests of employers and the future of the race in mind.

The rise of business and professional women in the post-war period tended to divert attention from the plight of women in lower-paying factory positions. Although starting clerks and stenographers were not uniformly well paid, they were better off than their unskilled counterparts who drifted from factory to factory. The National Council of Women of Canada played a significant role in promoting a minimum wage to protect these working girls from economic exploitation. As a result of femininst lobbying, the Ontario Department of Labour conducted a survey in 1918–19 to determine the minimum cost of wage-earning women's board and lodging. For Toronto, the estimate was $6 to $7 per week *excluding* the cost of clothing, recreation, and personal maintenance. With half of the city's laundry workers earning under $8 and almost 20 per cent of biscuit-makers receiving less than $7 per week, the inadequacy of that minimum estimate is stark. The results of this study, along with the recommendations of the 1919 Royal Commission on Industrial Relations, sent a clear message to the Ontario government that wage-earning women were paid less than they required to support themselves.[66]

The initial fanfare that greeted the passage of the Ontario Minimum Wage Act in 1920 was largely unwarranted, since the law was neither intended nor implemented to force employers to raise the standard of living for working girls. The terms on which a minimum wage were calculated were the same pro-capitalist, pro-family values that motivated MacMurchy and Knox. The Minimum Wage Board (MWB), composed of representatives from business and industry (but not labour) made no secret of its paternalistic orientation towards working girls: 'Old man Ontario is determined that none of his daughters shall lack the necessities of life.' The state, through the MWB, would permit business to 'borrow' its daughters' labour power while they were single, but ensure that they would leave the paid labour force prepared to make more significant contributions to the nation: 'Working girls of to-day are the mothers of to-morrow … No community can afford to stand aside and see them exploited.'[67]

There was very little muscle behind this moralizing, however. First, the MWB assumed that enlightened employers would perceive the benefits of treating their workers well, and therefore would not require policing. Second, the board determined the minimum wage through a moral rather than an economic calculus. The simplest method would have been to use existing figures on the minimum cost of living for a family to determine the costs for an individual. Instead, the MWB invented a base figure 'requisite to the proper conduct of life' for working girls. Just as the Bell Telephone managers and Timothy Eaton had explained that they paid their female employees less because they were 'girls,' so the marginality of women workers was encoded in the tabulation of minimum wages. The ability to balance a tight budget remained a moral test – not for employers who were permitted to pay women 'minimal' salaries, but for working girls who struggled to conduct themselves properly.

The MWB's initial estimate of a minimum wage was based on a detailed breakdown of living expenses for a typical Toronto working girl.[68] They considered the figure of $12.56 per week, based on $7.00 for room and board, $2.66 for clothing and $2.90 for sundries, to be fair both to employers and to employees.[69] As critics pointed out, however, these rates assumed a full year of employment, made no provisions for sickness, and set aside a mere 44 cents for recreation, a necessary restorative for young women. More significantly, the rate applied only to 'experienced' full-time workers, and excluded domestics, farm workers, bank employees, teachers, and nurses.[70] The minimum wage was actually reduced to $12.50 in 1923, when there was a slump in the price of clothing; it remained at that rate for the rest of the decade. The apparent limitations of the law did not seem to trouble the members of the MWB, who felt that Old Man Ontario's duty was simply to give his daughters a 'safe start toward success.' The board assumed that its 'friends' in industry would pay better workers higher wages. To its working-girl 'clients,' the MWB offered advice reminiscent of the Unemployment Commission's admonitions: 'Your own efforts will achieve the higher rewards.'[71]

The individualist philosophy of the Ontario Minimum Wage Board was remarkably consistent with the eugenic policies promoted by those battling feeble-mindedness. The minimum wage was designed to expose inferior workers who did not deserve to be paid at even the lowest rates. Efficient women had nothing to fear, according to the MWB. It was only a 'certain type' of woman worker – 'shy, timid, perhaps rather slow but faithful and steady' – who was likely to be let go, yet 'such dismissal [was] perhaps what the girl needed.' This weeding-out process worked in the interests of capital, which praised the Act for raising the standards demanded of women workers. The MWB advised the women who wrote 'piteous letters' begging to be paid less than the $12.50 minimum in order to keep their jobs to improve their efficiency to the level now demanded by business and industry. The 'few dismissals' were blessings in disguise, the MWB decided, since more spaces would open for 'competent worker[s].'[72]

In practice, the Minimum Wage Act did not throw out masses of inefficient women workers. The economic downturn of 1921–22 alone was responsible for more layoffs than the thinly enforced legislation. Nor did the Act ensure that eligible women would actually receive a minimum wage. Even in factories and department stores, which were major employers of women and easy targets of regulation, managers freely manipulated the law to their advantage by claiming that certain workers were not experienced or by shifting women from waged labour to piece rates. Most working girls decided not to report their substandard wages out of fear of reprisals, while workers in small offices and shops may never have known of its existence.[73]

Employers who regarded the Minimum Wage Act as unwarranted inter-ference in the free labour market were still, in some cases, willing to provide benefits designed to foster employee loyalty and improve their public image. The aftermath of the Toronto Bell Telephone strike proved that it was significantly cheaper to offer benefits than to raise wages. The company maintained its wage cutbacks, but it did eliminate some of the safety hazards and offered the 'hello girls' a lunchroom and tea service. Shortly after the strike ended, employees were granted a free medical examination, and by 1912 the operators could join a health benefit plan. Although few firms copied Bell's pioneering work in employee insurance in the 1920s, several employers of women did make relatively inexpensive improvements in working conditions and ex-panded the opportunities for employees' wholesome leisure.

Companies could not control their employees' free time, but they did offer incentives for women to engage in the sorts of pastimes considered to be beneficial to their health and welfare. In *Her Own Fault*, 'Elaine,' the efficient worker, takes advantage of all the opportunities her factory employer supplies for her. She eats a well-balanced lunch, prepared by a dietitian, in the company cafeteria, then relaxes in a lounge, doing fancy-work and socializing. During her break she lines up with her fellow working girls for a few minutes of calisthenics supervised by a physical instructor. Like boarding-houses, paternalistic companies encouraged young women to spend their leisure time on the premises. When Simp-son's built a women's restroom in its downtown store, a spokesperson explained the intended purpose of the facility: 'A recreation room … will help uplift the physical and moral welfare of our employees, and [provide a place] where they can spend their lunch hours instead of loitering through the store or being forced to walk the streets.'[74] Welfare schemes did more than serve the economic needs of capital; in the case of pro-grams offered to women, managers hoped that benefits might instil happiness, gratitude, and contentment in a work force routinely denied advancement policies or wages comparable to men's.

The provision of welfare services evidently quelled wage-earning women's discontent, but it did not necessarily lead women to behave as compliant daughters towards paternalistic employers. The con-testants in the Health Confessions contest revealed that they appreci-ated benefits for quite practical reasons. A comfortable chair, good ventilation, and adequate lighting simply made work more tolerable. 'Lucky Dog' appreciated her company lunch room because she could get 'a good, hot, well-cooked dinner in the middle of the day without any bother ... It's one thing done for you that saves contriving on your part.'[75] 'Olive Gray' thought that all large factories ought to have nurses and emergency rooms, since prompt health care reduced the risk of long-term illnesses that might lead to unemployment. Other women urged working girls to request workplace improvements for their own good. 'Helper' believed that 'intelligent girls' should appreciate good facilities as well as 'ask bad ones to be rectified.' Thus, if she found the heating or her desk to be unsatisfactory, a girl should speak up for her own and her fellow employees' good. 'No sensible employer should mind sensible requests – probably he'll think more of you,' she ended optimistically.[76] 'Helper' may have worked for Eaton's, an employer that actively sought suggestions that would increase efficiency. Eaton's, through its 'efficiency department,' encouraged its workers 'to become more interested, not only in their own line of work, but in the general improvement of the store.' Sales clerks might have found the one dollar reward for the best suggestion to be an even greater incentive.[77]

Company welfare schemes could offer women workers a sense of self-worth that their work, performed at minimal wages on factory lines or in typing pools, did not. Women were not duped or bought off by recreational programs so much as they were offered a context for making friends and discovering talents. Large factories sponsored women's softball teams, complete with uniforms and equipment – to say nothing of the thrills of competition and even fame. Games between teams in the Toronto Industrial Softball League drew more paying spectators than any other sporting event in the city, save the men's international league games. Factory operatives such as Billy Smith of the K & S Supremes became so skilled that US scouts tried to lure her south.[78] Eaton's employees who joined the Eaton Choral Society could develop their musical talents and sing before the cream of Toronto society at the prestigious Massey Hall. Others preferred the Eaton's Girls' Club, where they could make friends with coworkers to whom they were not allowed to speak during business hours.[79] Working girls and business-women may have played on company grounds under company rules, but they derived their pleasures on their own terms. They could only dream about equal pay or advancement possibilities, but they were not about to question subsidized lunchrooms or softball sponsors in the meantime.

MOTHERS OF THE RACE

Unprecedented efforts to meet the needs of single, wage-earning women were not tied to a sense of economic justice long delayed, but rather to a not so subtle anxiety about the future of the race. Despair over the human toll of the First World War added to earlier fears of race suicide. Worse still, the discovery of high rates of venereal disease infection among recruits to the Canadian Expeditionary Force suggested that a 'secret plague' had been unleashed, to the peril of the nation.[80] By the war's end the medical establishment, led by doctors Helen MacMurchy, Gordon Bates, and C.K. Clarke, convinced the provincial and federal governments to fund new ministries and professional organizations devoted to the fitness of the race. The most extreme lobbyists were eugenicists who were willing to quarantine and sterilize the 'unfit' and 'feeble-minded.' More moderate types advocated social hygiene, a philosophy of 'race betterment' through education and medical treatment. In either case, young Canadians and women in particular were sought out as key players in a project to foster a strong, vital nation.[81]

While some critics blamed the army's lax moral standards for the high rates of infection, the Canadian government, proud of its fighting men, was quick to deflect censure towards the civilian population.[82] Dr Gordon Bates, an associate of C.K. Clarke, was a captain in charge of the Venereal Section of the Toronto Base Hospital during the war. He claimed that most men had contracted infections *prior* to joining the CEF. Thus, although the diseased condition of male soldiers precipitated public alarm over the long-term dangers of sex, Canadian women were implicated, both as potential victims of returning profligate soldiers and as the suspected seducers of Canadian manhood. Under these circumstances, the prospects for race betterment after the war seemed dim.

The social hygiene movement, described by one advocate as a campaign for 'mental, moral, and physical as well as social health,' took up this challenge.[83] Its largely male medical leadership inherited the pioneering work of early sexual purity educators, but employed a more rigorous scientific approach to counter immorality. Knowledge united with faith was to be their great weapon in their state-supported battle against sexual ignorance and its devastating effects. As Angus McLaren has argued, social hygienists believed science would better the race through 'investigation, categorization and education.' They hoped that once young people knew the physical dangers of immorality, a 'more efficient form of self discipline could be instilled.'[84] Yet the moral impulse behind rational educational and regulatory schemes was equally important. Medical experts, with the continued assistance of religious authorities, created a 'dialogue between medicine and morality' and thereby 'redefined the terrain of moral problems.' Frank Mort concludes that the discourse of social hygiene 'produced a renewed moral emphasis within preventive medicine.'[85]

Prevention was a strategic element in the campaign against veneral disease, and social hygiene education, rather than the promotion of condoms, was the principal method used to reduce the number of newly infected persons. Even C.K. Clarke, a doctor with extreme eugenicist views, thought that properly conducted education provided 'a magnificent opportunity, not only for stamping out venereal disease but for making this Canada of ours a better place.'[86] Educating youth to forswear pleasure in favour of duty was essential to the project of race betterment. This was hardly a new message for urban working girls. Sounding much the same as recreation leaders, boarding-house supervisors, and ambitious busniesswomen, Clarke concluded: 'Our selfship in the past must develop into citizenship.'[87]

Social hygienists viewed sex hygiene education as a cure for ignorance and a buffer against reckless impulses. An Ontario Board of Health pamphlet, entitled 'Facts on Sex Hygiene for Girls and Young Women,' would have been handed out at public lectures and made available in doctors' offices and veneral disease clinics. Now that women of all classes had joined the workforce, it warned, they were bound to spend more time away from home, 'rubbing up against all kinds of persons.' Suggesting that venereal disease was as simple to contract as the common cold, the pamphlet described such women as 'unprotected' against physical and moral harm.[88] 'Young girls' who were 'accustomed to self-control' were safe, but those who showed a 'love of excitement or ignorance of certain of the fundamental facts concerning sex laws' were candidates for venereal disease.

Taking their cue from social purity talks, sex hygienists expounded a 'moralized medical ideology' tailored for males and females at various stages of life. Members of the public were all taught the same lesson of individual responsibility, yet the meaning of 'responsibility' differed for each group. Restraint and sublimation were recommended for men. The Dominion pamphlet 'Information for Men – Syphilis and Gonorrhoea' spelled out the benefits of male continence as higher will power along with 'physical and mental fitness.' The corresponding pamphlet for women promised no such personal benefits, save protection from the scourge of disease. The health and vitality of their future children was considered incentive enough for young women to avoid sexual contact.[89] They would not become great minds or great athletes as a result of their restraint, but they would go on to be fit mothers of the race.

Perhaps social hygienists' most radical departure from the social purity movement was their readiness to proclaim sex as a natural, positive force for men *and* women. It was wrongheaded and even dangerous to suppress the female sex drive lest the race die out, and it was equally foolish to leave heterosexuality to chance. Sex hygiene for single women teetered between warnings against undue familiarity with men and encouragement to form marital unions. 'Facts on Sex Hygiene' was a typical example. It urged young women to reject 'sports' or 'fast' men who tried to 'fondle or spoon.' They would thereby reduce their likelihood of catching syphilis from kissing and, more important, avoid 'being swept off [their] feet.' Avoiding men altogether, however, was not the answer, since most men allegedly led 'clean lives': 'It is important that girls should not get wrong ideas and think that because some men are not leading clean lives all men are bad.' It was 'normal' for women to find men sexually attractive, but potentially disastrous for them to heed the statistics on high rates of infection among soldiers. The pamphlet accordingly encouraged 'girls' to be 'full of fun and the best sort of a "good fellow."' With vague assurances to 'take for granted' that the men a woman knew and liked were 'all right,' the pamphlet concluded by promising self-controlled single women the reward of marital happiness: 'Girls should remember that real pure love between a man and a woman solemnized by marriage is a wonderful gift, a joy and a blessing, but those who indulge in their sex instinct before marriage cannot get the full blessings which should come later from real love.'[90] Thus while the pamphlet recognized and even valorized the female '[hetero]sex instinct,' it appealed to a higher force: women's love instinct.

Social hygienists owed a debt to Progressive recreationists as well as to the social purity movement. The most persistent refrain in government and private sex education materials was the necessity for wholesome recreation – the same call the Toronto Social Surveyors had issued in 1915. Ontario Appeal Court Judge William Riddell, the president of the Canadian Social Hygiene Council, believed that the diversion of youthful sex instincts into physical games would prove more fruitful than terrifying dictates against sinning. 'It is not the association of boys and girls together which does the harm,' he reasoned, 'it is such association in improper places, at improper times, without proper supervision.' Social hygienists applied lessons originally intended to prevent delinquency among impoverished inner-city youth to 'normal' young people. The supervised playground or dancehall, for instance, had come to be 'an imperative necessity of modern life.'[91] A pamphlet produced by the Toronto Social Hygiene Council explained that it stood for 'good, healthful recreation for old and young, well-supervised but sane.'[92] These unprecedented calls for Canadians to play illustrated their faith in a rational approach to leisure, one that encouraged self-restraint over self-indulgence. Only then could 'the primeval call of sex' be harnessed in service to 'the race.'[93]

At the same time, social hygienists began to see the city's single working women in a more positive light. It was clear, once Canada's urban population outstripped its rural population just after the War that the city would come to dominate the character of national life. The city was no longer simply a signifier of crime and disorder, but the centre of enlightenment and education in the eyes of sex educators. A film that illustrated the reformative powers of both the city and the single working girl was *The High Road*. Produced for the YWCA by the Canadian Educational Film Service in 1921, it exalted the moral value of recreation. In a complete reversal of earlier tales about the fate of women adrift from rural domesticity, it characterized small towns as breeding-grounds of immorality. Like *Her Own Fault*, it featured two young women, alike in every respect save their attitudes towards pleasure.[94] One dwells on 'unhealthy, small-town ideals of pretty clothes, chocolates and boys with motor cars'; the other leaves her home town to attend college in the city. She returns as a YWCA secretary, full of 'ideals of exercise and service to the community that were never before heard.'[95] Soon, her former pal and all the other girls in town go in for 'physical work, sports, out-door hikes and picnics.'

Dr Anna Brown of the New York Bureau of Education recommended *The High Road* because it presented 'a life for girls so filled with right activities of a happy sort and right relationships with boys that there is no room for wrong.' The education director of the American Social Hygiene Society was equally impressed with the film's wholesome portrayal of heterosexual relations. He summarized the fundamental purpose of the social hygiene movement in offering his praise for the film's portrayal of 'the healthy boy-and-girl relation, brought about by normal living, wisdom, and recreation of the right sort.'[96] It took a working girl, directly from the city, to transmit modern scientific theories of recreational reform and sex hygiene to the backward town of her childhood. The city still offered temptations, but it also provided amenities – including supervised boarding-houses, inexpensive recreational facilities, and self-improvement courses – that helped teach working girls how to think 'in the right way along sex lines.'[97]

Sex hygiene lessons for non-delinquent young women expressed an attempt to fill the gap between reformatory programs for 'delinquents' and the inadequate parental training and supervision of girls. The discipline of pleasure was no longer expounded solely for prostitutes, feeble-minded women, and sex delinquents but increasingly promoted as a creed for all wage-earning women. The supervised recreation movement and Progressive penology provided models for the management of working women who had never been labelled as sex delinquents and who had grown up with their own backyards to play in. Likewise, supervised boarding-homes and advice for women's self-management at work and play targeted 'normal' working women in an attempt to *keep* their lives normal. By the 1920s single, wage-earning women were no longer looked upon as symptoms of urban industrialization but as resources for national greatness. The emphasis in schemes as diverse as the Minimun Wage Act and sex education pamphlets accordingly fell on the ideal of preventing that precious resource from dwindling away. If young working women were to serve their country to the fullest, they were expected to contribute as efficient workers today while conserving their energy for the domestic duties of tomorrow. Thus, the ensemble of projects and legislation ostensibly aimed at improving the health, safety, and subsistence level of women workers in the 1920s projected to a time when single, wage-earning women would become mothers – their ultimate contribution to the nation and the race.

8

Conclusion

By the end of the 1920s Toronto's single working women had come into their own. A working girl's presence on a downtown street no longer elicited pity or fear of domestic breakdown. Perhaps she was bustling off to work at a garment factory or, more likely, one of the city's sky-scrapers or retail palaces. She might be waiting for a streetcar after having had her hair marcelled for a date with her boss. Or possibly she was returning to her boarding-house after a dip in a YWCA pool. Even the most conservative Torontonians realized that working girls had made the city their home and were there to stay.

In the early phases of industrialization and urban growth, Toronto's evangelical and civic leaders greeted the rise of wage-earning women with no such equanimity. The Royal Commission on the Relations of Labour and Capital gauged the transitions in men's and women's work by different sets of measures. Young single women were not 'workers'; instead, as the ladies of the YWCA and Toronto the Good's Mayor Howland concurred, they constituted a moral problem. Charting the fortunes of the woman adrift preoccupied both middle-class moral rescuers and labour men; although they differed when it came to ex-plaining her 'fall,' they agreed that single women's vulnerability sym-bolized the considerable moral costs of industrial progress. Still, they maintained their faith that respectable women would always, somehow, survive 'Satan's Kingdom,' even if the morally weak were doomed. Thus, although the first women wage-earners were identified as the prime victims of industrialization, very few received the benefit of doubt when they attempted to present themselves as victims in court. Extraordinary women, notably Carrie Davies and Clara Ford, did achieve, under equally extraordinary circumstances, merciful hearings, but their acquittals masked the dismissive treatment wage-earning women generally encountered in the criminal justice system.

By the turn of the century, as an army of single women took up employment in Toronto, the image of the woman adrift began to seem anachronistic. C.S. Clark and the police complained that working girls were not as innocent as their moral rescuers claimed. Young wage-earning women had, if anything, gained the upper hand in heterosexual relations. The Social Surveyors came to this surprising conclusion after failing to find evidence of a white slave trade in the city. Progressive penologists, social workers, and medical experts on 'feeble-mindedness' turned their attention, instead, to the sexually assertive working girl – a moral and medical menace.

This growing sense that the city's working girls had become sexually autonomous militated against women's credibility whenever they claimed to have been sexually assaulted. Although Toronto's civic leaders were committed to creating a City upon a Hill, free of crime and vice, working girls were no better protected against sexual danger than they were before the rise of Progressive reform. The discourse of the 'good times girl' was more than an idea disconnected from the 'reality' of working girls' lives: it was an effective defence strategy against charges of sexual assault, and it undoubtedly impeded countless working girls from coming forward with stories of sexual peril. The police and the correctional system proved to be more committed to creating a sexually ordered city through periodic brothel raids and the vigilant regulation of foreigners, homosexuals, and female morals offenders. Indeed, the case files of incarcerated working girls confirm that concerns about the girl problem significantly outweighed attempts to make city life safe for working girls.

Another side to the Progressive response to vice, however, was the optimistic belief that urban problems might be rendered manageable through the application of intellectual and bureaucratic resources. If working girls' leisure patterns were morally suspect, Toronto's settlement house workers and the Big Sisters suggested that they required alternative, well-regulated diversions. Wage-earning women who eschewed good times would not only avoid slipping into vice but would provide their employers and future families with a higher quality of service. Professional recreationists and advisers of women workers articulated a discipline of work *and* pleasure to guide single, wage-earning women towards their destiny as wives and mothers.

The girl problem inspired a wider range of responses by the 1910s and 1920s as the ranks of working girls came to include growing numbers of white-collar workers and single women from middle-class families. Working for wages while single had become an ordinary phase in the life cycle of virtually all women. The war merely accelerated the economic trend towards the integration of women workers in the tertiary sector, but it did provide an occasion for the exaltation of women's waged work as service to the nation. This message was resuscitated after the war in advice literature, which continued to articulate single women's work as a patriotic duty. Post-war advisers such as Knox and MacMurchy urged young women to think of their working lives both as a transitional period from childhood to adulthood and as a chance to play a vital role in fostering national greatness.

Lingering doubts about the viability of the race eroded this general sense of optimism about the New Day, however. Working girls evidently required expert help if they were to become fit mothers. Feeble-minded young women would never qualify, yet it seemed that the fit were alarmingly reluctant to assume the duties of marriage and mother hood, as Ruth Dembner's tragic fate revealed. The growing police and judicial vigilance over abortion and birth control showed that if single women's work was no longer considered an impediment to domesticity, the state was nevertheless unprepared to sanction sexual self-determination.

By the Depression, the working girl would fade from public consciousness, so ordinary had her work and presence in the city become. The concept of women's work as a moral problem had not, however, disappeared in the process; rather, the working *mother* now commanded greater concern. The rise of the post-war infant and child welfare movement, spearheaded by feminists, brought with it the keener scrutiny of mothers and mothering practices. Dr Helen MacMurchy's move from head of the Provincial Department of Feeble-mindedness to the Federal Division of Child Welfare symbolized a shift in tactics, from monitoring potentially profligate single women to educating and retraining inadequate mothers. This is not to say that married women had never worked before to the 1920s or 1930s, nor that the sexual practices of single working girls escaped regulation by the time of the Depression; rather, the working mother and the deleterious effects of her presumed irresponsibility towards her children and husband came to overshadow anxieties about the girl problem, particularly in the 1930s, when working mothers were accused of stealing jobs that 'rightfully' belonged to men. Along with unmarried mothers and abandoned wives, the working mother represented a deviant version of the 'fit and proper person' constructed by child welfare experts as the ideal mother. In the end, criticism of the working girl and the working mother sprang from a common current of anxiety over women's transgression of domestic boundaries. The greater acceptance of wage-earning and a measure of independence for single women was a bargain negotiated at the expense of married mothers who were counted on, more than ever before, to suppress their impulses towards autonomy at the risk of imperilling the psychological and physical fitness of their children.[1]

Toronto's Girl Problem shows that the urbanization and industrialization of Canadian life was more than a process of population concentration and economic restructuring: it was a profound cultural transformation that led urbanites, and rural holdouts, to view themselves and their nation differently. A handful of turn-of-the-century Torontonians may have been obsessed with adding up the number of power sewing machines in the city or its miles of electrically lit sidewalks, but most were preoccupied with trying to make sense of material progress and its apparent social costs. Did urban industrialization advance the race, or did it lure city dwellers from the moral values rooted in the not-so-distant past? The single, wage-earning woman seemed to offer clues. Her fate betokened the moral state of modern life.

By approaching the study of Toronto's working girls through the invention, analysis, and responses to the girl problem, I have recognized the materiality of language as an important, though not exclusive, determinant of material conditions that some historians still term 'reality.' The discourses of the YWCA and medical experts on feeble-mindedness, for instance, were produced through a specific set of institutional and social practices that gave voice and credibility to their understandings of single wage-earning women. Some actors – royal commissions, professional organizations – spoke from privileged positions, which invested their pronouncements with authority and facilitated the implementation of their recommendations. But there was no neat fit between what was said about working girls and what was done for them or to them. Wage-earning women were never actually made to go back to domestic work; the feeble-minded were never rounded up en masse and institutionalized; Toronto's red light district was never wiped out. There were always countervailing forces to the moral discourse on the working girl. The most obvious was the insatiable appetite of industrial capitalism for workers who could be paid very little yet whose labour was highly profitable. Aside from economic forces, of course, tens of thousands of working girls themselves proved that young single women could work in the city and, in some cases, live on their own without jeopardizing the future of the nation. Individual women who openly defied the moral discourse, however, did so at their peril, as the young women locked up for incorrigibility and delinquency soon discovered. That most working girls never encountered the punitive arm of the state or the intrusive gaze of moral rescuers could be read as confirmation that they conformed to the strict moral script set out for them. It is also possible that they simply devised subtler ways to seek pleasure without inviting censure (or leaving traces of their exploits for the equally intrusive gaze of the historian).

The relentless sexualization of working girls' behaviour is perhaps the most salient observation in this story. Through discourse and social practice, their morality was equated with and measured by their *sexual* morality. Understanding how that happened requires the problematization of female singlehood, a much understudied category of analysis among historians. Turn-of-the-century Torontonians were troubled by the emergence of a female wage-earning workforce precisely because it was comprised overwhelmingly of young *single* women. Those who opted for non-domestic work drew the most attention: Who would protect them? How easily might they give in to the temptations of city life? Would an independent wage spell sexual independence? Could working women be trusted to leave the workforce for marriage and motherhood? These were the questions that arose time after time, not only in philanthropic organizations' minutes but in official surveys of industrialization and urban life. That most of Toronto's women workers were single was not incidental – not to the first generations of women in the twentieth century to experience paid work as a definitive feature of young adulthood, nor to the employers who justified paying them less than men because they would supposedly leave paid work for marriage.

Single wage-earning women were reconstituted in successive images of 'modern' metropolitan life.[2] As women adrift, working girls, and businesswomen they marked the city's economic and social development from an inconsequential, overgrown town to a centre of manufacturing, distribution, commerce, and government. Young working women were at the cutting edge of change during this fifty-year period even as they stood on the sidelines and watched other workers and business owners reap the greatest profits of economic growth. As factory and shop workers, they shattered fragile ideals of domesticity; as pleasure-seekers, they forced a reappraisal of working-class women's right to leisure.

My analysis of Torontonians' obsession with wage-earning single women is not meant to imply that they fretted about little else when they puzzled over the changing face of the city. As I have suggested, 'foreigners,' and foreign men in particular, captured the Anglo-Celtic majority's fears about Toronto's shifting ethnic composition. Drunk and disorderly men, men who gambled and visited brothels, were also the targets of moral regulation. And when the city's clerics and judges fulminated against the threat of homosexuality, they focused on men, not on lesbians. In other words, I have suggested how historians might proceed to link the girl problem with what one might call the problems of the stranger and the 'moral pervert.' Some have already embarked on this complementary project. George Chauncey's *Gay New York*, for instance, is a superb study that builds upon feminist analyses of women, sex, and the city to examine male sexualities in the metropolis.[3]

To speak in terms of sexualities emphasizes that writing women's and men's histories is enriched when we think beyond unitary concepts of femininity and masculinity. As the editorial collective for the journal *Gender History* reminds us, divisions of 'race, class, religion, ethnicity and sexual orientation have redounded on both ideas about gender and the experiences of gender.'[4] Of course, other factors may be equally or more significant in particular contexts. As I have argued, female single hood was a characteristic that brimmed with economic and cultural significance in the early decades of industrial urbanization. Some feminists fear that underscoring differences between women and stressing the interstices of gender decentres the 'grand feminist tradition of critiquing and opposing the oppression of women.'[5] It need not. Wage-earning single women experienced unique forms of oppression at the turn of the century, but they also struggled against their oppression, seeking more tolerable and even pleasurable ways of life. Thus, I hope that working girls themselves would have recognized some of their stories in *Toronto's Girl Problem*.

The turn of a new century faces us now, yet the effects of industrialization and urbanization on woman and the sexual morality of the single working women have not disappeared from the political or social map. In Southeast Asia, an industrial 'miracle' is taking place: once again female migration to cities hungry for cheap labour is fracturing customary patterns of women's work and domestic life. In the electronics industry, young women workers are highly valued by employers for their 'nimble fingers,' patience, and docility, yet they are routinely paid less than male workers who, in many cases, perform less taxing work. Even more startling are contemporary parallels to historic disapproval of working girls' morality. The hypersexualized image of neophyte factory women in Malaysia, for instance, has been attributed to Malaysians' 'intense ... ambivalen[ce] about the social consequences of industrial development.' Similarly, single women in Communist Saigon are regarded as 'loose' if they wear makeup and adopt Western clothing styles. The women, however, protest that they are simply trying to make themselves appear more attractive to potential marriage partners, since marriages are no longer arranged as they once were in villages. The extent of prostitution and the sex tourism industry in countries such as Thailand confirm once again that women's sexuality is more highly prized on the open market than their 'legitimate' labour power.

The continuities between working girls' experience in late eighteenth-century Europe, turn-of-the-century Canada, and late twentieth-century Southeast Asia raise the question of why sexuality, and single wage-earning women's sexuality in particular, should become a critical concept in debates over the economic and social transformations of industrial capitalism. Historians and anthropologists show that unmarried women's ability to earn an individual wage violates female life cycle patterns that are based on the concept of patriarchal control and protection. Single women's autonomy, across a range of social and economic contexts, is bound up in their sexual autonomy and is invariably interpreted as a threat to domestic norms and thus to the stability of the wider community. However, pointing to continuities in wage-earning single women's experiences does not deny important material and historical distinctions in women's lives. In contemporary industrializing societies, for instance, modernization is taking place in the context of neo-colonialsm, and the 'foreigners' who are vilified are more likely to be white capitalist bosses than dark-skinned 'strangers.' Thus, anxiety over single women's work, its articulation, the forms of regulation it inspires and supports, and working girls' accommodations and resistance to it are manifested differently in specific historic and cultural settings.[6]

In our own time, and in a geographical and cultural context less far removed from turn-of-the-century Toronto, we now hear that single women are suffering from a shortage of suitable marriage partners and that career women are prone to severe mental depression as a result of the stress of singlehood and success. The feminist movement, smug conservatives assert, has offered women a false model of achievement that has left them with confused gender identities and empty wombs. Bitter career women have become not only self-destructive but homicidal, as the popular melodramas *Fatal Attraction*, *Misery*, and *Single White Female* suggest. Whether or not these allegations are attributable to a post-feminist 'backlash,' they are certainly linked to the historically ambivalent response to single wage-earning women and their aloofness from the institutions of marriage and motherhood.[7] After all this time, the girl problem appears to have a remarkable capacity for reinvention.

Single Women and Toronto's Industrial Development, 1880–1930

TABLE A.1
The Industrial Might of Toronto, 1881–1911

	Number of establish-ments	Percent-age[1]	Capital (dollars)	Percent-age[1]	Value of products (dollars)	Percent-age[1]
1881	932	12.7	11,691,700	21.6	19,562,981	19.5
1891	2401	19.1	31,725,313	28.3	44,963,922	28.7
1901	847	26.6	52,114,042	30.0	58,415,498	31.4
1911	1100	na	145,799,281	na	154,306,948	na

1 Values for Toronto industries, expressed as a percentage of the total for Ontario.
SOURCE: Census, 1911, vol. 3, table 11, 353.

TABLE A.2
Proportion of Single Women in Toronto, 1881–1931[1]

	Sex ratio of single adults in total population (females. 100 males)	Single women as a percentage total city population
1881[2]	105.4	16.3
1891	106.9	16.3
1901	120.9	18.4
1911[3]	105.5	15.5
1921	112.9	13.8
1931	110.6	14.7

1 The population figures for these years are based on the city of Toronto population as listed in each census year.
2 Estimates based on percentage of Torontonians over 15 as listed in 1891 census, vol. 2, table 1, 'Ages of the People,' 10.
3 Estimates based on averages of 28 per cent of males as children and 25 per cent of females as children (based on actual rates from 1901 and 1921).
SOURCE: Census, 1931, vol. 2, table 19, 160.

TABLE A.3
'Women Adrift' in Toronto, 1881

Sectors employing women	
Manufacturing	*3,218*
Service (domestic and personal)	*2,888*
Teachers	*301*

Total number of women workers	6,407
Total city workforce	31,764
Percentage of women in city workforce[1]	20.2

1 Outworkers and nurses were not counted; hence the total is
  more likely to be 21%.
SOURCE: Census, 1881, vol. 2, table 14, 292–303.

TABLE A.4
'Women Adrift' in Industry in Toronto and the Province, 1891

Total city manufacturing workforce	24,480

Percentage of women in the city manufacturing workforce	30

Female manufacturing workers in Toronto as a percentage of total female manufacturing workers in Ontario	20.8

SOURCE: Census, 1891, vol. 3, table 2, 365.

TABLE A.5
'Women Adrift' in Industry in Toronto, 1891 (specific sectors)

Manufacturing sector	Women and girls employed
Bag and box	170
Bakeries	215
Baking powder	29
Bookbinding	255
Boot and shoe	153
Brush/broom	26
Cabinet and furniture	52
Carpet	20
Confectionery	141
Cork-cutting	17
Dress/millinery	1,562
Dye and scouring	19
Embroidery (factory)	25
Engraving	16
Fancy goods	37
Fruit/vegetable canning	10
Fringe and tassle	43
Fur and hat	413
Glove/mittens	32
Knitting (factory)	94
Mattress	24
Mirrors	19
Paper pattern	10
Patent medicine	32
Photography galleries	41
Picture framing	10
Printing and publishing	447
Regalia	13
Rubber goods	150
Shirt, collar, and tie	535
Soap and candle	28
Stationery	18
Stereotyping	15
Tailors	1,592
Tent and awning	31
Thread	25
Tinsmithing	37
Tobacco	22

TABLE A.5 (continued)

Manufacturing sector	Women and girls employed
Trunk and box	19
Umbrellas	60
Watches/jewelry	36
Wig-making	13
Woollen mills	64
Yeast	12
Miscellaneous	147
Out workers	444
Total	7,350

SOURCE: Census, 1891, vol. 2, table 1, 2–379

TABLE A.6
The 'Working Girl' in Toronto's Workforce, 1911

Occupation	Number of females	Percentage of total female workforce
Agriculture	52	<1.0
Building trades	44	<1.0
Domestic and personal service	11,618	27.1
Civil and municipal government	273	<1.0
Forestry	1	<1.0
Manufactures and mechanical industries	15,097	35.2
Mining	1	<1.0
Professional	5,677	13.2
Trade and merchandising	8,945	20.9
Transportation	1,158	2.7
Office workers	7,716	18.0
Office and sales	12,431	29.0

SOURCE: Census, 1911, vol. 6, table 6, 262–75.

TABLE A.7
Female and Male Earnings in Toronto, 1921[1]

	Females	Males
Average number of weeks employed	46.9	45.4
Average earnings per person per week	$14.23	$26.60
Total average earnings per annum	$667.12	$1,208.73
Female earnings as a percentage of male earnings (annual)	55.2	

1 Earnings were calculated principally for manufacturing and service occupations, listed as 'selected occupations' in Census of Canada, 1921, vol. 3.
SOURCE: Census, 1921, vol. 3, table 40, 360–71.

TABLE A.8
'Working Girls' and 'Business Women' in Toronto's Female Workforce, 1931

Occupation	Number of females	Percentage of total female workforce
Agriculture	12	<1.0
Manufacturing	12,132	17.8
Building and construction	23	<1.0
Transportation/communication	2,233	3.3
Warehousing and storage	1,779	2.6
Trade	6,077	
Saleswomen	5,495	9.0
Service	23,067	
Public administration	46	
Professions	5,715	
Recreation	39	34.0
Personal	16,280	
Domestic	10,212	
Laundry	987	
Other	1,001	
Clerical	21,556	
Bookkeepers and cashiers	3,864	
Office appliance operators	249	31.7
Stenographers/typists	11,690	
Other clerical	5,753	
Other	1,208	1.2
Total	68,064	100.0

SOURCE: Census, 1931, vol. 7, table 41, 226–37.

APPENDIX B

Sex, Crime, and Policing, 1880–1930*

TABLE B.1
Female Arrests as a Percentage of Total Arrests, Toronto, 1880–1930[1]

1880–93	16.9
1894–1910	13.5
1911–19	7.6
1920–30	8.0
Total 1880–1930	11.5

1 Average number of arrests per annum within each period.

TABLE B.2
Arrests of Unmarried Women as a Percentage of Total Female Arrests, Toronto, 1880–1930[1]

1880–93	57.2
1894–1910	55.9
1911–19	52.7
1920–30	43.3
Total 1880–1930	52.3

1 Arrest reports did not distinguish between single, widowed, and divorced women.

*All figures in Appendix B are compiled from the Annual Reports of the Chief Constable of Toronto, 1881–1931.

TABLE B.3
Prostitution-Related Arrests, Toronto, 1880–1930[1]

| Period | Female | | | Male inmates and keepers |
	Inmates and keepers	vagrants	Inmates, keepers, and vagrants	
1880–93	75.0	106.0	181.0	42.0
1894–1910	91.0	109.0	200.0	68.0
1911–19	206.0	310.0	516.0	232.0
1920–30	123.0	157.0	280.0	161.0
1880–1930	123.8	170.5	294.3	125.8

1 Average number of arrests per annum in each period.

TABLE B.4
Prostitution-Related Arrests as a Percentage of Total Female Arrests, Toronto, 1880–1930

Period	Inmates and keepers	Vagrants	Inmates, keepers and vagrants
1880–93	5.4	7.6	13
1894–1910	5.8	7.2	13
1911–19	9.0	13	22
1920–30	3.0	4	7
1880–1930	5.7	7.7	13.4

TABLE B.5
Female Prostitution-Related Arrests as a Percentage of Total Prostitution-Related Arrests, Toronto, 1880–1930

| Period | Offence category | |
	Inmates and keepers	Inmates, keepers, vagrants
1880–93	61.6	82.8
1894–1910	57.2	75.6
1911–19	50.6	70.2
1920–30	43.2	64.3
1880–1930	53.2	73.2

224 Appendix B

TABLE B.6
Arrests of Males for Sexual Offences, Toronto, 1880–1930[1]

Offence	1880–93	1894–1910	1911–19	1920–30	1880–1930
Rape[2]	7.5	10.2	5.3	6.0	7.3
Indecent assault	6.2	15.6	45.0	44.1	27.8
Carnal knowledge	-	2.1	10.0	13.0	6.3
Seduction	1.6	6.1	14.3	13.6	8.9
Procurement	0.6	0.4	5.6	2.3	2.2
Offences against other males[3]	0.3	3.3	21.1	23.2	12.0

1 Average number of arrests per annum within each period.
2 Includes 'attempted rape.'
3 Sodomy, gross indecency, and buggery.

TABLE B.7
Female and Male Arrests for Abortion, Concealment of Birth, and Infanticide, Toronto, 1880–1930[1]

Period	Abortion[2]		Concealment		Infanticide	
	F	M	F	M	F	M
1880–93	5	15	4	–	5	1
1894–1910	7	29	–	–	–	–
1911–19	11	21	4	–	–	–
1920–30	22	29	8	1	–	–

1 Average number of arrests per annum in each period.
2 Includes 'aid to procure an abortion.'

Notes

CHAPTER 1 Introduction

1 Significant exceptions to these generalizations exist. Among Canadian women's historians to study single women workers are Strong-Boag, *New Day Recalled*; among labour historians, the best work on the place of working girls in urban culture remains Klein and Roberts, 'Besieged Innocence.' There is not yet a Canadian urban history that looks at wage-earning women beyond a demographic or economic context. See, for instance, Careless, *Toronto to 1918*. Bradbury, 'Family Economy and Work,' highlights the importance of daughters' work in the household economy and points to intrafamilial tensions over the same. For the most part, however, historians of women and work have concentrated on organized women. See, for instance, Frager, *Sweatshop Strife*.

2 See Careless, *Toronto to 1918*, at 200, for a comparison of Toronto's and Montreal's population growth in the late nineteenth and early twentieth centuries

3 On nationalism and the concept of 'northernness,' see Carl Berger, 'The True North Strong and Free,' in Peter Russell, ed., *Nationalism in Canada* (Toronto 1966), and the articles in his edited collection, *Imperialism and Nationalism, 1884–1914* (Toronto 1969). The Group of Seven's art, popularized at the very point at which Canada became a predominantly urbanized country, rested largely on its subject–matter – the uninhabited Canadian wilderness.

4 On 'masterlessness,' see Merry E. Weisner, *Working Women in Reformation Germany* (New Brunswick, NJ, 1986). Other important studies that look at patriarchal restrictions on independent female workers include Martha C. Howell, *Women, Production and Patriarchy in Late Medieval Cities* (Chicago

1986); Heath Dillard, *Daughters of the Reconquest: Women in Castilian Town Society, 1100-1300* (Cambridge 1984); and Barbara Hanawalt, ed., *Women and Work in Pre-Industrial Europe* (Bloomington 1986).

5 On France, see Joan Scott, 'L'Ouvrière! Mot impie, sordide ...': Women Workers in the Discourse of French Political Economy, 1840-1860,' in Scott, *Gender and the Politics of History*; on England, see Valverde, 'Domestic Turn.'

6 The supposed higher moral standards of domestic workers were belied by statistics on illegitimacy in industrializing England. See Gillis, 'Servants.' On the migration of single pregnant women from rural France to Paris, see Fuchs, *Poor and Pregnant*.

7 The literature on women and work is too extensive to review in detail. Among the more influential US works over the last two decades are Kessler-Harris, *Out to Work*; Baron, ed., *Work Engendered*; Milkman, ed., *Women, Work and Protest*. For Britain, see Alexander, 'Women, Class and Sexual Difference'; Cohn, *Occupational Sex-Typing*; Rendall, *Women in an Industrializing Society*; Rose, 'Gender at Work'; John, ed., *Unequal Opportunities*; and Taylor, *Eve and the New Jerusalem*. For Canada, see Bradbury, 'Women's History'; Cohen, *Women's Work*; Parr, *Gender of Bread-winners*; and Frager, *Sweatshop Strife*.

8 Farge and Klapisch-Zuber, eds, *Madame ou Mademoiselle?* 7. The authors do not confine themselves to young, potentially marriageable women (as I do), but also explore feminine solitude in respect to old women. The 'grisette' and the 'flaneuse' were French versions of public women who embraced the city but rejected feminine sexual restraint and circumspection. On the literary images of these single women, see Wolff, 'Invisible Flaneuse.'

9 See, for example, Jane Lewis, ed., *Labour and Love: Women's Experience of Home and Family, 1850–1940* (New York 1986); and Louise Tilly and Joan Scott, *Women, Work and Family* (New York 1978).

10 See, for instance, Cohen, *Women's Work*; Tentler, *Wage-Earning Women*; Bradbury, 'Women and Wage Labour.'

11 The classic work on intrafamilial tensions over daughters' work and play is Ewen, *Immigrant Women in the Land of Dollars*. Tentler explores this issue in native-born as well as immigrant families in *Wage-Earning Women*, 85–114.

12 In St Paul, Minnesota, for example, 33.6 per cent of adult working women in 1900 were boarders or lodgers: Meyerowitz, *Woman Adrift*, 4. On the different expectations imposed on daughters and sons, see Bradbury, *Working Families*, 118–51.

13 The first woman barrister in the British empire was a single woman from

Toronto who battled the Ontario legislature and the Law Society of Upper
Canada to gain admission to the profession. See Backhouse, '"To Open
the Way."' Similar battles were fought by the first women who struggled
against the male medical establishment.

14 Vicinus, *Independent Women*; Carroll Smith-Rosenberg, 'The New Woman
as Androgyne: Sexual Disorder and Gender Crisis, 1870–1936,' in Smith-
Rosenberg, *Disorderly Conduct*.

15 Stansell, *City of Women*; Peiss, *Cheap Amusements*; Meyerowitz, *Women
Adrift*. For an excellent review of literary depictions of wage-earning
women, see Hapke, *Tales of the Working Girl*.

16 Peiss, *Cheap Amusements*, 6.

17 Faderman, *Surpassing the Love of Men*, is most closely identified with the
body of work in lesbian history that identifies the nineteenth century as a
golden age of women's passionate friendships, replaced, by the 1920s, by
the pathologizing of women's same-sex love. For an analysis that links
this reaction to a more general backlash against first wave feminism, see
Jeffreys, *The Spinster and Her Enemies*. For the United States, see Smith-
Rosenberg, 'The New Woman as Androgyne.' On the pro-marriage
campaign in Canada, see Snell, 'The White Life for Two.'

18 On the concept of 'race suicide' and the schemes implemented to combat
it, see McLaren, *Our Own Master Race*.

19 Elizabeth Lunbeck contends that young single women whom psychiatrists
labelled 'hypersexual' were working-class versions of the New Woman.
While both violated norms of female dependency and respectability, it is
doubtful that they shared a similar consciousness of their violations of
behavioral norms. Lunbeck, '"A New Generation of Women."'

20 Two decades ago, Alice Klein and Wayne Roberts adopted this approach.
See their 'Besieged Innocence.'

21 Ryan, *Women in Public*, 71. See also Scott, 'L'Ouvrière ... Mot Impie.'

22 Walkowitz, *City of Dreadful Delight*, 21–2.

23 Palmer, *Descent into Discourse*, 5.

24 Walkowitz, *City of Dreadful Delight*, 8. Joan Scott has borne most of the
credit and criticism for introducing historians to poststructuralist theory;
see the essays in her *Gender and the Politics of History*. For hostile
responses based on the defence of material history, see the comments by
Bryan Palmer and Christine Stansell in *International Labor and Working-
Class History* 31 (Spring 1987), 14–23 and 24–9. Scott defended her work in
'A Reply to Criticism,' *International Labor and Working-Class History* 32 (Fall
1987), 39–45. For a defence of historical materialism, see Palmer, *Descent
into Discourse*. Deborah Thom has blamed discourse analysis for the rise of

gender as a opposed to women's history, see 'A Lop-Sided View: Feminst History or the History of Women?' in Kate Campbell, ed., *Critical Feminism: Argument in the Disciplines* (Buckingham 1992). Lorna Weir provides an incisive critique of historians' limited understanding of textual analysis in 'Wanderings of the Linguistic Turn.'

25 These records include assize minute books and criminal court indictment files (most of which included nothing more than the official complaint, but some of which included evidentiary material including coroner's inquest transcripts, depositions from witnesses and defendants, incriminating material – in one sexual assault indictment file, a used condom! – and correspondence from defence lawyers, Crown attorneys, and the attorney general of Ontario). All indictments bearing women's names as defendants or principal Crown witnesses were selected, numbering over 300 in total. Unfortunately, the records of the Police Magistrate's Court – the level at which most women encountered the criminal justice system, typically as vagrants, drunk and disorderly persons, or prostitutes – have been destroyed. Each of the reformatory case files from the Andrew Mercer Ontario Reformatory for Females, the Alexandra Industrial School, and the St Mary's Industrial School were examined (a total of more than 3,000 cases). Again, most case files provided little more than a brief admission description, but a few include correspondence between prison officials, parents, social workers, truancy officers, Big Sisters, Children's Aid workers, and inmates themselves.

26 Joan Sangster discusses the possibilities for uncovering women's 'voice' through court documents in '"Pardon Tales.' Karen Dubinsky reads court documents relating to sexual assault 'against the grain' in *Improper Advances*.

27 Allen, *Sex and Secrets*. Judith Allen does not assume that women are everywhere, at all times, in danger of being victimized, but she does argue, along with most feminists, that crimes against women tend to be underreported.

28 Two general histories that attempt to show the less seemly side of Toronto are Glazebrook, *Story of Toronto*, and Frederick Armstrong, *A City in the Making: Progress, People and Perils in Victorian Toronto* (Toronto 1988). The essays in Russell, ed., *Forging a Consensus*, also represent an attempt to move away from the onward-and-upward genre of urban history that has characterized the historiography. For a recent history in this traditional vein, see William Kilbourn, *Toronto Remembered: A Celebration of the City* (Toronto 1984).

29 Carol Lee Bacchi draws connections between the romanticization of rural

Canada and the resistance to feminism at the turn of the century in *Liberation Deferred?*

30 Williams, *City and Country*, 227. This is how writers such as Dickens, Hardy, and Mayhew depicted the 'city of darkness.' In contrast, metropolitan centres such as Paris and London could also appear as 'cities of light' and emblems of progress to more optimistic observers of urbanization and social change (229).

31 The two most noteworthy examples are Piva, *Condition of the Working Class*, and Kealey, *Toronto Workers Respond*. An early exception to this masculinist focus is Roberts, *Honest Womanhood*.

32 Valverde, *Age of Light*, 17. Valverde describes the enormously influential churchman as a stereotypical moral reformer, 'keen on prohibiting pleasures and uninterested in people's welfare' (54–6).

33 Ibid, chapter 5; McLaren, *Our Own*, chapter 4. For Europe, see Moss, *Nationalism and Sexuality*, and Nye, *Crime, Madness and Politics*. Concerns about race suicide and national decline were also evident in Australia in this period. See Judith Allen, 'Octavius Beale Re-considered: Infanticide, Babyfarming and Abortion in NSW, 1880–1939,' in Sydney Labour History Group, *What Rough Beast? The State and Social Order in Australian History* (Sydney 1982), 111–29.

34 Canadian historians prefer the term 'Social Gospel' to describe the broad-based reform movement that swept through rural and urban Canada in the late nineteenth and early twentieth centuries. I use 'Progressivism' because the movement in Toronto was so directly influenced by social and political changes in US cities. The Chicago Vice Commission, for example, not the city surveys conducted by the Canadian Board of Evangelism and Reform, was the model chosen by the promoters of a vice survey in Toronto.

35 Steven Maynard's excellent work confirms that the policing of gross indecency, buggery, and sodomy consumed an enormous amount of the Toronto force's time, particularly after the 1910s when the fight against organized prostitution was also at its height. 'Through a Hole in the Lavatory Wall: Homosexual Subcultures, Police Surveillance, and the Dialectics of Discovery, Toronto, 1890–1930,' *Journal of the History of Sexuality* 5, no. 2 (1994), 207–42.

36 Sharon Hartman Strom's finely textured account of white-collar women shows how differences in age, education, salary, position, and class background defined different classes of workers even within the ranks of businesswomen. *Beyond the Typewriter: Gender Class, and the Origin of Modern American Office Work* (Urbana 1992).

37 Denise Riley, *'Am I That Name?'* 16, 9.

CHAPTER 2 City Work, Moral Dilemmas

1 Marjorie Cohen has shown that among twenty to thirty-year-olds in
Toronto, there were 89.1 men for every 100 women in 1851. The sex ratio
for young adults gradually dropped to 76.1 over the following fifty years.
She does not, however, distinguish between single and married adults:
Women's Work, 163-4, 121.
2 Selected statistics from the 1871, 1881, and 1891 census as compiled by
Gregory S. Kealey, *Working-Class Toronto,* 4, table 1.
3 Canada, *Census,* 1901, vol. 3, table 2, 24–31.
4 In 1870, annual starting salaries for women teachers were approximately
$230, while men earned almost $600. As late as 1900, women teachers in
Toronto started at $324 per year – $100 less than male street-sweepers:
French, *High-Button Bootstraps* 20–1.
5 Kealey, *Toronto Workers Respond,* 50, 187–8.
6 Toronto *Daily Mail and Empire,* 3 October 1897, quoted in Frager,
Sweatshop Strife, 104
7 On class factions in the women's movement in Toronto, see Roberts,
Honest Womanhood.
8 Chris Weedon distils this Foucauldian insight in *Feminist Practice,* 107–11.
For Foucault's analysis of power and discourse, see *The History of
Sexuality,* volume 1: *An Introduction* (Harmondsworth 1981), 92–104.
9 Ryan, *Women in Public,* 63
10 An exception is Trofimenkoff, 'One Hundred and Two Muffled Voices.'
11 The royal commission uncovered evidence of food deprivation, confinement in dungeons and physical abuse of child workers in Canadian
factories. The investigators described this evidence as 'the darkest pages
in the testimony' of witnesses who appeared before the commission. For a
sketch of child labour in Ontario in this period, see Bullen, 'Hidden
Workers.'
12 Canada, *Report of the Royal Commission on the Relations of Labour and Capital*
(Ottawa 1889), vol. 1, Majority Report, 87 (hereinafter cited as *Labour and
Capital*).
13 Ibid., vol. 5, Ontario Evidence, 347.
14 Ibid., 291.
15 Many of Ontario's cigar-makers were unionized in the 1880s, and in some
cases women workers were also unionized. See evidence of August
Eichlorn, *Labour and Capital,* vol. 5, 306.
16 Ibid., 291.

17 Ibid., 338, 287.
18 Ibid., 358, 316.
19 Alexander, 'Women, Class and Sexual Differences,' 144. On the resistance of working-class men to the rights of women workers to organize, see Barbara Taylor, '"The Men Are as Bad as Their Masters": Socialism, Feminism and Sexual Antagonism in the London Tailoring Trade in the Early 1830s,' *Feminist Studies* 1 (Spring 1979), 7–40, 19.
20 *Labour and Capital*, 359, 1009.
21 Ibid., 1079, 1162.
22 Meyerowitz, *Women Adrift*, 44. The percentage of women living apart from their families in twenty-eight US cities in 1900 ranged from a high of 33.6 per cent in St Paul to a low of 10.8 per cent in Jersey City: ibid., 4. The Toronto YWCA's estimates of 'homeless' working girls never exceeded 20 per cent.
23 *Labour and Capital*, Minority Report, 36.
24 Ibid., 73.
25 Ibid., vol. 5, 168.
26 Ibid., Majority Report, 90, 91.
27 Ibid., vol. 5, 1009.
28 Ibid., Majority Report, 91. Aside from a few socialist women, the Canadian left maintained this class-based critique and failed to address both 'the sexual exploitation and the economic exploitation inherent in [prostitution].' Newton, 'Wage Slave to White Slave,' 233.
29 Canada, *Census*, 1911, vol. 6, table 6, 262–75.
30 Jean Scott, 'The Conditions of Female Labour in Ontario,' *Toronto University Studies in Political Science*, First Series (no. 3, 1892), 9–31, 19.
31 Ontario, Bureau of Industry, *Annual Report* (1887), 28.
32 Scott, 'Conditions of Female Labour,' 19.
33 Ibid.
34 Canada, *Report of the Royal Commission on a Dispute Respecting Hours of Employment between the Bell Telephone Co. of Canada, Ltd. and Operators at Toronto, Ontario* (Ottawa 1907), 32 (hereinafter cited as *Bell*).
35 Ontario, 'Report of the Bureau of Labour,' *Sessional Papers* (1907), 150–67. Men working in the shoe and fur industries, for example, earned approximately twice the wage of women workers, who in turn received almost twice as much as the regular staff at Bell.
36 Striking operators estimated food and board costs of $16 to $18 per month, leaving women who were self-supporting with a $6 shortfall that made overtime work essential. Joan Sangster, 'The 1907 Bell Telephone Strike,' 118, note 46.
37 Heron and Palmer, 'Prism of the Strike.'

38 *Bell*, 98–101, 97.

39 Eisenstein, *Give Us Bread*, 52, 49.

40 Quoted in Sangster, 'The 1907 Bell Telephone Strike,' 119.

41 *Bell*, 34. Dunstan's estimate of self-supporting operators in his employ at 30 to 40 per cent was undoubtedly low: ibid., 41.

42 Ibid., 98.

43 Studies of medical experts and urban Progressivism include Leavitt, *The Healthiest City*. For Toronto, see Heather MacDougal, '"Enlightening the Public": The Views and Values of the Association of Executive Health Officers of Ontario, 1886-1903,' in Charles Roland, ed., *Health, Disease, and Medicine: Essays in Canadian History* (Toronto 1984), 436–64. For the influence of doctors in formulating eugenic social policies in Canada, see McLaren, *Our Own Master Race*.

44 *Bell*, 42.

45 Ibid., 56–9.

46 Ibid., 68–9. These doctors were asked to testify because they had treated a number of 'telephone girls' for eye troubles, headaches, throat problems, and nervous strain.

47 Ibid., 72. Clarke later became instrumental in linking feeble-mindedness and criminality. In 1913, troublesome cases from the newly established Juvenile Court were sent to his Social Service Clinic, attached to the University of Toronto. Not surprisingly, he diagnosed the vast majority of boys and girls as feeble-minded. McLaren, *Our Own*, 41.

48 *Bell*, 75, 77.

49 Ibid., 97–8.

50 Ibid., 98.

51 Ibid., 6. Bell's chief office manager, Frank Maw, told the Toronto *Star* that the operators were already exhausted when they came to work because they spent their evenings roller-skating. *Star*, 7 February 1907.

52 *Bell*, 100.

53 The company taught operators how to use courteous speech in order to convey the company's respectable image. Martin, 'Subjugating the Voice'; *Bell*, 30

54 Chief Manager Sise to Hamilton manager, 1907, quoted in Sangster, 'The 1907 Bell Telephone Strike,' 121.

55 Canada, *Report of the Board of Inquiry into the Cost of Living* (Ottawa 1915), vol. 1, 71.

56 Of the thirty-eight participants in the commission, eleven were women. Miss Lucy Brooking, superintendent of the Alexandra Industrial School, Miss Carson of the Concord Industrial Farm for Women, and Mrs Emma

O'Sullivan of the Mercer Reformatory made up the correctional contingent. Mrs H.D. Warren, the convenor of the Committee on Women's Employments of the Toronto Women's Patriotic League, and Miss M.A. Fitzgibbon, the superintendent of the Women's Welcome Hostel, represented those who saw domestic labour as the solution to the problem of women's unemployment.

57 Ontario, *Report of the Ontario Commission on Unemployment* (Toronto 1916), 13 (hereinafter cited as *Unemployment*). MacMurchy was a provincial bureaucrat at the time of the 1916 commission. She was also the sister of Dr Helen MacMurchy, the country's leading exponent of eugenics and the founder of the provincial health branch that dealt with the feeble-minded.

58 *Unemployment*, 15, 16.

59 Ibid., 59 (emphasis added).

60 Ibid., 60, 61.

61 Ibid., 180.

62 Ibid., 183, 68.

63 This was the general conclusion of the 1915 federal investigation into the rising cost of living: 'The "gospel of ease" preached from every platform [has] permeated the national life of the Anglo-Saxon race and has had its influence in the formation of present conditions.' Canada, *Report of the Board of Inquiry*, 12.

64 *Unemployment*, 69.

65 Ibid., 181. The domination of the Toronto labour market in white collar work was equally apparent in the retail sales sector. The report estimated that approximately 6,000 of the province's 15,000 to 18,000 saleswomen worked in Toronto: ibid., 176

66 Ibid., 181, 182, 178.

67 Testimony of Emma O'Sullivan, ibid., 195.

68 The proportion of women working in service dropped dramatically in Canada, from 41 per cent of the female labour force in 1891 to 34 per cent in 1901, 27 per cent in 1911, and 18 per cent in 1921. Ontario led the provinces in this national trend, and Toronto led the trend in Ontario. Marilyn Barber, 'The Women Ontario Welcomed: Immigrant Domestics for Ontario Homes, 1870–1930,' *Ontario History* 72 (September 1980), 148–72, 148, 170–1.

69 The Toronto *Telegram* reported on 14 September 1914 that 'women who a few months ago had to advertize two or three times before getting one application for a maid now have from fifty to one hundred anxious applicants.'

70 *Unemployment*, 52.

71 Former servant's testimony in the Toronto *Star*, 29 March 1910, quoted in Roberts, *Honest Womanhood*, 14. See also Genevieve Leslie, 'Domestic Service in Canada, 1880–1920,' in Janice Acton et al., eds, *Women at Work* (Toronto 1974), 71–125, 93.

72 Goldwin Smith, quoted in Roberts, *Honest Womanhood*, 13.

73 See Davidoff, *Best Circles*, on rituals of deference in domestic work in Victorian England.

74 Quoted in Roberts, *Honest Womanhood*, 14.

75 MacMurchy's qualifications had come from her work as a journalist. She had been the literary editor of *The News* and had written in several journals and papers, including *Harper's Bazaar*, *Saturday Night*, the *Globe*, and *The Canadian Courier*, in which she had chronicled the problems of working girls in 1911. Henry Morgan, *Canadian Men and Women of the Time* (Toronto 1912), 714–15.

76 The census considered artists, teachers, law clerks, stenographers, trained nurses, typists, and 'office employees' to be professionals. Canada, *Census*, 1911, vol. 6, table 6, 262–75.

77 Stenographers and typists were among the least-well trained and the poorest paid of the 'professionals' listed in the 1911 census. As chapter 7 will show, they had become the most marginal of office workers by the post-war period.

78 Strong-Boag, 'Girl of the New Day.'

CHAPTER 3 Ruined Girls and Fallen Women

1 *Toronto Evening News* (hereinafter cited as *News*), 10 July 1888; PAO, Toronto (York) Coroner's Reports, 'Brown,' 1888. Irving had used the name 'Brown' as an alias.

2 For theoretical analyses of anti-urban and agrarian mythologies, see Smith, *The City and Social Theory*, and Williams, *The Country and the City*. Bacchi, *Liberation Deferred?* touches on rural nostalgia as an impetus behind turn-of-the-century moral reform movements in English Canada.

3 For a comprehensive study of the rise of police forces in the United States, see Monkkonen, *Police in Urban America*.

4 Boritch, 'Making of Toronto the Good,' York University, 87.

5 Jones, *Outcast London*, 280–90.

6 'Annual Report of the Chief Constable for the City of Toronto' (hereinafter cited as ARCC), *Toronto City Council Minutes* (1891), 21 (1890), 48–9.

7 Ibid., 1888, 414.

8 The staff inspector's office was, for many years, the only specialized division of the Toronto police force. The status of the office was shown as well in Staff Inspector David Archibald's salary which, at $1,218.25, was higher than any other inspector's in the 205-man force in 1887.
9 ARCC, 1892, 28.
10 ARCC, 1871, 13.
11 Until the 1880s clerks in police departments and correctional facilities continued to list 'prostitution' as a woman's trade. Whether arrestees themselves gave this reponse when asked their occupation is unclear.
12 Philippa Levine, 'Consistent Contradictions: Prostitution and Protective Labour Legislation in Nineteenth-Century England,' *Social History* 19, no. 1 (January 1994), 17–35, 21.
13 *News*, 18 May 1888.
14 Quoted in Pedersen, '"A Building for Her,"' 227.
15 Toronto YWCA, Minutes, May 1881.
16 Toronto YWCA, *Annual Report*, 1879, 19.
17 Toronto YWCA, Minutes, May 1883.
18 Boarding-house applicants were required to provide a letter of reference. Most women presented a letter from a minister or former employer.
19 Toronto YWCA, *Annual Report*, 1878, 10.
20 Ibid., 1879, 8.
21 Ibid., 1880, 32.
22 Toronto YWCA, Minutes, 7 December 1883.
23 Morton, 'Seduced and Abandoned.'
24 While boarding-houses received 'friendless girls,' the Haven took in women who could not supply a satisfactory reference vouching for their moral reputation: Toronto YWCA, Minutes, 1881.
25 Toronto YWCA, *Annual Report*, 1880, 28.
26 ARCC, 1870. In the same year, the police made 586 arrests of women for drunkenness and 219 for vagrancy.
27 Toronto YWCA, *Annual Report*, 1879, 18.
28 Toronto YWCA, Minutes, June 1881.
29 Toronto YWCA, *Annual Report*, 1888, 10.
30 On Britain, see Walkowitz, *City of Dreadful Delight*, chapter 1. On the United States, see Barth, *City People*, 58–110.
31 The vast majority of women charged with prostitution were tried summarily in Police Court. Unfortunately, these records were destroyed regularly and none survive from this period.
32 It appears from an analysis of indictments between 1880 and 1930 that approximately five such charges were laid in Toronto.

33 PAO, Toronto (York) High Court of Justice, Criminal Assize Indictments (hereinafter cited as HCJ, CAIs), Tate, 1886.
34 The maximum possible sentence for women sent to the Mercer was two years less a day. Most women in this period served sentences of less than one year. For an analysis of sentences and time served, see Strange, 'Velvet Glove,' University of Ottawa.
35 Mrs Bennet, the alleged procuress, sued the *News* for $10,000 in damages in May 1885, but she lost her suit. Although the Crown attorney did not prosecute her either as a procuress or as a keeper of a brothel, Bennett was later convicted on an unrelated perjury charge. She was sentenced to six months at the Mercer Reformatory on 29 June 1885. HCJ, CAIs, Bennet, 1885.
36 Ibid., Stewart, 1887.
37 In the 1880s and 1890s, seventy-one indictments for rape were filed in York County, resulting in only eight convictions. I have been unable to locate a successful prosecution of a rape committed upon a working girl. See HCJ, CAIs, Ryan and Christie, 1884, for examples of cases that led to convictions. Carolyn Strange, 'Patriarchy Modified: The Criminal Prosecution of Rape in York County, 1880-1930,' in Jim Phillips, Tina Loo, and Susan Lewthwaite, eds, *Essays in the History of the Criminal Law* (Toronto 1994).
38 HCJ, CAIs, Jones, 1892.
39 Ibid., Gibson, 1881.
40 Ibid., Burns and Mitchell, 1888.
41 Ibid., Fee, 1880.
42 Ibid., Graham, 1886.
43 Coroner's Reports, 1888.
44 For a typical range of abortion options, see HCJ, CAIs, Norfolk, 1886. Rachel Fuchs examines abortion and birth control in *Poor and Pregnant*, chapter 8.
45 HCJ, CAIs, Gamble, 1888.
46 Backhouse, 'Involuntary Motherhood,' 83. On the prosecution of abortionists in the nineteenth-century United States see Mohr, *Abortion in America*. For Britain, see Dickens, *Abortion and the Law*.
47 Constance Backhouse states that Andrews spent only 203 days at the penitentiary. It is unclear whether he was pardoned, became ill, or died after that point. In any event, another Dr Andrews did operate an abortion practice in Toronto in the 1890s: 'Involuntary Motherhood,' 91.
48 In 1888, a midwife who operated a home for unwed mothers on Teraulay

Street in the heart of the Ward was tried and acquitted for the murder of Lizzie Parker, a fur cutter engaged to be married to a fellow employee with whom she had been 'keeping company' for a year. Parker died with a detached fetus at her side. Toronto (York) HCJ, CAIs, Woods, 1888.

49 On infanticide, see Fuchs, *Poor and Pregnant*, chapter 9.
50 Backhouse, 'Desperate Women,' 477.
51 Judith Allen touches on several of these points in *Sex and Secrets*, 30–40.
52 Gordon, *Woman's Body;* McLaren, 'Birth Control and Abortion in Canada'; Backhouse, 'Desperate Women.'
53 The common abortifacients pennyroyal and tansy produced systemic toxicity and may, as a side effect, have induced miscarriages. On the use of abortifacients in Canada, see McLaren and McLaren, *The Bedroom,* 34. On the United States, see Gordon, *Woman's Body*, 36–7.
54 Women inserted anything from strips of slippery elm bark to catheters or knitting-needles to produce miscarriages: McLaren and McLaren, *The Bedroom,* 34.
55 Ward, 'Unwed Motherhood.' Infanticide rates were even greater earlier in the century. Only seven women were arrested in Toronto for infanticide in the 1860s, even though the coroner investigated the suspicious deaths of almost sixty infants in the same decade. Eric James Jarvis, 'Mid-Victorian Toronto: Panic, Policy and Public Response, 1857–73,' Ph.D. thesis, University of Western Ontario (1978), 134–5.
56 Backhouse, 'Desperate Women,' 456, 462. Included in arrest statistics are charges for murder, manslaughter, and concealment of birth. Murder was the only capital offence.
57 Toronto YWCA, *Annual Report*, 1880.
58 Coroner's Inquests, 1891.
59 HCJ, CAIs, 1884. In another case the mother was so quick to leave a lodging-house that she was never found. This time, neighbourhood children, playing in a snowbank, came upon the body of an infant who had been strangled to death with a piece of dress and buried in the snow; no charge was laid. Coroner's Inquests, 1887.
60 Infanticides were usually pinned on women who disposed of their infants in their own living quarters. Women placed infants in shoeboxes, trunks, and stovepipes, and under floorboards. In these cases, smells and blood stains proved too difficult for other residents to ignore. See HCJ, CAIs: Flanagan, 1881; Harris, 1888; and McGinnis, 1885.
61 Judith Allen, 'Octavius Beale.'
62 HCJ, CAIs, Berry, 1891.

63 Toronto *World*, 2 March 1891.
64 On the 'politics of the street' see Stansell, *City of Women*, 193–217.
65 *News*, 10 April 1883, 5 May 1881. On the rough and rowdy environment of Halifax's poorest quarters, see Fingard, *Dark Side of Life*, 19–20.
66 Police constables' records show that from 1880 to 1893 the Toronto police made an annual average of 78 arrests of women on assault charges. In 1883, for example, 102 assault arrests were made, second only to drunk and disorderly arrests. In addition, an average of 37 arrests were made per annum on the charge of using insulting language.
67 Several other Toronto women were charged with murder in this period, but they were married women who killed their children and were subsequently found to be insane.
68 Mary Hartman, *Victorian Murderesses: A True History of Thirteen Respectable French and English Women Accused of Unspeakable Crimes* (New York 1977); Ruth Harris, *Murders and Madness: Medicine, Law and Society in the Fin de Siècle* (Oxford 1989). The story of the most famous French muderess to be acquitted in this period is told in Edward Berenson, *The Trial of Madame Caillaux* (Berkeley 1992).
69 In the absence of confirmation of Ford's marital status, and in view of her independent living, I have categorized her as single. As Arlette Farge and Christine Klapich-Zuber argue, narrowly conceived notions of the single woman as simply 'la femme devant la mariage ou, tout au plus, la femme hors mariage' miss the wider cultural meanings of singlehood. See their *Madame ou Mademoiselle?* 9.
70 Census figures indicate that in the 1890s the black population in Toronto numbered less than five hundred. Most of the men worked in the railway industry as porters, while domestic service employed the bulk of Toronto's black women. I shall refer to Ford as 'black' except when quoting directly from contemporary sources.
71 Westwood's murder caused such a stir partly because murder was still relatively rare in Toronto. In several years in the 1890s, for instance, not a single murder was reported. Most murders were inflicted on victims closely related to the perpetrator – usually family or friends – and were therefore relatively easy to solve.
72 Ruth Harris, *Murders and Madness*, 213–14. Harris notes that most women who availed themselves of the crime-of-passion defence were members of the petit bourgeoisie with a highly developed sense of honour.
73 Testimony of Detective Reburn as recorded in Justice Sir John Boyd's bench book, 2 May 1895. Supreme Court of Ontario, Judge's Bench Books, Spring Assizes, 1895 (Criminal), 22 April–26 June 1895, Osgoode Hall. The

term 'insult,' used by several rape complainants in this period, was a euphemism for sexual assault.

74 Trial testimony of Clara Ford, quoted in Wallace, 'The Case of Clara Ford,' *Murders and Mysteries*, 78.

75 Robin Winks, *The Blacks in Canada: A History* (Montreal 1971). Winks notes that the black population in Canadian cities declined after the Emancipation Proclamation. For the racist paternalism that characterized white Torontonians' impressions of blacks, see Denison, *Recollections of a Police Magistrate*.

76 Peter Brooks, *The Melodramatic Imagination: Balzac, Henry James, Melodrama and the Mode of Excess* (New Haven 1976).

77 Charlesworth, *Candid Chronicles*, 242.

78 *Globe*, 24 November 1894. Earlier speculation was equally melodramatic. The police had believed that a woman must be involved somehow, and that the person who had shot Westwood was likely to have been the father of a young woman 'ruined' by the young man.

79 Detective Reburn's testimony, quoted in Justice Boyd's bench book, 2 May 1895.

80 *Empire*, 23 November 1894.

81 *World*, 29 November 1894.

82 On racist perceptions of black men and women as sexually aggressive and promiscuous, see Hall, *Revolt against Chivalry*.

83 *World*, 26 November 1894. In 1882 the *World* had reported on another case in which a woman had apparently gotten away with murder. In a 4 September letter to the Ottawa *Free Press*, which had reprinted the article, a correspondent stated that until women had the strength of Samson, 'men need not be surprised if the pistol is sometimes used.' I am grateful to Russell Prime for this reference.

84 Osler had been one of the prosecuting counsel in the trial of Louis Riel.

85 *World*, 1 May 1895.

86 Ibid., 6 May 1895.

87 HCJ, CAIs, 1915.

88 The article continued: 'Many of the women were well-dressed and evidently of the "upper" stratum, but they pushed and jostled with the rest, intent on satisfying a more or less morbid curiosity.' *Daily News*, 16 February 1915.

89 *Telegram*, 22 February 1915.

90 *News*, 26 February 1915.

91 Ibid., 27 February 1915.

92 *Telegram*, 27 February 1915.

CHAPTER 4 The Social Evil in the Queen City

1 C.S. Clark to Deputy Attorney Cartwright, 24 April 1898. PAO, RG4, Series 32, Attorney General, Files, Civil and Criminal, 557, 1898. Cartwright's response to Clark is not in the file.

2 On the interpretation of women's dress as a signifier of moral categories, see Mariana Valverde, 'Love of Finery.'

3 ARCC, 1894, 15.

4 Ibid., 1896, 11.

5 Clark was a journalist with the Montreal office of the Toronto Publishing Company. Although he is mentioned in virtually every history of Toronto, no further biographical information on him in secondary and archival sources appears to exist.

6 Judith Walkowitz studies the bourgeois male's fascination with urban exploration in *City of Dreadful Delight*, chapter 1.

7 Clark to Cartwright, c. 20 May 1898. Clark sent a copy of his book to York County Crown Attorney Curry for comment as well. Neither Cartwright's nor Curry's reply to this second letter is in the file.

8 Clark, *Of Toronto*, 131, 14.

9 Ibid., 89.

10 Ibid., 89, 91, 133 (emphasis added).

11 Ibid., 93, 102, 106. Clark's outlandish claim has often been cited uncritically to show that Toronto was as vice-ridden as cities such as Chicago, or that it was at least less pure than its reputation would suggest. Lori Rotenberg, for instance, opens her article on prostitution in Toronto at the turn of the century with this quotation to show the extent of the trade. See Lori Rotenberg, 'The Wayward Worker: Toronto's Prostitute at the Turn of the Century,' in Acton et al., eds, *Women at Work*, 33–69, 33.

12 Quoted in Clark, *Of Toronto*, 98. Clark merely updated the fifth-century BC text which, like all of the Proverbs, was written to instruct youth in the mysteries of leading a pure life in a wicked world.

13 Ibid., 101.

14 Lynda Nead explores the iconography of the prostitute's suicide in *Myths of Sexuality*, chapter 5, and 182–96. Suicide by drowning seemed to be British artists' favourite image.

15 Clark, *Of Toronto*, 118, 119.

16 On Stead's campaign and its legislative results, see Gorham, 'Maiden Tribute.'

17 Graham Parker, 'The Origins of the Canadian Criminal Code,' in David H. Flaherty, ed., *Essays in the History of Canadian Law*, vol. 1 (Toronto

1981), 249–81. Parker argues that the 1892 Code 'had and retains the most comprehensive system of offences for protecting young women and girls from sexual predators' (268).

18 *Criminal Code of Canada* (1892), c. 29, s. 185.

19 Ibid., sections 186, 187, 281, 282.

20 NCWC, *Handbook*, 1907, 83.

21 Ibid., 1910, 54.

22 NCWC, *Annual Report*, 1912, 49.

23 Mrs Gordon, the chairperson of the NCWC's Committee on the White Slave Traffic, recommended in her 1911 report that all council women read the book. NCWC, *Handbook*, 28.

24 Rev. Dr John Shearer, 'The Canadian Crusade,' in Ernest A. Bell, ed., *The War on the White Slave Trade* (Toronto [1911] 1980), 333–64, 334.

25 Ibid.

26 Ibid., 347.

27 Ibid., 348.

28 Ibid., 254–5.

29 Prior to the amendment, only women under the age of twenty-one could be deemed victims of procurement.

30 John McLaren provides a comprehensive review of the stiffer sanctions against prostitution and procurement introduced in the Criminal Code Amendment Act (1913), 3 & 4 Geo. V, c. 13, in 'White Slavers,' 83–4.

31 On the social gospel, see Allen, *Social Passion*. For an overview of reform sentiment in the period, see Cook, *The Regenerators*.

32 Leaders of the settlement house and reformatory movement in Toronto made regular visits to large US cities, and some were trained in the United States. Several mayors during the period made explicit comparisons between Toronto and US cities, rather than Canadian ones, to measure the extent and pace of municipal improvement in areas such as health and recreation. For the Canadian movement see Rutherford, ed., *Saving the Canadian City*. The classic study of American Progressivism remains Robert Wiebe's *Search for Order*.

33 ARCC, 1897, Mayor's address, 10.

34 I elaborate this argument in Strange, 'From Modern Babylon.'

35 The Committee of Fifteen, *The Social Evil, with Special Reference to Conditions Existing in the City of New York* (New York 1902), 8.

36 Rosen, *Lost Sisterhood*, 214–27.

37 Chicago, The Vice Commission of Chicago, *The Social Evil in Chicago: A Study of Existing Conditions* (Chicago 1911), 1.

38 Ibid., 231

39 Toronto Council of Women, *Nothing New Under the Sun*. This concise hagiographic account of the council provides a sketch of the TLCW's preoccupations over its early years.
40 Toronto Local Council of Women, Minutes, PAO, Series A, Box 1, MU 6362, December 1912
41 Ibid., 19 March 1913.
42 Mrs Campbell Meyers of the 'Survey Committee.' Ibid., May 1913.
43 Only one other woman was appointed. Adelaide Plumptre represented the St James (Anglican) Cathedral Rectory, where she was engaged in social work.
44 Toronto, Social Survey Commission, *Report of the Social Survey Commission, Toronto, Presented to the City Council, October Fourth, 1915* (Toronto 1915), 7 (hereinafter cited as Toronto *Report*)
45 Chicago, *The Social Evil*, 32.
46 Toronto *Report*, 7.
47 Ibid., 15, 14.
48 Ibid., 15–16.
49 On the Western identification of Asians with 'exotic' forms of sensuality, see Said, *Orientalism*.
50 Toronto *Report*, 34
51 Ibid., 35. The quotation was taken from a report in *Leslie's Weekly*. Kaufman was not a member of the commission, nor were there any representatives from the labour movement who participated in the survey.
52 Toronto *Report*, 34.
53 Ibid., 34, 35, 36.
54 Ibid., 36, 37.
55 Ibid., 38.
56 Ibid.
57 Valverde, *Age of Light*, 108–10.
58 For France, see Nye, *Crime, Madness and Politics*. For Germany, see Moss, *Nationalism and Sexuality*. For England, see Weeks, *Sex, Politics and Society*. For Australia, see Allen, 'Octavius Beale.'
59 Toronto *Report*, 41, 42. The Presbyterian and Methodist churches both established departments of 'the stranger' in the 1910s to deal with overseas immigrants, including British people. Valverde, *Age of Light*, 120–8
60 Toronto *Report*, 42, 43.
61 Ibid., 14–15. The Surveyors believed that 'the opportunities for the establishment of a "white slave" system are nowhere so favourable as in the foreign sections of a great city.' Ibid., 42.

62 In 1913 MacMurchy had strongarmed the Ontario government into establishing a Department of the Feeble Minded and installing her as its director. Her eugenic proclivities became more pronounced as her career proceeded: see her *Sterilization?*

63 Toronto *Report*, 47–8, 47.

64 Roberts, 'Purely Administrative Proceedings,' 207–27. Some were deported simply for being 'immoral,' a code that included a range of transgressions but usually referred to single motherhood.

CHAPTER 5 Good Times and Bad Girls

1 Petit was a graduate of the University of Toronto, a journalist, a Methodist church worker, and a member of the University Women's Club. *Star*, 1 June 1912.

2 Marjory MacMurchy, who would later write *The Canadian Girl at Work*, also wrote a series of articles for the *Canadian Courier* between May and August 1912. On the phenomenon of professional women posing as working girls to expose the 'realities' of working-class life, see Hapke, *Tales of the Working*. A classic example of 'feminine cross-class' writing is Richardson, *The Long Day*.

3 Toronto *Star*, 1 and 6 June 1912.

4 Figures tabulated from the City Directory. Included were theatres, rinks, concert halls, nickelodeons, and amusement parks.

5 For a critique of Marxist approaches to the study of working-class leisure, see Jones, 'Class Expression,' 162–4.

6 Kathy Peiss has observed that nineteenth-century commercial amusements were 'homosocial' spaces. Poolrooms, bowling alleys, cigar shops, and saloons were among the urban spaces 'colonized by men' in late nineteenth-century cities: *Cheap Amusements*, 16–17.

7 Armstrong and Nelles, *Methodist Bicycle Company*. Those who opposed Sunday cars feared that Toronto would adopt a 'wide-open' Sunday and become indistinguishable from the sinful cities to the south: ibid., 61.

8 Toronto YWCA, Minutes, 1883.

9 *Globe*, 28 March 1903.

10 Excerpts from the 'amusements' columns of Toronto daily newspapers, 1880–1900. For Hanlan's point, see Gibson, *More Than an Island*, 96.

11 Clark, *Of Toronto*, 93, 106, 133. In his list of public assemblies he included band concerts, religious street shows, and Salvation Army parades.

12 Ibid., 122, 111–12, 114. On courtship conventions among literate, property-holding English Canadians in the nineteenth century, see Ward, *Courtship, Love and Marriage.*

13 Central Neighbourhood House, Headworker's Report (hereinafter cited as CNH), April 1913, City of Toronto Archives, SC 5-B, Box 1. Neufeld's research team compiled a list of thirty-five 'houses of ill-repute' and recorded the names of the owners; in addition, they took down the names of fifteen prostitutes 'and some of the causes of their downfall.'

14 Toronto *Report,* 54–9.

15 In New York, these women were known as 'charity girls.' For the definitive study of working girls' leisure as a moral problem, see Peiss, *Cheap Amusements.*

16 Toronto *Report,* 12.

17 Hapke, *Tales of the Working Girl,* 50–2. Richardson's *The Long Day* was particularly contemptuous of the boisterous paper-box workers with whom she had worked in New York.

18 Toronto *Report,* 12.

19 Lenton, 'Vaudeville in Toronto,' University of Toronto.

20 Filey, *I Remember Sunnyside,* chapter 1; Gibson, *More Than an Island,* 141–2; excerpts from the amusement columns of Toronto daily newspapers, 1900–1920. Exhibition attendance generally exceeded 100,000 on Labour Days alone in the early twentieth century. In the summer of 1902 Sunny-side Beach was the only free bathing spot in the city open to women and girls. Over that season, Sunnyside hosted 31,475 visitors: *News,* 2 September 1902.

21 Toronto *Report,* 13.

22 Ibid., 51.

23 The Methodists were anxious about the 'grave danger of [modern] dancing both to health and morals.' Department of Evangelism and Social Service of the Methodist Church, 'The Methodist Church and Dancing,' 1921, Baldwin Room, Broadside Collection.

24 The classic Progressive tract on recreation is Addams, *Spirit of Youth.* On the playground movement in the United States, see Cavallo, *Muscles and Morals.*

25 By 1914 there were nine supervised playgrounds in Toronto where there had been none only five years earlier. Over the same period, Toronto spent $1.35 million on new and improved parks. Hocken, 'New Spirit,' 86.

26 CNH, Board Minutes, 25 April 1911, Headworker's Summer Report, 1912.

27 Ibid., Headworker's Report, October 1913.
28 Reports about the 'well supervised weekly dance' indicated 'goodly' crowds in the first few weeks. After January 1914, however, there was nothing more said in the minutes about the scheme.
29 Peiss uses this term to describe the culture of 'sexual expressiveness and social interaction' between men and women in their leisure pursuits in turn-of-the-century New York City: Cheap Amusements, 6.
30 Municipalities were empowered to establish separate juvenile courts after the passage of the federal Act Respecting Juvenile Delinquents, 1908. Canada, Statutes, 1908, 7–8 Edw., c. 40, s. 35.
31 Robinson, Decades of Caring, 9, 20, 37, 32.
32 The Toronto WCTU made this estimate in 1912. Klein and Roberts, 'Besieged Innocence,' 216.
33 Valverde, Age of Light, 67–76.
34 Headline of announcement flyer, Board of Evangelism and Social Service Papers, Methodist Church of Canada, United Church Archives, Box 3, 1915.
35 Toronto Slur, 1 May 1912.
36 Foucault, History of Sexuality, 122.
37 Lunbeck, 'New Generation of Women,' 513.
38 Schlossman and Wallach, 'Precocious Sexuality,' 49.
39 Starr, 'First Annual Report of the Juvenile Court,' 201.
40 M.J. Clarke, 'The Attitude of the Neighbourhood Worker,' Public Health Journal 7, no. 12 (December 1916), 498–500, 498. The biographical information about Miss Clarke was provided by Jennifer Stephen.
41 Linda Gordon discusses a similar institution in Boston staffed by psychiatric social workers who treated 'sex delinquents' sent by the courts and social work agencies. Linda Gordon, Heroes of Their Own Lives, 13, 68.
42 C.K. Clarke, 'A Study,' 11–24
43 Most of the women were unwitting subjects who had gone to the hospital simply to be treated for venereal diseases and gynaecological disorders. C.K. Clarke, 'Toronto General Hospital Psychiatric Clinic,' 30–7.
44 Clarke, 'A Study,' 12.
45 Ibid., 12–13.
46 Starr, 'Charities and Corrections,' 569.
47 Foucault, Discipline and Punish, 293–308. On juvenile delinquency, see Platt, Child Savers.
48 Toronto Report, 30–1.

49 Ibid., 31–2.
50 Canada, Act Respecting Juvenile Delinquents, preamble. The Act applied to minors under sixteen who violated the Criminal Code, statute laws, or municipal bylaws, and empowered local jurisdictions to establish a separate juvenile court to try all cases involving children.
51 Canada, House of Commons, *Debates*, 8 July 1908, 12404.
52 Toronto was the only city in the province to have industrial schools for both boys and girls. By 1893 Toronto's industrial schools were supervised by the Children's Aid Society, which reported to provincial authorities.
53 If children were deemed neglected, dependent, or immoral, CAS agents could recommend that they be sent to reformatories for a maximum of two years or until they reached the age of eighteen. Ontario, Act for the Prevention of Cruelty to and better Protection of Neglected and Dependent Children, 1893, c. 45, s. 14(2).
54 Canada, House of Commons, *Debates*, 8 July 1908, Mr Graham, 12404.
55 For the United States, see Estelle Freedman, *Their Sisters' Keepers: Women's Prison Reform in America, 1830–1930* (Ann Arbor 1981), chapter 3.
56 The campaign for a women's reformatory and girls' refuge is covered in Strange, 'Velvet Glove,' chapter 1.
57 The first provincial reformatory for men, at Guelph, was not built until 1916.
58 Minors were to be tried summarily, and evidentiary standards were lower than they were in adult criminal courts unless they were charged with indictable offences. Even then, the police magistrate could change the venue to juvenile court in the interest of the child and of justice. Canada, Act Respecting Juvenile Delinquents, 1908, s. 17.
59 In adult reformatories, an indeterminate sentence could technically last no longer than two years less a day. In practice, juvenile sentences were seldom limited to a particular term; rather, most were 'indefinite' and could last until a minor reached the age of twenty-one. Strange, 'Velvet Glove,' 75–7.
60 All statistics are based on the analysis of the Mercer Reformatory prisoner register in Strange, 'Velvet Glove.' Analyses of the Alexandra and St Mary's inmate registers were not conducted.
61 Schlossman and Wallach state that the courts 'did not distinguish between actual delinquency and predelinquency because they saw their mission as the treatment of underlying causes:' 'Precocious Sexuality,' 55.
62 Ontario, An Act Respecting the Andrew Mercer Ontario Reformatory for Females, 1913, 3 & 4 Geo. V, c. 78, s. 9. Under the BNA Act, the provinces were responsible for the administration of the criminal law.

63 According to the Criminal Code, those charged under section 228, 'Keeping a Disorderly House,' could be sentenced to one year's imprisonment; those charged under section 229, 'Being found in any Disorderly House,' could be sentenced for terms not exceeding twelve months; and those convicted under section 238, 'Vagrancy,' could be sentenced for maximum terms of six months.

64 Ontario, 'Annual Report of the Superintendent of the Andrew Mercer Ontario Reformatory for Females' (hereinafter cited as ARS in OSP), 1919, *Ontario Sessional Papers*, 1920, 48.

65 It is not possible to give accurate committal figures because the case files did not always indicate how an inmate ended up behind bars. Over half the files examined, however, indicated that the parents or other relatives had at least cooperated in sending a young woman to prison. Once the juvenile court opened in 1912 it referred the bulk of Alexandra and St Mary's inmates, even though parents remained the principal instigators of complaints.

66 Ontario, Ministry of Correctional Services, 'Alexandra Industrial School for Girls, Case Files' (hereinafter cited as AISG Case Files), PAO, RG 60, D-3, Reel 1, 1-303, 'Neale,' 5 August 1892. Sentences at Alexandra and later at St Mary's ranged from six months to as much as ten years. Names cited are pseudonyms.

67 David Garland discusses the intersection of welfare and penal strategies in *Punishment and Welfare*.

68 AISG Case Files, PAO, RG 60, D-3, Reel 1, 1-303, 'Dupont,' 3 March 1923.

69 The conflicts between immigrant parents and their daughters over wages are explored in Tentler, *Wage-Earning Women*, 109–11, and in Ewen, *Immigrant Women*, 106–8. Many of the inmates of the St Mary's (Catholic) Industrial School were daughters of European immigrants.

70 Gordon, *Heroes*, 244. Gordon bases her interpretation on records from social work agencies and only incidentally on police and prison records.

71 St Mary's Industrial School for Girls, Case Files (hereinafter cited as SM Case Files), PAO, RG 60, 'Flambeau,' Report of Mr O'Connor, 13 March 1917.

72 Donzelot, *Policing of Families*.

73 SM Case Files, 'Lavallée,' excerpt from juvenile court transcript, 13 May 1919.

74 The employment of white women by Chinese men was technically illegal. Ontario, An Act to amend the Factory, Shop and Office Building Act, 1914, c. 40, s. 2. None the less, the provincial minister of labour reported in 1923 that 126 white 'girls' worked in 121 Chinese restaurants in Toronto alone. Ontario, *Journals of the Legislative Assembly*, vol. 57, 1923, 28.

75 SM Case Files, 'Lavallée,' 1919.
76 Ibid. Hincks worked with Clarke and was a leader in the local and national campaign against venereal disease and feeble-mindedness. He founded the Canadian National Committee on Mental Hygiene in 1918. McLaren, *Our Own*, 109–10.
77 SM Case Files, 'Lavallée,' 1919.
78 Sample release form from 'Jean Nolan's' file, SM Case Files, 28 March 1906.
79 As an informal precedent for the position of parole officer at the Mercer Reformatory, Chief Inspector Rogers introduced 'field officers,' the first of whom was Margaret Howe. Although the Parole Board was operational by 1917, Mercer maintained field officers until 1921.
80 SM Case Files, 'Chisholm,' 1919; CAS inspector John Simpson to J.J. Kelso, 16 September 1919.
81 Ibid., Report of Mr O'Connor, 10 June 1907.
82 Ibid., 4 October 1907.
83 Andrew Mercer Reformatory for Females, Case Files (hereinafter cited as AMORF Case Files), PAO, RG 20, Series D-13, 'Camden,' 28 July 1904.
84 Ibid., 'Fergus,' extract from Dr King's Day Book, 3 November 1913.
85 Ibid., February and June 1916; Howe's reports on released inmates.
86 Ontario, Provincial Secretary's Correspondence, PAO, RG8, 1-1-B-1, Box 10, Howe to O'Sullivan, 14 October 1916.
87 AMORF Case Files, 'Cook,' letter of O'Sullivan to employer, 22 July 1912.

CHAPTER 6 Temptations, Crimes, and Follies

1 Wodson, *Whirlpool*, 147, 149.
2 A. Baldwin Sloane, composer, and Edgar Smith, lyricist. Copyright, Charles K. Harris, 1910. The chapter title is borrowed from a line in the chorus: 'From temptations, crimes and follies Villains, taxi-cabs and trolleys Oh! Heaven will protect the working girl.' On the image of white slavery in films, see Meyerowitz, *Women Adrift*, 63–4.
3 Song titles listed in the Apex Records 'New Releases for December 1924.' Baldwin Room, Ephemera Collection.
4 For the United States, see Rosen, *The Lost Sisterhood*; Connelly, *Response to Prostitution*; and Peiss, *Cheap Amusements*. For Canada, see Rotenberg, 'Wayward Worker'; Valverde, *Age of Light*; and McLaren, 'White Slavers.' On the regulation of homosexual acts, see S. Maynard, "Through a Hole in the Lavatory Wall: Homosexual Subcultures, Police Surveillance, and the Dialectics of Discovery, Toronto, 1890–1930,' *Journal of the History of Sexuality* 5, no. 2 (1994), 207–42.

5 McLaren, 'White Slavers,' 85–101. On the attack on male sexual licence, see Gilfoyle, *City of Eros*, 181–221.

6 ARCC, 1897, 33, and 1904, 26.

7 The police refused to cooperate with the Social Survey Commission in its investigation, and ultimately refuted the conclusions of the report: *Telegram*, 4 October 1915.

8 ARCC, 1916, 17.

9 Although the number of people arrested for being found in a brothel fluctuated from the 1890s to the 1920s, the number of arrestees in 1915 was more than ten times greater than in any other year. Not until the 1940s did the annual number of arrests again reach this level.

10 Men who gambled or lived off the avails of prostitution for a living could be charged under specific provisions of the Criminal Code rather than under the general category of vagrancy.

11 Boritch does not include any female vagrancy charges in the category of prostitution arrests: 'Making of Toronto,' 59. A study that errs in the opposite direction is Watts, 'Police Response.'

12 From 1910 to 1915, vagrancy charges accounted for 59 per cent of possible prostitution offences. During the 1920s it remained high at 54 per cent, with the charges of frequenting and operating brothels accounting for the remainder.

13 ARCC, 1915, 16.

14 Bylaws and police ordinances were supplemented by rules imposed by individual New York City dancehall operators intent on maintaining a respectable image: Peiss, *Cheap Amusements*, 104–5.

15 The force of two consisted of Mary Minty, formerly a guard at the Mercer Reformatory, and Margaret Leavitt of the Methodist Fred Victor Mission.

16 ARCC, 1915, 17 and 1920, 29–30. There were already several women who worked for the police department as 'matrons,' but their duties were confined to in-house station work.

17 Ibid., 1925, 8.

18 Ibid., 1924, 24.

19 *Globe*, 30 December 1912.

20 *Star*, 13 January 1913; *Telegram*, 14 January 1913.

21 Backhouse, 'Canadian Rape Law,' 200–47.

22 One study that suggests the expansion of the middle class and the rising status of women account for the rise in sexual assault arrests is Ferdinand, 'Criminal Patterns.'

23 Boritch, 'Making of Toronto,' 231

24 Lane, 'Urban Police'; Gurr, 'Historical Trends,' 28.

25 The city's foreign-born, non-British immigrants comprised 9.1 per cent of the population, but in 'the Ward' they accounted for one-third of the inhabitants. Bureau of Municipal Research, 'What Is "The Ward" Going to Do with Toronto? Report on Undesirable Living Conditions in One Section of the City of Toronto – "The Ward" - Conditions Which are Spreading Rapidly to Other Districts,' Toronto, 1918, CTA SC 3, 37

26 Elizabeth Neufeld, 'Life in the Ward,' CTA, SC 5-D, Box 1, typescript, 1. Her draft article went on to urge Torontonians that the Ward was really the 'safest and friendliest place on earth.'

27 Woodsworth, *Strangers within Our Gates*. Woodsworth was a Methodist minister and the founder of the All Peoples Mission in Winnipeg, where half the population was foreign-born.

28 Wodson, *Whirlpool*, 147, 156.

29 Denison, *Recollections*. Denison found blacks 'a source of amusement in the court because of their many peculiarities' (39). Toronto lawyer J. Cleland Hamilton and Ontario Court of Appeal Justice William Renwick Riddell also publicly portrayed blacks as incompetent, uncivilized people. Winks, *The Blacks in Canada*, 298, 291–4.

30 HCJ CAIs, 1901. On the myth of the black rapist in this period, see Hall, *The Revolt against Chivalry*.

31 *Globe*, 9 November 1901. Although death was the maximum penalty for rape prior to 1873 and an optional maximum (with the alternative of life in prison) after that year, not one man was executed for rape after Confederation.

32 *World*, 12 November 1901.

33 Toronto *Star*, 11 November 1901; *News*, 11 November 1901. In Toronto, for instance, the police made 20 arrests for rape and sexual assault in 1901, but only 12 were tried at the assizes. In the entire first decade of the century, only 35 men were tried for rape and 8 were convicted. Hawes's sentence was the stiffest.

34 Supreme Court of Ontario Criminal Assize Indictment Files (hereinafter cited as SCO CAIs), 1920; *Star*, 30 October 1920. It is not clear whether or not the men were later pardoned.

35 *Jack Canuck*, 1, no. 4 (16 September 1911).

36 ARCC, 1911, quoted ibid. For anti-Asian sentiment in law enforcement circles, see Emily Murphy, *Black Candle* (Toronto), 188, 186. Murphy was the Police Court magistrate of Edmonton.

37 CCJCC, CAI, 1913. In a similar case, Horace Wing was convicted for procuring white women who had answered his advertisement in the *Telegram* for girls to fill positions. Two working girls testified that he had

asked them to sleep with him. Wing was given a suspended sentence after he appealed the verdict in November 1913: ibid.

38 General Sessions (hereinafter cited as GS CAIs), 1910.

39 By the 1890s, Jews represented the single largest religious group after Protestants and Catholics: Harney and Troper, *Immigrants*. Men from eastern and southern European countries were also vulnerable to charges of sexual assault. See GS CAIs, Peskalis, 1918.

40 SCO CAIs, 1923.

41 In another case, Clarence Short lured Goldie McGuire from a dancehall to a deserted field. McGuire managed to free herself when Short tried to attack her, and ran to the protection of nearby rail workers: GS CAIs, 1930. Short was convicted of indecent assault and sent to the Guelph Reformatory for one year determinate and six months indeterminate. He was also given twenty lashes.

42 The idea of an informal women's vigilance patrol was introduced by the YWCA and approved by the Toronto police in 1917 as a means of keeping young women from going astray and as an effort to curb venereal disease among recruits. The patrol was disbanded in 1918. ARCC, 1919, 25.

43 SCO CAIs, 1919.

44 Supreme Court of Ontario Indictment Reports, York, Fall 1919, Minutes, 9. PAO, RG 22, Series 391, Box 141. The witnesses and court officers were the only people allowed at the trial. O'Hara's accomplice appears to have been allowed to plead guilty to a lesser charge.

45 O'Hara was not tried because he pleaded guilty. He received a sentence of fifteen years along with ten lashes after three months' detention, followed by ten more after nine months. Ibid., Box 143, 1928–9.

46 The percentage of men found guilty of rape in York County was 7.4 per cent in 1890–1899; 22.9 per cent in 1900–9; 33.3 per cent in 1910–19; and 25 per cent in 1920–9. Strange, 'Patriarchy Modified.'

47 GS CAIs, 1918.

48 In a 1918 case involving a fifteen-year-old woman and a fifty-four-year-old man, Robinette managed to have Alex Kene's conviction for 'unlawful intercourse' quashed on appeal because the jury and judge had both misunderstood the 'previously chaste' clause. He showed that Elsie Stoner could not have been chaste, since Kene had had sex with her when she was only twelve. GS CAIs, 1918.

49 GS CAIs, 1910, Aylesworth to Winchester, November 1910. Ewers appears to have been the son of a small-town Ontario mayor, and his family was able to afford this expensive appeal process.

50 Ibid., 1910, Winchester to Aylesworth, 17 November 1910.

51 CCJCC CAIs, 1913. Ferris was acquitted.

52 Ibid. The word 'sobbing' appears in the verbatim transcript.

53 The movement for racial purity and a precipitous decline in national birth rates were both evident throughout the Western world from the mid-nineteenth to the mid-twentieth century. For France see McLaren, *Sexuality and Social Order*; on the United States see Gordon, *Woman's Body*, and Reed, *Private Vice*; on Australia see Allen, 'Octavius Beale'; on Canada see McLaren and McLaren, *Bedroom and the State*, and Backhouse, 'Involuntary Motherhood.'

54 McLaren, 'Birth Control.' Quebec's higher birth rate was known among Anglo-Protestant nationalists as the 'revenge of the cradle' and was cited as further evidence of racial degeneration.

55 Linda Gordon argues that the period from 1905 to 1910 was the high-water mark of 'race suicide' hysteria in the United States, although the eugenics movement carried those fears into scientific schemes for 'race betterment' over the following two decades. Gordon, *Woman's Body*, 136–8.

56 Mrs Louisa Simmons, a part-time waitress at the New York Lunch, received a three-month sentence at the Concord Industrial Farm for Women for helping out fellow waitresses 'in trouble.' In another instance, a young box maker, Ivy Atchinson, sought help from a married co-worker whose brother had put her 'in the family way.' GS CAIs, 1919, and CCJCC CAIs, Leonard, 1929.

57 Clark, *Of Toronto*, 127. Clark had slipped a condom into his letter to the deputy attorney general to make his point. He also asked that it be returned.

58 Ibid., 331.

59 Home abortions were in many instances more dangerous than procedures performed by professionals. Overdoses of pennyroyal, ergot, or cotton root could easily lead to the death of the woman before the fetus. See CCJCC CAIs, Eldred, 1903.

60 Backhouse, 'Involuntary Motherhood,' 82–3, n. 82. Backhouse contends that 'the primary enforcement focus ... was upon the provision of medical services' and that abortion laws were enforced as 'a method of regulating the practice of medicine.' Ibid., 85.

61 It appears that one of the city's policewomen, Mary Mayhew, was used in a sting operation against Margaret McKenzie, a thirty-two-year-old married woman who performed an abortion on Agnes Bethel in 1928. The police threatened Bethel, her mother, and two other working women with $500 fines if they refused to testify against McKenzie. The abortionist

received one year definite and two years less a day indefinite at the Mercer Reformatory: GS CAIs, 1928.

62 GS CAIs, Coulter, 1916. Sweet was a charity patient, so it is not clear whether paying patients would have been subject to such scrutiny. This method of medico-legal regulation was also employed in the investigation of knife and gun wounds as well as venereal diseases.

63 GS CAIs, 1912.

64 Greer countered that the Crown had simply to show that Backrack had had reason to believe he was the father and that he, along with his older brother, shared a motive for 'conspiring to procure an abortion.'

65 Most were owners or general managers of financial or manufacturing firms. Included among the supporters were the millionaire piano manufacturer Heintzman, the clothing wholesaler Fairweather and the president of Goldsmith's Stock Company.

66 In another case involving a Jewish defendant, the crown doggedly pursued the prosecution of Dr Benjamin Cohen, a professional who had apparently provided his clients with safe, effective service. After his conviction for performing an abortion and subsequent appeal, however, he went free. SCO CAIs, 1927.

67 Canada, *Census*, 1931, vol. 5, tables 11, 12, and 13. The average earnings for women in Toronto in 1921 were $15.13 and $15.56 in 1931. In 1931 housekeepers earned just under $10, while cooks, waitresses, and cleaners earned slightly more. Low-skilled factory workers did not fare much better: packers and wrappers earned just over $11, and box, bag, and envelope workers earned approximately $12 per week. Ibid., vol. 5, table 23.

68 *Globe*, 22 June 1927.

69 Ibid.

70 Withrow devoted his post-war practice to the promotion of sexual hygiene and 'race betterment.' McLaren, *Our Own*, 82–3. Withrow was appointed the national secretary for sex education by the Dominion YWCA in 1918; his work involved lecturing and distributing pamphlets on sex hygiene.

71 This procedure, which involves the dilation and scraping of the cervix, was routinely used by the 1920s to relieve irregular or painful menstrual periods, but Withrow seemed to treat more than his share of patients with this affliction.

72 'Report of Inspector John Miller, Criminal Investigation Division, Ontario Provincial Police,' PAO, RG 4, Attorney General Files, no. 470, 1927.

73 The Ontario Provincial Police, called in at the behest of the attorney general to coordinate the investigation into Withrow's practice, discovered

that the doctor had performed fourteen D and C's in the month prior to Dembner's operation. Ten of these patients had given married names, but so had Dembner. In her ante-mortem statement, Dembner claimed that she and Brooks had been secretly married in September of 1926.

74 *Star*, 22 March 1927.

75 *Telegram*, 18 May 1927.

76 Brooks appealed his conviction for 'counselling in favour of abortion' on the grounds that he had been acquitted on the charge of manslaughter and because 'the excitement that was voiced everywhere' unduly influenced the jury members to convict, no matter what the evidence. The appeal was granted on the basis of Justice Logie's misdirection and nondirection. At his retrial, a hung jury resulted in his release. *Star*, 20 November 1927; *Mail and Empire*, 20 April 1928.

77 PAO, RG 4, Attorney General Files, no. 470, Price to Hincks, 29 December 1928.

78 McLaren, *Our Own*, 83. By 1933, Withrow regained his medical licence. He continued to supply his patients with contraceptives and established contact with Marie Stopes. Ibid., 194, note 76. On Stopes, see Reed, *Private Vice*.

79 Ontario, HCJ CAIs, 1897.

80 GS CAIs, 1918.

CHAPTER 7 Citizens, Workers, and Mothers of the Race

1 Coombs, 'White Collar Work Force,' York University, 93. For an outline of transitions in the city's economy in the period, see Lemon, *Toronto since 1918*, 12–13.

2 City of Toronto Archives, SC 5, Georgina House, Annual Report (hereinafter cited as GH Annual Report), 1910. In 1914 the annual report mentioned ten other subsidized homes in the city, including those maintained by the WCTU, the Girls' Friendly Society, 'Barbara's House,' Rosary Hall (a Catholic home), and the King's Daughters' Homes, operated by the IODE. Most homes had a sliding scale that ranged from $3.50 to $6.00 per week.

3 *Evening Telegram*, 30 January 1917; GH Annual Report, 1912, 4.

4 Miss Bollert, address before the Halcyon Club in Ottawa, *Ottawa Citizen*, 20 October 1920; Bollert had an MA in social work. *Woman's Century*, January 1917, 8; *Ottawa Citizen*, 20 October 1920.

5 GH Annual Report, 1910, 14. Sherbourne House Club (hereinafter cited as SHC), Scrapbooks, 1917, Fisher Rare Book Library, University of Toronto. Ibid., ca. 1918, 3–4.

6 These lecture titles appeared in the GH Annual Report of 1910. *Star*, 30 January 1917, *Globe*, 2 August 1919.
7 'Rules and Regulations for Boarders,' GH Annual Report, 1919, 37–8, 39. Toronto YWCA, Home Department Minutes, 13 April 1922.
8 GH, 'Correspondence and Miscellaneous,' Superintendent's Report, December 1909. Twenty-four of fifty-five boarders left in the first year.
9 *Star Weekly*, 22 September 1917.
10 GH Annual Report, 1910, 9.
11 Toronto YWCA, 'Minutes,' 17 January 1924.
12 GH, 'Girls' Club Journal,' 1922.
13 Toronto YWCA, Home Department, 'Minutes,' 8 February 1923. This report also referred to 'problems of runaway girls,' presumably young women who left without informing the staff of their whereabouts.
14 GH, 'Girls' Club Journal,' 1923.
15 Ibid.
16 Ibid.
17 Hamilton *Spectator*, 27 February 1920. SHC, 'Scrapbooks,' vol. 11, 1926, 'Sherbourne House Club,' 2.
18 Smith-Rosenberg, 'New Woman.' On 'New Women' see also Vicinus, *Independent Women*. Others have shown how the attack was focused most directly on spinsters and lesbians and their sexual autonomy from men. On the 'morbidification' of lesbianism, see Faderman, *Surpassing the Love of Men*, and Jeffreys, *The Spinster and Her Enemies*, for sexologists' suspicions about feminists and single women.
19 GH, 'Girls' Club Journal,' March 1923.
20 SHC, Scrapbooks, 1925. On the meanings of dress-up parties see Fine, 'Between Two Worlds.'
21 On images of subordination and superordination in public rituals see Natalie Zemon Davis, *Society and Culture in Early Modern France* (Stanford 1975).
22 SHC, Scrapbooks, 1927, 12 October 1929.
23 Toronto's female workforce numbered 68,064 in 1931. Canada, *Census*, vol. 5, table 34, 452.
24 TLCW, 'Minutes,' 18 November and 20 May 1919.
25 Toronto YWCA, 'Minutes,' 15 January 1920, 17 March 1921. The placement rate seems to have increased over time. In October 1920, 297 of 367 applicants were referred to registered rooms.
26 Toronto YWCA, 'Minutes,' Dominion Council of Canada, 'Home Field,' n.d., ca. 1920, 8.
27 Ibid.
28 Toronto YWCA, 'Minutes,' 16 March 1922. A further 349 women used the Room Registry and Employment Bureau.

29 Toronto YWCA, Home Department, 'Minutes,' 12 December 1918, 28 February 1919.
30 Lowe, 'Mechanization,' 182.
31 Ed Andrew remarks that it was not until the war and the training of 'hitherto untrained women who lacked the know-how and solidarity required to resist the speed-up methods' that Tayloristic management techniques took hold: *Closing the Iron Cage*, 72. Most Marxist theorists have overlooked the importance of female clerical workers in carrying out new administrative policies. See Harry Braverman, *Labor and Monopoly Capital*.
32 Taylor, *Principles of Scientific Management*. On the impact of scientific management on the reorganization of Canadian business in the 1920s, see Palmer, *Working Class Experience*, 197.
33 For a discussion of Knox and MacMurchy's guidance literature see Strong-Boag, 'Girl of the New Day.'
34 Ontario, Provincial Board of Health, Division of Industrial Hygiene, *Health Confessions of Business Women by Business Women* (Toronto 1923), 17, 18. The contest organizers edited the letters to correct spelling and grammatical errors and to 'clarify meaning.' It would be questionable, then, to accept every word as authentic, but it is reasonable to assume that businesswomen, and not DIH managers, wrote the letters.
35 The DIH's 1924 annual Report declared that 'The idea of producing a book for a selected group of workers actually written by that group is, it is thought, distinctly original and might well be more widely adopted.' *Health Confessions* was 'favorably reviewed in Canada, England and the United States,' and over 12,000 copies were distributed in the year after its publication. Ontario, *Sessional Papers*, 'Annual Report of the Provincial Board of Health,' 1924, 44; 1925, 42.
36 In 1929, Ruth Shonle Cavan conducted a survey of businesswomen who had attended YWCA clubs and summer camps in the Chicago area. The responses were remarkably similar to those received by the DIH. Their single greatest concern was their appearance, followed by difficulty in achieving a comfortable level of socializing, the demands of families, overwork, and lack of advancement possibilities. Sharon Hartman Strom, *Beyond the Typewriter: Gender, Class, and the Origins of Modern American Office Work* (Urbana 1992), 370, 378.
37 Ontario, *Health Confessions*, 9, 5.
38 Knox, *Girl of the New Day*, 19–29, 29, 28.
39 Ontario, *Health Confessions*, 157.
40 Ibid., 157, 177. Several writers recognized that single men could either afford to have their laundry and housework done for them or count on

their female relatives to maintain them. 'Double Life' put it bluntly: 'The real trouble about a business girl ... is that she's not a man' (123).

41 Ontario, Division of Industrial Hygiene, *Her Own Fault* (Toronto 1921). Mamie has to hide her poor personal hygiene with make-up, perfume, and false curls.

42 Knox, *Girl of the New Day*, 112, 181.

43 Chris Rojek, *Capitalism*, 16. Most feminist analyses of women and leisure focus on married women's 'double day.' See Oakley, *Sociology of Housework*, and, Hargreaves, *Sport*.

44 MacMurchy, *Canadian Girl*, 26, 118, 120.

45 In the second appendix to *Health Confessions*, 'charts to assist in "stock-taking" were provided to guide business women on the science of "Time Accounting."'

46 Knox, *Girl of the New Day*, 130.

47 Members of the Sherbourne House chapter of the IODE donated personnel and money to run a girls' camp for impoverished teenaged factory workers. The *Globe* praised the Sherbourne House women, who themselves knew 'the strain of responsibility and the meaning of weariness at the close of a hard day. Nevertheless, in their spare time these strenuous young women work for those less favoured than themselves.' *Globe*, 27 June 1927.

48 GH, Girls' Club Journal, 1925–7.

49 Ontario, *Health Confessions*, 224–5, 224

50 Hubert Groves, *Toronto Does Her 'Bit'* (Toronto 1918). Groves reported that, as of 1 March 1918, 3,124 Toronto men had died in action: ibid., 7. Approximately 44,000 Toronto residents enlisted over the course of the war, more than any other city in the dominion.

51 MacMurchy, *Canadian Girl*, vi.

52 Knox, *Girl of the New Day*, 12–13

53 Ibid., 117.

54 MacMurchy, *Canadian Girl*, 108.

55 Ibid., 1, 8.

56 Watson, 'Cotton Stockings.'

57 Redpath, 'Galleons of Spain.'

58 Ontario, *Health Confessions*, 10.

59 Ibid., 17.

60 Lowe, 'Mechanization,' 196. Lowe restricts this observation to smaller offices and private secretaries who could forge strong relationships with individual men. In large corporations with steno pools, the work relations more closely resembled the gender hierarchies of factories.

61 Ontario, *Health Confessions*, 42, 38.
62 Ibid., 218, 224, 26.
63 Ibid., 256.
64 Weedon claims that patriarchal culture poses multiple 'subject positions' or 'ways of being' for women so that, at any moment, women might embrace, reject, or resist prescriptive messages of femininity through, for example, dress or deportment: *Feminist Practice*, 86–7.
65 Ontario, *Health Confessions*, 37, 36.
66 The 1919 royal commission was launched after the Winnipeg General Strike in an attempt to seek the causes of industrial unrest and to prevent its recurrence. Minimum wage legislation for women was already in force in Alberta (1917), British Columbia and Manitoba (1918), and Quebec and Saskatchewan (1919). Ontario and Nova Scotia joined in 1920. Strong-Boag, 'The Girl,' 159.
67 Ontario, 'Report of the Minimum Wage Board,' *Sessional Papers*, vol. LV, no. 89 (1923), 24, 25.
68 Toronto was chosen because it was the most industrialized city in the province and because it had the greatest number of wage-earning women in its paid labour force. The estimates were based on the budget for a typical saleswoman: ibid., vol. LIV, no. 73 (1922), 6.
69 The figure of $7 for room and board was based on responses to ads in Toronto papers for a room for a respectable 'working girl.' The replies, none of which was investigated, ranged from $6 to $8 per week (ibid).
70 Resistance to the new law was strongest on the left. The *Worker*, the official organ of the Communist Party of Canada, advocated organizing over accepting the extremely limited provisions of the Minimum Wage Act. Hobbs, '"Dead Horses,"' University of Toronto, 83.
71 Ontario, 'Report of the Minimum Wage Board,' 1923, 25. In 'A Word to Employers,' the MWB stated: 'Your co-operation has helped make strong the work of the Ontario Minimum Wage Board. We count you our friends and believe most of you regard us in the same fashion.'
72 Ibid., 22. Hobbs, '"Dead Horses,"' 86; Ontario, 'Report of the Miniumum Wage Board,' 1927, 5.
73 Strong-Boag, 'The Girl,' 160–3. See also McCallum, 'Keeping Women in Their Place.'
74 *Star Weekly*, 22 September 1917.
75 Ontario, *Health Confessions*, 151.
76 Ibid., 147.
77 'Early Notices of R.W. Eaton,' T. Eaton Company, PAO, Series 61, ca. 1903.

78 Raine, 'Girls Invade Track.'
79 'Company Personnel Office – Recreation Office, 1920-1930,' T. Eaton Company, PAO, Series 182, Box 1. The choral society began in 1919 and had over 150 members by the mid 1920s. In 1924, only 4 out of 100 women in the chorus were married.
80 *Globe*, 7 June 1917.
81 Buckley and McGinnis, 'Venereal Disease.'
82 Cassell, *Secret Plague*, 156–7.
83 Riddell, 'Social Hygiene.' This was his presidential address, delivered at the annual meeting of the Canadian Social Hygiene Council in 1928.
84 McLaren, *Our Own*, 68–9
85 Mort, *Dangerous Sexualities*, 173.
86 Quoted in Cassell, *Secret Plague*, 159.
87 Ibid.
88 Ontario, Provincial Board of Health, Division of Preventable Diseases, Sex Hygiene Pamphlets, PAO, RG 62, Box 467, 1923. The full list of titles prepared in 1923 was 'Facts on Venereal Disease – General'; 'Facts for Boys and Young Men'; 'Facts for Girls and Young Women'; 'Short Description of Venereal Diseases'; and 'Instructions to those Having Venereal Diseases.'
89 Canada, Dominion Department of Health, National Archives of Canada, RG 29, vol. 217, 1920; ibid., 'Information for Young Women About Sex Hygiene,' 1920.
90 Ibid., 'Facts on Sex Hygiene,' 10, 9, 11.
91 William Riddell, 'Presidential Address,' 197.
92 Toronto Social Hygiene Council, 'What Social Hygiene Means to You,' ca. 1923, in Provincial Board of Health, 'Correspondence (York),' PAO, RG 62, A-1, Box 372.
93 Riddell, 'Presidential Address,' 196.
94 A US film, *The End of the Road*, featured two young women from the same town who both went to New York for work. One pure-hearted woman preserves her sexual integrity and goes on to marry a doctor, while the other fun-loving, materialistic woman becomes a sport's paramour and contracts a disease. This film opened in Toronto and toured the country in 1920 to 1921. A total of 500,000 Canadians saw it. Cassel, *Secret Plague*, 207–9.
95 Promotional letter advertising *The High Road*, Ontario, Provincial Board of Health, 'Correspondence (York),' PAO, RG 62, A-1, Box 324, 1921.
96 Ibid.
97 Canada, Dominion Department of Health, 'Facts on Sex Hygiene,' 10.

CHAPTER 8 Conclusion

1 Lynn Y. Weiner, *From Working Girl to Working Mother*, elaborates this shift for the United States. For the changing discourses of motherhood in Canada and other nations, see Katherine Arnup, Andrée Lévèsque, and Ruth Roach Pierson, eds, *Delivering Motherhood: Maternal Ideologies and Practices in the Nineteenth and Twentieth Centuries* (London 1990). For the rise of the child welfare movement in Canada, see Veronica Strong-Boag, 'Intruders in the Nursery: Childcare Professionals Reshape the Years One to Five, 1920–1940,' in Joy Parr, ed., *Childhood and Family in Canadian History* (Toronto 1982), and Strong-Boag, *New Day Recalled*, 145–78. On models of deviant motherhood, see Margaret Little, '"A Fit and Proper Person": The Moral Regulation of Mothers through Ontario Mothers Allowance, 1920–1993' (Ph.D. thesis, York University 1993); Andrée Lévèsque, *La Norme et les deviantes: Des femmes au Québec pendant l'entre deux-guerres* (Montreal 1989).
2 On a similar equation between female emancipation and modernity in this period, see Sato, '*Moga* Sensation.'
3 George Chauncey, *Gay New York: Gender, Urban Culture, and the Making of the Gay Male World, 1890–1940* (New York 1994).
4 Editorial Collective, 'Why Gender History?' *Gender and History* 1, no. 1 (Spring 1989), 1–6, 1.
5 Judith Bennett, 'Feminism and History,' *Gender History* 1, no. 3 (Autumn 1989), 251–72, 259.
6 Ong, *Spirits of Resistance*, 4, 6. This excellent study, which incorporates Marxist, Foucauldian, and feminist analyses of capitalism and colonialism, looks at the phenomenon of 'spirit possession' among the young women recruited into factory labour as 'part of a non-capitalist critique of capitalist practices.' See also Christine Pelzer White, 'Vietnam: War, Socialism and the Politics of Gender Relations,' in Sonia Kruks, Rayna Rapp, and Marilyn B. Young, eds, *Promissory Notes: Women in the Transition to Socialism* (New York 1989), 172–92; Linda Lim, 'Capitalism, Imperialism and Patriarchy: The Dilemma of Third World Women Workers in Multinational Factories,' in June Nash and Patricia Maria Fernandez Kelly, eds, *Women, Men and the International Division of Labor* (Albany 1983); Sally Errington, *Power and Difference: Gender in Island Southeast Asia* (Stanford 1990); and John P. Neelson, ed., *Gender, Caste and Power in South Asia: Social Status and Mobility in Transnational Society* (New Dehli 1991).
7 Susan Faludi demolishes contemporary myths about the dangerousness of women's independence in *Backlash: The Undeclared War against American*

Women (New York 1991). Critics have suggested that there was never a 'pre-backlash' era when feminist calls for women's independence were greeted sympathetically. Perhaps the most notorious example is Freda Adler, *Sisters in Crime: The Rise of the New Female Criminal* (New York 1975), a study that attributed the rise in certain forms of female offending to feminism.

Bibliography

ABBREVIATIONS

BR Baldwin Room, Metropolitan Toronto Reference Library
CTA City of Toronto Archives
FRD Thomas Fisher Rare Book Library, University of Toronto
NAC National Archives of Canada
PAO Public Archives of Ontario
UCA United Church Archives
UTA University of Toronto Archives

NEWSPAPERS AND PERIODICALS

Globe
Empire
Mail
World
Star
Telegram
Jack Canuck
Chatelaine, vols 1–4, 1928–30
Social Welfare, vols 1–12, 1918–30
The Woman Worker, 1926–9

ARCHIVAL HOLDINGS

Apex Records, 'New Releases for December 1924,' BR, Broadside Collection
Central Neighbourhood House, 'Board Minutes,' CTA, SC 5-B, Box 1, 1911–30

Children's Aid Society of Toronto. Complaint Books, 1892–1930. CTA, SC 1, D6

Company Personnel Office – Recreation Office, 1920–30, PAO, T. Eaton Co., Series 182, Box 1

Department of Social Service, University of Toronto, *Calendar*, 1918–19. UTA

Early Notices of R.W. Eaton, PAO, T. Eaton Co., Series 61, 1900–30

Georgina House. Annual Reports. 1909–29. CTA, SC 9

– 'Girls' Club Journal,' 1925–7. CTA, SC 9, Box 5

Lyons, Florence, 'The Story of a Tea Room in the 1920s,' n.d. CTA Papers and Theses, Box 10

Methodist Church, Department of Evangelism and Social Service, 'The Methodist Church and Dancing,' 1921. BR, Broadside Collection

– Papers, UCA, 1915–20

Neufeld, Miss Elizabeth, 'Life in the Ward,' CTA, SC 5-D, Box 1

Patterson, Norman, 'Evolution of a Department Store,' c. 1907. CTA Papers and Theses, Box 11

Recreational Department, Annual Report, 1930, PAO, T. Eaton Co., Series 183, Box 1

Robert Simpson Co., 'Thumbnail Sketches,' 1927. PAO Pamphlets, No. 5

'Shea's Yonge St Theatre Programme, 1 October 1900,' BR Broadside Collection

Sherbourne House Club, Scrapbooks, 1916–47. FRB

'Some Canadian Authors of Today, Facing the Public with New Books,' 1922. BR Broadside Collection

'Toronto between the Wars,' BR Oral History Project, 192

Toronto East End Day Nursery and Settlement Papers. BR Manuscript Collection, S51

Toronto Local Council of Women, Minutes, 1903–28. PAO, MU 6362, Series A

– Annual Reports, 1925–6. PAO, MU 6373

Toronto Young Women's Christian Association. Annual Reports, 1874–95, 1918–19. PAO, B-1 MU 3527–8

– Boarding House Committee, 1885–92. PAO, A-2, MU 3523

– Cafeteria Committee – Minutes, 1920–30. PAO, A-2, MU3525, Box 9

– Home Department – Minutes, 1916–30. PAO, A-2, MU 3525

– Minutes, 1873–1929. PAO, A-1, MU 3517

GOVERNMENT RECORDS

City of Toronto

'Annual Report of the Chief Constable of the City of Toronto,' CTA, RG 9, 1870–1931

Board of Police Commissioners, 'Minutes,' 1880–1930
Bureau of Municipal Research, 'Municipal Police Service,' 14 December 1927.
CTA, SC 3
– 'What Is 'The Ward' Going to Do with Toronto? A Report on Undesirable
Living Conditions in One Section of the City of Toronto – 'The Ward' –
Conditions Which are Spreading Rapidly to Other Districts,' 1918. CTA SC 3
Toronto. Social Hygiene Council. 'What Social Hygiene Means to You,' c.
1923, in Provincial Board of Health, 'Correspondence (York),' PAO, RG 62,
A-1, Box 372
Toronto. Social Service Commission. *Report Dealing with Origins, Duties,
Growth and Work since November 1912* (Toronto 1921)
Toronto. Social Service Commission. *Report of the Social Survey Commission of
Toronto.* UCA, Doc HN 29, M4TO

Ontario
'Annual Report of the Superintendent of the Andrew Mercer Ontario
Reformatory for Females,' 1919, *Sessional Papers*, 1920
Attorney General. Criminal and Civil Files, 1880–1930 PAO, RG4, 4-3a
– Minister's Correspondence, 1926-30. PAO, R.G. 4, 4-02
County Court Judges Criminal Court, Criminal Assize Indictments, County of
York, 1886–1930. PAO, RG 22
Court of General Quarter Sessions of the Peace, Criminal Assize Indictments,
County of York, 1880–1930. PAO, RG 22
Hodgins, Frank Egerton, 'Report on Venereal Diseases,' *Sessional Papers*, no.
59 (1919): 3–25
Minimum Wage Board, 'Annual Reports,' *Sessional Papers*, 1921–31
Ministry of Correctional Services, Alexandra Industrial School for Girls. Case
Files, 1892–1930. PAO, RG 20, D-3, Reels 1–16, 22, 23
– Alexandra Industrial School and St Mary's Industrial School Miscellaneous
Records, 1900–30. PAO, RG 20, D-3, Reel 25
– Mercer Reformatory for Females, Case Files, 1880–1928. PAO, RG 20, D-13
– Mercer Reformatory for Females, Prison Register, 1898–1930. PAO, R.G. 20,
E-13
– St Mary's Training School for Girls, Case Files, 1900–30. PAO, RG 60, D-12,
Reels 1–11
Provincial Board of Health. Correspondence (York), 1907–26. PAO, RG 62,
A-1
– Circular Letters, 1925–6. PAO, RG 62, A-2
– Departmental Memoranda, 1925–6, PAO, RG 62, A-2
– Division of Industrial Hygiene. *Health Confessions of Business Women.*
Toronto: Provincial Board of Health, 1923. PAO, RG 62, E-1

- Division of Industrial Hygiene. Correspondence and Memoranda, 1921–6. PAO, RG 62, E-1
- Division of Industrial Hygiene. *Her Own Fault.* 1921. PAO RG 62, Series 1-E, Box 468
- Division of Preventable Diseases. Circular Letters, Memoranda and Reports of Clinicians, 1920–7. PAO, RG 62, C-1
- Division of Preventable Diseases. Questionnaires and Publications, 1920–3. PAO, RG 62, C-2-c
- Division of Preventable Diseases. Reports of Clinicians, 1920–7. PAO, RG 62, C-2-c
- Division of Preventable Diseases. Reports of Social Service Nurses, 1925–7. PAO, RG 62, C-2-c
- Division of Preventable Diseases, Sex Hygiene Pamphlets, 1923. PAO, RG 62, Box 467
- Division of Preventable Diseases. Special Clinic Reports, 1921–6. PAO, RG 62, C-2-c

Provincial Police Files. 'Ruth Dembner Case,' PAO, RG 23, E-93, Box 1, item 1.11
Report of the Ontario Commission on Unemployment (Toronto 1916)
Supreme Court of Ontario. Criminal Assize Indictments – Toronto (York) Case Files, 1880–1930. PAO, RG 22
- Indictment Reports, York County, PAO, RG 22, Series 391, 1880–1930
Toronto (York) Coroners Inquests. PAO, RG 22, 05/124, 1877–1907
- Crown Attorney. General Sessions Court Books, 1916–29. PAO, RG 22, 05/b/36

Canada
Census. 1881–1931
Dominion Department of Health, National Archives of Canada, RG 29, vol. 217, 'Information for Young Women About Sex Hygiene,' 'Facts on Sex Hygiene,' 1920
Report of the Board of Inquiry into the Cost of Living, vol. 1 (Ottawa 1915)
Report of the Royal Commission on a Dispute Respecting Hours of Employment between the Bell Telephone Company of Canada Ltd., and Operators at Toronto, Ontario (Ottawa 1907)
Report of the Royal Commission on the Relations of Labour and Capital, vols 1 & 5 (Ottawa 1889)

UNPUBLISHED THESES

Bell, Marion M. 'The History of the Catholic Welfare Bureau,' MSW thesis, University of Toronto, 1949
Boritch, Helen. 'The Making of Toronto the Good: The Organization of Policing

and Production of Arrests, 1859–1955,' Ph.D. thesis, York University, 1985
Brett, Fred. 'A History of the Big Brother Movement of Toronto, 1912–1939,' MSW thesis, University of Toronto, 1953
Coombs, David G. 'The Emergence of a White Collar Work Force in Toronto, 1895–1911,' Ph.D. thesis, York University, 1978
Fiser, Vladimir. 'The Development of Services for the Juvenile Delinquent in Ontario, 1891–1921,' MSW thesis, University of Toronto, 1966
Hobbs, Margaret. '"Dead Horses" and "Muffled Voices": Protective Legislation, Education and the Minimum Wage for Women in Ontario,' MA thesis, University of Toronto, 1985
Kilgallin, Anthony T. 'Toronto in Fiction, Poetry, and Occasional Prose,' M.Phil. thesis, University of Toronto, 1966
Knight, Andrea. 'Educating Working Women for the Vote: The Response of the Toronto Labour Movement to Woman Suffrage, 1900–1917,' MA thesis, University of Toronto, 1912
Lenton, Gerard Bartley Bruce. 'The Development and Nature of Vaudeville in Toronto: From 1899–1915,' Ph.D. thesis, University of Toronto, 1983
MacDougall, Heather. 'Health Is Wealth: Development of Public Health Activity to 1834–1890,' Ph.D. thesis, University of Toronto, 1981
Maehey, Thomas Clyde. 'Red Lights Out: A Legal History of Prostitution, Disorderly Houses and Vice Districts, 1870–1917,' Ph.D. thesis, Rice University, 1984
Meen, Sharon Patricia. 'The Battle for the Sabbath: The Sabbatarian Lobby in Canada, 1890–1912,' Ph.D. thesis, University of British Columbia, 1979
Meyerowitz, Joanne. 'Holding Their Own: Working Women apart from Family in Chicago, 1880–1930,' Ph.D. thesis, Stanford University, 1983
Morrison, Terrence. 'The Child and Urban Social Reform in Late Nineteenth-Century Ontario,' Ph.D. thesis., University of Toronto, 1971
Munro, Don. 'Care of the Dependent Poor in Ontario, 1891–1921,' MSW thesis, University of Toronto, 1966
Roberts, Barbara. 'Purely Administrative Proceedings: The Management of Canadian Deportation, Montreal, 1900–1935,' Ph.D. thesis, University of Ottawa, 1980
Strange, Carolyn. 'The Velvet Glove: Maternalistic Reform at the Andrew Mercer Ontario Reformatory for Females, 1874–1927,' MA thesis, University of Ottawa, 1983

UNPUBLISHED PAPERS

Brown, Philip. 'Jarvis Street, Toronto, 1890–1930: Neighbourhood Change in a High Status District,' CTA Papers and Theses, 1976

Cohen, Sharon. 'The Bureau of Municipal Research: An Historical Survey and Evaluation,' CTA Papers and Theses, 1970

Corrigan, Philip. 'Doing Mythologies,' paper presented at the 'Mythologies: Myths We Live By' conference, University of Toronto, 21 January, 1988

Fulford, Robert. 'Myth Canada: Images Signifying a Nation,' paper presented at the 'Mythologies: Myths We Live By' conference, University of Toronto, 21 January 1988

Hobbs, Margaret. 'The Image of the Family and Parent-Child Relationships in English-Canadian Novels, 1920–1929,' Trent University, Department of History, 1979

Lipkin, Mary Jane. 'Immigrants and Education for Citizenship, 1900–1919, the Experience of Central Neighbourhood House and Frontier College,' CTA Papers and Theses, n.d.

Mah, Valerie Ann. 'The 'Bachelor Society': A Look at Toronto's Early Chinese Community, 1878–1924,' CTA Papers and Theses, 1978

Martin, Michele. 'Subjugating the Voice: Telephone Companies' Regulation of Workers' and Consumers' Self-Expression,' paper presented at the Canadian Historical Association, Université Laval, June 1989

Meyerowitz, Joanne. 'Working Women's Alternatives to the Family Economy, Chicago, 1880–1930,' Berkshire Conference on the History of Women, Smith College, 1984

O'Connor, Patricia. 'History of the University Settlement House,' CTA Papers and Theses, 1985

Parker, Ethel A. 'A History of the Settlement Movement in Canada,' 1965. BR Manuscript Collection, S54

– 'Things in Common to the Three Toronto Settlements,' CTA Papers and Theses, 1962

Pitsula, James. 'The House of Industry and the Poor of Late Nineteenth-Century Toronto,' CTA Papers and Theses, n.d.

Price, Linda. 'Women Factory Workers in Toronto, 1890–1919,' CTA Papers and Theses, 1982

Sobel, David M. 'Household Economics and Material Life: Family Survival in Southern Saint John's Ward, 1879–1885,' CTA Papers and Theses, 1982

Stephen, Jennifer. '"For the Good of Coming Generations": The Toronto Public Health Campaign against V.D., 1920–1917,' Ontario Institute for Studies in Education, January 1990

– The "Incorrigible," the "Bad," and the "Immoral": Toronto's "Factory Girls" and the Work of the Toronto Psychiatric Clinic,' Ontario Institute for Studies in Education, May 1990

Valverde, Mariana. 'Constructing National and Sexual Purity: The 'White

Slave' Panic in Canada, 1910–1925,' Centre of Criminology, University of
    Toronto, 13 October 1987
Weaver, John C. 'Tidying Up Toronto: Civic Reform, 1900–1915,' CTA Papers
    and Theses, 1973
Weir, Lorna 'Sexual Regulation and Prostitution,' Marxist Institute Workshop,
    Toronto, 12 February 1987

PRIMARY SOURCES

Articles
'Address by Miss Addams.' *The Playground* 2, no. 13 (April 1908), 25–8
Bell, Ernest A., *The War on the White Slave Trade* (Toronto [1911] 1980)
Bowman, LeRoy E., and Maria Ward Lambin, 'Evidence of Social Relations as
    Seen in Types of New York City Dance Halls,' *Journal of Social Forces* 3
    (January 1925), 286–91
Brooking, Lucy. 'Conditions in Toronto,' in Ernest A. Bell, ed., *War on the
    White Slave Trade* (Toronto [1911] 1980)
Clarke, C K 'Occupational Wanderers,' *Maclean's Magazine* 13 April 1922.
– 'The Story of the Toronto General Hospital Psychiatric Clinic,' *Canadian
    Journal of Mental Hygiene* 1 (1919–20), 30–7
– 'A Study of 5,600 Cases Passing through the Psychiatric Clinic of the
    Toronto General Hospital. A Special Study of 188 Clinic Cases – Also a
    Survey of 767 Cases of Illegitimacy,' *Canadian Journal of Mental Health* 3
    (1921–2), 11–24.
Clarke, Mary Joplin. 'The Attitude of the Neighbourhood Worker,' *Public
    Health Journal* 7, no. 12 (December 1916), 498–500
– 'Sunday in the Ward,' *Ward Graphic* 1919, 8
Codding, Mrs J.K. 'Recreation for Women Prisoners,' *American Prison
    Association Proceedings* (1912), 312–19
Crawford, Willena 'YWCA Industrial Work,' *Social Welfare* 5 (August 1923),
    232–3
Dennison, Mrs. John. 'The Young Woman Problem,' *Missionary Outlook* (June
    1905), 139
Ford, Marjory A. 'Housing the Wage-Earning Woman,' *Social Welfare* 4
    (September 1922), 267–8
Harrison, S. Francis. 'A Philanthropic Failure,' *Acta Victoriana* 32, no. 3
    (December 1908), 206–20
Hart, Hastings. 'The New Penology,' *American Prison Association Proceedings*
    (1925), 116–31
Hincks, Clarence M. 'Feeblemindedness in Canada: A Serious Social
    Problem,' *Social Welfare* 1 (November 1918), 29–30

Hocken, Horatio C. 'The New Spirit in Municipal Government,' Canada
Club, Ottawa, *Addresses* (1914–15)

Lapp, Eula. 'When Ontario Girls Went West,' *Ontario History* 60, no. 2 (June
1968), 71–9

Miner, Maude E. 'The Problem of Wayward Girls and Delinquent Women,'
Academy of Political Science Proceedings 12, no. 4 (1912), 604–12

O'Sullivan, Emma. 'Recreation for Women Prisoners,' *American Prison
Association Proceedings* (1912), 319

– 'Some Difficulties in Reformatory Work among Women,' *American Prison
Association Proceedings* (1907), 235–9

Plumptre, Adelaide N. 'What Shall We Do with 'Our' Flappers?' *Maclean's
Magazine* 35, no. 11 (June 1922), 64–5

Raine, Norman Reilly. 'Girls Invade Track and Diamond,' *Maclean's Magazine*
38, no. 16 (15 August 1925), 12–13, 62–3

Reckless, Walter C. 'The Distribution of Commercialized Vice in the City: A
Sociological Analysis,' in Ernest Burgess, ed. *The Urban Community*
(Chicago 1926), 192–206

Redpath, Beatrice. 'The Galleons of Spain,' *Chatelaine* 1, no. 1 (March 1928),
20–1, 48–50

Riddell, William Renwick, 'Moral Prophylaxis against Venereal Disease,'
National Hygiene and Public Welfare 13, no. 1 (January 1922), 52–4

– 'Presidential Address, Canadian Social Hygiene Council,' *The Public Health
Journal* 15, no. 5 (May 1924), 193–7

– 'Social Hygiene,' *Medical Record and Journal* (March 1928), 1–3

– 'Venereal Disease: A Public Peril,' *New York Medical Journal* (December
1921), 1–5

Scott, Jean. 'The Conditions of Female Labour in Ontario,' *Toronto University
Studies in Political Science*, First Series (no. 3, 1892), 9–31

Shearer, J.G. 'Canada's War on the White Slave Trade,' in Ernest A. Bell, ed.,
Fighting the Traffic in Young Girls (n.p. 1911), 333–64

Shearer, Rev. Dr John. 'The Canadian Crusade,' in Ernest A. Bell, ed., *The
War on the White Slave Trade* (Toronto [1911] 1980), 333–64

Starr, Rev. J. Edward. 'Charities and Corrections,' *The Public Health Journal* 4,
no. 10 (October 1913), 567–70

– 'First Annual Report of the Juvenile Court,' *Public Health Journal* 4, no. 4
(April 1913), 194–205

Watson, Muriel. 'Cotton Stockings,' *Chatelaine* 1, no. 3 (May 1928), 21-2, 43-4

Wicket, Morley S. 'City Government in Canada,' *University of Toronto Studies*
2, no. 1 (1902), 3–23

Books and Pamphlets

Addams, Jane. *The Spirit of Youth and the City Streets*. Allen R. Davis, intro. (Urbana [1909] 1972)
Beard, Mary Ritter. *Women's Work in Municipalities* (New York [1915] 1972)
Callaghan, Morley. *A Native Argosy* (New York 1929)
– *Strange Fugitive* (Toronto [1928] 1970)
Canadian Social Hygiene Council. *A Special Investigation: Summary of 156 Social Histories Taken of Venereal Disease Patients* (Toronto 1922)
Charlesworth, Hector. *Candid Chronicles: Leaves from the Book of a Canadian Journalist* (Toronto 1925)
– *More Candid Chronicles* (Toronto 1928)
Chicago. Vice Commission of Chicago. *The Social Evil in Chicago: A Study of Existing Conditions* (Chicago 1911)
Civic Committee of the University Women's Club of Winnipeg. *The Work of Women and Girls in the Department Stores of Winnipeg* (Winnipeg 1914)
Clark, Christopher St George. *Of Toronto the Good, a Social Study: The Queen City of Canada as It Is* (Toronto 1970 [1898])
The Committee of Fifteen, The *The Social Evil, with Special Reference to Conditions Existing in the City of New York* (New York 1902)
de la Roche, Mazo. *Jalna* (Montreal [1927] 1945)
Denison, George T. *Recollections of a Police Magistrate* (Toronto 1920)
Donovan, Frances. *The Woman Who Waits* (New York [1920] 1974)
Dreiser, Theodore. *Sister Carrie*. Alfred Kazin, intro. (New York [1900] 1981)
Fitzroy, Yvonne. *A Canadian Panorama* (London 1929)
Galloway, Lee. *Factory and Office Administration* (New York 1918)
Groves, Hubert. *Toronto Does Her 'Bit'* (Toronto 1918)
Hale, Katherine. *Canadian Cities of Romance* (Toronto 1922)
Heaton, Ernest. *Toronto: An Encyclopaedia with Maps and Street Car Directory* (Toronto 1924)
Knox, Ellen M. *The Girl of the New Day* (Toronto 1919)
Laughlin, Clare E. *The Work-a-Day Girl: A Study of Some Present-Day Conditions* (New York [1913] 1974)
MacDougal, John. *Rural Life in Canada, Its Trends and Tasks*. Robert Craig Brown, intro. (Toronto [1913] 1973)
MacMurchy, Helen. *Sterilization? Birth Control? A Book for Family Welfare and Safety* (Toronto 1934)
MacMurchy, Marjory. *The Canadian Girl at Work: A Book of Vocational Guidance* (Toronto 1919)
Middleton, Jesse Edgar. *Toronto's 100 Years* (Toronto 1934)
Moody, Walter. *What of the City?* (Chicago 1919)
Morgan, Harry. *Canadian Men and Women of the Time* (Toronto 1912)

Mulvany, C. Pelham. *Toronto: Past and Present: A Handbook of the City* (Toronto 1884)

Municipal Handbook (Toronto 1880–1930)

Murphy, Emily. *The Black Candle*. Brian Anthony and Robert Soloman, intro. (Toronto [1922] 1973)

National Council of Women of Canada. *Yearbook* (1919–30)

Nichols, J.L. *Safe Counsel: Practical Eugenics* (Naperville, Ohio 1922)

Pruette, Lorine. *Women and Leisure: A Study of Social Waste* (New York [1924] 1972)

Reeves, Margaret. *Training Schools for Delinquent Girls* (New York 1929)

Richardson, Dorothy. *The Long Day: The Story of a New York Working Girl* (New York 1905)

Schlessinger, Arthur. *The Rise of the City: 1878–1898* (Chicago [1933] 1971).

Stein, Leon, and Annette K. Baxter, eds. *Working Girls of Cincinnati* (New York [1930] 1977)

Taylor, Frederick Winslow. *The Principles of Scientific Management* (New York 1911)

The Toronto Theatres: Season 1904–5 (Toronto 1904)

Wallace, W. Stewart. *Murders and Mysteries: A Canadian Series* (Toronto 1931)

Wodson, Harry M. *The Whirlpool: Scenes from Toronto Police Court* (Toronto 1917)

Woodsworth, James Shaver. *My Neighbour: A Study of City Conditions, A Plea for Social Service* (Toronto 1911)

– *Strangers within Our Gates, or Coming Canadians* Marilyn Barber, intro. (Toronto [1909] 1972)

SECONDARY SOURCES

Articles

Alexander, Sally. 'Women, Class and Sexual Differences in the 1830s and 1840s: Some Reflections on the Writing of a Feminist History,' *History Workshop* 17 (Spring 1984), 125–49

Allen, Judith. 'Octavius Beale Re-considered: Infanticide, Babyfarming and Abortion in NSW, 1880–1939,' in Sydney Labour History Group, *What Rough Beast? The State and Social Order in Australian History* (Sydney 1982), 111–29

Anderson, Michael. 'The Social Position of Spinsters in Mid-Victorian Britain,' *Journal of Family History* 9, no. 4 (Winter 1984), 377–93

Backhouse, Constance B. 'Desperate Women and Compassionate Courts: Infanticide in Nineteenth-Century Canada,' *University of Toronto Law Journal* 34 (1984), 447–78

- 'Involuntary Motherhood: Abortion, Birth Control and the Law in Nineteenth-Century Canada,' *Windsor Yearbook of Access to Justice* 3 (1983), 61–130
- 'Nineteenth-Century Canadian Rape Law, 1800–1892,' in David H. Flaherty, *Essays in the History of Canadian Law*, vol. 2 (Toronto 1983), 200–47
- 'Nineteenth-Century Canadian Prostitution Law: Reflection of a Discriminatory Society,' *Histoire Sociale / Social History* 18, no. 36 (November 1985), 387–423
- '"To Open the Way for Others of My Sex": Clara Brett Martin's Career as Canada's First Woman Lawyer,' *Canadian Journal of Women and the Law* 1, no. 1 (1985), 1–41.
Bajor, Stephan. 'Illegitimacy and the Working Class: Illegitimate Mothers in Brunswick, 1900–1933,' in Richard J. Evans, ed., *The German Working Class, 1888–1933: The Politics of Everyday Life* (London 1982), 142–73
Barber, Marilyn. 'The Women Ontario Welcomed: Immigrant Domestics for Ontario Homes, 1870–1930,' *Ontario History* 72, no. 3 (September 1980), 148–72
Bator, Paul A. '"The Struggle to Raise the Lower Classes": Public Health Reform and the Problem of Poverty in Toronto, 1910-1921,' *Journal of Canadian Studies* 14, no. 1 (Spring 1979), 43–9
Bedarida, François. 'The French Approach to Urban History: An Assessment of Recent Methodological Trends,' in Derek Fraser and Anthony Sutcliffe, eds, *The Pursuit of Urban History* (London 1983), 395–407
Beeby, Dean. 'Industrial Strategy and Manufacturing Growth in Toronto, 1880–1910,' *Ontario History* 76, no. 3 (September 1984), 199–232
Bennett, Paul W. 'Taming "Bad Boys" of the "Dangerous Class": Child Rescue and Restraint at the Victoria Industrial School, 1887–1935,' *Histoire Sociale / Social History* 21, no. 41 (May 1988), 71–96
Bercuson, David. 'Through the Looking Glass of Culture: An Essay on the New Labour History and Working-Class Culture in Recent Canadian Historical Writing,' *Labour / Le Travailleur* 7 (Spring 1981), 95–112
Berger, Carl. 'The True North Strong and Free,' in Peter Russell, ed., *Nationalism in Canada* (Toronto 1966)
Bradbury, Bettina. 'The Family Economy and Work in an Industrializing City: Montreal in the 1870s,' *Canadian Historical Association Historical Papers* (1979), 71–96
- 'Women and Wage Labour in a Period of Transition: Montreal, 1861–1881,' *Histoire Sociale / Social History* 17, 33 (May 1984), 116–30
- 'Women's History and Working-Class History,' *Labour / Le Travail* 19 (Spring 1987), 23–43

Brunet, J.R. 'The Urban Community and Changing Moral Standards,' in Michiel Horn and Ronald Sabourin, eds, *Studies in Canadian Social History* (Toronto 1974), 298–325

Buckley, Suzann, and Janice Dicken McGinnis. 'Venereal Disease and Public Health Reform in Canada,' *Canadian Historical Review* 63, no. 3 (September 1982), 337–54

Bullen, John. 'Hidden Workers: Child Labour and the Family Economy in Late Nineteenth-Century Urban Ontario,' *Labour / Le Travailleur* 18 (Fall 1986), 163–87

Corrigan, Philip. 'Doing Mythologies,' *Borderlines* (Fall 1984), 20–2

Cranz, Galen. 'The Sharon Building: The Transformation of Women's Recreational Needs in the Late Nineteenth-Century City,' *Heresies* 3, no. 2 (1981), 77–9

– 'Women in Urban Parks,' *Signs* (Supplement) 5, no. 3 (Spring 1980), S79–S95

Craven, Paul. 'Law and Ideology: The Toronto Police Court, 1850–1880,' in David H. Flaherty, ed. *Essays in the History of Canadian Law*, vol. 1 (Toronto 1983), 248–307

Darrock, A. Gordon. 'Early Industrialization and Inequality in Toronto, 1861-1899,' *Labour / Le Travailleur* 11, no. 1 (Spring 1983), 31–61

Denning, Michael. 'Cheap Stories: Notes on Popular Fiction and Working-class Culture in Nineteenth-Century America,' *History Workshop Journal* 22 (Autumn 1986), 1–17

Dubois, Ellen Carol, and Linda Gordon. 'Seeking Ecstasy on the Battlefield: Danger and Pleasure in Nineteenth-Century Feminist Sexual Thought,' in Carol Vance, ed., *Pleasure and Danger: Exploring Female Sexuality* (Boston 1984), 31–49

Erenberg, Lewis A. 'Everybody's Doin' It: The Pre-World War I Dance Craze, the Castles and the Modern American Girl,' *Feminist Studies* 3, nos. 1–2 (Fall 1975), 155–71

Ferdinand, Theodore N. 'The Criminal Patterns of Boston since 1849,' *American Journal of Sociology* 73, no. 1 (1967), 84–99

Fine, Lisa. 'Between Two Worlds: Business Women in a Chicago Boarding House, 1900–1930,' *Journal of Social History* 19, no. 3 (Spring 1986), 511–21

Freedman, Estelle B. 'The New Woman: Changing Views of Women in the 1920s,' *Journal of American History* 61 (September 1974), 372–93

Gillis, John. 'Servants, Sexual Relations, and Illegitimacy in London, 1801–1900,' *Feminist Studies* 5, no. 1 (1979), 142–73

Goheen, Peter G. 'Currents of Change in Toronto, 1850–1900,' in Gilbert Stelter and Alan Artibise, eds., *The Canadian City: Essays in Urban History* (Toronto 1979), 54–92

Goldin, Claudia. 'The Work and Wages of Single Women, 1870–1920,' *Journal of Economic History* 40 (March 1980), 81–8

Gordon, Loraine. 'Doctor Margaret Norris Patterson: First Woman Police Magistrate in Eastern Canada – Toronto – January 1922 to November 1934,' *Atlantis* 10, no. 1 (Fall 1984), 95–109

Gorham, Deborah 'The Maiden Tribute of Modern Babylon Re-examined: Child Prostitution and the Idea of Childhood,' *Victorian Studies* 21, no. 3 (Spring 1978), 353–80

Grace, Sherrill E. 'Quest for the Peaceable Kingdom: Urban / Rural Codes in Roy, Laurence and Atwood,' in Susan Merill Squier, ed., *Women Writers and the City: Essays in Feminist Literary Criticism* (Knoxville 1984), 193–209

Gullet, Gayle. 'City Mothers, City Daughters, and the Dance Hall Girls: The Limits of Female Political Power in San Francisco, 1913,' in Barbara J. Harris and JoAnn K. McNamara, eds, *Women and the Structure of Society* (Durham, NC 1984), 149–60

Gurr, Ted. 'Historical Trends in Violent Crime: A Critical Review of the Evidence,' in N. Morris and M. Tonry, eds, *Crime and Justice: An Annual Review of Research* (Chicago 1980), 1–43

Harris, Ruth. 'Melodrama, Hysteria and Feminine Crimes of Passion in the Fin-de-Siècle,' *History Workshop Journal* 25 (Spring 1988), 31–63

Heron, Craig, and Bryan Palmer. 'Through the Prism of the Strike: Industrial Conflict in Southern Ontario, 1901–1914,' *Canadian Historical Review* 58 (December 1977), 423–58

Hodgetts, J.E. 'Royal Commissions of Inquiry in Canada,' *Public Administration Review* 9 (1949), 22–9

Homel, Gene Howard. 'Denison's Law: Criminal Justice and the Police Court in Toronto, 1877–1921,' *Ontario History* 73, no. 1 (March 1981), 171–86

– 'Sliders and Backsliders: Toronto's Sunday Tobogganing Controversy of 1912,' *Urban History Review* 10, no. 2 (October 1981), 25–34

Hufton, Olwen. 'Women without Men: Widows and Spinsters in Britain and France in the Eighteenth Century,' *Journal of Family History* 9, no. 4 (Winter 1984), 355–76

Jarvis, Julia. 'The Founding of the Girl Guide Movement in Canada, 1910,' *Ontario History* 62, no. 4 (December 1970), 213–20

Jones, Andrew. 'Closing Penetanguishene Reformatory: An Attempt to Deinstitutionalize Treatment of Juvenile Offenders in Early Twentieth Century Ontario,' *Ontario History* 70, no. 4 (December 1978), 227–44

Jones, Gareth Stedman. 'Class Expression versus Social Control? A Critique of Recent Trends in the Social History of "Leisure,"' *History Workshop Journal* 4 (Autumn 1977), 162–70

Kealey, Gregory S. 'Labour and Working-Class History in Canada: Prospects in the 1980s,' *Labour / Le Travailleur* 7 (Spring 1981), 67–9

Kealey, Linda S., 'Women and Labour during World War I: Women Workers and the Minimum Wage in Manitoba,' in Mary Kinnear, ed., *First Days, Fighting Days: Women in Manitoba History* (Regina 1987), 76–99

Kessler-Harris, Alice. 'Independence and Virtue in the Lives of Wage-Earning Women: The United States, 1870–1930,' in Judith Friedlander, Blanche Wiesen Cook, Alice Kessler-Harris, and Carroll Smith-Rosenberg, eds, *Women in Culture and Politics: A Century of Change* (Bloomington 1986), 3–18

Klaczynska, Barbara. 'Why Women Work: A Comparison of Various Groups – Philadelphia, 1910–1930,' *Labor History* 17 (Winter 1976), 73–87

Klein, Alice, and Wayne Roberts. 'Besieged Innocence: The 'Problem' and Problems of Working Women – Toronto, 1896–1914,' in Janice Acton et al., eds, *Women at Work: Ontario, 1850–1930* (Toronto 1974), 211–59

Lampard, Eric. 'American Historians and the Study of Urbanization,' *American Historical Review* 67 (October 1961), 49–61

Lane, Roger, 'Urban Police and Crime in Nineteenth-Century America,' in N. Morris and M. Tonry, eds, *Crime and Justice: An Annual Review of Research* (Chicago 1980), 295–353

Leonardo, Micaela de. 'Women's Work, Work Culture and Consciousness,' *Feminist Studies* 11, no. 3 (Fall 1985), 491–5

Leslie, Genevieve. 'Domestic Service in Canada, 1880–1920,' in Janice Acton et al., eds, *Women at Work* (Toronto 1974), 71–125

Lofland, Lyn. 'The "Thereness" of Women: A Selective Review of Urban Sociology,' in Marcia Millman and Rosabeth Moss Kanter, eds, *Another Voice: Feminist Perspectives on Social Life and Social Science* (Garden City, NY 1975), 144–70

Lowe, Graham. 'Mechanization, Feminization and Managerial Control in the Early Twentieth Century Canadian Office,' in Craig Heron and Robert Storey, eds, *On the Job: Confronting the Labour Process in Canada* (Montreal 1986), 177–209

Lunbeck, Elizabeth. '"A New Generation of Women": Progressive Psychiatrists and the Hypersexual Female,' *Feminist Studies* 13, no. 3 (Fall 1987), 513–43

McCallum, Margaret. 'Keeping Women in Their Place: The Minimum Wage in Canada, 1910–1925,' *Labour / Le Travailleur* 17 (Spring 1986), 29–56

MacDougal, Heather. '"Enlightening the Public": The Views and Values of the Association of Executive Health Officers of Ontario, 1886–1903,' in Charles Roland, ed., *Health, Disease, and Medicine: Essays in Canadian History* (Toronto 1984), 436–64

MacDougall, Donald V. 'Popularized Canadian Trials: A Bibliography,' *The Law Society Gazette* 10, no. 3 (September 1976), 248–55

McLaren, Angus. 'Birth Control and Abortion in Canada, 1870–1920,' *Canadian Historical Review* 49, no. 3 (1978), 319–40

McLaren, John P.S. 'Chasing the Social Evil: Moral Fervour and the Evolution of Canada's Prostitution Laws, 1867–1917,' *Canadian Journal of Law and Society* 1 (1986), 125–65

– 'White Slavers: The Reform of Canada's Prostitution Laws and Patterns of Enforcement, 1900–1920,' *Criminal Justice History* (1988), 53–119

MacNab, John E. 'Toronto's Industrial Growth to 1891,' *Ontario History* 47, no. 2 (Spring 1955), 59–79

Mercer, John. 'On Continentalism, Distinctiveness and Comparative Urban Geography: Canadian and American Cities,' *Canadian Geographer* 23, no. 2 (1979), 119–39

Morton, Marion J. 'Seduced and Abandoned in an American City: Cleveland and Its Fallen Women, 1869–1936,' *Journal of Urban History* 11, no. 4 (August 1985), 443–69

Murphy, Marjorie. 'Work, Protest, and Culture. New Work on Working Women's History,' *Feminist Studies* 13, no. 3 (Fall 1987), 657–67

Newton, Janice. 'From Wage Slave to White Slave: The Prostitution Controversy and the Canadian Left,' in Linda Kealey and Joan Sangster, eds, *Beyond the Vote: Canadian Women and Politics* (Toronto 1989), 217–36

O'Brien, Patricia. 'Crime and Punishment as Historical Problem,' *Journal of Social History* 11 (June 1978), 508–20

Parker, Graham. 'The Legal Regulation of Sexual Activities and the Protection of Females,' *Osgoode Hall Law Journal* 21, no. 2 (1983), 187–244

– 'The Origins of the Canadian Criminal Code,' in David H. Flaherty, ed., *Essays in the History of Canadian Law*, vol. 1 (Toronto 1981), 249–81

Pedersen, Diana. '"A Building for Her": The YWCA in the Canadian City,' *Urban History Review* 15, no. 3 (February 1987), 225–41

– '"Keeping our Good Girls Good:" The YWCA and the 'Girl Problem,' 1870–1930,' *Canadian Women's Studies* 7, no. 4 (1986), 20–4

Peel, Mark. 'On the Margins: Lodgers and Boarders in Boston, 1860–1900,' *Journal of American History* 72, no. 4 (March 1986), 813–34

Pitsula, James. 'The Emergence of Social Work in Toronto,' *Journal of Canadian Studies* 14, no. 1 (Spring 1979), 35–42

Poovey, Mary. 'Feminism and Deconstruction,' *Feminist Studies* 14, no. 1 (Spring 1988), 51–66

Rapp, Rayna, and Ellen Ross. 'The Twenties Backlash: Compulsory Heterosexuality, the Consumer Family, and the Waning of Feminism,' in

Amy Swerdlow and Hannah Lessinger, eds, *Race, Class and Sex, the Dynamics of Control* (Boston 1983), 93–107

Rawling, Bill. 'Technology and Innovation in the Toronto Police Force, 1875–1925,' *Ontario History* 80, no. 1 (March 1988), 53–72

Reekie, Gail. '"Humanising Industry:" Paternalism, Welfarism and Labour Control in Sydney's Big Stores, 1890–1930,' *Labour History* 53 (November 1987), 1–19

Richter, Linda. 'The Ephemeral Female: Women in Urban Histories,' *International Journal of Women's Studies* 5, no. 4 (September–October 1982), 312–29

Rose, Sonya. 'Gender at Work: Sex, Class, and Industrial Capitalism,' *History Workshop* 21 (Spring 1986), 113–21

Rosenzweig, Roy. 'Middle-Class Parks and Working-Class Play: The Struggle over Recreational Space in Worcester, Massachusetts, 1870–1910,' *Radical History Review* 21 (Fall 1979), 31–46

Rotenberg, Lori. 'The Wayward Worker: Toronto's Prostitute at the Turn of the Century,' in Janice Acton et al., eds, *Women at Work: Ontario, 1880–1930* (Toronto 1974), 33–69

Rothman, David J. 'The State as Parent: Social Policy in the Progressive Era,' in Willard Gaylin, Ira Glasser, Steven Marcus, and David Rothman, eds, *Doing Good: The Limits of Benevolence* (New York 1978), 67–97

Sangster, Joan. 'The 1907 Bell Telephone Strike: Organizing Women Workers,' *Labour / Le Travailleur* 3 (1978), 109–30

– '"Pardon Tales" from Magistrate's Court: Women, Crime and the Court in Peterborough County, 1920–1950,' *Canadian Historical Review* 74, no. 2 (June 1993): 161–97

Sato, Barbara Hamill. 'The *Moga* Sensation: Perceptions of the *Modan Garu* in Japanese Intellectual Circles during the 1920s,' *Gender and History* 5, no. 3 (Autumn 1993), 363–81

Schlossman, Stephen, and Stephanie Wallach. 'The Crime of Precocious Sexuality: Female Juvenile Delinquency and the Progressive Era,' in D. Kelly Weisberg, ed., *Women and the Law: A Social Historical Perspective*, vol. 1, *Women and the Criminal Law* (Cambridge, Mass., 1982), 45–84

Scott, Joan Wallach. 'Deconstructing Equality-Versus-Difference: Or, the Uses of Poststructuralist Theory for Feminism,' *Feminist Studies* 14, no. 1 (Spring 1988), 33–50

– 'Language, Gender, and Working-Class History,' *International Labour and Working-Class History* 31 (Spring 1987), 1–13

Shepard, Catherine J. 'Court Records as Archival Records,' *Archivaria* 18 (Summer 1984), 124–7

Shumsky, Neil. 'Tacit Acceptance: Respectable Americans and Segregated
Prostitution, 1870–1910,' *Journal of Social History* 19 (Summer 1986), 665–79
Simmons, Christina. 'Companionate Marriage and the Lesbian Threat,'
Frontiers 4, no. 3 (Fall 1979), 54–9
Smith-Rosenberg, Carroll. 'The New Woman as Androgyne: Sexual Disorder
and Gender Crisis, 1870–1936,' in Carroll Smith-Rosenberg, *Disorderly
Conduct: Visions of Gender in Victorian America* (New York 1985)
Snell, James. 'The White Life for Two: The Defence of Marriage and Sexual
Morality in Canada, 1890–1914,' *Histoire Sociale / Social History* 16, no. 31
(May 1983), 111–28
Sochen, June. 'Myths and Realities about Urban Women,' *Journal of Urban
History* 8, no. 1 (November 1981), 107–15
Stansel, Christine. 'Women, Children, and the Uses of the Streets: Class and
Gender Conflict in New York City, 1850–1860,' *Feminist Studies* 8, no. 2
(Summer 1982), 308–35
Strange, Carolyn. 'From Modern Babylon to a City upon a Hill: The Toronto
Social Survey Commission and the Search for Sexual Order in the City,' in
Roger Hall et al., eds, *Patterns of the Past: Interpreting Ontario's History*
(Toronto 1988), 255–77
– 'Patriarchy Modified: The Criminal Prosecution of Rape in York County,
1880–1930,' in Jim Phillips, Tina Loo, and Susan Lewthwaite, eds *Essays in
the History of the Criminal Law*, vol. 5 (Toronto 1993)
Stricker, Frank. 'Cookbooks and Law Books: The Hidden History of Career
Women in the Twentieth Century,' *Journal of Social History* 10, no. 1 (Fall
1976), 1–20
Strong-Boag, Veronica. 'The Girl of the New Day: Canadian Working Women
in the 1920s,' *Labour / LeTravailleur* 4 (1979), 131–64
Thom, Debra. 'A Lop-sided View: Feminist History or the History of
Women?' in Kate Campbell, ed., *Critical Feminism: Argument in the
Disciplines* (Buckingham 1992)
Toews, John. 'Intellectual History after the Linguistic Turn: The Autonomy of
Meaning and the Irreducibility of Experience,' *American Historical Review*
92, no. 4 (October 1987), 879–907.
Trofimenkoff, Susan Mann. 'One Hundred and Two Muffled Voices:
Canada's Industrial Women in the 1880s,' *Atlantis* 3 (Fall 1977), 66–84
Valverde, Mariana. 'Giving the Female a Domestic Turn,' *Journal of Social
History* 21 (Summer 1988), 619–34
– 'The Love of Finery: Fashion and the Fallen Woman in Nineteenth-
Century Social Discourse,' *Victorian Studies* 32, no. 2 (Winter 1989), 169–
88

Valverde, Mariana and Lorna Weir. 'The Struggles of the Immoral: More Preliminary Remarks on Moral Regulation,' *Resources for Feminist Research* 17, no. 3 (September 1988), 31–5

Walkins, Susan Corts. 'Spinsters,' *Journal of Family History* 9, no. 2 (Winter 1984), 310–24

Walkowitz, Judith R. 'Jack the Ripper and the Myth of Male Violence,' *Feminist Studies* 8, no. 3 (Fall 1982), 542–74

Wallace, Elisabeth. 'The Origin of the Social Welfare State in Canada, 1867–1900,' *Canadian Journal of Economics and Political Science* 15, no. 3 (August 1950), 383–93.

Ward, Peter. 'Unwed Motherhood in Nineteenth-Century English Canada,' Canadian Historical Association, *Historical Papers* (1981), 34–56

Watts, Eugene J. 'Police Response to Crime and Disorder in Twentieth-Century St Louis,' *Journal of American History*, 70, no. 2 (1983), 340–58

Weeks, Jeffrey. 'Foucault for Historians,' *History Workshop Journal* 14 (Autumn 1982), 106–20

Weir, Lorna. 'The Wanderings of the Linguistic Turn in Anglophone Historical Writing,' *Journal of Historical Sociology* 6, no. 2 (June 1993), 227–45

Wolff, Janet. 'The Invisible Flaneuse: Women and the Literature of Modernity,' *Theory, Culture and Society* 2, no. 3 (1985), 37–47

Wortman, Marlene Stein. 'Domesticating the Nineteenth-Century American City,' *Prospects: An Annual of American Cultural Studies* 3 (1977), 531–72

Yeo, Eileen and Stephen. 'Perceived Patterns: Competition and License versus Class and Struggle,' in idem, eds, *Popular Culture and Class Conflict, 1500-1914: Explorations in the History of Labour and Leisure* (Sussex 1981), 271–307

Books

Allen, Judith. *Sex and Secrets: Crimes Involving Australian Women since 1880* (Melbourne 1990)

Allen, Richard. *The Social Passion: Religion and Social Reform in Canada, 1914-1928* (Toronto 1971)

Allen, Richard. ed. *The Social Gospel in Canada* (Ottawa 1975)

Andrew, Edward. *Closing the Iron Cage: The Scientific Management of Work and Leisure* (Montreal 1981)

Armstrong, Christopher, and H. Vivian Nelles. *The Revenge of the Methodist Bicycle Company: Sunday Streetcars and Municipal Reform in Toronto, 1888-1897* (Toronto 1977)

Armstrong, Frederick H. *Toronto: The Place of Meeting* (Toronto 1983)

Artibise, Alan, and Paul-Andre Linteau. *The Evolution of Canada: An Analysis of Approaches and Interpretations* (Winnipeg 1984)

Bacchi, Carol Lee. *Liberation Deferred? The Ideas of the English-Canadian Suffragists, 1877–1918* (Toronto 1983)

Bailey, Peter. *Leisure and Class in Victorian England: Rational Recreation and the Contest for Control, 1830–1885* (London 1978)

Baron, Ava, ed. *Work Engendered: Toward a New History of American Labor* (New York 1991)

Barth, Gunther. *City People: The Rise of Modern City Culture in Nineteenth-Century America* (New York 1980)

Beattie, John M. *Attitudes toward Crime and Punishment in Upper Canada* (Toronto 1977)

– *Crime and the Courts in England, 1660–1800* (Princeton 1986)

Berenson, Edward. *The Trial of Madame Caillaux* (Berkeley 1992)

Berg, Barbara. *The Remembered Gate: Origins of American Feminism: The Woman and the City, 1800–1860* (New York 1978)

Boyer, Paul S. *Urban Masses and Moral Order in America, 1820–1920* (Cambridge, Mass 1978)

Bradbury, Bettina, ed. *Canadian Family History: Selected Readings* (Toronto 1992)

– *Working Families: Age, Gender and Daily Survival in Industrializing Montreal* (Toronto 1993)

Brandt, Allan M. *No Magic Bullet: A Social History of Venereal Disease in the United States since 1880* (New York 1985)

Braverman, Harry. *Labor and Monopoly Capital* (New York 1975)

Brenzel, Barbara. *Daughters of the State: A Social Portrait of the First Reform School for Girls in North America* (Cambridge, Mass. 1983)

Brown, Desmond H. *The Genesis of the Canadian Criminal Code of 1892* (Toronto 1989)

Brunwald, Jan Harold. *The Vanishing Hitch-Hiker: American Urban Legends and their Meaning* (New York 1981)

Bumsted, J.M., ed. *Interpreting Canada's Past*, vol. 2: *After Confederation* (Toronto 1986)

Burnet, Jean, ed. *Looking into My Sister's Eyes: An Exploration in Women's History* (Toronto 1986)

Cantor, Milton, and Bruce Laurie, eds. *Class, Sex and the Woman Worker* (Westport, Conn. 1977)

Careless, J.M.S. *Toronto to 1918* (Toronto 1984)

Cassel, Jay. *The Secret Plague: Venereal Disease in Canada, 1838–1939* (Toronto 1987)

Cavallo, Domenick. *Muscles and Morals: Organized Playgrounds and Urban Reform, 1880-1920* (Philadelphia 1981)

Chambers-Schiller, Lee Virginia. *Liberty, a Better Husband: Single Women in America: The Generations of 1780–1840* (New Haven, Conn. 1984)

Cohen, Marjorie Griffin. *Women's Work, Markets, and Economic Development in Nineteenth-Century Ontario* (Toronto 1988)

Cohn, Samuel. *The Process of Occupational Sex-Typing: The Feminization of Clerical Labour in Great Britain* (Philadelphia 1985)

Connelly, Mark. *The Response to Prostitution in the Progressive Era* (Chapel Hill 1980)

Cook, Ramsay. *The Regenerators: Social Criticism in Late Victorian English Canada* (Toronto 1985)

Cunningham, Hugh. *Leisure in the Industrial Revolution, c. 1780–c. 1880* (London 1980)

Davidoff, Leonore, *The Best Circles: Society, Etiquette and the Season* (London 1973)

Davis, Allen F. *Spearheads for Reform: The Social Settlements and the Progressive Movement* (New York 1967)

Davis, Natalie Zemon. *Fiction in the Archives: Pardon Tales and their Tellers in Sixteenth-Century France* (Stanford 1987)

D'Emilio, John, and Estelle B. Freedman. *Intimate Matters: A History of Sexuality in America* (New York 1988)

de Lauretis, Teresa, ed. *Feminist Studies / Critical Studies* (Bloomington 1986)

Dickens, Bernard. *Abortion and the Law* (Bristol 1966)

Donzelot, Jacques. *The Policing of Families: Welfare versus the State* (London 1980)

Dubinsky, Karen. *Improper Advances: Rape and Heterosexual Conflict, Ontario 1880–1929* (Chicago 1993)

Dublin, Thomas. *Women at Work: The Transformation of Work and Community in Lowell, Massachusetts, 1826–1860* (New York 1979)

Dyhouse, Carol. *Girls Growing Up in Late Victorian and Edwardian England* (London 1981)

Eisenstein, Sarah. *Give Us Bread, but Give Us Roses: Working Women's Consciousness in the United States, 1890 to the First World War*, Harold Benenson, intro. (Boston 1983)

Ewen, Elizabeth. *Immigrant Women in the Land of Dollars: Life and Culture on the Lower East Side, 1890–1985* (New York 1985)

Faderman, Lillian. *Surpassing the Love of Men: Romantic Friendship and Love between Women from the Renaissance to the Present* (New York 1981)

Farge, Arlette, and Christiane Klapisch-Zuber, eds. *Madame ou Mademoiselle? Itinéraires de la Solitude Féminine, 18è–20e siecle* (Paris 1984)

Fass, Paula. *The Damned and the Beautiful: American Youth in the 1920s* (New York 1977)

Filey, Mike. *I Remember Sunnyside: The Rise and Fall of a Magical Era* (Toronto 1981)

Fingard, Judith. *The Dark Side of Life in Victorian Halifax* (Porter's Lake, NS 1989)

Foucault, Michel. *The History of Sexuality*, vol. 1: *An Introduction*. Robert Hurley, trans. (New York 1978)

– *The History of Sexuality*, vol. 2: *The Use of Pleasure*. Robert Hurley, trans. (New York 1985)

– *Discipline and Punish: The Birth of the Prison*. Alan Sheridan, trans. (New York 1979)

Frager, Ruth. *Sweatshop Strife: Class, Ethnicity and Gender in the Jewish Labour Movement of Toronto, 1900–1939* (Toronto 1992)

Freedman, Estelle. *Their Sisters' Keepers: Women's Prison Reform in America* (Ann Arbor 1981)

French, Doris. *High-Button Bootstraps: Federation of Women Teachers' Associations of Ontario, 1919–1968* (Toronto 1968)

Fuchs, Rachel. *Poor and Pregnant in Paris: Strategies for Survival in the Nineteenth Century* (New Brunswick, NJ 1992)

Garland, David. *Punishment and Welfare: A History of Penal Strategies* (Aldershot 1985)

Gibson, Sally. *More Than an Island: A History of the Toronto Island* (Toronto 1984)

Gilfoyle, Thomas. *City of Eros: New York City, Prostitution, and the Commercialization of Sex, 1790–1920* (New York 1992)

Gillis, John R. *For Better, For Worse: British Marriages, 1600 to the Present* (New York 1985)

Girouard, Mark. *The Return to Camelot: Chivalry and the English Gentleman* (New Haven, Conn. 1981)

Glazebrook, George P. de T. *The Story of Toronto* (Toronto 1971)

Glenn, Susan. *Daughters of the Shtetl: Life and Labor in the Immigrant Generation* (Ithaca 1990)

Gordon, Linda. *Heroes of Their Own Lives: The Politics and History of Family Violence* (New York 1988)

– *Woman's Body, Woman's Right: A Social History of Birth Control in America* (New York 1976)

Hall, Jaquelyn Dowd. *The Revolt against Chivalry: Jessie Daniel Ames and the Women's Campaign against Lynching* (New York 1979)

Hapke, Laura. *Tales of the Working Girl: Wage-Earning Women in American Literature, 1890–1925* (New York 1992)

Hargreaves, Jennifer, ed. *Sport, Culture and Ideology* (London 1982)

Harney, Robert F., ed. *Gathering Place: Peoples and Neighbourhoods of Toronto, 1834–1945* (Toronto 1985)

Harney, Robert F., and Harold Troper. *Immigrants: A Portrait of the Urban Experience, 1890–1930* (Toronto 1975)

Harring, Sydney L. *Policing a Class Society: The Experience of American Cities, 1865–1915* (New Brunswick, NJ, 1983)

Heron, Craig, and Robert Storey, eds. *On the Job: Confronting the Labour Process in Canada* (Montreal 1986)

Jeffreys, Sheila. *The Spinster and Her Enemies: Feminism and Sexuality* (London; Boston 1985)

John, Angela, ed. *Unequal Opportunities: Women's Employment in England, 1800–1918* (New York 1986)

Jones, Andrew, and Leonard Rutman. *In the Children's Aid: J.J. Kelso and Child Welfare in Ontario* (Toronto 1981)

Jones, Frank. *Master and Maid: The Charles Massey Murder* (Toronto 1985)

Jones, Gareth Stedman. *Languages of Class: Studies in English Working-Class History, 1832–1982* (Cambridge 1983)

– *Outcast London: A Study in the Relationship Between Classes in Victorian Society* (London 1984)

Katz, Michael B. *The People of Hamilton, Canada West: Family and Class in a Mid-Nineteenth-Century City* (Cambridge, Mass., 1975)

Katz, Michael B., Michael Ducet, and Mark Stern. *The Social Organization of Early Industrial Capitalism* (Cambridge, Mass., 1982)

Kealey, Gregory S. *Canada Investigates Industrialism* (Toronto 1973)

– *Toronto Workers Respond to Industrial Capitalism, 1867–1892* (Toronto 1980)

– *Working-Class Toronto at the Turn of the Century* (Toronto 1973)

Kessler-Harris, Alice. *Out to Work: A History of Wage-Earning Women* (New York 1982)

– *A Woman's Wage: Historical Meanings and Social Consequences* (Lexington 1990)

Krahn, Harvey, and Graham S. Lowe. *Work, Industry and Canadian Society* (Toronto 1988)

Lemon, James. *Toronto since 1918: An Illustrated History* (Toronto 1985)

Lowerson, John, and John Myerscough. *Time to Spare in Victorian England* (Sussex 1977)

Mahood, Linda. *The Magdalens: Prostitution in the Nineteenth Century* (London 1990)

Masters, D.C. *The Rise of Toronto, 1850–1890* (Toronto 1947)

McKelvey, Blake. *The Emergence of Metropolitan America, 1915–1966* (New Brunswick, N.J. 1968)

McLaren, Angus. *Our Own Master Race: Eugenics in Canada, 1885–1945* (Toronto 1990)

– *Sexuality and Social Order: The Debate over the Fertility of Women and Workers in France, 1770–1920* (New York 1982)

McKelvey, Blake. *The Emergence of Metropolitan America, 1915–1966* (New Brunswick, N.J. 1968)

McLaren, Angus, and Arlene Tigar McLaren. *The Bedroom and the State: The Changing Practices and Politics of Contraception and Abortion in Canada, 1880–1980* (Toronto 1986)

Meller, Helen E. *Leisure and the Changing City, 1870-1914* (London 1976)

Meyerowitz, Joanne. *Women Adrift: Independent Wage Earners in Chicago, 1880-1930* (Chicago 1988)

Mohr, James C. *Abortion in America* (New York 1978)

Monkkonen, Eric. *The Dangerous Class: Crime and Poverty in Columbus, Ohio, 1860–1885* (Cambridge, Mass., 1975)

– *Police in Urban America, 1860–1920* (Cambridge 1981)

Mort, Frank. *Dangerous Sexualities: Medico-Moral Politics in England since 1830* (London 1987)

Morton, Desmond. *Mayor Howland: The Citizen's Candidate* (Toronto 1973)

Moss, George. *Nationalism and Sexuality* (New York 1985)

Nead, Lynda. *Myths of Sexuality: Representations of Women in Victorian Britain* (London 1988)

Nye, Robert A. *Crime, Madness & Politics in Modern France: The Medical Concept of National Decline* (Princeton 1984)

Oakley, Anne. *The Sociology of Housework* (Oxford 1974)

Palmer, Bryan. *Descent into Discourse* (Philadelphia 1990)

– *Working Class Experience: The Rise and Reconstruction of Canadian Labour, 1800–1980* (Toronto 1985)

Parr, Joy. *The Gender of Breadwinners: Women, Men, and Change in Two Industrial Towns, 1880–1950* (Toronto 1990)

Peiss, Kathy. *Cheap Amusements: Working Women and Leisure in Turn-of-the-Century New York* (Philadelphia 1986)

Peiss, Kathy, and Christina Simmons, with Robert A. Padgug, eds. *Passion and Power: Sexuality in History* (Philadelphia 1989)

Piva, Michael. *The Condition of the Working Class in Toronto: 1900–1921* (Ottawa 1979)

Platt, Anthony. *The Child Savers: The Invention of Delinquency* (Chicago 1977)

Raban, Johnathan. *Soft City* (London 1974)

Rafter, Nicole Hahn, and Elizabeth Anne Stanko, eds. *Judge, Lawyer, Victim, Thief: Women, Gender Roles and Criminal Justice* (Boston 1982)

Reed, James. *From Private Vice to Public Virtue: The Birth Control Movement and American Society since 1830* (New York 1978)

Rendall, Jane. *Women in an Industrializing Society: England, 1750–1880* (Oxford 1990)

Riley, Denise. *'Am I That Name?' Feminism and the Category of 'Women' in History* (Minneapolis 1988)

Roberts, Wayne. *Honest Womanhood: Feminism, Femininity and Class Consciousness among Toronto Working Women, 1896–1914* (Toronto 1976)

Robinson, Helen Caister. *Decades of Caring: The Big Sister Story* (Toronto 1979)

Rojek, Chris. *Capitalism and Leisure Theory* (London 1985)

Rosen, Ruth. *The Lost Sisterhood: Prostitution in America, 1900–1918* (Baltimore 1982)

Rosenzweig, Roy. *Eight Hours for What We Will: Workers and Leisure in an Industrial City, 1870–1930* (Cambridge 1983)

Rothman, David J. *Conscience and Convenience: The Asylum and Its Alternatives in Progressive America* (Boston 1980)

Russell, Victor, ed. *Forging a Consensus: Historical Essays on Toronto* (Toronto 1984)

Rutherford, Paul, ed. *Saving the Canadian City: The First Phase, 1880–1920* (Toronto 1974)

Ryan, Mary P. *Women in Public: Between Banners and the Ballots, 1825-1880* (Baltimore 1990)

Said, Edward. *Orientalism* (New York 1979)

Scott, Joan Wallach, and Louise Tilly. *Women, Work and the Family* (New York 1978)

Sennett, Richard. *The Fall of Public Man: On the Social Psychology of Capitalism* (New York 1975)

Smith, Cecil, and Glen Litton. *Musical Comedy in America* (New York 1981)

Smith, Michael Peter. *The City and Social Theory* (Oxford 1980)

Smith-Rosenberg, Carroll. *Disorderly Conduct: Visions of Gender in Victorian America* (New York 1985)

Snitow, Ann, Sharon Thompson, and Christine Stansell, eds. *Powers of Desire: The Politics of Sexuality* (London 1983)

Splane, Richard. *Social Welfare in Ontario, 1791–1893: A Study of Public Welfare Administration* (Toronto 1965)

Stansell, Christine. *City of Women: Sex and Class in New York, 1789–1860* (New York 1986)

Stelter, Gilbert A., and Alan F.J. Artibise, eds. *The Canadian City: Essays in Urban History* (Toronto [1966] 1979)

Strong-Boag, Veronica. *The New Day Recalled: Lives of Girls and Women in English Canada, 1919–1939* (Toronto 1988)

– *The Parliament of Women: The National Council of Women of Canada* (Ottawa 1976)

Tentler, Leslie Woodcock. *Wage-Earning Women: Industrial Work and Family Life in the United States, 1900–1930* (New York 1979)

Tobias, John J. *Crime and Industrial Society in the Nineteenth Century* (London 1967)

– *Nineteenth-Century Crime: Prevention and Punishment* (New York 1972)

Toronto Council of Women. *Nothing New under the Sun: A History of the Toronto Local Council of Women* (Toronto 1978)

Valverde, Mariana. *The Age of Light, Soap and Water: Moral Reform in English Canada, 1885–1925* (Toronto 1991)

Vance, Carol. *Pleasure and Danger: Exploring Female Sexuality* (Boston 1984)

Vicinus, Martha. *Independent Women: Work and Community for Single Women, 1850–1920* (London 1985)

Walkowitz, Judith R. *City of Dreadful Delight: Narratives of Sexual Danger in Late-Victorian London* (Chicago 1992)

– *Prostitution and Victorian Society* (Cambridge 1980)

Ward, Peter William. *Courtship, Love and Marriage* (Montreal 1990)

Weedon, Chris. *Feminist Practice and Poststructuralist Theory* (Oxford 1987)

Weeks, Jeffrey. *Sex, Politics and Society: The Regulation of Sexuality since 1800* (London 1981)

Weiner, Lynn. *From Working Girl to Working Mother: The Female Labor Force in the United States, 1820–1980* (Chapel Hill 1985)

Wiebe, Robert. *The Search for Order, 1877–1920* (New York 1967)

Williams, Raymond *The Country and the City* (London 1973)

Wilson, Barbara, ed. *Ontario and the First World War, 1914–1918: A Collection of Documents* (Toronto 1977)

Wilson, Margaret Gibbons. *The American Woman in Transition: The Urban Influence, 1870–1920* (Westport, Connecticut 1979)

Wilson, Patrick. *Murderess: A Study of the Women Executed in Britain since 1843* (London 1971)

Winks, Robin. *The Blacks in Canada: A History* (Montreal 1971)

Yeo, Eileen, and Stephen Yeo, eds. *Popular Culture and Class Conflict, 1590–1914: Explorations in the History of Labour and Leisure* (Sussex 1981)

Picture Credits

Ontario, Annual Report of the Inspector of Prisons and Public Charities, *Sessional Papers* 35 (1903), 87: 'Fallen women' learn the virtues of domesticity.

City of Toronto Archives: Girl workers toil in factory-like conditions (N137A); Winter sports (N462A); Young women congregate on the boardwalk (N149); Working girls adorned in the latest fashions (N1199); A working-class entertainment district (N288).

Public Archives of Ontario, RG 4, Series 32, File 583: Toronto Vigilance Committee notice.

Public Archives of Ontario, Eaton's Photograph Collection: Eaton's switchboard operators (220); Shift change at Eaton's (1764); Working girls relax in the Eaton's Junior Girls' Recreation Club (1765).

Daily News, 30 August 1902: A 'good times girl'?

University of Toronto, Thomas Fisher Rare Book Library, Sherbourne House Club scrapbooks: The well-educated Miss Bollert (1917); two winners of the Sherbourne House Club's Hallowe'en costume contest (1925).

Ontario, Provincial Board of Health, Division of Preventable Diseases, Sex Hygiene Pamphlets, 1928: Page from *Facts on Sex Hygiene* (PAO 62, Box 467).

Index

Ford, Clara 11, 54, 55, 78, 87, 145,
152, 153, 173; trial 79–83
Foucault, Michel 127, 128

Georgina House 177, 180, 181, 182,
184, 184, 193–4; Business Women's
Club 178; Girls' Club Journal 181–
4, 193–4
Girl of the New Day, The (Knox) 188,
190, 191, 192, 195, 196, 200, 202
'girl problem': defined 3, 10–20; and
commercial amusements 117–18;
contemporary parallels 214–16;
historiography of 3, 214–15;
identification and response to 23,
53–5, 200–16; methodology 16–20;
moral discourse of 17-20, 213–14;
studies and investigations 22, 23,
39, 50–2, 104–6. *See also* pleasures,
criminalization; women wage-
earning
'Good times girl' 116–43, 152, 153.
See also pleasures, criminalization
Gordon, Linda 136

Hanlan's Point. *See* Parks, Toronto
Island
Hapke, Laura 122
Harris, Ruth 77–8
Hartman, Mary 77–8
Haven, The 60, 61, 87
Health Confessions of Business Women
189–91, 192, 194, 197–9, 202–3
Her Own Fault 189, 191, 193, 207
homosexuality 146, 151, 214–15, 224.
See also lesbianism
House of Industry, The 49, 73
Housing: wage-earning women and
95–6, 177, 180, 184–5, 196. *See also*
boarding-homes, supervised

Howland, William 17, 34–6, 37, 38,
45, 46, 55, 93, 131
Hughes, Crown Attorney, 163–4, 168

immigrant men 138, 152–7, 174. *See
also* racism
immigrant women 108, 112–15. *See
also* racism
immigration 165. *See also* racism
Imperial Order Daughters of the
Empire (IODE) 179
incest: and juvenile delinquency
charges 137
indecent assault. *See* sexual assault
industrial schools 91, 118, 131–40.
See also correctional institutions;
reformatories
Industrial Schools Act 131
infanticide 72–6, 87, 88, 93, 112–13,
224
'Information for Men – Syphilis and
Gonorrhoea' 205
International Council of Women
98–9

Jack Canuck 155
Jeffreys, Sheila 9
Johnston, E.F.B. 'Blackie' 81–3, 154,
173
Juvenile Court 125, 128, 134, 136,
138
Juvenile Delinquents Act 131, 132–3
juvenile offenders 131–2, 133, 134–9,
140

Kelso, J.J. 131, 140
King, William Lyon Mackenzie 41,
43, 44
Klapisch-Zuber, Christiane 7
Knights of Labor 26, 32, 36

Knox, Ellen 188, 190, 191, 192, 195, 196, 200, 202

labour legislation 29–30, 34. *See also* minimum wage
Lane, Roger 151
lawyers: and abortion cases 167; and Ford murder trial 77–83; and sexual assault cases 66, 67, 157, 160–4
leisure and recreation 5, 9, 15, 116, 117; and class 118, 121, 176–7, 192; as deviant 127–33, 137–9; provision of for wage-earning women 178, 186–7; and leisure discipline 90, 118–19, 124–5, 126, 129, 130, 131; self-management techniques for, 187–99, 202–3; and sex education 206–8; and Social Survey Commission 120–3. *See also* commercial amusements
lesbianism 10, 183–4, 214–15. *See also* homosexuality
Levine, Philippa 56
Lunbeck, Elizabeth 127

McLaren, Angus 16, 204
MacMurchy, Helen 10, 114, 115, 195, 196, 200, 202
MacMurchy, Marjory 47, 50–1, 178, 188, 192
'Maiden Tribute of Modern Babylon' (Stead) 62
Mann Act 105
marriage and motherhood: as civic duty 193, 194, 196; as women's natural role 27–8, 32; efforts to ensure fitness for 58, 118, 122, 124, 186, 190, 200; encouragement in supervised boarding-homes 183;

historiography of 9; wage work as temporary phase prior to 38–9, 41, 42, 48, 176, 195, 197, 208. *See also* eugenics; single mothers
Massey, Charles 83–6
medical profession: and abortion 69, 166–8, 169–72; and leisure reform 127; and sexual delinquency 127–8; and social hygiene 204–5. *See also* eugenics; psychiatric profession; race, Anglo-Celtic; social hygiene
men 29, 36; and abortion cases 172–4; arrest rates of 148–9, 151; civil liberties of 160, 163; criminality of 131; and infanticide 224; and prostitution 94–6, 112, 174; ratios to women 21–2, 23–4, 217; and sexual delinquency 127, 130, 174; single 24; as 'stranger' in sexual assault cases 152–3, 224; and unemployment 46–7; as victims of women 90, 94–6; as 'villains' 62–5, 70, 96, 100; and wage-earning women's leisure 118, 121, 125, 149–50; and wages 221. *See also* immigrant men; racism; trade unions; sexuality, wage-earning women and; victims, women as; white slavery
Mercer Reformatory: *See* Andrew Mercer Ontario Reformatory for Females
Methodist Church of Canada 98, 124, 126
Meyerowitz, Joanne 33
midwives 69. *See also* abortion
minimum wage 176–7, 199–202, 208
Minimum Wage Act (Ontario) 176–7, 200, 201–2, 208